Global Perspectives on Technology Transfer and Commercialization

We dedicate this work to Professor George M. Kozmetsky, founder of the IC^2 Institute. George taught us the importance of creating wealth and jobs from science and technology. As we ride through the sands of time, he will always be cherished and remembered.

Global Perspectives on Technology Transfer and Commercialization

Building Innovative Ecosystems

Edited by

John Sibley Butler

The University of Texas at Austin, USA

and

David V. Gibson

The University of Texas at Austin, USA

Edward Elgar

Cheltenham, UK • Northampton, MA, USA

Published by
Edward Elgar Publishing Limited
The Lypiatts
15 Lansdown Road
Cheltenham
Glos GL50 2JA
UK

Edward Elgar Publishing, Inc.
William Pratt House
9 Dewey Court
Northampton
Massachusetts 01060
USA

A catalogue record for this book
is available from the British Library

Library of Congress Control Number: 2010939218

ISBN 978 1 84980 977 1

Typeset by Servis Filmsetting Ltd, Stockport, Cheshire
Printed and bound by MPG Books Group, UK

Contents

Kamau Gachigi is Chairman and Coordinator at the University of Nairobi Science and Technology Park Co. Ltd, University of Nairobi. He lectures in the Department of Mechanical and Manufacturing Engineering at the University of Nairobi, and is also a member of the National Steering Committee for Science and Technology Parks, Ministry of Higher Education, Science and Technology, Government of Kenya.

David V. Gibson is a Senior Research Scientist at The University of Texas at Austin and Associate Director of the IC² Institute. He has been an IC² Institute Senior Research Fellow since 1992.

Boaz Golany has been a Senior Research Fellow since 1994, and is a professor in the Industrial Engineering and Management Faculty at the Technion Institute of Technology, Haifa, Israel.

Patricia G. Greene has been a Senior Research Fellow of the IC² Institute since 2003. She is a Chaired Professor in Entrepreneurship at Babson College, Wellesley, MA, USA, where she formerly served as Provost (2006–08) and Dean of the Undergraduate School (2003–06).

Manuel Heitor was appointed an IC² Institute Senior Research Fellow in 1996. He is Secretary of State for Science, Technology, and Higher Education, Lisbon, Portugal.

Robert Hodgson was inducted as a Senior Research Fellow in 2000. He is the Managing Director of Zernike (UK) Ltd in Sawston, Cambridge, UK.

Byung-Joo Kang is a professor in the Department of Urban and Real Estate Development in the College of Social Science at Hannam University in Daejon, Republic of Korea, and is Chairman of the Advising Committee for the World Technopolis Association (WTA).

Crispus M. Kiamba is Permanent Secretary, Ministry of Higher Education, Science and Technology, Government of Kenya.

Michael F. Korpi has been an IC² Institute Senior Research Fellow since 2003. He is Professor of Film & Digital Media at Baylor University, Waco, TX, USA, a Fellow of the Society of Motion Picture and Television Engineers and a member of the Academy of Digital Television Pioneers.

Paul Kukubo, CEO ICT Board Kenya, in the Ministry of Information and Communications in the Government of Kenya.

Marc LeGare, is President and Chief Executive Officer of Proactive Communications, Inc., Killeen, TX, USA.

Deog-Seong Oh is a professor at the College of Engineering, Chungnam National University, Daejeon, Republic of Korea and is Secretary General of the World Technopolis Association (WTA).

Mark P. Rice is the Inaugural Dean of Business at the School of Business, Worcester Polytechnic Institute, Worcester, MA, USA.

Nikolay Rogalev has been an IC^2 Senior Research Fellow since 1996, and is Deputy Chief Executive Officer of GAZPROM 'Gazprom energoholding' Company, Moscow, Russia.

Dariusz Trzmielak is Executive Director of the Center for Technology Transfer, University of Łódź, Poland, and is responsible for technology commercialization and the business development of the university high-tech incubator.

Lan Xue has been a Research Fellow since 1996. He is Professor and Dean of the School of Public Policy and Management at Tsinghua University, Beijing, China.

Ling Zhou School of Development and Public Policy, Beijing Normal University, China.

Foreword

It is indeed a pleasure to write a foreword for *Global Perspectives on Technology Transfer and Commercialization: Building Innovative Ecosystems.* Anyone who has traveled the world with their eyes and ears open and tuned to their surroundings experiences those moments of realization that someone else does something better than any other country or locale or culture or institution in the world. Wise travelers bring those observations home and try to influence positive change in the direction of the best practices they have observed. Relatively recently, societies and their private sector and government institutions have tried to organize systems and methods (even ecosystems) to successfully and consistently stimulate and nurture technology transfer and commercialization as components of economic development strategies. Their efforts are not only relatively new, but they are highly varied as well. Thus, it is way too soon to make the call as to who does this best. That is not the intent of this volume. Rather, my distinguished colleagues, John Sibley Butler and David Gibson and IC² Institute's formidable worldwide faculty affiliates, have brought to the rest of us a most insightful (armchair) tour of the great variety of efforts and methods that have been developed or are being explored worldwide. I can think of no better manifestation of the IC² mission at this moment in time when population size and depletion of natural resources central to global economic activity are colliding and challenges are exploding from the collision. The rest of the twenty-first century will bring a huge succession of sometimes brutal and urgent tests of mankind's ingenuity. The world must pick up the pace of discovery and invention and their application and commercialization if mankind is to thrive within the bounds of our finite natural resources.

The IC² Institute is a research unit at The University of Texas at Austin with a transdisciplinary focus. Since its inception, it has brought together scholars from many disciplines to solve unstructured problems in economic development within market economies. One of its great strengths is its Global Fellows Network, composed of scholars worldwide who share the research vision of the Institute in many areas. The Global Fellows, in turn, interact with many additional scholars and leaders bringing them into contact and collaboration with the Institute and greatly expanding the total network of affiliated faculty dedicated to the same or related objectives.

This volume has been produced by that network, drawing on the expertise and experiences of scholars from thirteen countries who examine the infrastructures for technology transfer and commercialization in their countries. Significantly, it allows scholars, business leaders and government leaders to compare countries on an important dimension of technology transfer and commercialization, the business ecosystem. As George Kozmetsky, the founder of the Institute, admonished, 'Technology continues to shrink the world. There is no choice other than to participate in the global community. Science and technology is too precious a resource to be restricted from drawing the world together. That is what the twenty-first century is all about.'

Robert G. May, PhD
Former Dean, McCombs School of Business
Faculty Coordinator, Master of Science in Technology Commercialization
The University of Texas at Austin

Acknowledgments

The editors acknowledge a long tradition of scholars at the IC^2 Institute who have dedicated their research to examining the process of technology transfer. The list begins with George Kozmetsky, Professor of Management, former Dean of the McCombs School of Business, and founding director of the IC^2 Institute, who provided the early vision for the integration of econ-systems, technology transfer, and job creation. IC^2 Institute Fellow, Everett M. Rogers, integrated early research from Rural Sociology and helped the Institute apply it in a theoretical way to our general understanding of the importance of how science and technologies are transferred from university laboratories to the world of commerce. Ray Smilor and David V. Gibson helped formulate the concept of the science city, or Technopolis, which has informed this research tradition for over three decades. Ideas, like rivers, flow through time and influence the continued quest for understanding through systematic research. This is certainly the case of the scholars associated with the IC^2 Institute at the University of Texas at Austin.

We cannot say enough about Coral Franke, the professional staff member at IC^2 Institute, who is responsible for the management of this publication and for conference processes at the Institute. We acknowledge the significant contribution of Coral, whose dedication produced and delivered this manuscript in a timely fashion. We also acknowledge and thank Juan Sanchez, Vice President for Research and Robert A. Peterson, Associate Vice President for Research at the University of Texas at Austin, who have long supported the creative and innovative activities of the IC^2 Institute.

Introduction: technology transfer in global perspectives – issues for the twenty-first century

John Sibley Butler and David V. Gibson

This edited volume is dedicated to the continued understanding of technology transfer, commercialization, and regional technology-based development with an emphasis on how issues converge or diverge in global context. All of the contributors are Research Fellows or associated scholars of the Institute for Innovation Creativity and Capital (IC²) at the University of Texas at Austin. For over three decades the IC² Institute has studied technology transfer and how it impacts the development of new companies, the enhancement of established companies, and the transformation of cities, regions, and countries. In 1986, George Kozmetsky, the founder of IC² and one of its greatest Fellows, noted,

> Since the First Industrial Revolution, technology has been a basic motor for economic growth. The management of technology as a resource for economic development and wealth generation is a recent phenomenon. The lessons from the utilization of technology over the past two decades are clear. Those who manage technology creatively and innovatively will reap the benefits of sustained economic growth. They can also play an important leadership role in dealing with new issues regarding competition and cooperation. (1986, 1)

Over the last three decades policy makers, academicians, and those in government have shown an increased awareness of the importance of technology transfer.[1] This is a dynamic area of study that examines traditional topics such as intellectual property management, risk management, market identification, the role of public and private labs, and the role of universities.[2] The study of technology transfer can also be found in the literature on technology diffusion, which has its roots in the early agriculture literature as new technologies moved from agricultural labs to the market.[3] This volume presents a collection of essays detailing how government, business, and academia influence technology transfer in different nations: how the infrastructure of a country enhances the technological and contributes to the economy. The countries examined range in size and development and include China, Kenya, the United Kingdom, Iraq, Israel, Japan, Korea, Malta, Mexico, Poland, Portugal, Russia, and the United States of America. In an earlier effort, IC² Fellows established the groundwork for our perspective in a book entitled, *Creating the Technopolis: Linking Technology Commercialization and Economic Development.*[4] As Global IC² Fellows, the authors utilized elements of this framework, or what we call the IC² Model of economic development, to understand how support systems from government, business, and academia influence the movement of science to the market and thus influence economic development. Although each country presented has its unique history, there is a considerable degree of overlap in the chapters.

The IC² Model of research and real-world experiments are in a series of publications starting in the 1980s.[5] Perhaps the greatest real-world experiment was done in Austin, Texas. The 'Technopolis Framework', or the science city, became the driving theoretical paradigm. The force of the technopolis paradigm is the interlocking relationships among governments (quasi-public, private, and public institutions, respectively) to enhance technology-based economic development in regions. The paradigm is dependent on the continuous improvement of four major steps: (i) achievement of scientific pre-eminence in technology-based research; (ii) development of new technologies for emerging industries; (iii) attraction of major technology companies; and (iv) creation of homegrown technology companies.[6] Nested within the theoretical framework are the mechanisms of the technopolis that include elements such as incubators, capital formation, networking, and the characteristics of the city or region (for example, uniqueness, pleasant place to live and so on). Research shows that Austin, Texas, moved rapidly to the forefront of literature that ranks cities according to their entrepreneurial opportunity, wealth creation, and job creation.[7] The IC² Model of economic development through technology transfer served as the catalyst for 'experiment Austin'. This paradigm has been applied worldwide as countries and regions create strategies for technology-based economic growth.

To be sure, government laboratories and universities, as movers of the technology transfer process, have a prominent place in the growing research literature in the United States.[8] Also becoming prominent is the literature on how technology transfer in the United States is influencing economic development in regions in different countries.[9] With the IC² Model as the guiding theoretical force, this volume is in the tradition of how to research technology transfer as it moves through different stages in different countries. Contributors in this work combine the history of their country with issues of scientific knowledge, technology transfer, and economic development. Although each country is a diversity of richness, there is uniformity to the volume when it comes to the importance of technology transfer for countries as we enter the twenty-first century.

Lan Xue and Ling Zhou's contribution on China (Chapter 1) examines technology transfer and the development of university–market linkages. This development is wrapped around the history and restructuring of universities from the founding of the People's Republic of China to the national restructuring of today's innovation system. This is a system of technology transfer that combines university–market–government interactions; government is seen as improving public infrastructures that will allow innovation and the enhancement of the high-tech business ecosystems. This contribution is an interesting study of how technology transfer contributes not only to the growth and continued development of China's economy but also to the development of intellectual property. The theme of the importance of government support and ecosystem development for technology transfer is continued in Kamau Gachigi and Crispus M. Kiamba's chapter on Africa (Chapter 2). Although the final focus is on Kenya, the authors stress the point that the overall understanding and success of technology transfer in the continent will depend on the economic and political ecosystem. The chapter concentrates on challenges of the creation of knowledge-based economies and then uses Kenya's data to illustrate how infrastructure is enhancing the development of that country. The relationship between developed and developing countries is also a lesson of this chapter.

An interesting finding of Robert Hodgson's chapter on the United Kingdom (Chapter 3) is how England's traditional universities, with an emphasis on academic teaching and academic research, have to transform themselves so that they can contribute to a knowledge-based, technology transfer economy. This means working with businesses to enhance the country's national competitiveness with a concentration on innovation. In a real sense, this is also a study of how a country rebuilds itself by changing policy that enhances economic development. In contrast, Uzi De Haan and Boaz Golany's chapter (Chapter 5) starts with the proposition that Israel has built a country that is the model for technology transfer and economic stability. The authors utilize a strong sense of history to show how Israel went from a poor, developing country or start-up in 1948 to one of the world's leading centers for economic development through technology transfer.

Technology transfer and business development are put to a great test in Corey P. Carbonara, Michael F. Korpi and Marc LeGare's work on Iraq, a country that is at war (Chapter 4). At the center of the IC^2 Model for economic development is creative and innovative management. This research universities. Greene and Rice examine emerging trends and the role of the office of technology transfer in the context of the future of the relationship between technology transfer and the university. This dynamic area of study becomes critical as regions are increasingly seeing universities as significant drivers of regional economic development.

The IC² Institute, its Research Fellows, and associated scholars around the globe understand that in the technology transfer and commercialization arena the study of the regional ecosystem in which it takes place is as important as the traditional emphasis on entrepreneurship as 'small business'. We hope that this volume will continue to influence policy makers and managers of regions about the importance of a transfer ecosystem. Silicon Valley, California, and Austin, Texas, are two exemplary regions where regionally based science and technology research has occurred and has been linked to economic development that teaches us how business principles interact with emerging technologies, knowledge, and know-how to launch and grow companies, enhance profit centers of established companies, and thus continue to create wealth and jobs.

NOTES

1. For an excellent review of the emergence of technology transfer in both academia and the public square, see Bozeman (2000); see also Godkin (1988); Zhao and Reisman (1992).
2. For excellent reviews of major concerns, see *Journal of Technology Transfer*. See also Shane (2005).
3. For a review, see the classic *Diffusion of Innovations* (Rogers, 2003), and Butler (2010).
4. Smilor et al. (1988b); see also Smilor et al. (1988a) and Gibson et al. (1992).
5. See, for example, Kozmetsky and Smilor (1986).
6. For a review of the model, see Butler (2010). An examination of the growth of Austin, Texas can be found in Harvard Business School Case Study (1998).
7. For an overview of the rise of the Austin Technopolis, see Gibson and Rogers (1994) and Gibson and Butler (n.d.).
8. For a contrast between university and federal laboratories in the technology process, see Crow and Bozeman (1987). For the history of the relationship between government and universities, see Fellwe (2005).
9. See, for example, Rosenberg (2001).

REFERENCES

Bozeman, Barry (2000), 'Technology transfer and public policy: a review of research and theory', *Research Policy*, **29**, 627–55.
Butler, John Sibley (2010), 'Diffusion theory and technology transfer systems: an application of the IC² Model', in Mark Rice, Patricia Gene Greene and John Sibley Butler (eds), *Comparative Business Eco-System*, Cheltenham, UK and Northampton, MA, USA: Edward Elgar, pp. 99–121.

Crow, M. and B. Bozeman (1987), 'R&D laboratories' environmental context; are the government lab–industrial lab stereotypes still valid?', *Research Policy*, **13**, 329–55.

Fellwe, Irwin (2005), 'An historical perspective on government–university partnerships to enhance entrepreneurship and economic development', in Shane (ed.), pp. 6–32.

Gibson, David V. and Everett M. Rogers (1994), *R&D Collaboration on Trial: The Microelectronics and Computer Technology Corporation (MCC)*, Cambridge, MA: Harvard Business School Press.

Gibson, D., G. Kozmetsky and R. Smilor (eds) (1992), *The Technopolis Phenomenon: Smart Cities, Fast Systems, and Global Networks*, Lanham, MD: Rowman & Littlefield.

Gibson, David V. and John Sibley Butler (n.d.), 'Sustaining the technopolis: high-technology development in Austin, Texas 1988–2009', Working Research Paper, IC^2 Institute, University of Texas at Austin.

Godkin, L. (1988), 'Problems and practicalities of technology transfer: a survey of the literature', *Journal of Technology Transfer*, **13** (1), 20–26.

Harvard Business School Case Study 9-799-038 (1998), 'Austin, Texas: building a high-tech economy', Harvard University, Boston, MA.

Kozmetsky, George (1986), 'Economic growth through technology: a new framework for creative and innovative managers', in Eugene B. Konecci, George Kozmetsky, Raymond W. Smilor and Michael D. Gill, Jr (eds), *Commercializing Technology Resources for Competitive Advantage* Austin, TX: IC^2 Institute, Monograph, pp. 1–49.

Kozmetsky, George and Raymond W. Smilor (1986), 'Building indigenous companies: private/public infrastructures for economic growth and diversification', in Eugene B. Konecci, George Kozmetsky, Raymond W. Smilor and Michael D. Gill, Jr (eds), *Commercializing Technology Resources for Competitive Advantage*, Austin, TX: IC^2 Institute, Monograph, September.

Rogers, Everett M. (2003), *Diffusion of Innovations*, 5th edn, New York: Free Press.

Rosenberg, David (2001), *Cloning Silicon Valley: The Next Generation High Tech Hotspots*, New York: Reuters, 2001.

Shane, Scott (ed.) (2005), *Economic Development Through Entrepreneurship: Government, University and Business Linkages*, Cheltenham, UK and Northampton, MA, USA.

Smilor, R., David V. Gibson and G. Kozmetsky (1988a), 'Creating the technopolis: high-technology development in Austin, Texas', *Journal of Business Venturing*, **4**, 49–67.

Smilor, Raymond W., George Kozmetsky and David V. Gibson (eds) (1988b), *Creating the Technopolis: Linking Technology Commercialization and Economic Development*, Boston, MA: Ballinger.

Zhao, L.M. and A. Reisman (1992), 'Toward meta research on technology transfer', *IEEE Transactions on Engineering Management*, 39 (1), 13–21.

1. Technology commercialization in Chinese universities: an innovation system approach*

Lan Xue and Ling Zhou

1 INTRODUCTION

In recent years, the rise of the knowledge economy has led to the recognition of the essential role of technological innovation in economic development. The concept of an 'innovation system' has been adopted to explain mechanisms of knowledge creation and dissemination at the national, regional, and sectoral levels (Freeman, 1987; Lundvall, 1992; Nelson, 1993; Saxenian, 1994; Breschi and Malerba, 1997; Edquist, 1997). A primary focus of these studies is on the role of different actors of innovative activities and the interaction among them. In particular, many have focused on the new roles of universities in the division of labor in national innovation systems and their roles in technology commercialization.

While the innovation system approach presents a useful framework for examining the role of universities from an institutional perspective, most of these studies are based on the experience of industrialized countries. In recent years, researchers have already considered these issues sporadically within the setting of a developing country such as China. However, comprehensive and systematic descriptions of the whole system remain absent. The Chinese experience is interesting not only because China is a large developing country, but also because it is moving toward a market economy with a centralized innovation system in transition. The university–market linkage in China offers a unique case to study the evolving institutional relationships between academia and industry, since China's innovation system has experienced dramatic change over the last two decades. The development of university–market linkages has been greatly influenced and conditioned by such change.

In addition, as the trend of globalization of science and technology (S&T) continues, academic communities in developing countries will increasingly become important partners in a global innovation system.

1

The academy–market interface in these countries therefore matters not only because such experience can shed new light on the ongoing debate, but also because the evolution of such a relationship will also have an impact on the interlinked global innovation system.

This chapter will focus on the evolution of university–market linkages in China with a special focus on technology commercialization. In the next section, we shall give a brief account of the linkages between universities and the market, followed by summaries of the reforms of China's higher education system, the changing role of universities in its national innovation system, as well as R&D activities in universities and their relationship with other innovative entities. Section 3 will present an analysis of forms of university–market linkages, such as contract research or incubation services, based on recent data collected by the Ministry of Education. The chapter will then focus on the evolution and reform of China's national innovation system and the lack of fundamental reform in its higher education system, as the general background against which Chinese universities interact with the market in various forms. Section 4 focuses on the unique form of university technology commercialization, the university–owned enterprises. Finally, the implications of the current university–market linkages for the overall Chinese innovation system will be explored.

2   UNIVERSITIES IN CHINA'S NATIONAL INNOVATION SYSTEM

Reforms in China's Higher Education System

Shortly after the People's Republic of China was founded in 1949, a new education system was directly imported: the Soviet model. However, this model did very little to address the problem of mass illiteracy that was a prevalent phenomenon in China at that time. By 1956, it was still the case that less than half of the age cohort was able to attend primary and secondary school. During the 1950s, most energy was devoted to the development and restructuring of higher education and a so-called 'traditional higher education system' of New China was formed during this period.

As a result of restructuring, the number of comprehensive universities decreased, while the number of specialized colleges showed a significant increase. The newly established Ministry of Higher Education was given a stronger role in overseeing the administration of both the comprehensive and polytechnic universities as well as the teacher-training institutions, which made up the main parts of this traditional system. In addition, numerous colleges directly under the supervision of different government ministries were also established, focusing mainly on training talents for relevant social sections, which greatly limited the knowledge scope of those colleges (World Bank, 1998).

Beginning in the late 1980s, universities in China entered a new era of large-scale readjustment, cooperation, and merging. From 1994 to 1998, the total number of universities decreased from 627 to 590; the average number of students per college increased from 2,591 to 3,335; the ratio of teachers to students increased from 8:8 to 11:601; and the number of comprehensive universities also increased significantly (Shao, 2002).

Administrative rights were largely transferred back to universities over time. In 1999, a decision was made to encourage the further adjustment of the administrative system of higher education. With the exception of those universities directly under the supervision of certain government departments such as the Ministry of Education, the Ministry of Foreign Affairs, the Ministry of Public Security, Customs of PRC, and the State Sport General Administration, the majority of universities were given independent administration rights (State Council, 1999).

Unlike the traditional higher education system, in which government was the only funding channel for universities, during the process of adjustment more parties were encouraged to invest in the universities; however, government funds remained the dominant share. In addition, reforms were also carried out in the administrative systems, including enrollment, employment, and tuition. Currently, the new model of the higher education system is in the process of formation.

The Traditional Role of Universities in China's National Innovation System

The national innovation system of New China began to take shape in the 1950s. As mentioned above, it was adopted directly from the Soviet model which emphasized centralized management and planning, with government playing a major role: (i) as the sole source of financial support for research work; (ii) as a 'grand master' defining the division of labor among different institutional players, project planning and execution, direct supervision over research institutes, and unified deployment of research resources; and (iii) as the pivot for the knowledge flow among different research entities (see Figure 1.1; Feng,1999).

Under such a model, research and development (R&D) had been undertaken by a research network composed of the Chinese Academy of Science (CAS) and a number of research institutes directly under the supervision of the central government and different ministries or local governments with projects and funds being directly deployed by the government. As the pillar of this research network, the Chinese Academy of Sciences was

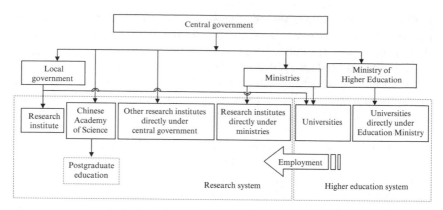

Figure 1.1   China's national innovation system and universities since the 1950s

founded in December 1949, developing from both the Central Research Institute and the Peking Research Institute. In the early years of its operation, the Academy also took on such administrative responsibilities as providing guidelines for research activities, including drafting and executing the national science research plans. Although it was later deprived of these administrative responsibilities, this independent research network, in which the CAS served as the core force, has always been the dominant player in China's S&T activities such as basic research and technology development (CAS, 1949–1954).

Universities at this time were mainly set up to train talent for the country's other sectors. The university-based research function was further weakened when the teaching function of the higher education system was re-emphasized and the research resources reorganized, particularly between 1950 and 1955. The only contact between universities and research institutes was when research institutes accepted graduates from universities. At the same time, the industrial sector did not take up research responsibilities nor did it connect with the research network directly. Its connection with universities was limited to the acceptance of graduates and its interaction with the research system was under the guidance of government.

The reason why China chose to adopt the centralized model in the 1950s was closely related to the fact that its national economic system was also centralized. In addition, the country had little technical infrastructure at the time and was in urgent need of development in many technological fields. Only when the research resources were pulled together could the country make the best use of available resources in its technology development, thus further boosting the growth of the economy (SSC, 1986).

The Transition of China's National Innovation System and the Changing Role of Universities

Beginning in 1978, China's national innovation system entered a new era with a series of institutional reforms, the technology market being set up and further developed with a range of laws on patents and technology contracts, and technology transformation being successively enacted. Meanwhile, another important action was the 1979 regulation, which had explicitly prescribed universities as the center for both teaching and scientific research. This marked universities' formal entrance into China's national science research system (Li and Zeng, 2000).

Significant changes also occurred in research institutes, which were formerly, under the Soviet model, the only players in China's R&D activities. Public research institutes (PRIs) prior to the reform could be further divided into three groups (all figures are 1985 statistics from SSTC, 1986). The first group comprised 122 research institutes affiliated and administrated by the CAS. Each of these institutes specialized in a particular field, such as physics, mathematics, semiconductors, and chemistry. In 1985, close to 60,000 research staff were employed by these institutes. Research institutes under CAS were engaged in a wide spectrum of activities including basic and applied research, development, design, and other S&T services. The second group of PRIs comprised research institutes and facilities under China's national ministries. In 1985, there were 622 state-level research institutes administered by more than 50 ministries and commissions and employing just over 200,000 researchers. Most of these researchers were engaged in various R&D activities with an emphasis on the experimental and development work required by their particular industry. The third group of PRIs consisted of research institutes and facilities subordinated to the government at the provincial level. In 1985, 3,946 provincial research institutes employed more than 310,000 researchers providing services in R&D, engineering design, and technology transfer.

As a focus for China's 1985 resolution on the reform of the S&T system, the internal management of PRIs changed greatly. In April 1986, the State Council issued Temporary Provisions on Extending the Decision-Making Power of Research Units (SSTC, 1986), granting PRIs far greater autonomy in areas such as personnel, finance, property management, and international exchanges. Not until late 1992, however, was the contract responsibility system, already widely used in industrial enterprises and in some PRIs, formally introduced into the technology development of PRIs. Under this new system, the director of a PRI could sign a contract with the state and take responsibility for achieving certain goals in research, income, assets, and other areas within a period of three or more years. In return, the director was allowed to exercise greater control over the PRIs and receive a mutually agreed reward when the contract was successfully fulfilled.

Such contracts turned out to be far more difficult to implement in research institutes than in industrial enterprises. In December 1993, the SSTC, together with the Ministries of Personnel and Treasury, therefore issued another document specifying what research and financial indicators should be used in such contracts. The contract system also began to be adopted by PRIs engaged in basic and public interest research at the level of research divisions or projects within a PRI. By the end of 1993, about 71 percent of PRIs had implemented the R&D contract system at either the level of a research institute or the level of research projects (SSTC, 1994, 1995).

In terms of the reform on institutional structure, the government moved carefully to avoid forcing drastic changes to the existing institutional structure due to the complexity and difficulty of the issues involved (Zhao, 1986). For the first few years after the 1985 resolution, the SSTC issued only one document on how to manage the operating cost of PRIs merged into state-owned enterprises. At the same time, various government-initiated national S&T programs created many opportunities for PRIs to foster horizontal linkages with other sectors of the economy. In addition, the government encouraged the continuing growth of technical enterprises, many of which were spin-offs from PRIs or universities. These enterprises typically offered their products or services in the growing high-tech market. In the 1990s, the government had encouraged mergers and acquisitions between applied PRIs and such enterprises to form new enterprises with strong R&D centers or new PRIs with strong application arms.

As these policies were all market oriented, they generated concerns about the negative impact on academic research. To balance this, the government initiated a major national research program called the 'Knowledge Innovation Program' (KIP), which focused support on the CAS to enable it to regain its strength in basic and strategic research. A unique government initiative, the KIP is a reform and funding program targeted at the research institutes in the CAS.

In order to promote the national capability in S&T innovation in a comprehensive fashion, the government approved a proposal submitted by the CAS in 1998 to initiate a pilot project to strengthen China's KIP in CAS. By implementing the program, The CAS was to be transformed into a research institute with a flexible management system and much improved innovative capacities. The program is divided into three phases: the Initial Phase (1998–2000); the All-Round Implementation Phase (2001–05); and the Phase of Optimization (2006–10). The pilot project initiated a new era for the development of CAS, as well as a new stage for the building up of a national knowledge innovation system. At the same time, the government also made appropriate restructuring efforts in other kinds of research institutes, with the intention of generating a more flexible operating mechanism and more powerful innovative capacities.

In 1999, the Ministry of Science and Technology and the Economic and Trade Commission announced restructuring plans for 242 PRIs, followed by plans for another 664. These restructuring plans included merging PRIs into existing companies, reorganizing them into companies, or turning them into non-profit research institutes for which the government no longer provided guaranteed financial support. Although only 14 percent of all PRIs were restructured, their share of the research funding and human resources constituted almost one-fourth of the total (STS, 1999). Reforms of research institutes were then further accelerated. By the end of 2002, 1,185 applied research institutes had completed the restructuring program or were in the process of being restructured. These efforts helped strengthen China's industrial R&D capability and fostered better linkages between PRIs and industry.

Through these reform initiatives, China's national innovation system has changed fundamentally. Government-affiliated research institutes are no longer the only major player in the nation's research system; both universities and the industrial sector have also become significant participants. Recently, another new phenomenon emerged. After the government made a serious decision to encourage the development of the non-public economic sector, both non-profit and private research institutes restructured on the basis of the former government-affiliated research institutes. Meanwhile, private universities have also been set up, particularly with the formal launch in 2003 of the Law on Promoting Private Education. Although these new organizations make up only a small proportion of the nation's total number of universities and are not involved in research activities at all, the establishment of private universities will help accelerate reforms in China's research system.

During this transition period, China's universities have shown their great potential in knowledge innovation and the commercialization of high-tech research, and they have become a major force in the country's knowledge production activities. In 2004, over 437,000 researchers were involved in S&T work in universities, taking up 12.55 percent of the national share. In the nation's R&D expenditures on basic research, universities accounted for 40.6 percent. Meanwhile, universities accounted for 64.4 percent of the papers published domestically.

The relationship between universities and other players in the national innovation system has also changed. Universities are cooperating more closely with the industrial sector and research institutes, and the means for them to interact with each other have diversified to include joint research, human resource training, and people exchange (see Figure 1.2; Shao, 2002).

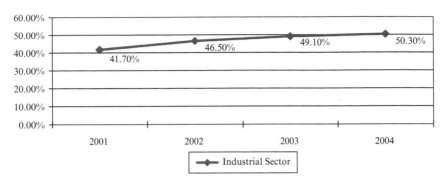

Source: www.sts.org.cn.

*Figure 1.4   Domestic service invention granted by SIPO, shares of
industrial sector to the total number for 2001–2004 (%)*

Analysis of Push and Pull Factors of the Interactions between U&Cs and the Industrial Sector

The pull factor: opportunities due to lack of industrial R&D capability

One of the major problems with China's innovation system is its weak
industrial R&D capacity. In general, the crucial players in the innovation
process are business enterprises that translate R&D results into profitable
products or processes. Without a strong and effective industrial R&D
capability, efforts by universities, research institutes, or other organizations often become futile. The current status of industrial R&D capability
in China can be illustrated by the results of a 1996 innovation survey of
large and medium-sized industrial firms in six provinces and cities conducted by the Ministry of Science and Technology.

The provinces and cities covered include Beijing, Shanghai, Guangdong,
Jiangsu, Liaoning, and Haerbin. They are either China's economic pow-
erhouses (such as Beijing, Shanghai, Guangdong, and Jiangsu) or its
traditional industrial bases (such as Liaoning and Haerbin). In addition,
the average firm size ranges from 21,622 employees (for 'Special Large
Class' in the Chinese classification system) to 796 employees (for 'Medium
2'). Small firms are not included. Even for this somewhat selective group,
the situation is not encouraging. It was found that while 73 percent of the
firms surveyed had engaged in some form of innovative activity in which
R&D accounted for a small part, they spent only 3.7 percent of the total
sales for these activities, of which more than half (54.7 percent) was spent
on purchasing equipment. Only 0.5 percent of total sales were spent on
R&D (MOST, 1999).

One reason for this situation is that many large and medium-sized state-owned enterprises (SOEs) are undergoing governance and managerial reforms. Such reform has become the top priority of China's overall economic reform. However, such a challenging task cannot be expected to be completed overnight. Under such circumstances, many SOEs simply do not have the financial resources needed for R&D investment. Without some fundamental change in the external financial environment and internal management in these SOEs, there is little hope that they can be active in R&D and commercialization activities. While in recent years non-state-owned industrial enterprises are playing increasingly more important roles in China's economy, most are still relatively small compared to large and medium-sized SOEs, and their R&D activities are limited at present. However, in the long run, the non-state sector will become one of the most important forces in R&D commercialization.

The lack of in-house R&D capability in most Chinese industrial enterprises means that they cannot rely on themselves to solve more complex technical problems in production. They are also incapable of acquiring external knowledge in tacit and more dynamic forms given that some form of in-house R&D capability is a prerequisite for being able to absorb knowledge from outside (Cohen and Levinthal, 1989, 1990). These enterprises need technical services from research institutes and universities. Because most of these firms do not have significant in-house R&D capabilities, technology contracts have become major forms of collaboration between them and universities.

Weak industrial R&D capabilities also means that firms find it difficult to commercialize much potentially useful research work in universities, particularly those conducted in engineering schools and departments. At the same time, rapid technological change in many high-tech and traditional industries has also created many technical and economic opportunities for this research. Some faculty with entrepreneurial spirits naturally see the opportunities and begin to 'jump into the sea'. Some universities have also provided support such as establishing specific funds for enhancing working conditions and salaries, helping staff to cooperate with the industrial sector by means of a technology contract and joint research, and enabling departments to set up small-sized technology development companies. However, few faculty are willing to give up their university job. Most want a 'safe cushion' in case their ventures fail. Interestingly, for a period, many universities did indeed provide such a safe cushion, and to understand why universities would be willing to do this, we need to examine the push factor of the equation.

Push factor: slow reform in the higher education system and government policy orientation

Since the mid-1980s, a number of related factors have helped push universities to establish closer linkages with the market. These factors include slow reform in the higher education system and government policy orientation.

The major difficulties in the higher education system lie in its heritage of a planned economy in which central government played a key role in determining everything from faculty salaries to the number of students to be admitted to a specialty in a particular university. Chinese universities are far less autonomous than SOEs in other industries. At the same time, the environment in which universities operate has changed dramatically, becoming very market oriented. The mismatch between the centralized system and its market-oriented environment has created many tensions and pressures that have prevented China's higher education system from adapting to meet new challenges.

One constant challenge is the funding shortage. Table 1.1 shows the income structure of a nationally recognized university in selected years in the 1990s. As can be seen, government appropriation, often closely tied to the number of undergraduate admissions, represented only about one-third of the total budget and declined slowly throughout the 1990s. The largest sources of income were research, including government research projects, industrial collaborations, and so on. The contribution of university-owned enterprises to universities comes in two forms: one is through contract research; the other is payback to universities through the profit gained from the operation of the enterprises (see Section 4). The former is included in the 'Research' category, while the latter is included in the 'Other' category. Unfortunately, detailed data on the payback of university-owned enterprises to universities are difficult to obtain.

Heavy reliance on research funding was mainly due to slow reform in the higher education system. Reform proposals to grant universities more autonomy and take a more market-oriented approach to financing the higher education system were debated and not implemented until 1999 when the policy on enrollment expansion in higher education was launched (Xue, 1999). Dramatic changes have taken place in universities ever since: from 1998 to 2001, the number of students in universities jumped from 6,430,000 to 12,140,000, and annual average tuition for each student increased from 2,500 yuan to 5,000 yuan. While tuition and fees increased rapidly, they started from a low base and government regulations prevented them from increasing substantially. Universities in China were therefore placed in a difficult position: they were not provided with enough funding to operate, and nor did they have enough autonomy

*Table 1.1   Example of the income structure of a well-known Chinese
university*

	1990	1992	1994	1996	1998
Total income (in millions of yuan)	152.1	222.6	342.3	532.7	741.9
Government appropriation (%)	36	30	32	32	29
Tuition and fees (%)	2	4	8	10	11
Research (%)	48	53	49	45	41
Donations (%)	0.2	0.0	0.0	2.5	4.2
Others (%)	13	12	12	11	15

Source: Compiled by author.

to take a more market-oriented approach to financing their operation.
Providing S&T services was therefore a very attractive and legitimate way
for many universities to finance their operations.

A further analysis of sources of research funding for universities from the
mid-1980s to the late 1990s shows an interesting pattern. In 1985, when the
S&T reform and educational reforms started, funding from the government
for university S&T activities accounted for about 75 percent of the total.
The rest came mainly from industry. Since then, the government proportion has declined steadily, while the industry proportion has risen steadily.
By the mid-1990s, funding from industry surpassed government slightly,
becoming the largest source of funding for university S&T activities. While
there have been fluctuations, industrial sources continue to provide close to
half of the funding of university S&T activities. To a certain degree, universities, particularly those with an engineering focus, have begun to depend
on industrial research income to support their daily operations.

Government policy orientation also played an important role in pushing
universities to participate in the market (Shao, 2002; Chen, 2004). Since
the central government issued the policy documents on S&T system
reform and education system reform in 1985, the government's policy
orientation has been consistently focused on pushing universities to offer
their research service to the market in order to help the economic and
social development of society. University high-tech industrial development has become one of the top priorities for university administration.
Both central and local governments at various levels have seen universities
as engines of economic development and tried to provide various incentives and supportive policies to encourage universities to forge closer ties
with local industry.

To summarize, government appropriation for Chinese universities has been far from adequate over a long period. Research funding from industry has become a major source of income for universities. Given that research funding from industry accounts for almost half of the total research income, universities naturally encourage their faculty members to develop closer ties with industry or even to become entrepreneurs themselves in order to commercialize technologies quickly. In addition, the endorsement of the central government and the fact that university-owned enterprises have become a priority of university administrations have also played important roles. These factors may help to explain why university-owned enterprises have become so popular in China, but not in other developing countries with similar push and pull factors.

3 UNIVERSITY AND ENTERPRISE LINKAGES WITH A SPECIAL FOCUS ON TECHNOLOGY COMMERCIALIZATION

General Introduction

It should be recognized at the outset that the most important forms of university–market linkage are the flow of university graduates into the market, as well as the flow of new knowledge generated by university-based research into society through public channels. China is no exception to this.

In fact, the university–market linkage can be traced back to the time before the establishment of the People's Republic of China (PRC) when universities already had a direct interaction with the market. After the PRC was founded in the 1950s, the central government successively asked universities: to organize short-term training for talent (1950); to set up university-owned enterprises for student internship and R&D activities (1957); and to combine the educational process with production and research activities (1959). All these linkages have reflected the basic functions of universities for enterprise education and research. This traditional connection to the productive world is a specific feature of socialist countries.

However, linkage forms have changed greatly over the past two decades. Since the 1985 S&T system reform, university faculty members, particularly those in engineering and other applied disciplines, have worked aggressively to develop closer ties with industry. The government has formally encouraged universities to conceive of different ways to serve society, which was particularly evident in 1988 when the Third National Higher Education Working Conference was held. Over the years, universities have developed various linkages to the market, including informal consulting by university researchers to industry, technology contracts, technology transfer and licensing, joint research centers, university-run enterprises, and university-based science parks.

Of all the forms of university–enterprise linkage, technology contracts and university-run enterprises are the most common and flexible. While university licensing activities have been on the rise, they are limited to universities with strong engineering disciplines, which are the major players in patenting. Joint research centers are also making their appearance as a mechanism for cooperation between universities and international companies, as well as carrying out joint research online. This has gained considerable support from the Chinese government, with the Law on Promoting the Transformation of Scientific and Technological Achievements in 1996. This law encourages different means of joint research. In addition, university-based science parks have gained popularity in recent years, but have been built mostly in major cities with dynamic entrepreneurial activities.

Technology Contracts

Of all the forms of linkage, technology contracts have become the most important source of research funding for universities. An examination of R&D spending in Chinese universities reveals that a very high percentage, close to 80 percent, is on applied research and development (Table 1.2). Most of this spending will be funded by industry through different forms of technology contracts.

Technology contracts in China are usually composed of categories such as technology development, technology transfer (non-patent technology transfer and patent licensing), technical services, and technical consultancy (see Table 1.3).

The table shows that technology contracts signed in China have witnessed a stable year-by-year growth between 2001 and 2004. Among the contracts, the category of technology development always ranks first.[3] Technology development is usually in the form of 'joint research' in which enterprises entrust universities with technology tasks or combine with universities to jointly conduct research on a specific topic or even set up an entity with universities for long-term research in a special field.

Among the different service providers, it is clear that industrial enterprises play the most dynamic and important role in the technology contract business, with the trade sum exceeding 56 percent of the total in 2004. However, the percentage of research institutions doing contract business decreased from 23 percent in 2001 to 14 percent in 2004. This is partly due to the change of status of many research institutes that underwent a restructuring process and have been turned into stand-alone enterprises.

Table 1.4 Technology contracts of Tsinghua University

	1991	1992	1993	1994	1995	1996	1997	1998	1999
Technology development (%)	72.43	69.03	86.55	94.09	83.56	75.06	76.20	79.16	79.11
Technology transfer (non-patent) (%)	9.54	24.64	7.22	1.58	5.74	5.61	13.33	6.02	7.26
Patent licensing (%)	0.00	0.00	0.00	0.00	4.51	0.00	0.00	4.43	0.09
Technical service (%)	16.79	5.83	5.19	4.10	5.19	17.97	9.14	8.05	11.21
Technical consultancy (%)	1.24	0.49	1.05	0.24	1.01	1.36	1.33	2.34	2.32
Total (million yuan)	1.497	5.168	6.621	12.789	8.866	12.304	13.100	17.520	25.287

Source: Compiled by author from data from the Contract Office of the Department of S&T Development, Tsinghua University.

*Table 1.5   S&T research centers by type of university in China,
(1999–2002)*

	1999	2000	2001	2002
Total	1,456	4,432	4,599	4,842
Comprehensive universities	243	1,122	1,073	1,099
Engineering universities	541	1,972	1,958	2,117
Agriculture universities	193	420	452	481
Medical universities	381	635	604	579
Normal universities	94	390	434	476
Others	4	73	78	90

Source: S&T Development Centre, Ministry of Education.

over 1,000 research centers for technology development in universities
have developed a very close relationship with both public and private
enterprises.

A new trend for joint research in China's universities is to set up
research centers with multinational companies. Tsinghua University provides a good example as in 1992 the university set up its first joint research
center with the Japanese company Panasonic. Over the next decade, joint
research centers in Tsinghua University increased quickly, in terms of both
numbers and scale. By the end of 2002, multinational companies from nine
countries and regions jointly set up 48 research centers with the university,
18 of which were with Fortune 500 companies (see Tables 1.6 and 1.7).

In the course of a decade, over 1.6 billion yuan have been invested in
12 research areas, such as information technology, machinery, automation, automobiles, and biology. Overall, Tsinghua University has a 29
percent share in these centers. Multinational companies own 4 percent,
with the rest being jointly owned by both sides (see Table 1.8).

Cooperation over the last 10 years has also enabled these research
centers to generate the achievement of 36 domestic patents, 23 international patents, over 500 published papers, and 12 products. Among the
145 projects undertaken by these centers, 77 were jointly developed by
both sides. Altogether, over 5,000 students have benefited from such joint
research. Such cooperation has also proven that joint research centers
of high quality and with high standards can provide significant benefit
to a university in terms of: (i) accelerating the commercialization of the
technology developed; (ii) providing adequate funding support for S&T
research; (iii) providing opportunities for students to interact with industry and put theory into practice; and (iv) accumulating advanced management experience. Meanwhile, multinational companies have found that

Table 1.6   International joint research centers in Tsinghua University

Year	New centers	With Fortune 500	Total sum (10,000 yuan)	With Fortune 500
1992	1	0	80	0
1993	1	0	100	0
1994	5	2	3,531.19	250.22
1995	3	2	3,018	540
1996	4	3	1,192.5	1,102.5
1997	4	1	647.7	320
1998	5	1	1,653.28	397.8
1999	5	1	1,777.88	600
2000	7	4	1,933.61	1,025.81
2001	9	3	5,268.92	812.34
2002	4	1	147,250	1,652
Total	48	18	166,453.08	6,700.67

Source: S&T Department of Tsinghua University.

Table 1.7   Regional distribution of international partners

Country/region	Number	Total sum (10,000 yuan)
America	23	142,584.8
Japan	10	6,337.52
Germany	5	734.8
Canada	2	1,136.9
South Korea	2	3,057.82
Taiwan (China)	2	10,619.5
Hong Kong (China)	2	173.4
Britain	1	1,652
Switzerland	1	156.34
Total	48	166,453.08

Source: S&T Department of Tsinghua University.

Table 1.8   Ownership of research centers (%)

	Tsinghua Uni.	International Co.	Jointly owned
Research center	29	4	67
Project	29	4	67

Source: S&T Department of Tsinghua University.

taking advantage of the intangible assets of a well-known university is a good way of expanding the market share of their products in China (Zhou and Zhu, 2004; Fan, 2005).

Another new trend for China's universities is the virtual research center. In 1999, the Ministry of Education initiated its experiment with virtual research centers by setting up 10 such centers online among different universities, mainly focusing on the fields of mathematics, chemistry, computer and information science, and life sciences. In 2001, these research centers finished the experimental stage and entered into formal operation. By 2002, the Ministry of Education had formally approved 20 virtual research centers, of which three centers are being set up jointly by universities and enterprises, with the rest being mainly established by universities and research institutions.

By making full use of modern calculation and communication tools, such as the internet, these virtual centers can help reduce the waste of time and human resources spent travelling among different research sites, integrate relevant resources to the maximum, and also operate far more flexibly than the regular joint centers. However, determining ownership of the intellectual property rights developed under this modality has become a challenging question (Liu et al., 2002).

Technology Commercialization through Technology Transfer and Licensing

When a technology is well developed by the university and begins the process of commercialization, technology transfer occurs in two ways: patent licensing and non-patent technology transfer. When compared with the US, where patent licensing and sales are one of the most important methods for universities to transfer technology, patenting activity in China's universities has been relatively weak. According to a 1998 survey, the total revenue generated by American universities through patent licensing was US$576 billion, greatly outnumbering the total revenue (RMB 0.19 billion) generated by Chinese universities in 2001, which was the highest in the past two decades (see Table 1.9). The weakness of China's universities in patent licensing and sales can be attributed to weaknesses in the country's innovation system, such as inadequate patent awareness, the shortage of patents with commercial value, a lack of original innovation strength, and weakness in government support structures to help researchers commercialize their inventions (Shao, 2002). For example, 1,653 patents were granted to domestic applicants in China in 2001, as compared to 125,704 in Japan or 35,900 in Korea.[4]

Although the absolute number is not very high, patent licensing and

is focused on establishing and developing new and high-tech development zones (NHTZs). Since China formally launched the Torch Program in 1988, high-tech development zones have witnessed a fast pace of development and a wide range of expansion. To date, a total of 53 new NHTZs have played an increasingly important role in China's national economic growth and social development. Located in a knowledge-intensive and open environment while relying on China's S&T capability and economic strength, these NHTZs are providing an optimal environment to transform R&D achievements into actual productivity. From the very beginning, NHTZs have attached much importance to linkages between high-tech development and market demand both at home and abroad. Establishing NHTZs is one of the most important initiatives in commercializing S&T in China.

Unlike NHTZs, science parks make full use of the advantages of universities in terms of innovative capability, talent, and solid research foundations. Instead of a place for mass production, university-based science parks have been launched mainly for high-tech entrepreneurship. Since most of these universities themselves are also located in NHTZs, companies located in science parks can also enjoy preferential policies offered in NHTZs (Mei et al., 2005).

University-based science parks have played an important role in three main areas. First, in incubating spin-offs created by faculty or students from universities which is their core function as well as the key difference from NHTZs. Second, by widening and increasing channels to integrate and commercialize all kinds of scientific outcomes from local markets as well as other places. In addition to providing incubators for spin-offs, these parks have also become a magnet to attract other high-tech start-ups, including those created by expatriates. Third, by providing services to enterprises located in the science park, this means that they are obliged not only to manage the real estate of the park, but also to provide a sound environment for innovation, ranging from fundraising to legal counsel as well as talent absorption (He and Zhang, 2005).

Table 1.11 shows the function of university-based science parks as important incubators for university-owned spin-offs. In 2004, of the 4,563 enterprises affiliated with universities over 24 percent were located in the science parks. Although relatively small in number, these enterprises have operated far more successfully than those outside science parks in terms of income, profit, and tax paid, taking up over 60, 64, and 49 percent of the total figures generated by the university-owned enterprises.

While science parks have developed very quickly over the last few years, there are also some relevant problems that need to be addressed. First, many parks were not very clear of their mission and strategy and accepted

Table 1.11   *General statistics of university-owned enterprises in science parks 2004 (billion yuan)*

	Enterprises in science parks	Total university-owned enterprises
Number	1121 (24.57%)	4563
Income	58.26 (60.10%)	96.93
Profit	3.24 (64.95%)	4.99
Tax paid	2.39 (49.26%)	4.87
Income to university	0.45 (25.56%)	1.75

Note: Figures in brackets indicate the ratio to the total number for the year.

Source: S&T Development Centre, Ministry of Education.

all kinds of enterprises without careful selection due to their thirst for short-term economic achievements. Only when the parks ascertain the specific area for development according to the strengths of the university will they obtain comparative advantages and long-term development. Second, there are problems in the mechanism of management and operations, especially when parks must simultaneously accept guidance from several administrative bodies including district, municipal, and provincial governments. This will place a great burden on the smooth development of the parks. Third, a lack of talent has curbed the rapid growth of the parks, which are in urgent need of professionals who are good at management or specialized in certain areas such as technology assessment, technology transfer, and capital operation. All three challenges have become important factors in determining the development of science parks (ibid.).

As an important part of the national innovation system, a successful science park has become a symbol of a first-rate university, which will not only help increase the regional economy and boost technology innovation, but also provide an important platform for the university to serve society.

4   TECHNOLOGY COMMERCIALIZATION THROUGH UNIVERSITY-OWNED ENTERPRISES (UOEs): A UNIQUE CHINESE EXPERIENCE

UOEs refer to those enterprises that are still in one way or another controlled by the universities with which they are affiliated. Legitimacy of this control derives from the fact that many of the enterprises were created through funds from universities and many universities are still the largest shareholders in these companies. In other cases, enterprises willingly submit their management control to universities so that they can generate intangible benefits for themselves.

UOEs are not new for Chinese universities. Many, particularly those that are engineering and science based, have had university-owned factories since the 1950s. These were mainly used for students to obtain short-term internships or apprenticeships in a real production environment. Moreover, under the 'work unit system' (a self-sufficient organizational system for enterprises, universities, and other social institutions in China after the founding of the PRC), many universities had their own service providers such as print shops, publishers, guest-houses, and so on (for a detailed discussion of this system, see Lu, 1990). What is new is the market environment and the new roles these enterprises are playing (or are expected to play) and the complex relationships they have developed with their parent universities.

The development of UOEs can be divided into three stages. The first stage was from the early 1980s to 1990. During this period, China had just begun to implement its reform and open-door policy. Faced with the commercial opportunities in society and their own internal financial needs, traditional university-owned service providers began to open up society while many new services were created. Most of these operations were focused on technology transfer, technology development, technical consultancy, and technical services (MOST, 1999).

UOEs during this first stage were run under three models: the first was that of university-owned factories or print shops; the second was to create joint commercial entities with enterprises outside universities; and the third was technology development companies created by universities and departments. By 1989, sales of UOEs had reached 470 million yuan (Li, 2000).

Many UOEs in the early stage were short term, profit oriented, and poorly managed. This generated controversy as to whether it was appropriate for Chinese universities to run such enterprises. In order to address this issue, the State Commission of Education, the State Science and Technology Commission, and the Investigation Office of the General Office of the Party formed a joint investigation team in November 1990. The team visited over 30 universities in Beijing, Shanghai, Nanjing, and other cities to look into the issue, and submitted a report that endorsed the development of UOEs.

The second stage of UOEs was from 1991 to 2000. In 1991, China's State Council issued its endorsement of UOEs in a document submitted by the Commissions on Education and Science and Technology to provide guidelines for administering UOEs. In 1993, another document submitted by the Commission of Education was endorsed by the State

Table 1.12 Growth of university-owned enterprises (billion yuan)

Year	Number	Sales	Profit	Tax paid	Income to universities
1997	–	29.55	2.72	1.23	1.58
1998	5,928	31.56 (6.8)	2.59 (–5.6)	1.35 (9.7)	1.50 (–5.1)
1999	5,444	37.90 (20.1)	3.05 (18.0)	1.66 (18.6)	1.59 (6.0)
2000	5,451	48.46 (27.9)	4.56 (49.5)	2.54 (53.3)	1.69 (6.2)
2001	5,039	60.30 (24.4)	4.81 (5.5)	2.84 (11.8)	1.83 (8.3)
2002	5,047	72.01 (19.4)	4.59 (–4.6)	3.63 (27.8)	1.72 (–6.0)
2003	4,839	82.67 (14.8)	4.29 (–6.4)	3.87 (6.61)	1.8 (4.7)
2004	4,563	96.93 (17.3)	4.99 (16.3)	4.87 (25.8)	1.75 (–2.8)

Note: Figures in brackets indicate growth rate.

Source: S&T Development Centre, Ministry of Education.

Council to expedite the reform and development of higher education. This document prescribed that university-affiliated enterprises of a high-tech nature should be actively developed. Since then, particularly after Deng Xiaoping's southern tour in 1992, UOEs have been developing at an accelerated speed. In 1992, sales of such enterprises jumped to 2.9 billion yuan from 1.76 billion yuan in 1991, rising to 37.9 billion yuan by 1999.

The third stage started in 2000, when new controversies began to surface over the appropriateness of universities getting involved in running enterprises. There were also concerns about the potential financial risks that universities were exposed to by UOEs being traded on stock markets. Furthermore, many UOEs felt the need to change the governance structure in order to allow them to operate as commercial enterprises. Recently, the government has begun to encourage universities and their affiliated enterprises to 'de-link' by clarifying property rights and obligations, separating management from administration, reforming the shareholding structure to establish a modern enterprise system, and standardizing the operating quality and investment actions to achieve scientific management. Clearly, Chinese UOEs are currently at a new crossroads.

In 2004, there were 4,563 enterprises affiliated with regular Chinese universities. Table 1.12 presents an overall picture of the development of UOEs. As can be seen, over the past several years and in particular between 1998 and 2000, UOEs have maintained their growth momentum in terms of sales, profit, and tax paid. Since 2001, however, the growth rate has slowed with the profit and income to universities decreasing in 2002 and 2003.

Given university-affiliated enterprises, S&T-based enterprises were the

Table 1.15   Provinces and cities with profits exceeding 100 million yuan from university-affiliated enterprises, 2004 (in millions of yuan)

Rank	P/C	Profit	Rank	P/C	Profit
1	Beijing	1,964	6	Zhejiang	225
2	Shanghai	705	7	Shanxi	151
3	Liaoning	585	8	Sichuan	139
4	Jiangsu	313	9	Shanxi	122
5	Hubei	229	10	Guangdong	112
	Total profit			4,545	

Source: S&T Department Centre, Ministry of Education.

can be traced back to 1993 when 'Fuhua Shiye' of Fudan University in Shanghai went public on the Shanghai Stock Exchange. Like other kinds of university-affiliated enterprises, these publicly listed companies have played an important role in commercializing technological achievements as well as in solving the problem of capital shortage in university operations. However, as the number of such enterprises increased and their scale expanded, university-affiliated enterprises have also revealed their inherent problems, such as unclear property rights, the risks universities were exposed to by these business operations, the lack of a mechanism for universities to exit, and interference of the university administration with the enterprise's management. These challenges were part of the reason why their business achievements in recent years have declined almost year by year. To guarantee the healthy development of the business operations of these enterprises as well as the education and S&T activities of universities, it has been widely suggested that the enterprises should sever their connection with universities and be given full autonomy of operations. In 2001, the State Council, formally endorsed a document submitted by the Ministry of Education to clarify the property rights and standardize the management mechanism of university-affiliated enterprises. Tsinghua University and Peking University were designated as trial cases (State Council, 2001).

By 2005, the number of such companies listed on the stock market reached 40 and about two-thirds went public through their own initial public offering (IPO), while the rest went public through purchasing the 'shells' of existing public companies. The 'university bloc' has become a significant player in China's stock market, which has also been a source of controversy.

Of the 30 companies listed in Table 1.16, half were in the business

Table 1.16   Industry distribution of university-owned listed enterprises, 2000–2002

Industry	Number
Comprehensive	8
Computer application and service	7
Chemical material and products	3
Equipment manufacture	3
Medicine manufacture	3
Telecommunication and relevant equipment manufacture	1
Computer and relevant equipment manufacture	1
Biomedical products	1
Light Industry – office equipment & utensils	1
Other manufacture	1
Retail	1
Total	30

categories of 'comprehensive' and 'computer application and service'. Of the remaining companies, most were in other techno-business categories such as chemicals, equipment manufacture and medicine. Of these listed companies, universities are either the majority shareholders or the largest shareholders.

Many forms of university–market linkage, including informal consulting, technology contracts, licensing, and university science parks are universal. The most controversial university–business linkages are university-affiliated enterprises that are, to a certain degree, unique to China. Indeed, university-affiliated enterprises, along with high-tech enterprises affiliated with government research institutes, have grown into a major force in China's high-tech industry. Such enterprises have made major contributions to the development of the Chinese high-tech industry.

A close examination of high-tech enterprises reveals two types. The first is best represented by the Pearl River Delta in Guangdong province. Many of these enterprises are joint ventures with foreign capital and technologies. They basically follow the traditional path of how developing countries catch up with the developed countries (Amsden, 1989). Hobday (1995) asserts that such a path typically begins with low-cost labor assembly, progressing from OEM (original equipment manufacturing) through to ODM (original design manufacturing) and OBM (original brand manufacturing). It is a 'bottom-up' upgrading process in which different kinds of skills are acquired sequentially according to increasing levels of sophistication. The second type is best represented by high-tech enterprises that were either spin-offs from or affiliated with universities or research institutes, such as Legend, Founders, or Tongfang. Many such enterprises follow a 'top-down' process where they start with some R&D results and then 'move down' to the process of manufacturing and marketing. Both of these types of high-tech enterprises have played a major role in bringing knowledge generated in academia into the market.

Accelerated commercialization of R&D results from universities has clearly yielded benefits to society. One such case is the nuclear imaging device used for screening smuggling activities at customs. This technology was developed by Tsinghua Tongfang, an enterprise affiliated with Tsinghua University. The initial research work was done by professors at the Engineering Physics Department in the late 1990s, who saw the market potential but did not have the resources and capabilities to bring a viable product to the market. They could not find an industrial partner who would be willing to take on the research needed to bring the idea to the production stage. Over time, Tsinghua Tongfang worked closely with the Engineering Physics Department and brought the product to the market; it has become a huge commercial success and plays an important role in the fight against smuggling. An important institutional arrangement that played a central role in the success of this case was that key faculty members became full-time employees of Tsinghua Tongfang in order to bring needed tacit research knowledge to manufacturing.

While recognizing the benefits, there are still many serious problems that must be addressed before university-affiliated enterprises can be endorsed without reservation. The first issue is related to the division of labor between different social institutions. Are there comparative advantages inherent to universities in carrying out the basic mission of education and research? What are the explicit and implicit social contracts in such a social division of labor? Is there a change in the comparative advantages of universities in such a new social and technical environment? Currently, these issues are not well thought-through in China. Policy orientation and institutional design are also somewhat confusing. For example, universities are supposed to be the only social institutions responsible for higher learning but the government does not provide enough funding to universities to fulfill this main purpose. Nor are universities allowed to raise tuition fees to become self-sufficient. It is these inconsistencies in policy that force many universities and faculty members to engage in activities that might or might not be in the best interests of their organization in the long run.

Another problem related to university-affiliated enterprises is the impact of such activities on the academic environment and their potential for defining directions for university research. Some academics complain that there are too many commercial activities on campus and that this has changed the academic environment, making it harmful for basic research.

Others consider this an inefficient way of allocating R&D resources. Many faculty members and graduate students are no longer engaged in academic research. Rather, they are carrying out applications work whose commercial value is far greater than its perceived academic value. Furthermore, the university administration often devotes much time and energy to running university-affiliated enterprises.

A related question is to what degree one could attribute the slow improvement in the quality of university teaching to university-affiliated enterprises. This is a complicated question to answer, and there is little systematic data to support the argument one way or another. On the one hand, in the years prior to the reform, one of the missions of many university-affiliated enterprises was to improve teaching by providing students with better 'hands-on' opportunities. This mission seems to have become less important in recent years. Particularly since the late 1990s, many people involved in university-affiliated enterprises have become full-time employees in the enterprises rather than professors in their original academic departments. On the other hand, there is general agreement that along with the reform in the S&T system since 1985, Chinese academia, including public research institutes and universities, has become more commercially and application oriented. Government policies in general have supported this trend. The university-affiliated enterprise is one of many outlets for faculty and researchers to foster their commercial talents. While it is somewhat unfair to blame university-affiliated enterprises for the slow improvement in teaching quality, it is reasonable to say that such enterprises have contributed to the overall trend of commercialization of academia.

Some people believe that university-affiliated enterprises expose universities to undue financial risks. Of all such enterprises, only a small percentage has made a profit. Many are losing money and are running huge debts, which generate a significant financial burden for the universities. Such risks are not limited to financial concerns. They may also have an impact on the reputation of the university. For example, in analyzing university-affiliated enterprises on the stock market, many investors automatically linked the 'university concept' to the concept of high-tech. But most of the UOEs listed on the stock market have not transformed their technology advantages into commercial successes. Some argue that these companies used the university name improperly to attract potential investors, which might be helpful to the company in the short term, but could be damaging for the university in the long term.

Partly as a result of these concerns, beginning in the late 1990s many university-affiliated enterprises began to reform their governance structures. Discussions have shifted from whether universities should run enterprises to what should be their 'exit strategy', leading to two sets of problems. First, for public companies where universities have controlling a share, the question is how to reduce the share owned by the universities, a problem similar to many SOEs on the stock market. Theoretically, universities can use the money to build their endowment for long-term development in a similar manner to many European and US private universities.[6] In reality, China's vulnerable financial market might not be able to absorb the share owned by universities, which was why the government's 2001 attempt to reduce its share of many public SOEs failed.

The second problem is how to sort out the ownership structure of those university-affiliated enterprises that are not listed on the stock market. Universities started these companies by investing some seed money or by providing some equipment, office space, and other non-tangible support. Managers also contributed to the success of their companies by taking a salary below the market rate. How should one count the contribution of universities and individual managers, and for those companies in bad shape, who is responsible for the debt?

In summary, over the past two decades, UOEs have built up a reputation as a powerful engine for economic development and as a useful conduit for commercializing university research. Even so, it is now time for UOEs to reflect on their future development given that China's market economy has become more mature, the R&D capabilities of industrial enterprises have made important progress, and the business climate for entrepreneurship has improved substantially.

After years of ups and downs in running UOEs, it is important for universities in China to recognize that business management is a commitment that requires knowledge and experience that universities might not have as part of their institution. In addition, running a business in a market economy is full of commercial risks that many universities are not prepared, and in many cases not designed, to assume. As a case in point, the leadership of Tianjin University was recently implicated in a business scandal.[7] There have been other similar cases in recent years.

5   CONCLUSIONS

In this chapter, we have reviewed China's economic reforms, the changing roles of its universities in the national innovation system, and the various ways in which universities and the market interact, with a special focus on technology commercialization from universities. We have also analyzed various forces that shaped the current relations among universities, the market, and the government. Some preliminary conclusions follow.

Economic reform and other related reforms in China have changed the overall environment in which universities and the market interact. Over the last two decades, the government not only has initiated some major policies to reform its innovation system and introduced market instruments, but it has also set up many programs to complement these policies. These programs were systematic and wide-ranging, so that different institutions and sectors could all benefit. More importantly, the implementation of these programs has often induced changes in institutional culture. For example, many national programs aimed at supporting basic research or solving key national bottlenecks were not automatically allocated to research institutes or universities. Rather, a competitive system based on peer review was adopted.

Since the government is no longer the sole source or even the major source of funding for university operations, universities must finance their operations through multiple channels, including charging tuition fees and providing services to industry. Nor is the government the main employer of university graduates, who have to find jobs for themselves in the new economic environment. While the Ministry of Education is still playing an important role in administering the university system and providing partial funding for university educational services, it mostly has to rely on indirect policies rather than on direct financial measures with regard to university research functions. The expansion of higher education enrollment in recent years has generated new dynamics that will further complicate relationships between the government and the universities.

China's innovation system has also undergone important structural change. PRIs are no longer the main R&D service providers; in most cases, universities are equal competitors in the market. In addition to the public research programs set up by the government, the rapid economic growth and weak industrial R&D capabilities from the mid-1980s to the late 1990s also created strong demand for applied industrial research and services. Universities and PRIs learned, adapted, and created many ways of collaborating with industry and fulfilling the roles expected by industry. However, as the industrial R&D capabilities of Chinese firms are improving, the expectations of industry from the universities and PRIs are also becoming more demanding. These changing environments and market conditions have also brought new challenges to the universities.

The evolving relationship of universities with the market is not without controversy. Some have argued that some of the reforms and programs related to university–industry interactions have gone too far by mixing the market with academia, which poisons the academic environment and distorts long-term research. Such critiques are not without foundation. The potential downside of the overemphasis on the university–market linkage

China's Academy of Sciences (CAS) (1949–1954), Annual Report of China's Academy of Sciences.

China Statistical Bureau (Various years), *China Statistical Yearbook on Science and Technology*, China Statistical Press.

Cohen, W. and D.A. Levinthal (1989), 'Innovation and learning: the two faces of R&D', *Economic Journal*, September, 569–96.

Cohen, W. and D.A. Levinthal (1990), 'Absorptive capacity: a new perspective on learning and innovation', *Administrative Science Quarterly*, **35**, 128–52.

Edquist, C. (1997), *Systems of Innovation: Technologies, Institutions and Organizations*, London: Pinter.

Fan, Z. (2005), 'Analysis of the cause of TNCs' quickening investment to R&D center in China', *China Business and Market*, **9**, 19–22.

Feng, Z. (1999), *Theories and Policies on National Innovation Systems*, Economic Science Press.

Freeman, C. (1987), *Technology Policy and Economic Performance: Lessons from Japan*, London: Pinter.

He, J. and Y. Zhang (2005), 'Function of university-based science parks', *Chinese University Technology Transfer*, **8**, 27–9.

Hobday, M. (1995), *Innovation in East Asia: The Challenge to Japan*, Aldershot, UK and Brookfield, VT, USA: Edward Elgar.

Li, G. (2000), 'A Research Report on the Tenth Five Year Plan for Beijing's University High-Tech Industries' (draft).

Li, Z. and G. Zeng (2000), 'Analysis on the transitional process of China's innovation system', *Studies in Science of Science*, **3**, 12–19.

Liu, X., J. Xiao and Q. Hui (2002), 'Virtual research center and its function in national technology innovation system', *Science and Technology Progress and Policy*, **2**, 18–19.

Lu, F. (1990), 'On work unit system', *China Social Science*, **9** (1).

Lundvall, B. (1992), *National Systems of Innovation: Towards a Theory of Innovation and Interactive Learning*, London: Pinter.

Mei, M., J. Xu and J. Luo (2005), 'Pondering on the construction of China's university-based science parks', available at: www.tsinghua.edu.cn (accessed 5 April 2007).

Ministry of Education (MOE) (1999), *Action Scheme for Invigorating Education towards the 21st Century*, Beijing: MOE.

Ministry of Science and Technology (MOST) (1999), *China's New and High-tech Industrialization Development Report*, Science Publishing House.

Nelson, R.R. (ed.) (1993), *National Innovations Systems: A Comparative Analysis*, Oxford: Oxford University Press.

Netbig (2001), 'Chinese university ranking', available at: http://www.netbig.com (accessed 5 April 2007).

Saxenian, A. (1994), *Regional Advantage: Culture and Competition in Silicon Valley and Route 128*, Cambridge, MA: Harvard University Press.

Science and Technology Statistics (STS) (1999), 'Technology activities of independent R&D institutes nationwide in the fields of natural science and technology', available at: www.sts.org.cn (accessed 5 April 2007).

Science and Technology Statistics (STS) (2002), 'Reforms on R&D institutes', available at: www.sts.org.cn (accessed 5 April 2007).

Shao, Y. (2002), 'Reports on China's higher education in the national innovation system' (post-doctoral research report).

SSTC (eds) (1986), 'Guidelines for China's science and technology policy', Science and Technology White Paper No. 1, Science and Technology Documentary Press.

SSTC (1994, 1995), 'China's science and technology indicators', Science and Technology Yellow Paper No. 2, No. 3.

State Council of China (1999), 'Resolution on further adjustment on the management system and deployment of State Council-affiliated universities'.

State Council of China (2001), 'Guidelines on the management standardization of university-affiliated enterprises in both Peking and Tsinghua universities'.

State Science Commission (SSC) (1986), 'Guideline on China's science and technology policies', Scientific and Technical Documents Publishing House.

World Bank (1998), *Reforms on China's Higher Education* (in Chinese), China Financial and Economic Publishing House.

Xue, L. (1999), 'The knowledge-based economy and its challenge to China's higher education', paper presented at the First US–China S&T Policy Seminar, Beijing, October 25–26.

Zhao, Z. (1986), 'Speech at the National Working Conference on Science and Technology', SSTC (ed.).

Zhou, L. and M. Zhu (2004), 'A study on transfer to China of multinational corporations' R&D facilities', *Academic Exploration*, **4**, 70–74.

2. Perspectives on technology transfer and commercialization in Africa: a focus on Kenya

Kamau Gachigi, Paul Kukubo and Crispus M. Kiamba

> The piecemeal engineer will adopt the method of searching for, and fighting against, the greatest and most urgent evil of society, rather than searching for, and fighting for, its greatest ultimate good.
>
> Karl Popper

1 INTRODUCTION

The basis for economic success in the world today is knowledge. The challenge for any nation seeking economic success can therefore be thought of as twofold: first, to facilitate the acquisition of knowledge from within (or without) its borders and second, to facilitate the conversion of that knowledge into benefits for its citizens by the most efficient means available. This is the essence of technology transfer. Not only is it necessary that these two conditions are met but that they are met consistently and competitively.

An overview of the situation in Africa south of the Sahara is a Herculean task largely because of lack of data. It would therefore be misleading to present this chapter as comprehensive in detail; rather it seeks to describe the common practice on the continent where factors that influence policy making and implementation are concerned. A brief discussion is provided on some current thoughts and debates regarding what can be termed the challenge of Africa's economic development, so as to contextualize the idea of technology transfer. Anecdotal examples are provided of activities toward technology transfer in a number of countries in terms of the scant data available. A key objective of this chapter is to propose a model for how technology transfer might be effected in Africa in light of specific developments in digital technologies where information and communication technology (ICT) applications and hardware fabrication are concerned. The approach taken pays special attention to factors not widely understood or even known when African issues are reported in the media. By the same token poor governance and corruption, factors that deservedly receive copious media attention, are not given much consideration. In addition, it is broadly assumed that technology transfer is a fixed vector pointing inwards from outside. While this is mostly true, the place of indigenous knowledge, which can provide and indeed has provided in some instances (an example is the development of appetite suppressant P57 by Pfizer Phytopharm from plant Hoodia gordonii, traditionally used by the San of the Kalahari Desert: Lee and Balick, 2009), significant exceptions to this, is not considered.

William Easterly (2006) of New York University dichotomizes the types of interventionists in Africa's economic challenge: the first group he calls the 'planners', who he describes as being wont to impose top-down solutions, on a massive scale, on the problematic populations; the second group he terms the 'searchers', who are those who seek bottom-up solutions to specific needs, following the realism of Karl Popper's piecemeal interventions. The ideas presented in this chapter fall more under the latter, albeit from an African and not a 'foreign' source. (Easterly, in fact, was classifying foreign interventionists.) The interventionists are presented within the context of plans still in the formative stages in Kenya, which is the UNESCO pilot project for science and technology parks in Africa south of the Sahara (excluding South Africa).

2 ASSESSING TECHNOLOGY TRANSFER IN AFRICA

Before going into a discussion on how Africa can earn the prize of effective technology transfer, it is important to present some discussion of the tacit assumptions embedded in the idea of technology transfer that make some qualifications necessary.

Environmentally Sustainable Technology-based Growth

Copious evidence exists for an ailing earth (Millennium Assessment, 2005; World Resources Institute, 2009), with the average per capita eco-footprint worldwide in terms of global hectares[1] standing at 2.2 global hectares per person, against the availability of only 1.8 acres per person. This translates to an excess of about 20 percent over the earth's carrying capacity. Any discussion on technology transfer should therefore take these dire figures into account as a necessary overarching backdrop, as policies and actions that fail to do so are likely to exacerbate the situation further in light of the large populations seeking to improve their material livelihood. While the carrying capacity of ecologies can be augmented by judicious use of technology, the assessment of such technologies in practice today is usually based on optimization and efficiency within a limited and localized scope.

Emerging economies need to heed the lessons from the past where modernization is concerned, and as broad-based a cost–benefit analysis as possible ought to be sought when considering the ways in which technology transfer might be effected in places such as Africa. Developed countries need, at the very least by moral obligation, to bear a significant portion of the financial cost for developing nations to emerge from underdevelopment in as an environmentally benign a manner as possible. Such considerations are indeed the objective of programs under international bodies such as the UN[2] and the African Union (AU). A particularly balanced approach is captured in resilience theory (Holling and Gunderson, 2002), which proposes ways in which competitive economic development can proceed while being overtly considerate of environmental concerns. Having at least mentioned the importance of the environment, other issues relating to Africa's technology transfer challenges can be considered.

Does 'One-Size-Fits-All' Apply to National Innovation Systems?

Creating an environment conducive to technology transfer is, according to the UN (2007, 42), tantamount to establishing a national innovation system. What actually comprises such a system will differ from nation to nation, though they will share certain basic features. There must exist, for example, the supply side of the system that acquires, creates, or in some other way provides the knowledge. There must also be mechanisms that ensure that the knowledge diffuses from the point of source to the point of consumption, which will tend to be the marketplace, though could equally be government (civil service, military and so on). The consumer must then accept and utilize the products of the knowledge for the exercise to be considered successful. Government is expected to facilitate this process, and such structures are usefully called a national innovation system. Much current thinking revolves around the idea that successful technology transfer requires more than the government effort; one notable notion being the 'triple helix' that effectively conveys the notion of the need for a near genetic interplay between government, academia, and the private sector. More is said about this in the case study on Kenya.

In considering the actions necessary by governments in developing countries to achieve the goals of a national innovation system, Calestous

Juma (2005) points out three basic steps that can be paraphrased thus: that the government designs specific programs for mainstreaming technology in economic development; that the government restructures government machinery to serve these programs; and that the government promotes the programs through the creation of new institutions where necessary, along with providing incentives for their application.

According to Nick Segal (2008) there are 10 basic evolutionary steps that track the thinking around what is necessary to make possible economic development, including: a realization of the importance of small and medium-sized enterprises (SMEs); a recognition of the role of technology and innovation; and an application of Michael Porter's theory of economic clusters (1990). Segal also differentiates between the concept of a 'national innovation system' and the 'triple helix', defining the former as being focused on the entrepreneur and the latter as being focused on the inventor. Segal points out that the consequence of this differentiation can be very significant in terms of policy making. However, the basic point is that a complex system of interlinked entities is necessary for a successful knowledge-based economy.

Many governments are increasingly opting to actively create national innovation systems rather than hoping that they might somehow evolve spontaneously (Parry and Oh, 2008). This involves actions and activities including the creation of science and technology parks (STPs), special economic zones (SEZs), export processing zones (EPZs) and so on. Like the rest of the world, African countries are interested in implementing national innovation systems by a variety of means including these, though for reasons that range from the obvious to the rather subtle, most are barely beginning the process.

General Economic Indicators for Africa

According to the *World Development Indicators* (WDI) publication from the World Bank Group (2008), Africa as a region lags behind all other regions of the world in most of the important economic indicators. For example, the number of people living in extreme poverty on the continent increased from about 300 million in 1990 to 388 million in 2005. Related statistics indicate that the urban population in Africa has almost doubled over the last two decades and stood at 209 million in 2007, representing 36 percent of the population, many of whom live in appalling slums. The number of students completing their primary education was only 60 percent in 2006. Of the 50 officially recognized 'least developed nations' in the world, 34 are in Africa. Africa contributes a mere 3 percent or so of international trade (WTO, 2007), and 90 percent of trade in Africa is to external nations, with only 10 percent being within the continent, leaving it highly exposed to the state of the international economy.

And yet it is also true that large populations in African countries subsist on agriculture and are therefore not unduly interconnected to that international trade; for them life therefore proceeds largely unaffected by changes in the global economy. Indeed, many activities of trade in the continent are not recorded by the formal structures and thus cannot be accurately included in any estimation of national GDP.

Sub-Saharan Africa achieved a growth rate of 6.2 percent in 2006 and 2007, experiencing a small drop to just below 6 percent in 2008.[3] This was attributed to higher prices for its oil and commodity exports, which is indicative of an overdependence on the export of unprocessed commodities. So while such growth rates are positive, the truth is that most of the income the continent continues to receive is from raw materials, which underscores clearly the need for the transfer of technology necessary for local value-addition activities with due attention to the important linkages pointed out in Michael Porter's cluster theory (1998). According to John Mugabe (2007), between 2000 and 2007 Africa's economic growth averaged 5 percent of GDP, with some countries posting higher growth than the United States and Japan; however, this growth was unsustainable, as it was based on the export of raw materials and thus vulnerable to global economic instabilities. Indeed, forecasts at present are that Africa is set to suffer significant adverse effects due to the current global crisis. However, recent indications (Blas, 2009) are that commodity prices have begun to rally. Mugabe (2007) also points out that foreign direct investment (FDI) inflows have risen from approximately US$20 billion in 1998 to US$53 billion in 2007. He points out that there is evidence that FDI is neither a source of new technologies nor does it promote local technological learning in Africa.

Some Proposed Solutions to the Development Challenge

Considerable effort is being applied to seeking solutions to the world's development challenge, which can be distilled into two complementary objectives: poverty alleviation and sustainable economic growth (wealth creation). A well-known example of this is Ernst Schumacher's (1973) 'world of a million villages' dependent on appropriate technologies, which seeks to provide the same villagers with the technological means to being self-sufficient as far as possible and is predicated on their retaining a traditional world outlook, defined by sustainable coexistence with nature and one's neighbors.

Jeffrey Sachs (2005) proposed 'clinical economics', which seeks to eradicate poverty at the village level by providing in essence, *per capita* aid of US$100 per year for five years. His plan is based on using the money to make available seven key factors, including seeds and fertilizer and healthcare interventions, to poor villagers worldwide, after which they can be expected to make their own fortune. This leans perilously close to the 'aid that kills' variety of action described in greater detail in the sub section 'What really is the role of aid?', below.

Perhaps the most widely referenced, if not universally accepted, framework for development is found in the Millennium Development Goals (MDGs) prepared through the UN Millennium Project, which happens to be closely associated with Sachs. Practical interventions and policy measures for achieving these goals have been proposed, one of which is the application of science, technology, and innovation. The findings by the Task Force, led by Calestous Juma and Yee-Cheong Lee, assigned to develop proposals within the context of science and technology were presented in the report (2005), 'Innovation: Applying Knowledge in Development'. Their primary recommendations for policy action revolve around the following:

- focus on platform technologies;
- improve infrastructure as a foundation for technology;
- improve science and technology education;
- promote knowledge-based business and industry;
- improve accessibility for science and technology experts to policy makers; and
- increase research and development (R&D).

Key policy direction for Africa is being provided by the outcomes of the World Summit on Sustainable Development (WSSD, 2002) that was convened by the UN and the UN General Assembly in 2005, and being implemented through the AU's New African Partnership for Economic Development (NEPAD).[4] Through NEPAD the AU has set specific science technology and innovation (STI) goals for implementation. These are meant to harness and apply science and technology for Africa's sustainable development and envisage that Africa will also contribute to the world's global pool of innovation and science. They have identified challenges that include confidence building and the creation of policy instruments that are shared across borders. Other challenges specified in the program are the need to improve the infrastructure for R&D and to build civic and political constituencies for technology. AU/NEPAD has created three elements to the program: the first involves gathering knowledge and information, which includes creating profiles of institutions, identifying funding instruments, garnering STI indicators, creating STI policy for agriculture and health, doing an inventory of STPs, and generating a list of good practice for regional STI cooperation. The second element involves the launching of flagship R&D programs listed as follows:

- The African Biosciences Initiative: creating a network of world-class laboratories dedicated to biotechnology. About 70 percent of the countries in Africa have ratified the Cartagena Protocol on Bio-safety (CPB) and are formulating their bio-safety frameworks with assistance from UNEP-GEF. Approximately 12 countries have bio-safety legislation, and in 2009 Kenya became the fourth African country to put laws in place to manage the introduction of commercial GM crops. The other three are Burkina Faso, Egypt, and South Africa.
- The African Institute for Mathematical Sciences (AIMS): started by Cambridge physicist Neil Turok, the first college in Cape Town is a resounding success, and NEPAD is planning to build 15 more, in collaboration with Turok, for the rest of Africa.
- The African Laser Center.
- A drug research, discovery and manufacturing system.
- The African Water Sciences Network.

Furthermore, under this second element of the program, 12 flagship areas have been identified (ICTs, biotechnology, biodiversity, laser technologies, space science, post-harvest food technologies, water sciences and technologies, drought research, indigenous technologies, mineral sciences, and energy).

The third and final element involves creating a common set of strategies aimed at improving policy conditions. These include:

- the African Biotechnology Panel;
- listing common African Science, Technology and Innovation (ASTII) Indicators;
- creating a regional science and technology cooperation protocol;
- promoting stakeholder dialogues on STI, for example African Policy Dialogues on Biotechnology, parliamentary fora on STI and the like; and
- a strengthening of the capacity of regional economic communities to address science and technology issues.

But for any plan intended to raise Africa from its economic underdevelopment to be successful, it must first recognize as completely as possible the situation in which Africa finds itself, that is the symptoms within the continent and the total raft of causes, both within and outside Africa. For many developing countries, the outstanding success in economic growth demonstrated by the so-called 'Asian Tigers' represents the ideal model, worthy of emulation.

The fact is that the world that Africa finds itself in as it seeks to develop is quite unlike the world that the Asian Tigers faced on their climb into economic development or indeed that in which the nations in the West developed. The dominant ideological prescription for poor nations to achieve this type of economic growth, recommended most notably by the World Bank, the International Monetary Fund (IMF), and the World Trade Organization (WTO), is captured in the term 'neo-liberal economics'. This process in effect opposes any semblance of protectionism, instead recommending the sacrifice of equity in exchange for economic growth through the attraction of FDI. It espouses small government, free markets and so on for all nations alike, regardless of the size of their GDP or their history. And it is being challenged perhaps as never before.

Challenging the Prevailing International Economic Order

Historically, African political and economic commentators such as Frantz Fanon (1961), Kwame Nkrumah (1965), and Walter Rodney (1973) have exposed exploitative economics, though in the context of the colonial milieu. More recently authors such as former World Bank employees David Korten (1995) and Joseph Stiglitz (2002) and others including Ha-Joon Chang (2002, 2007) and John Perkins (2004) have presented a challenge to the neo-liberal viewpoint of economics. The very fact that the Asian Tigers *have* managed to lift themselves up by their bootstraps begs the question: 'Why not Africa?'.

In a recent article, Sachs and McArthur (2009) mention some significant reasons which they believe contribute to the difference. The authors list the fact that Africa had not yet undergone a green revolution as Asia had. Africa was, and to a large extent remains, dependent on rain-fed irrigation. Much of Asia already had river-fed irrigation systems before the modern era. Additional reasons include the 'tropical disease burden, heavy concentration of landlocked countries, decline of aid for infrastructure during the 1980s and 1990s, and misguided attempts by Africa's creditors to collect debt servicing under "structural adjustment programs" during the 1980s and 1990s all played their part'. All these appear to be reasonable causes to explain the current status quo in Africa.

Another major difference gaining currency is related to one of the key features of the success of the Asian Tigers. This has been the imposition of protectionist policies for long enough to ensure adequate strength for their industries to compete: that is, the creation of a level playing field where it is manifestly absent to start with.

Is there a place for protectionism?

Ironically, as Chang (2002, 2007) clearly demonstrates, developed nations historically built their own economies through highly protectionist public support of private business and often even through state-owned companies, far from the neo-liberal economic viewpoint they now insist on for poor countries. Two examples he cites are the growth of the wool industry in eighteenth-century England, which was the start of modern industrialization, and the early protectionism championed by Alexander Hamilton that enabled the United States to build a competitive manufacturing sector.

Japan and the newly developed nations of the Far East, the Asian Tigers, have all employed distinctly protectionist policies in order to ensure that their fledgling new industries were protected until such a time that they were able to stand on their own in the international marketplace, at which time neo-liberal policies of free market economics hold true. Similarly economic development in South Korea, far from being the result of the recognition of free market forces and small government, leaned decidedly in the direction of public–private partnerships aimed at creating an advantage for local businesses on an international stage on which it would otherwise have been impossible to compete.

Chang and authors of his ideological standpoint are ushering in the advent of hitherto less well-known revisionist historo-economic evaluation of the rich–poor divide among countries on a broader stage. The result of these books is likely to be a greater resistance by poor countries, alongside the thousands of citizens in rich nations who have created a formidable lobby to expose unfair trade practices of much of the corporate sector in their countries in conjunction with the Bretton Woods organizations. The net result could be science parks in which the activity is organized in a much more purposeful and directed manner aimed more aggressively at greater local and regional self-sufficiency and at winning market share on the global 'battlefield' for poor countries in a non-zero-sum manner.

What really is the role of aid?

Another commonly held view is that development aid is necessary and indispensable. Indeed the development aid activities that have grown around Africa have evolved into a veritable industry in their own right. In an academic space dominated by non-African commentators such as

Sachs, Easterly, Collier, and even non-academicians such as Bono and Bob Geldof, the voices of African authors such James Shikwati, Allan Mwenda (2006), and Dambisa Moyo (2009b) are a welcome intervention increasingly making themselves heard as they call for a cessation of all aid. In a 2005 interview with *Spiegel*, Shikwati argues that aid promotes poverty in Africa by encouraging complacency, and that the individuals hired by the aid agencies are faced with the knowledge that success in their work would necessarily render them jobless.

This viewpoint, and in particular the book *Dead Aid* by Dambisa Moyo (2009b), has gained support from African heads of state such as Paul Kagame of Rwanda and Abdoulaye Wade of Senegal (Moyo, 2009a). Moyo makes it clear that it is development aid as opposed to charity and emergency aid that she is arguing against. Other voices, such as that of William Easterly (2002), (who coined the term 'cartel of good intentions' to represent those organizations he sees as central to the foreign aid milieu that is, according to this viewpoint, crippling Africa), have long held that because it is not accountable to the people that it contends to be helping, aid is a failure. The statistics are that US$60 billion of aid has been spent on Africa over decades; a period over which Africa has actually become poorer. The main arguments against Moyo's contentious views on aid are that the statistics she uses to defend her thesis are not accurate and that she does not justify her ultimate conclusion, that aid to Africa be cut forthwith, and ignores what they say is copious evidence that aid does often work. It is contended that as long as the major development organizations continue to insist on policies that require liberalized markets and harmful aid continues, any real technology transfer with its attendant benefits cannot take place.

The Status of STI in Africa

It has long been held that STI holds the key to economic development. As the world continues to experience enormous flux driven by continued advances in science and technology, it has become increasingly necessary to take stock of indicators and statistics that enable the characterization of a given economy in terms of the state of science and technology within its borders. Technologically developed nations have identified the need for such data and developed frameworks for conducting surveys for R&D (Frascati Manual), innovation (Oslo Manual), and human resources (Canberra Manual). The Organisation for Economic Co-operation and Development (OECD) nations regularly post reports (2007) in order to keep abreast of the STI readiness of its members. This particular scoreboard includes:

- the current situation of investment in R&D;
- the continuing growth of human resources in science and technology (HRST); and
- recent policy changes in the field of research and innovation.

The report also examines the efficacy of investments in knowledge (ICTs, nanotechnology, biotechnology, and so on), according to identified measures, while keeping abreast of significant trends in the general field of scientific and technological advancement. Ultimately they are meant to measure the impact of investment on productivity and trade.

One of the difficulties with regions of low economic development is that statistics are difficult to come by. This in itself presents a further barrier to solving the economic challenges, as policy making becomes that much more difficult to accomplish. In Africa, which by most economic indicators is a region of low economic productivity, such analyses have not been in any sense systematic. In 2006, in a paper presented at the International Conference on Science, Technology and Innovation, Frank Teng-Zen (2008) reviewed the status of STI indicators in African countries. He affirms this point of view, citing only a handful of exercises in South Africa, Mozambique, and Nigeria aimed at collecting such data. He also describes a very poor response from African governments to attempts by UNESCO and the World Bank to gather such statistics. He assesses the reasons for the dearth in such data as twofold: a lack of prioritization of STI at government level and a lack of the necessary manpower to conduct the research necessary. He points out, for example, that few universities in Africa have programs aimed at this objective that are adequately funded by their governments, and that until recently all such research was paid for by external agents.

However, today it is widely recognized by governments of the AU member states, as evidenced by the regular meetings of the African Ministerial Conference on Science and Technology (AMCOST), which as its name implies is an AU secretariat at cabinet level, that the key to unlocking the benefits of STI in Africa lies in creating effective STI systems. NEPAD is receiving assistance from a number of organizations in this regard, and several conferences have been organized around the theme of collating STI indicators through surveys. This process is called the African Science and Technology Innovation Indicators Initiative (ASTII), and is being steered within the AU through AMCOST.

Its broad objective is 'to build Africa's capacity to develop and use STI indicators', while the specific objectives are to:

- develop and enable the adoption of internationally compatible STI indicators;

- build human and institutional capacities for STI indicators and related surveys;
- enable African countries to participate in international programs for STI indicators; and
- inform African countries on the state of STI in Africa.

The process is still underway and the results are yet to be released. In the absence of this much anticipated data, the following sub section pools information from documents in the public domain to paint a picture that is hopefully of some value.

Some Indicators of STI Preparedness in Africa

A recent paper (Pouris, 2007) commissioned by UNECA concluded that for the best chances of success, the STIs in Africa should be structured in a three-tiered pyramidal arrangement, with the highest policy makers at the top, a middle layer of largely autonomous agencies whose role is to organize the lowest tier, and then the research laboratories themselves, under broad thematic groups. The UNECA paper presents publication and patent information as indicators of Africa's footprint in the world of research and innovation. It reports that in fact Africa accounts for only 1.8 percent of the world's publications, which is half as many as Latin America and fewer than India alone. It also finds that Africa is responsible for only 0.1 percent of all patents produced worldwide. It is worth qualifying these facts further first by pointing out that much economic innovation in Africa goes on without formal recognition, partially due to ignorance of intellectual property rights and partially out of suspicion that the system of justice would be unable to apply the law in the face of an infringement. A second qualification is required regarding the comparison of patent production with India, which might be misleading as the population of India exceeds that of Africa (Africa's population in 2005 was estimated at 921 million, while that of India is approximately 1.3 billion: United Nations, 2009).

Further analysis in the UNECA paper indicates that of all Africa's patents, half are attributed to South Africa and Egypt, and that South Africa alone is responsible for 88 percent of all the inventions emanating from the continent. However, it is also suspected that many African countries store much good-quality research in reports that never get published in peer-reviewed journals and are therefore not included in such data as is mentioned above (Kahn, 2001). Other indicators include the usual economic indicators such as R&D budgets as a percentage of GDP, the number of people engaged in R&D, and so on.

Table 2.1   Selected % GDP expenditure on R&D (GERD), 2000–2005

Country	% GERD	Country	% GERD
South Africa	0.76	Madagascar	0.12
Mozambique	0.59	Seychelles	0.11
Sudan	0.34	Zambia	0.01
Uganda	~0.25	Lesotho	0.01
Burkina Faso	0.17		

Source: UNDP Human Development Report, 'Technology: Diffusion and Creation', 2007/2008.

In terms of expenditure on R&D as a percentage of GDP, Africa's figures are more difficult to come by. However, the International Comparison of Research and Development report covering the period between 1999 and 2000 places Africa's expenditure at US$5.8 billion. It indicates that approximately half of the countries in Africa did not at the time have data available (see Table 2.1).

As dire as some of these figures appear, there is a certain amount of activity on the ground in many African countries that offers a positive glimpse at the future. As is described in the following section, STPs are a proven means to achieving economic development, though they have only recently been applied in developing countries. In the following are highlighted some of the positive developments on the African scene that have an impact on the potential for technology transfer.

Development of STPs in African Countries

A recent study carried out at the behest of the Economic Commission for Africa under the UN began by questioning the suitability of STPs in all African countries. In the report they present criteria for whether or not a nation is capable of implementing an STP, which are summarized by whether a viable national innovation system pertains in that country. The latter involves the ability to conduct research and, critically, the ability for the economy to transfer that research into the market place. By examining key economic indicators (KEI) for 30 African countries (the remainder had insufficient data to be included), they concluded that 21 out of 31 countries in Africa did not have the requisite resources to create STPs.

They studied the best practice and business model development among STPs in Southern Africa (South Africa, Botswana, Mauritius, Mozambique) and Northern Africa (Algeria, Egypt, Morocco, Tunisia) and found that of the eight countries, five had integrated STPs in their science and technology policies, while six (Algeria, South Africa, Egypt, Morocco, Botswana and Tunisia) had actually initiated parks (all being public-private partnerships, except for Elgazala in Tunisia, which is fully public), just four of which were fully operational and six more under construction at the time of publication. Most were focused on the ICT sector, except for Casablanca Park and the Innovation Hub in South Africa, both of which are diversified. In terms of numbers of companies hosted at each park, they reported Casablanca Technopark, the smallest in terms of physical space, actually hosted the largest number of companies (140). Smart Village in Cairo was found to be host to about 100 companies, while the number of companies hosted at The Innovation Hub and Elgazala hovered at around 50. These researchers went further to create a business model for how such parks should operate and rated the parks studied against their model. Their model took into account the park's location, its vision and mission, governance and operation management, the park's champion(s), and performance indicators (including the number of hosted companies, the rate of graduation of incubatees, jobs created, etc.) An interesting statistic with regard to these factors was the large gap between the highest performer in terms of job creation (Smart Village in Cairo with 12 000 jobs) and the others (the next best was the Innovation Hub in Pretoria with 1400 jobs).

As of 2005 there were about 30 business incubators in Sub-Saharan Africa (Dolun, 2005). As the current number in South Africa has now reached 38, the total number must be in excess of 46 (South Africa was home to at least 22 of the 30 in 2005). It is important to note that South Africa is also home to six of MIT's Fab Labs, the most in any nation in the world. South Africa also is home to SunSpace, the company that produced the world's first micro-satellite, developed at Stellenbosch University. Others include Zamnet, Zambia's premier ISP that was developed at the University of Zambia and the drive to promote alternative energies, such as biogas at the Kigali Institute of Science, Technology and Management (KIST.).

A sample of activities in Africa related to STPs and technology transfer is provided in Table 2.2. The specific case of Kenya is presented in the next section as a model for how other countries in Africa might progress in this field.

Possible Indicators for the Future of Technology Transfer in Africa

The record of poor performance mentioned in the previous sub section, though factual, masks positive developments of significance that are more encouraging. In a recent survey by the Institute for the Future in Palo Alto

Table 2.2   Summary of developments in specific African nations at the Africa Regional Workshop

Stage	Country	Developments
Advanced development	South Africa (Phindile Tshabangu, phindile@sabtia.org.za)	• The Technology Innovation Hub (Pretoria) is already a member of the IASP • 38 business incubators in S. Africa, 75% govt funded, 25% private • SABTIA (South African Business and Technology Incubator Assoc.), founded in 2004, had 20 members by 2007 • Notable spin-offs: SunSpace & Information Systems (Pty) Ltd (launched world's first micro-satellite in 2005)
Moderate development	Mozambique (Carlos José Tamele, ctamele@micti.co.mz) Kenya (Kamau Gachigi, kamaug@uonbi.ac.ke)	• Technology Development Center and Science and Technology Park in Moamba • US$4 million govt investment • The main national document Vision 2030 identifies ST&I as foundation of development • US$10 billion Ol Donyo Malili Technopolis. Construction starts August 2010, including the Mzalendo National Science and Technology Park (which is the UNESCO/WTA pilot project for Sub-Saharan Africa) – presidential support • Two business parks (EPZ, Sameer), one govt. incubator (KIE) • Life Sciences incubator launched by ICIPE and Bridgeworks Africa Co. Ltd • 4 private ICT incubators • University of Nairobi Science and Technology Park is incubating technology companies and uses a rapid-prototyping center built around a MIT Fab Lab. Network

Table 2.2   (continued)

Stage	Country	Developments
		of small, inter-linked incubators modeled on this planned for tertiary institutes nationwide
	Zimbabwe (Q C Kanhukamwe)	• Harare Institute of Technology conducts incubation of hi-tech businesses. Presidential support
	Rwanda (Albert Mutesa, amutesa@mineduc. gov.rw)	• Presidential support. 0.5% annually of the national budget goes to R&D activities. Focus on ICT (ICT Park started) • Notable spin-off: CRET Sarl has constructed 25 biogas plants
	Uganda (Dick M. Kamugasha, dkamugasha@uiri. org)	• Kampala Industrial and Business Park (KIBP) located at Namanve – 700 Ha. World Bank funding US$27 million. Being implemented. Presidential support
	Nigeria (Umaru Bindir, ubindir@yahoo.com)	• Unprecedented $5 billion (US) endowment fund pledged for the establishment of a National Science Foundation (NSF) in 2006 • $500,000 (US) from UNESCO/ Japan Funds for policy reform. Matched by Govt of Nigeria http://allafrica.com/ stories/200801240348.html • Plans for six S&T Parks
Planning stage	Ethiopia (Shumu Teferra, shumu_ teferra@ yahoo.com)	• Ethiopian National Research, Science and Technology Plan is in process
	Tanzania (Rose Kingamkono, rkingamkono@ costech.or.tz)	• R&D Intensity (2007 Current Prices) for Year 2007 • GERD-1[a] 0.02% • GERD-2[b] 0.49% • GERD-3[c] 0.86% • GERD-4[d] 1.01% • Researchers per million population – 61 (head count, 2200) • Indications of policy framework for STI and Parliamentary acts on patent protection, incentives

Table 2.2   (continued)

Stage	Country	Developments
		for innovation (presidential STI Advisory Committee planned)
		• ST&I given place of high priority in several national documents, including Vision 2025, National Social Growth and Poverty Reduction (NSGPR – Kiswahili abbreviation: *MKUKUTA*), Ruling Party Manifesto
		• Eight clusters formed, each around a specific industry. NM-AIST World Bank initiative – one of 4 campuses in Africa
	Namibia (Israel Tjizake, tjizake@mhevtst.gov)	• Implementation of the Science Policy through the Commission and the National Research and Innovation Fund
	Malawi (Alfred O. Maluwa, aomaluwa@mistmw. org)	• Several locally developed innovations (appropriate technology)
Non-existent	Cameroon	• Free zone for higher education
	Lesotho (Spirit B. Tlali, sb.tlali@nul.ls)	• The establishment of S&T parks is listed in the Science and Technology Policy, 2006–2011
	Swaziland (Mgidi Donald Dlamini, mgidi@ uniswacc.uniswa.sz)	• National STI policy being formulated
	Burundi	• Policy includes development of science park

Notes:
a   Refers to GERD based on government funds flow to R&D programs only.
b   Refers to GERD based on all government fund flow to R&D activities (recurrent and developmental funds.
c   GERD-3: =GERD2 plus internal sources (Self Generated Fund and Local Donor Fund).
d   GERD-4: =GERD2 plus external & internal sources (Foreign Donor Support).
    Presenters at the Africa Regional Workshop on Science and Technology Park Development, Windhoek, Namibia, 9–11 May 2007, were: UNESCO, WTA, ISESCO, KOICA & Govt of Namibia. The above information was mostly sourced from their presentations at that meeting. Botswana and Ghana were not represented at the conference.

seeking to obtain indications of future directions, especially in the area of STPs, Gachigi lists some signals that he believes are important for Africa (2009), which are summarized in the following.

During 2007–08 three of the top 10 reformers in business were Sub-Saharan countries (World Bank). This is a reflection of policy adjustment on the parts of those governments to reforms that have precipitated improved competitiveness. Indeed, Mauritius is among the top 15 nations in the world measured in terms of favorable business regulations. Furthermore, while entrepreneurs in Sub-Saharan countries face greater bureaucratic barriers to doing business than in any other part of the world, 58 of the region's nations implemented reforms during 2007–08 in what has been a growing trend.

There has also been positive development on the investment front. Historically Africa has never been very attractive to international arbitrage investors because of perception problems. That is changing. The following quote is taken from Jerome Booth's article (2008) in *The Daily Telegraph*, a respected newspaper in the UK:

> African markets aren't nearly as tiny as you'd think. With a market capitalization of well over $100 billion, Africa's markets are substantially larger than Central Europe and Russia were in the mid-1990s when they opened up to foreign investors. More importantly, African markets have been on a strong bull run. Between 1995 and 2005, African stocks showed compound annual growth of 22%.

The same attractiveness seen by arbitrageurs for African stock markets, if based on fundamentals, should reflect a general growth in economic development which means that in time a venture capital sector will arise, of which local high-tech venture companies can take advantage. While some of the investor confidence may be based on speculation, the fundamentals are encouraging, as described by Booth:

> Emerging markets represent 85pc of the world's population and emerging market asset classes could account for 50pc of global market capitalization in 15 years. It is possible to argue with a straight face that pension funds should put 35pc of their assets in emerging markets now. All markets are risky. The emerging markets are those where this is priced in.

(Note that this statement was made in January 2008 – before the recent current financial crisis.)

Perhaps even less well known is the fact that African stock markets are experiencing significant growth in terms of traded volumes based mostly on local investment. For example, Safaricom's initial public offering (IPO) in Kenya managed to raise over $3 billion, representing an oversubscription rate of 532 percent, most of which was from a large number of small-sized local investors.[5]

Another particularly encouraging trend is the Kenyan government raising money for specific projects through infrastructure bonds. In 2010, US$225 million was targeted for such a bond and US$325 million raised, mostly from local sources. This is the first time in the country that a government bond is to be pegged to specific projects and for which transparent accountability has been offered to investors. Indications are therefore that private equity within the country is at levels that could convert, even if only partially, into venture capital. Whether or not these types of inflows into innovative venture companies happen hinges on the capacity of local champions to sell the cause effectively.

Mobile telephony, broadband, and cheap transportation are today all very basic functions that any and every economy requires in order to be competitive. In many parts of Africa, where abject poverty and poor infrastructure conspire to confine life to a space a couple of centuries behind the technologically developed world, even old technology is big news. Plenty has been written on the impact of mobile telephony on developing economies, as it is certainly much more glamorous than the quieter revolution taking place in transportation. Inasmuch as the mobile phone is bringing the twenty-first century to many Africans, cheap motorcycles and scooters primarily from China are now widespread and have ushered in massive change.

The arrival in 2009 of the first undersea cables in East Africa (TEAMS and SEACOM) and the landing of the Eassy cable in 2010 marks events of great import, as the prospect of affordable bandwidth is finally within reach, with obvious benefit to all economic activity. And yet the true extent of such technology is closely dependent on the availability of electricity (UNCTAD, 2007).

In a recent paper, Bell and Juma (2008) suggest that African countries should implement new ICT functionality by interconnecting with other existing infrastructures as varied as power grid systems and sewers, an approach which they report has been in practice in Europe, Japan, and South Africa for the last two decades. South Africa is implementing power line communication (PLC), which uses power line cables to provide broadband internet, and the same South African company has already begun work to do the same in Uganda and Rwanda. In Kenya, multi-media firms are competing to provide last-mile access to supply triple play access to homes via co-axial (along existing electricity cables) and optical fiber cable (for example, GPON).

Increasingly, accessible rapid-prototyping technologies can serve a hugely empowering role in industries in poor countries. In the industrialized nations of the north the idea of fabricating products in the home has been envisaged (Burns, 1998). In Africa these technologies may help to usher in a grassroots technological transformation, whereby laboratories stocked with relatively inexpensive rapid-prototyping equipment can be dotted throughout the region. They can serve as the cores of business incubators linked to one another and to centers of academic excellence anywhere in the world through video-conferencing facilities, thereby taking technology to the people.

It is likely that especially the drop-on-demand variety of 3D printers will have an enormous impact on the capacity of scientists and engineers in poor countries to make what they hitherto could only imagine. Batteries, capacitors, inductors, printable electronics, solar cells, and so on are examples of devices that can be fabricated using such technologies. However, there are limitations to these technologies as well. First, there is the very real threat that the lack of economies of scale has on market viability. Second, there is limited access to materials from which to make products, and there is a hampering absence of broad-band connectivity.

China has shown a very significant interest in strong trade relations with Africa. In 2006 China hosted the heads of state of 40 African countries. It has backed its stated interest in Africa with a US$5 billion Sino-Africa fund for Chinese companies investing in Africa (China Daily, 2007). This policy and the new relationships it has been creating reflect a pragmatism that has the potential to bear fruit for both Africa and China.

The fragmentation in Africa in terms of the size of the nation states is a major impediment to economic growth. Too many nations are simply not viable in a world of regional economic blocs and large, powerful nations such as India, China, the United States, and Russia. The result of such small size is usually a 'scramble for the bottom' as neighbors try to outdo one another in their competition for often over-rated FDI – longer tax holidays followed by give-away tax rates, and so on. This leads to the typical situation where significant FDI precipitates insignificant reward, as documented in a 2005 UNCTAD report with regard to FDI in Africa.

Perhaps the best way for nations to reap the potential benefits that accrue from STPs is to enhance the efficacy of regional economic blocs, joined by a common economic policy, and the unfettered flow of people, goods, and services. The negotiations between investor and host nation are then more likely to yield non-zero-sum gains.

3   AN OVERVIEW OF TECHNOLOGY TRANSFER IN KENYA

This section is dedicated to an overview of STI developments in Kenya. The country has adopted a plan for development termed 'Vision 2030' that stands on three pillars (economic, social, environmental) all based on a foundation of science and technology. Kenya's Vision 2030 envisages the transformation of the country into a modern and prosperous middle-income country by the year 2030. However, while the commonly held theme that the key to economic progress in developing nations lies in establishing science-based innovation systems for technology transfer is taken as axiomatic, it is important first to examine the constraints that are external to such systems that might serve as barriers to this goal. While an in-depth examination of education systems in Africa is beyond the scope of this chapter, it should suffice to mention that most such systems were inherited from the colonial milieu which sought to train personnel to run colonial economic machinery, and as such did not emphasize pedagogies that may develop critical thinking skills. Curricula in many African universities are being revised and reformed to better suit modern needs.

In Section 2, the prevailing world economic environment was looked at. This section discusses what might be the ideal structure of a 'knowledge ecosystem' in Africa by considering an overview of the history and plans for promoting technology transfer in Kenya, specifically around real-estate-based interventions.

Science and Technology Parks as a Means for Technology Transfer

Some fundamental shifts in thinking regarding the trends that result in successful technology transfer include the idea that not all technologies follow the same track – for example, it is popular to refer to the icon of real-estate-based development, Silicon Valley, with regard to the growth of any type of technology, but what is necessary for the growth of IT-based technologies, for instance, is not necessarily the same for biotechnologies. The challenge therefore, is to base policies for a particular country or region on a careful understanding of the needs and strengths (established and potential) in that region, and to apply global experience and acquired knowledge to this task.

In an interesting article, Anthony Townsend and Alex Soojung-Kim Pan (both from the California-based Institute for the Future) and Rick Weddle (Research Triangle Park, North Carolina) (2009) paint informed scenarios on future directions of real-estate-based STPs. In it they challenge the notion that STPs, which are real-estate-based interventions initiated in the 1950s and designed to garner the perceived necessary ingredients for technology transfer within a specified locality (which range in scale from an incubator in a building to a technology-based city or 'technopolis'), are still relevant today. The criteria they list for relevance are: that they actively manage activities and knowledge creation, the ability to repeatedly reinvent themselves to suit changing needs, and that they focus on linking local assets to global markets. On the basis of 14 emerging trends they arrive at *three scenarios for the future of technology-based economic development over the next two decades*, which are as follows:

1. that the current trend of real-estate-based parks continues and evolves steadily and incrementally as technological advances continue to increase rapidly;
2. that the a new ecosystem they call a 'research cloud' develops based on virtual networks of R&D entities, challenging current systems fundamentally; and
3. that the current real-estate-based model, with its 'legacy cost structure' dies out as it becomes increasingly irrelevant to new companies, and R&D functions enter virtual space.

Kenya's current reality for the creation of an effective national innovation system, or knowledge ecosystem, is an organic mixture of government-led initiatives, university innovation, and private sector (both formal and informal) ingenuity. Current plans include both the more traditional, real-estate-based STPs, and an already piloted project involving much 'lighter-weight' centers of innovation and prototyping. The latter are loose associations of innovation centers providing an environment for flexible technical learning for innovators, R&D activity, technological prototyping, science and technology-based community outreach, and technology-business incubation. They comprise a central component of Kenya's plans for STP development. Both approaches are described in the following, but are first contextualized by taking a comparative look at business incubation specifically in other *developing* countries, and by reviewing the history of business incubation in Kenya. Business incubation is considered in particular because it is at present the only component of a real-estate-based innovation system in which there is significant history in Kenya.

Business incubation in developing countries: Brazil and India
As stated above, the launch of a business incubator is not in any way a guarantee that it will succeed. Awareness of factors that might determine the difference between success and failure is vital, and a study of successes in other developing countries such as Brazil, India, and China is

instructive. Brazil is a sterling example of what can go wrong with business incubators and how it can be turned around into a success. The first incubator project in Brazil was the Technological Development Company (CODETEC), started in 1978 at the State University of Campinas (UNICAMP). Despite many efforts to organize it along the lines of Silicon Valley, including proximity to leading universities and industries, nothing of value happened for almost two decades. There are a variety of reasons why, ranging from poor institutional structure, financial stress, and national economic recession, to the loss of key personnel. However, since 1994, 297 new and successful incubators had developed by 2005 which have graduated an impressive total of 1,678 businesses to date and hosted a total of about 2,327 companies. This can be attributed to the judicious focus on key industries, major private sector participation, and strong university ties. Robust funding from both government and venture capital (US$2 billion) is also a key ingredient.

Of approximately 4,000 business incubators worldwide, about 80 are in India. The drive to establish them has come principally from the government, with 35 business incubators being affiliated to the Department of Science and Technology (DST). Tiruchi Regional Engineering College Science and Technology Entrepreneurs Park (TREC-STEP) was the first business incubator in India. It was launched in 1985 and was fully operational by 1989 with 15 nursery incubators. India is examining four different models for encouraging business growth in hi-tech industries: (i) the anchor company model; (ii) the hand-holding model; (iii) the student entrepreneur's model; and (iv) a model leveraging the entrepreneurial drive of a pool of motivated and technically educated graduates.

Lessons from these two developing giants can be summarized as follows:

- Government support is necessary in order for business incubators to be launched on a scale necessary for them to make an impact on the economy and society by adequately offering the opportunity to as many members of society as possible.
- Links with high-tech R&D leaders, which in Kenya are mainly universities, polytechnics, and government research centers, are essential.
- In spite of the necessity for government support, structural and organizational autonomy must be protected to allow the leadership the flexibility necessary to respond to organically changing market needs and social conditions.
- The population must be trained in order to be able to take advantage of available means for converting ideas into products, which covers the gamut from an understanding of science and technology, to business plan writing, marketing and ethnographic studies.

In light of these examples, the findings of researchers such as Juma (2005), Mwamadzingo (1995) are instructive. For example, Mwamadzingo found in a study of the R&D capacity of Kenyan universities that structural changes are necessary before meaningful progress can be made. These are already underway in many of Kenya's universities, for example, University of Nairobi, Strathmore University, and Jomo Kenyatta University of Agriculture and Technology (JKUAT).

Business incubation in Kenya
Historically Kenya has sought to promote technological advancement through the Industrial Survey and Promotion Center of the Ministry of Commerce and Industry, the East African Industrial Research Organization, the Kenya Industrial Estates Technical Service Center, the National Research Institutes (KIRDI, KARI, KEFRI, KEMFRI and so on), and the universities and polytechnics. Historically, numerous small-scale associations have developed in the country around specific sectors and subsectors, such as vehicle repair technicians, wood-carving artisans, and so on, but those will not be covered here, though they are well described in a recent book edited by by Oyelaran-Oyeyinka and McCormick (2009).

The Kenya Industrial Estates (KIE), started under the Industrial and Commercial Development Corporation (ICDC) with support from the Danish International Development Agency (DANIDA), and the Swedish International Development Agency (SIDA) has been on the scene since 1967, with Mareba Rooftiles Co. Ltd and Kuguru Foods Co. Ltd as two of its more famous graduate companies. Other more recent developments include:

- The Kenya Kountry Business Incubator (KeKoBI), which was started through a grant from the World Bank Group's Information for Development Program (infoDev) in 2004 totaling about US$230,000. It developed from JKUAT's Center for Business Innovation (JKUAT-CBI) eventually evolving, independently of the university, into a national umbrella institution with the objective of establishing business incubators countrywide. KeKoBI aims to support the Kenyan government in achieving the Poverty Reduction Strategy Paper (PRSP) objectives.
- ICTPark.com represents a consortium of local, regional, and global organizations with the stated aim of partnering to make Kenya the Business Processing Outsourcing (BPO) hub of Africa. Their stated goal is to set up a network of community-based ICT centers, both urban and local, to create jobs, especially for the youth.

- C4IDEA (Center for Innovative Development East Africa), has existed since 2004. It is a private sector resource network that seeks to use incubation to help companies create and manage innovative development initiatives.
- Bridgeworks Africa (associated with the Swiss venture capital company incubating and commercializing technologies) is a fairly recent incubator that aims at enabling technology transfer and the commercialization of research through relationships with life sciences institutes throughout Africa, particularly those involved in the fields of soils and health. They have already developed an anchor partnership with the world-renowned International Center of Insect Physiology and Ecology (ICIPE) in Nairobi.
- The University of Nairobi (UoN) seeks to fast-track the launch of its STP by consolidating the MIT Fab Lab (newly acquired through a government grant, and currently serves as a model for the planned national network of innovation centers, discussed in detail below) with other technology transfer units at the university such as the recently launched Nokia Research Center (School of Computing and Informatics) and the Center for Biotechnology and Bioinformatics (CEBIB), and its partial ownership of the Numerical Machining Complex at Kenya Railways. The science park is already incubating over 10 client companies and expects many more during the year. These vary from automation contractors that have, for example, converted sophisticated numerical control machines into computer numerical control machines, an inexpensive biogas digestor manufacturer, inexpensive sanitary towels, and so on. A wireless networking project for internet access in partnership with JoinAfrica and MIT is fast gaining ground.
- Strathmore University has launched the Strathmore Innovation & Technology Transfer (SITT) program aimed at supporting the commercialization of ICT technologies developed anywhere in Kenya. This support is directed through a business incubator and revolves mainly around business skill enhancement. Strathmore also hosts the MIT-based African Information Technology Initiative (AITI), which teaches mobile phone application development in a six-week program and promotes business start-ups by graduates.
- Skunkworks – 'Skunkworks' is a term referring to a small group of like-minded individuals who got together in 2007 with the objective of innovating around technology. This loosely gathered group of IT-savvy individuals would meet to share ideas on the latest developments in IT and to teach each other new skills and so on. Since its early days the group has developed into a significant entity

of about 600 members, at last count. It has attracted government support, complete with offices in a prominent building in downtown Nairobi, and regular visits from prominent government personalities. It was featured in the *New York Times* (Zachary, 2008), today it is a well-known entity within the local ICT-related community; several businesses have developed through members teaching and learning, sharing technical and market information and undertaking joint projects. They recently held their latest annual event (Barcamp 2010) which was a resounding success, attended by a wide spectrum of local and international innovators.

- The iHub is a recently launched incubator focused on the ICT sector. It is described as an open space where technologists, investors, tech companies and hackers can gather to commercialize good ideas and projects around web and mobile applications. Following a widely publicized and well-attended launch in March 2010, the iHub hosted the most recent Barcamp (June 2010) for Skunkworks. Within the iHub is Zuku Startup Index, a community-managed database of start-ups designed to link ideas and investors.
- The NAILAB is also an ICT Business Incubation Laboratory, focusing on start-ups in Nairobi. They offer assistance to young entrepreneurs who are unlikely to have the necessary initial capital for office space and services.

As is the case in many developing countries, many of the incubators focus on ICT. Recent trends in this sector demonstrate that this focus is well founded, as many young people are very interested in this sector. In a study of internet consumer habits in Kenya conducted by TNS Research and commissioned by the Kenya ICT Board, the following was revealed:

- Internet penetration in Kenya is highly concentrated in Nairobi compared to the other regions. The effect of this is a risk of continued marginalization of people outside the city from the digital world. This may in turn discourage high level investments in the digital arena in regions outside the city and, consequently, the level of development may remain relatively low.
- Interaction with the internet for most users is a daily affair, with 62 percent of the internet accessing it up to five times a day. This easily surpasses the duration spent on traditional media such as radio, television or newspapers.
- Online chatting is the most common way of staying 'together' in the digital world and is used by 89 percent of internet users. However, social networking is encroaching into this space especially because

the instant messaging service is integrated within social networking sites.

Venture capital and private equity in Kenya and the region

This is a fast expanding space since 2002 as more and more private equity firms enter into the market, often providing venture capital to local companies. The general focus is around SMEs including start-ups, which holds much promise for general economic growth. Historically funding has been available at the micro-finance (<US$50,000) and large-scale (>US$2 million) levels, but now it is the 'missing middle' between these scales that is drawing the most attention. It is the view of these types of investors that because the choices among the large corporations in the region are fewer, the very large number of SMEs that are actively looking for funding become more attractive, despite presenting a larger management load as business development services are necessary and can be laborious to provide. According to a local private equity investment expert, Tony Wainaina, returns of 30 to 40 percent year on year can be expected and have been proven. Dividends between 10 and 15 percent are common and exit strategies need not take the form of public listings alone, as the likes of Google Inc. and other large international corporations are seeking to expand their presence through local acquisitions (Ratio Magazine, 2010). While political risk is seen as less of a barrier to entry than in the past, the investment environment can be made more attractive by government intervention, which the lobby group East Africa Venture Capital Association, a chapter of the Africa Venture Capital Association, seeks to pursue.

The Capital Markets Authority has recently received funding from the Rockefeller Foundation to support the work of the impact investing taskforce. The vision of the impact investment taskforce is to establish a working framework for the development and support of the venture capital industry in Kenya, which is indicative of the role that the government is playing in supporting entrepreneurship there. The Kenya ICT Board, working with other partners locally, was able to organize two major venture capital events in October and November 2010. One of the companies involved was New Market Ventures from USA working through their local representatives, Savannah East Africa.

Some interesting players on the Kenyan and regional scene are as follows:

1. Donor government funds such as Norfund, the Dutch FMO, Swedfund, the American Overseas Private Investment Corporation (OPIC), and the World Bank's International Finance Corporation (IFC), have been operational on the continent as a whole for

decades, focused on development related financing that does not always make pure business sense. These have been historically funded, government-backed large projects, but have also recently moved onto the privatization wave and support private sector projects directly or through venture capital funds.

2. Actis Capital Fund (one of the oldest and largest on the continent), Aureos Capital (with US$381 million for SMEs in Africa, reportedly the largest such fund on the continent), Acacia Fund (recently purchased by Swedfund), and Acumen Fund (provides development funding with a large portfolio defined as 'pro-poor').

3. TBL Mirror Fund (fund size: €6 million fund, provides between €100,000 and €1 million), and presently has a portfolio of four companies.

4. Grofin East Africa has a US$25 million fund and invests between US$50,000 and US$1 million per company (29 percent of which are start-ups).

5. Business Partners International has a US$14.1 million fund size, and invests between US$50,000 and US$500,000 as debt.

6. InReturn Capital manages a US$20 million East Africa Fund for Jacana Venture Partnership and deals in risk capital and lends on the basis of cash flow (EMPEA, 2010). They also provide business development assistance.

7. A development on the Kenyan investment scene is the trend that has many emerging groups of individuals who jointly create investment clubs traditionally aimed at investments in real estate and stocks. More recently such groups have gained an interest in funding SMEs, usually related to some members through family or friendship. The flagship such group is TransCentury, which began when almost 30 relatively high-net worth individuals jointly created an investment vehicle which today stands at US$150 million. This fired the imagination of the Kenyan public and has ignited a wave of copycat groups. Perhaps the best known of these is the Baraka Africa Fund.

8. Fanisi Fund (fund size $55 million, making equity investments between US$500,000 to US$3 million), serves the East Africa region, and was set up by the global player Small Enterprise Assistance Funds (SEAF) which operates in emerging markets, and is managed by local teams with assistance from Norfund.

9. African Technology Media and Telecoms (ATMT) Fund – a US$100 million fund. Launched in 2008, it is managed by East Africa Capital Partners and partly funded by the US government (through OPIC).

10. Kibo Fund – a €30 million fund, only a year old was launched by Mauritius-based CIEL Capital.

11. eVA (eVENTURES Africa Fund BV) is a new venture capital firm
     in East Africa which focuses on ICT. It invests between €25,000 and
     €250,000 in any company that qualifies according to their criteria
     and invested in five to six companies in the six months since they
     launched.

Successes in technology-related business
The Kenya ICT Board has received a grant from the World Bank towards
the development of the local digital content in Kenya, an essential driver
of internet adoption and enterprise development in the ICT sector. This
project, branded 'Tandaa', is backed by a grant size of US$3 million to be
disbursed over three years. Grantees compete and winners are awarded the
money against an approved business plan. The initial grant winners had
ideas covering various social aspects. The five examples below from the
original group of winners illustrate Kenya's growing pool of entrepreneurship and its strong link with our social reality:

● Octopus Solutions Ltd is developing a project that improves HIV
   and AIDS e-learning in the workplace;
● JBA Advertising Ltd is developing a project that enables citizens to
   use technology to report, post and track lost identification;
● Ibid Labs is developing Kenya's first online museum;
● Infotrack Strategic Solutions is developing a Teachers' Portal,
   allowing Kenya's 200,000-odd pool of teachers to be better served
   by online means;
● Media Edge is developing a farmer mobile banking and mobile
   e-services transaction platform.

MPesa, a product of Kenya's dominant mobile phone operator Safaricom,
was the first such service offered anywhere in the world, and they achieved
another first when they launched the service for international money
transfers. Today more than one such service is offered to the Kenyan
public, and recently a fully-fledged mobile bank service M-Kesho was
launched by the Safaricom Co. Ltd and award-winning Equity Bank.
Another recent first occurred when international giant Barclay's Bank
engaged local innovative company Cellulant to design the back-end for
mobile money transfers for its customers. Cellulant has also won the contract to do the same for Standard Chartered bank, another large bank in
the region.
   A local innovation company called Homeboyz recently made local
history when they were engaged by Disney to produce a 52-episode anima-
tion for children called, 'Tinga-Tinga Tales', which they did in partnership

with Tiger Aspect productions (UK) (Amid, 2010). Homeboyz has a similar arrangement to supply the UK-based Ceebeebies with an animated series for pre-school children. Kenya also recently witnessed its first viral-video experience unfold with locally produced short movies called 'Makmende'. One of the largest local software firms, Seven Seas, is a beneficiary of local venture capital investment. Local filmmaker Wanuri Kahiu's science fiction film was recently awarded a prize at the Sundance film festival.

Another high-profile Kenyan innovation is Ushahidi, the crowd-sourcing software developed during the nation's 2007–08 post-election violence débâcle, a summary of which can be read at Kenyan IT magazine CIO's website. This software, developed by Juliana Rotich, Eric Hersmann, and Joshua Goldstein, gathered information from individuals using SMS on their mobile phones which it then displayed on a map, serving as an instantly updated picture of hot-pots and other newsworthy events during what was a very tense period. It quickly gained international fame, including through a TED Talk, and has since been deployed in the earthquakes in Haiti and Chile, during the last Iranian and Indian elections, and by 11 different organizations including the International Center for Transitional Justice (ICTJ), Peace heroes, and even by Al Jazeera during the War on Gaza.

These stories have captured the imagination of the public in Kenya, especially among the increasingly technology-savvy youth, and they serve as excellent encouragement. From the above it is clear that Kenya's technology landscape is undergoing a renaissance of sorts. However, many of these companies have succeeded in spite of what has historically been mostly a difficult business environment, particularly for start-ups. In the following we look at some of the steps being taken by the government to facilitate more such successes.

Konza Technology City

The Government of Kenya is in the advanced stages of the planning of a major technopolis about 50 km south-east of Nairobi, set to cost an estimated US$10 billion, and the World Bank has been invited to partner with the government in this endeavor. Already 5,000 acres have been purchased along Mombasa Road for this project, and construction is set to start in August 2010. The master plan includes a science and technology park, and BPO park, a financial district, a convention center, a mega mall, hospitals, hotels, schools and residential areas and so on, and a high-speed mass transport system connecting it to Nairobi. The central driver of this project, the Ministry of Information and Communications, has set as a strategic objective an increase in the contribution of the ICT sector GDP from a current level of 3 to 10 percent by the year 2013. In support of this, three out of the five planned-for fiber-optic cables have already been launched in the country. At the time of publication the International Finance Corporation arm of the World Bank had completed a feasibility study of this project and it is expected that ground will be broken once final government approval is given. The long-term vision of Permanent Secretary Dr Bitange Ndemo for this project is that it acts as a nucleus for Kenya's ICT Sector, directly employing 80,000-odd people in the business process outsourcing sector by 2030.

The Ministry of Higher Education, Science and Technology is responsible for planning the STP within the Malili Technopolis (as it is often referred to). The planned park, the Mzalendo Science and Technology Park, has been granted the status of the Africa Pilot Project for STPs by UNESCO and the World Trade Association.

The new national STI policy is centered on self-reliance, sustainable and equitable development embedded in a national system that will ensure that functioning institutions, and organizations and policies interact constructively in pursuit of Kenya's social and economic goals. In pursuing the goals of Vision 2030, STI is seen as the foundation of the social, economic, and political transformations. A National Steering Committee for Science and Technology Parks in Kenya, comprising individuals from the three components of the triple helix, has been created within the Ministry of Higher Education, Science and Technology to oversee the implementation of the STP system. The latter committee has identified a two-pronged approach to developing the STP structure within the country. The first is a traditional perspective, which is a real-estate-based development that will include the main features of STPs: R&D centers of excellence, business incubators supported with business development services, an industrial park, and so on. The second is more accurately described as a virtual STP that is envisaged as a network of rapid-prototyping workshops that can be set up all through rural and urban centers nationwide. Both are described in the following.

The National Steering Committee for Science and Technology Parks has proposed four thematic areas on which the STP program should focus: (i) biotechnology; (ii) energy; (iii) ICT; and (iv) materials. These areas are subject to modification as the need arises through inclusive stakeholder consultations using the triple-helix approach. This policy-driven approach is delicate, with the role of the government being to lead the strategic planning. For example, South Korean expert Deog-Seong Oh (Parry and Oh, 2008) cautions that its regional innovation hub, Daedeok Innopolis, 'would never have succeeded as a Technopolis were it not for the conscious shift from government-controlled, bureaucratic management to business management in the clustering mode', where all stakeholders contribute to the success of the management team that is nevertheless independent. The Korean model was a case of central strategic operation, but not planned control, and their model in fact allows much flexibility.

With this in mind the Ministry of Higher Education, Science and Technology approached UNESCO for assistance in developing a proposal for an STP in Kenya. The ministry presented Kenya's case at a UNESCO-organized workshop in Namibia (Southern Africa) (Africa Regional Workshop, 2007) and at the UNESCO General Conference in Paris in 2007. The former was part of a series of workshops held in partnership with the Korean International Cooperation Agency (KOICA) and the World Technopolis Association (WTA), which were attended by delegates from many developing countries in Africa, Western and Eastern Asia, Europe and South America. Through these workshops, UNESCO chose one country in each region to host a pilot project for STP development in each region. Kenya was selected in the Africa region.

Proposal for a Backbone of Digital Technology Incubators

The idea of the Fab Labs rests on a convergence of the access to technological development at a low price, with a pronounced onus on rapid-prototyping and hands-on technical education in an atmosphere of collaborative interaction and entrepreneurship. Rapid-prototyping, which is the fabrication of an initial model of an engineering design, is a key part of the modern industrial process. Machines for this purpose are available in a wide range of sophistication, though all share the feature that they are computer numerical control (CNC) machines, that is, that the prototype is machined from material using tools that are controlled by computer to precisely reproduce a computer generated drawing. The type of CNC machine proposed for use in the network of workshops comprises inexpensive tabletop versions of the machine. The existence of such small CNC machines, as opposed to their much larger relatives, represents an important paradigm shift in that their relatively low cost reduces the barrier to sophisticated machining capacity for a large, new market of designers. Specifically, the government has chosen to purchase equipment modeled by the 'Fab Lab' concept developed at the MIT Media Lab by Prof. Neil Gershenfeld (MIT, 2010).

The proposal is for the use of a nationwide network of Fab Labs as a platform for technology-based grassroots transformation. The Fab Labs, focused on practical state-of-the-art, computer-based engineering for fabrication, hold significant potential as a vehicle for transfer of technology by tapping into the enormous potential of any nation's most precious resource – its people. The approach is twofold:

- *First*, to provide hands-on human capacity training at these incubators, covering modern engineering technologies, business development services, in addition to a strong focus on values (relating particularly to national unity, cooperation and integrity), the absence of which potentially erodes any material developmental gains, as was so tragically exemplified in the post-election violence in Kenya, 2007–08. Also provided is the capacity to conduct useful R&D.
- *Second*, to create a network of business incubators built upon high-tech, relatively inexpensive CNC machines with significant capabilities in precision production. Key parts and devices can be produced cost-effectively using these technologies and can serve as 'platform technologies' by means of which a host of other wealth-generating products and industries can be developed. The sectors with the greatest potential for rapid application include ICT, materials (including nano-materials) and energy. Applicability to biotechnology will also follow, especially through the development of electronics-based sensors and diagnostic kits, and of course in the diverse ways in which ICT can serve to promote it.

The vision is to deploy rapid-prototyping units throughout the country, primarily through the network of Technical Industrial Vocational and Entrepreneurship Training (TIVET) institutions, which fall under the Ministry of Higher Education, Science and Technology's national program on Science Technology and Innovation. Each Fab Lab in the network will stand as a nexus point for technology proliferation throughout the country. The Fab Labs are intended to be centers of rapid-prototyping and proof-of-concept activities, with the express intention not only of nurturing innovation but also of churning out small and medium-sized businesses critical to Kenya's development.

The Fab Labs can also serve as launch pads into the high schools through programs being developed at the UoN Fab Lab so that high-school students are introduced to modern digital technology in a hands-on manner long before they get to university. The recent availability of broadband connectivity via the fiber-optic cable means that video-conferencing between the Fab Labs in the network will be possible and affordable, and carries enormous attendant benefits. Perhaps the most obvious of these is distance learning, which is already being done at the UoN Fab Lab as part of the MIT-centered international Fab Lab network.

The University of Nairobi Fab Lab as Model

The following is a summary of activities at the UoN Fab Lab since it was set up. It is located in the Engineering Building on the Main Campus, and forms the core of the Technology Business Incubator (TBI) at the newly instituted UoN STP. The key achievements to date can be listed as follows:

1. Engagement with 12 companies under virtual incubation at various levels of development, including one that was engaged by the Kenya Army on a critical national defense project. Other incubated business projects include:
    a. a home automation system that is being showcased at Kenya's most prestigious housing development;
    b. an image analysis system using artificial neural networks for monitoring traffic. Negotiations are underway with a large local company that wishes to license this product;
    c. a set-top box which will enable Kenyans to watch newly broadcast digital signals without buying a digital TV. The hardware in this product is from China whereas the software is partially developed in Kenya. The plan is to increase local content in time;
    d. extraction of material from local agricultural waste that can be used to develop proteins for biomedical use, and biofuel. Negotiations with foreign companies are underway;
    e. software companies offering customized database applications to local customers. One in particular is supplying an international church network. Another is supplying software that enables school students to practice their lessons online for a small fee, and monitors performance for the school system to evaluate students and its own delivery;
    f. a local entrepreneur learned about the open-source software package Asterisk while attending a Skunkworks meeting and developed a wifi phone system that has been demonstrated to government officials for possible inclusion in government offices (government as buyer of locally developed technology is a critical encouragement to innovation);
    g. a sophisticated software package for accessing and following markets (stocks, commodities, currencies, futures). A video of this can be viewed at the website. Given the current attention Africa is receiving from countries without enough arable land as one of the last agricultural frontiers on earth, commodities trading alone can be a great application for this software;

    h.   a company producing cheap and easy-to-erect biogas generators, for which there is an enormous potential market in the country and beyond;

    i.   a company at the proof-of-concept stage of a carbon-neutral, biomass electricity generator using a unique vortex design for combustion, and producing 150 kW output and more;

    j.   a sanitary towel maker using local raw materials in a local process. This recently won the Wharton Africa Business Forum Business Plan Competition; and

    k.   a CNC machine maker targeting machines primarily for use by low-income carpenters. A laudable vision of Neil Gershenfeld is for the Fab Labs to reproduce themselves. Projects such as this are the forerunners of this vision.

2.   The Fab Lab serves as a center of innovation and learning, and at present several interdisciplinary student projects are underway, including the impressive UoN Robotics Team preparing for the National Robotics Competition.

3.   International linkages are implicit in the Fab Lab network, including the founding Fab Lab at MIT, and opens opportunities for high-caliber collaboration. At present preparations for collaboration with MIT on designing and building digital fabrication machines are at an advanced level.

4.   Flexible and highly practical tech-education being provided through the Fab Academy. Each Fab Lab is equipped with a video-conferencing unit for, besides other inter-communication, the teaching of technical skills through classes offered remotely through the Fab Academy, launched in September 2009.

Association with Institutes of Higher Education

Students enrolled at such institutions will be instructed on the use of the equipment as a part of their degree or diploma course, in a regime providing for plenty of practical work. All the training will be provided by the faculty who, depending on the particular intellectual property arrangements, might benefit through publications where research findings are publishable or directly through revenue-sharing schemes. Graduate students are likely in some cases to do research that can result in their obtaining higher degrees. Engineering graduates will supply the technical engineering know-how, business graduates the business development services, social science graduates the ethnographic background studies, graduates of law the intellectual property advice, and so on. The incubator will have the responsibility of providing financing to incubatees (with developed business plans) selected in accordance with specific criteria aligned to the national thematic areas through networks developed with local venture capital funds, banks, and micro-credit organizations. Each incubator would be expected to be self-sustaining through unique and agreeable profit-sharing arrangements with their incubatees, besides offering courses and commercial services using the equipment without compromising access for innovation-related activities. An economic revolution can thus be precipitated through knowledge-based industries with the proceeds spreading through the economic multiplier effect.

Science outreach to schools and the general public
Enrolled students will also be involved in outreach to the public, especially to high schools and even primary schools, with the aim of developing an interest in science and engineering in the school population and in the public at large.

The fundamental objective is to develop a new generation of innovators by imparting critical thinking skills through engineering 'games', an idea pioneered at the MIT Media lab by Seymour Papert (1971). The first such program was launched in July 2009 at the University of Nairobi Fab Lab, using tools such as Picocricket and the Gogo Board. The Gogo Board is of great potential applicability and has been tested in Brazilian schools with interesting results (Sipitakiat et al., 2004).

Proposed metrics for evaluation of success
The evaluation is best done with reference to the primary objective of the project, which is the launch of a distribution of high-tech incubators across the country. These incubators have as their simplified objective the creation of knowledge-based businesses based upon ideas from a productive R&D base at host institutions or within surrounding communities. The metrics for evaluation (per year) which follow are: (i) number of businesses produced; (ii) number of jobs created; (iii) number of patents; (iv) number of publications; and (v) number of students trained in CAD/CAM and related topics.

Sustainability
Of primary concern is the sustainability of the Fab Labs. It is paramount that each be independently self-sustaining. The operation costs of the centers include consumables such as tool bits, materials for fabrication, electronic devices, staff, electricity, rent and so on.

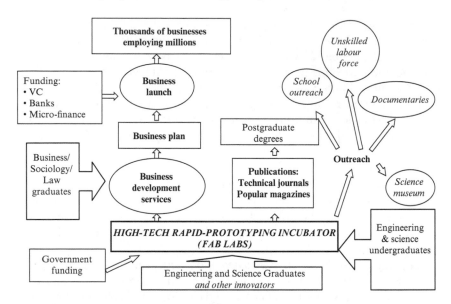

Figure 2.1   Proposed model of high-tech, rapid-prototyping centers

4   SUMMARY

The solution to the challenge of developing Africa is directly related to African nations adding value to their resources through the adoption of technology. However, technology transfer can only thrive in the correct atmosphere. The adoption of technology needs to be as close to the grassroots as possible. Education in relevant with hands-on courses taking advantage of the new paradigm of accessible digital technologies for ICT and manufacturing needs to proliferate, statistically increasing the odds for innovation. Innovation at such levels is also likely to directly meet more local needs accurately and provide greater wealth generation through entrepreneurship. These same technologies can be effectively utilized through a network of centers where this training can take place leading to business incubation for emergent innovations. Concurrently, a whole host of activities can take place at these centers including interactions that challenge a negative mindset including corruption and inter-ethnic animosity through the arts and even simple town-hall meetings, all enhanced by video-conferencing facilities.

At the level of policy making, government must become more accountable, in which Kenya is thankfully a progressing reality, as evidenced by a series of international awards, most recently being placed in the top 20 global programs for 'Innovations in Transforming Government' award by the Ash Institute for Democractic Governance at Harvard's Kennedy School of Government. Debilitating foreign aid (as opposed to well-meaning charity and emergency aid) should be decreased and efforts made to turn the attention of leaders in rich nations to creating a truly level playing field in international trade, rather than focusing on neo-liberal economics that seek to treat developing countries on the same footing as wealthy nations in the marketplace, removing all protectionism that they themselves benefited so manifestly from in their own development process.

Kenya has launched a dual strategy for a real-estate-based technopolis alongside a network of technology business incubators spread through the country. The signs are very encouraging.

NOTES

1. A global hectare is a hectare of biologically productive space with the world-average productivity.
2. For example, the requirement under chapter 8 of Agenda 21 of the Earth Summit, which calls on countries to adopt national strategies for sustainable development (NSDS) that should build upon and harmonize various sectoral economic, social and environmental policies that are operating in the country (http://www.un.org/esa/dsd/dsd_aofw_nsds/nsds_index.shtml).
3. The Action Plan of the Environment under NEPAD (New Partnership for African Development) was developed in 2003 in association with the African Ministerial Conference on the Environment (AMCEN), UNEP and the Global Environmental Facility (GEF).
4. NEPAD was born out of the AU as an internally hatched plan for the redevelopment of Africa, to be executed by African countries.
5. Safaricom is partially owned by Vodafone and the Kenya government. It was the latter that sold off a portion of its stock to the public.

BIBLIOGRAPHY

Africa Regional Workshop on Science and Technology Park Development, Windhoek, Namibia, UNESCO-WTA_ISESCO-KOICA & Govt of Namibia, 9–11 May 2007.

Akogun, K. (2008), 'Nigeria: FG plans six science parks to boost tech development', allAfrica.com, available at: http://allafrica.com/stories/200801240348.html.

Amid (2010), 'Tinga Tinga Tales' produced by Kenya's homeboyz, *Cartoon Brew*, January 23, available at: www.cartoonbrew.com/tv/tinga-tinga-tales-produced-by-kenyas-homeboyz.html.

Bell, B. and C. Juma (2008), 'Bundling critical information infrastructure in Africa: implications for science and innovation policy', *International Journal of Technology and Globalisation*, **4** (2), 186–205.

Blas, J. (2009), 'Rising raw material prices fuel surge in hedging', *Financial Times*, May 8, p. 13.

Booth, Jerome (2008), quoted in *The Daily Telegraph*, available at: http://www.telegraph.co.uk/finance/economics/2782149/Emerging-markets-still-a-good-investment.html.

Burns, M. (1998), 'Fabbing the future: developments in rapid manufacturing', Plastics Product Design & Development Forum, Chicago, IL, May 30.

Chang, H.-J. (2002), *Kicking Away the Ladder: How the Economic and Intellectual Histories of Capitalism Have Been Re-written to Justify Neo-liberal Capitalism*, London: Anthem Press.

Chang, H.-J. (2007), *Bad Samaritans: The Guilty Secrets of Rich Nations and the Threat to Global Prosperity*, New York: Random House Business Books.

China Daily (2007), 'US$5b African fund launched', June 27, available at: www.china.org.cn/english/BAT/215196.htm.

Dolun, Müge (2005), *Role of Universities in Business Generation in Kenya*, Proceedings of the Globelics Conference Tshwane University of Technology, South Africa, available at: http://www.globelics2005africa.org.za/papers/p0010/index.php.

Easterly, W. (2002), 'The cartel of good intentions: bureaucracy vs. markets in foreign aid', Center for Global Development Working Paper No. 4, May available at SSRN: http://ssrn.com/abstract=999981.

Easterly, W. (2006), *The White Man's Burden: Why the West's Efforts to Aid the Rest Have Done So Much Ill and So Little Good*, New York: Penguin Press.

EMPEA (2010), News Watch: Industry news. Emerging market private equity online, available at: www.empea.net/News/industry-news.aspx.

Fab Lab Executive Board (2008), 'The Fab Academy: Executive Summary', MIT, available at: fab.cba.mit.edu/about/academy.

Fab Lab Inventory (2010), 'Fab Lab 2.0', MIT, available at: http://fab.cba.mit.edu/about/fab/inv.html.

Fanon, F. (1961), *Wretched of the Earth* (Les Damnés de la Terre), London: Macgibbon & Kee.

Financial Times, http://www.ft.com/cms/s/0/0d1218c8-3b35-11de-ba91-00144feabdc0.html.

Gachigi, K. (2009), '10 signals on Africa', *Future of Science & Technology Parks*, Palo Alto, CA: The Institute for the Future (IFTF), available at: http://scienceparks.iftf.net/mysignals.

Holling, C.S. and L. Gunderson (eds) (2002), *Panarchy: Understanding Transformations in Human and Natural Systems*, Washington, DC: Island Press.

Juma, C. (2005), Interview by M. Lanzarotta, March 10, available at: http://www.hks.harvard.edu/new-events/publications/insights/markets/calestous-juma.

Juma, C. and Yee-Cheong Lee (2005), 'Innovation: Applying Knowledge in Development – task force on science, technology, and innovation', UN Millennium Project, UNDP.

Kahn, M.J. (2001), 'Developing mechanisms to promote South–South research in science and technology: the case of the Southern African Development Community', *African Sociological Review*, **5** (1), 17–35.

Korten, D. (1995), *When Corporations Rule the World*, West Hartford, CT: Kumarian Press.

Lee, R. and M. Balick (2009), 'Indigenous use of Hoodia Gordonii and appetite suppression', *Journal of Science and Healing*, **3** (4), 404–6.

Mark, O. and M. Bang (2008), 'Dawn of e-commerce looms as banks leap into mobile banking', July 15, available at: www.africa.co.ee/2008/07/dawn-of-e-commerce-looms-as-banks-leap-into-mobile-banking.html.

Millennium Assessment (2005), Millennium Ecosystem Assessment, available at: http://www.millenniumassessment.org.

Ministry of Information (2010), 'Economy', available at: www.information.go.ke./index2.php

MIT (2010), 'Welcome to fab central. Center for Bits and Atoms', available at: http://cba.mit.edu/projects/fablab.

Moyo, D. (2009a), 'Aid ironies: a response to Jeffrey Sachs', *The Huffington Post*, May 26, available at: http://www.huffingtonpost.com/dambisa-moyo/aid-ironies-a-response-to_b_207772.html

Moyo, D. (2009b), *Dead Aid: Why Aid Is Not Working and How There Is A Better Way for Africa*, New York: Farrar, Straus & Giroux.

Mugabe, J. (2007), 'Knowledge and innovation for Africa's development: priorities, programmes and policies', Zimbabwe.

Mutua, A. (2007), 'Kenya's public service recognized again', Office of Public Communications, October 9, available at: www.communication.go.ke/media.asp?id=435.

Mwamadzingo (1995), 'The impact of university research on industrial innovations: empirical evidence from Kenya', in Osita M. Ogbu, Banji O. Oyeyinka and Hasa M. Mlawa (eds), *Technology and Practice in Africa*, IDRC, pp. 211–37.

Mwangi, S. (2010), 'Kenya's IT talent comes of age', *CIO*, May 19, available at: www.cio.co.ke/index.php?option=com_content&view=article&id=897:kenyas-it-talent-com.

Mwenda, A. (2006), 'Aid only feeds Africa's corruption', *The Times*, 8 July, available at: http://business.timesonline.co.uk/tol/business/markets/africa/article684563.ece.

Nkrumah, K. (1965), *Neo-Colonialism, the Last Stage of Imperialism*, London: Thomas Nelson & Sons.

Nwogu, Udochi (2009), 'Focus on African entrepreneur – Zana Africa', *The Wharton Journal*, December 7, available at: media.www.whartonjournal.com/media/storage/paper201/news/2009/12/07/Perspectives/Focus.On.African.Entrepreneur.Zana.Africa-3847155.shtml.

OECD (2007), 'Science, Technology and Industry Scoreboard', Paris.

Oyelaran-Oyeyinka, B. (2006), *Learning to Compete in African Industry: Institutions and Technology in Development*, Burlington, VT: Ashgate.

Oyelaran-Oyeyinka, B. and D. McCormick (eds) (2009), *Industrial Clusters and Innovation Systems in Africa: Learning Institutions and Competition*, Tokyo: United Nations University Press.

Papert, S. (1971), 'Teaching children thinking', Artificial Laboratory Memo no. 247, Cambridge, MA: MIT Massachusetts Institute of Technology.

Parry, M. and D.-S. Oh (2008), 'A broad based business plan for science and technology parks in Kenya', UNESCO Report.

Perkins, J. (2004), *The Confessions of an Economic Hitman*, San Francisco, CA: Berrett-Koehler.

Popper, K. (1971), *The Open Society and Its Enemies*, Princeton, NJ: Princeton University Press.

Porter, M.E. (1990), *The Competitive Advantage of Nations*, London: Macmillan.

Porter, M.E. (1998), 'Clusters and the new economics of competition', *Harvard Business Review*, November–December, 77–90.

Pouris, Anastassios (2007), 'Building science, technology and innovative systems for sustainable development in Africa', United Nations Economic Commission for Africa, ISTD Division.

Ratio Magazine (2010), available at: www.wap.ratio-magazine.com.

Rodney, W. (1973), *How Europe Under-developed Africa*, Dar-Es-Salaam: Tanzanian Publishing House and London: Bogle-L'Ouverture Publications.

Sachs, J. (2005), *The End of Poverty: Economic Possibilities for Our Time*, New York: Penguin Press.

Sachs, J. and J. McArthur (2009), 'Moyo's confused attack on aid for Africa', *The Huffington Post*, May 27, available at: http://www.huffingtonpost.com/jeffrey-sachs/moyos-confused-attack-on_b_208222.html.

Schumacher, E.F. (1973), *Small Is Beautiful: Economics As If People Mattered*, New York: Harper & Row.

Scott, N., N. Batchelor, J. Ridley and B. Jorgensen (2004), available at: www.commissionforafrica.org/english/report/background/scott_et_al_background.pdf.

Segal, N. (2008), 'Science and technology parks and economic development: lessons from European experience', TCI – The Global Practitioners Network for Competitiveness, Clusters and Innovation, 11th TCI Annual Global Conference, Cape Town.

Sipitakiat, A., P. Blikstein and D.P. Cavallo (2004), 'GoGo Board: augmenting programmable bricks for economically challenged audiences', International Conference on Learning Sciences, Proceedings of the 6th International Conference on Learning Sciences, Santa Monica, CA, pp. 481–8.

Spiegel (2005), Spiegel interview with African economics expert: 'For God's sake, please stop the aid!' Spiegelonline, July 4, available at: http://www.spiegel.de/international/spiegel/0,1518,363663,00.html.

Stevenson, T. (2008), 'Emerging markets still a good investment', *The Daily Telegraph*, January 7, available at: http://www.telegraph.co.uk/finance/economics/2782149/Emerging-markets-still-a-good-investment.html.

Stiglitz, J. (2002), *Globalization and Its Discontents*, New York: W.W. Norton.

TBL Mirror Fund (2010), Home, available at: www.tblmirrorfund.com.

Teng-Zen, F. (2008), 'A discussion on Jacques Galliard's comments on the regional report on Sub-Saharan Africa', Symposium on the Comparative Analysis of National Research Systems, UNESCO 16–18 January, available at: http://portal.unesco.org/educvation/en/files/55706/12005736365Teng_Zeng_DISCUSSANT.pdf/Teng 2BZeng_DISCUSSANT.pdf.

Townsend, A., A. Soojung-Kim Pang and R. Weddle (2009), 'Future knowledge ecosystems: the next twenty years of technology-led economic development', IFTF Report Number SR-12361, available at: http://intelligentcommunity.org/index.php?src=news&refno=409&category=Facts%20%26%20Figures%20Library%20-%20Knowledge%20Workforce.

UN (2007), 'Creating a conducive environment for higher competitiveness and effective national innovation systems-lessons learnt from the experiences of UNEC countries', United Nations.

UNCTAD (2005), 'Economic Development in Africa, Rethinking the Role of Foreign Direct Investment', UNCTAD/GDS/AFRICA/2005/1.
UNCTAD Secretariat (2007), 'Mobile telephony in Africa: cross-country comparison', in *Information Economy Report 2007–2008: Science and Technology for Development: The New Paradigm of ICT*, New York: United Nations, pp. 243–68, available at: www.unctad.org/en/docs/sdteecb20071ch6_en.pdf.
UNESCO, 'Improving STI policy conditions and building mechanisms for innovation in Africa 2008–2013', available at: http://www.unesco.org/science/psd/thm_innov/africa_sc_park.shtml.
United Nations (2009), 'World Population Prospects: The 2008 Revision', available at: http://esa.un.org/unpp/
World Bank Group (2008), *World Development Indicators*, Washington, DC, available at: siteresources.worldbank.org/DATASTATISTICS/.../ssa_wdi.pdf.
World Resources Institute (2009), 'Earth trends environmental information', available at: http://earthtrends.wri.org.
World Summit on Sustainable Development (WSSD): Live (2002), Johannesburg, available at: http://www.un.org/events/wssd/.
World Trade Organization (WTO) (2007), 'World trade developments', Geneva.
Zachary, G. (2008), 'Inside Nairobi, the next Palo Alto?', *The New York Times*, 20 July, Business, available at: www.nytimes.com/2008/07/20/business/worldbusiness/20ping.html.

3. Some UK experience of technology transfer and commercialization

Robert Hodgson

1   INTRODUCTION

In the debate about competitiveness in the global economy, Europe is sometimes characterized as continuing with old ideas with an emphasis on social capital in contrast to the United States with its emphasis on individual-oriented market-driven change. The United Kingdom, in relation to this characterization, perceives itself to be somewhere between the two with one foot in each camp – we are a little more open to change than the European norm, but not much, and we enjoy a little more continuity than the US norm, but not much. This position also applies in many regards to the UK experience with technology transfer and commercialization that is the focus of this chapter.

Along with the EU and the so-called Lisbon agenda,[1] the United Kingdom has recognized for some time that as a high-wage, high-consumption economy it needs to accelerate its adoption of new technologies to achieve productivity gains in its current activities and to build a strong position in terms of new and emerging economic sectors or clusters. The so-called 'knowledge economy' is therefore seen as crucial to the UK competitive future. Plus, perceived long-term weaknesses in linking high-quality R&D, particularly in our leading universities and public research bodies, with product development and process improvement in the commercial world have to be addressed.

An additional significant change in understanding in the field of innovation has been a move away from the simplistic characterization of the processes involved in technology transfer and commercialization from the old, and in some quarters still appealing, notion of a linear science push to a much more complex characterization of an interactive process with both push and pull forces and subtle and important linkages among the components of the national innovation system (NIS).[2] Even the relatively sophisticated models that have built on the work of Nelson (1993) to show the interconnectedness of the main components of the NIS have been realized to be only partial models with insufficient emphasis on the multi-directional flow of information and the more complex sociology of hybrid communities that are needed to ensure that the traditional silos in the system can communicate clearly and transact efficiently.

In some ways, biological models, such as those describing symbiotic relationships and the imprecisely understood interactive linkages that are emerging from research on the workings of the human genome, are proving more insightful in conceptualizing innovation than the traditional engineering optimization analogies of earlier commentators. However, useful analogies are still being drawn from chaos models[3] and complexity analyses.

In this chapter the emphasis will be placed on the transactions and processes linking those with advanced science and technology (S&T) knowledge to those with commercial knowledge of where and how to invest to achieve commercial value and how to transfer new scientific findings into applications. The key actors in these processes are well known: first, universities and research institutes on the supply side; second, financial, technical and professional service providers and intermediaries on the transactional side; and third, corporate users and entrepreneurs on the demand side.

Inevitably, there are additional areas where the public sector is the main direct client for new innovations, much of public health, security, defense, and environment-related activities being the most important examples, and where the channels of commercialization might differ but the principles remain the same so no special reference is made to these areas. Appropriate examples will be drawn from particular institutions and programs largely but not solely from the Cambridge area,[4] which is where I have lived and worked for the last quarter-century. However, the analysis and comments apply to most other regions and institutions in the UK rather than being peculiar to Cambridge.

2   MAIN POLICY AREAS OF INTEREST

There is no single and self-contained innovation policy that shapes initiatives in technology transfer and commercialization because of the interdependency and connectivity of the different aspects. Instead, there is a need to integrate at least six complementary and reinforcing policy areas, and particularly relevant initiatives in each of these are described below. Being distinct policy areas it is inevitable that they neither necessarily proceed at the same pace nor are they each pursued with the same vigor. However, together the impact of change in each has changed the landscape for technology transfer and commercialization in the United Kingdom. The six areas are:

- enterprise in education;
- third-leg funding of universities;
- research quality and selectivity;
- international orientation;
- regional policies and diversity; and
- applications and mature industries.

In each of these areas the challenges faced, the thinking behind the developing policy, and the lessons learned are described briefly with an emphasis on how each area impacts on technology transfer and commercialization. However, all should be regarded as continuing works in progress rather than completed tasks. Following these sections a review of the more specific challenges of the commercialization process in the United Kingdom will be presented before we introduce some outstanding issues on which the next generation of policy and analysis are concentrating.

Enterprise in Education

The raw materials of the knowledge economy are people and ideas, so one of the main underlying policy areas relates to education. In this field, myriad initiatives have been pushed forward over the last 20 years with a persistent refrain on quality standards, relevance and life skills, inclusion of disadvantaged groups, funding innovations, and entitlements. We have moved from a *laissez-faire*, decentralized system reliant on individual teaching professionals with significant freedom and influence exercised through local governance, first, in the 1980s and 1990s, to a fully prescribed, centrally determined national curriculum with little local discretion and subsequently, after the millennium to a highly structured but looser specification of what and how to teach, which is some way between the two extremes.

The broader social context within which these changes have taken place within the United Kingdom has been an aging population, increased rates of participation in higher education, a growth of employment in services, and job shedding, particularly in traditional manufacturing. Within education there has been a movement of sentiment away from the natural sciences and mathematics, and a growing gender divide with girls significantly outperforming boys across the board. Two areas that are particularly relevant to technology transfer and commercialization are science, technology, engineering, and mathematics (STEM) education and the encouragement of entrepreneurship across all ages and across the curriculum.

In relation to STEM education there has been a deliberate effort to stimulate interest from a larger cohort of students as without this effort a declining proportion of students were coming forward to take science and engineering courses. These subjects were perceived to be harder and more demanding of students than alternative courses in the social sciences and humanities. Courses in STEM lead to careers that on average do not pay as well as alternative courses and for historic-cultural reasons are more oriented to boys than to girls.

All of these factors made STEM courses relatively less attractive to the best students as well as coinciding with a time when the level of hope embodied in the contribution of science to a prosperous future was declining. This latter effect was a result of mistaken presentations by spokespersons for science in a series of media stories, who were themselves culpable in some of the misrepresentations that undermined credibility.[5] Scientists were projected to be: either unable to answer key questions or, in some areas, to project comforting levels of certainty that were subsequently disproved by events; divided and contradictory in their views on either the causes or cures of particularly widely discussed topics; and incomprehensible when they did express views because of their overreliance on esoteric jargon rather than using plain English.

A number of initiatives were taken to reverse these trends, one of the most striking of which was the Royal Society's Seize The Initiative! (STI) program. STI established a roster of scientists drawn from the academy's membership[6] and provided their names to the serious media who were encouraged to contact them for comments, advice, and informed views on specific topics that had been brought up by the news. Each of these scientists was trained in how to relate to the media, how to communicate clearly, and what balance to strike between presenting the conventional wisdom of the established scientific mainstream in their subject and acknowledging the incompleteness of knowledge and the areas of risk and uncertainty of the current state of the art without undermining confidence in the value of their expert contribution to the discussion. The perception of the scientist has improved but there are still areas where there is a lack of credibility.

A much more systematic effort was also involved on a new priority emphasis on entrepreneurship in education. There was and still is a debate about whether entrepreneurs are born or can be taught, but this did not stop the recognition that a strong cultural change was needed to develop both higher levels of knowledge about enterprise and a higher social status for the entrepreneur. This recognition was acted upon at all levels in the education system, from the primary to the tertiary, with practical activities that gave an experience of business as well as tackling the social side of entrepreneurship. Some examples that illustrate the range of initiatives include:

● In primary education (4 to 11) reliance has often been on the enthusiasm of individual head teachers. Much of the provision was delivered by Young Enterprise (http://www.young-enterprise.org.uk/pub/) but there is an expanding role for Enterprise Network, see below.

● In secondary education (11 to 19) the government white paper, 'Enterprise Britain', published in 2002 paved the way for the introduction of enterprise education for all 14- and 15-year-olds and many others within the 11–16 age bracket. Enterprise educations has been coordinated by the Schools Enterprise Education Network since 2006, and the contract for the management of the network has recently been expanded and renamed the Enterprise Network. Its remit has been extended to 5- to 19-year-olds. (http://www.school-snetwork.org.uk/Article.aspa?NodeId=0&PageId=236209).

● In further education (16 to 19+ vocational education) there is very little enterprise education. Five centers of excellence have been established around the United Kingdom but funding has now dried up, and it is unclear what the next step will be. Make Your Mark (see below) is trying to stimulate more activity in this sector.

● In higher education (18 to 21+) a major government initiative in 1999 (Science Enterprise Challenge: SEC) established 13 science enterprise centers around the United Kingdom. Many of these centers led consortia of universities and 43 universities (out of a total of approx 140) were involved with this initiative in one way or another. The focus was on enterprise education for scientists, and a national network UKSEC was established to share best practices. SEC funding ended in 2004 and most universities then used part of their Higher Education Innovation Fund (HEIF) to fund further development. As HEIF is not specific to science, many institutions introduced some aspect of enterprise education for students across a range of curriculum areas. Universities that benefited from SEC funding (for example, the University of Nottingham, see http://www.nottingham.ac.uk/enterprise/) tend to have enterprise education well-established and partially embedded within the curriculum whereas others who have introduced it more recently still struggle to establish and embed. UKSEC has now expanded hugely and become Enterprise Educators UK (see www.enterprise.ac.uk).

- The National Council for Graduate Entrepreneurship was established in 2003 to increase the number of students and graduates starting businesses. They run mass participation 'Flying Start' events for students, carry out research, and are increasingly moving into the area of training and supporting enterprise educators. (See http://www.makeyourmark.org.uk/ for a lot of useful research reports.)
- Make Your Mark is the only government-backed organization that has an enterprise remit across all education sectors. They are a campaigning organization and much of their activity takes place around enterprise week in November. (See http://www.makeyourmark.org.uk/.)

Third-leg Funding of Universities

Third-leg funding refers to the systematic change that has been pushed through in society's expectations of universities in their contribution to S&T development and the commercial business sector. The classic Humbolt University[7] model, concurrently pursuing the two legs of academic research and academic teaching with each reinforcing the other, was the model to which all leading universities previously aspired. The requirements of the knowledge economy led to an extension to a third role of working with and for business to contribute to national competitiveness and innovation. Some saw this as a natural extension of the role of universities and merely recognition of what had been widely practiced by many for some time. Concurrently, the knowledge economy led to a need for an expansion of the participation in higher education by a larger proportion of each year's cohort of students who needed a higher level of education to contribute fully to new knowledge-intensive activities with a stronger flavor of vocational rather than academic content.

The benign view of these changes as a natural extension of the established model was not, however, shared by all academics, including a significant group for whom the changes were seen as a radical departure from their traditional purpose. They saw it on the research side as leading to the threat of undermining the original dual purpose by diverting effort from long-term pure academic excellence towards short-term applied work of commercial relevance. On the teaching side, greater participation led to debates about standards and dumbing down of higher education. There was, therefore, a need to address the legitimacy of the new activity with the core academic community and to embed the changes in institutional value systems and operating procedures.

While this legitimacy debate was progressing, initial activity was stimulated through elective programs, working with the willing, which offered targeted discretionary funding to be allocated on a competitive basis with innovative programs by an individual university or by alliances among a group of universities working together. The first round of this funding (the Science Enterprise Challenge mentioned in the previous section) gave rise to a number of interesting experimental programs such as the UNIEI programme[8] at University of Nottingham and the White Rose Fund[9] at three Yorkshire universities based in Leeds, Sheffield, and York. A second round of funding both deepened the interaction at certain universities[10] and drew in an additional cohort with new programs. In some ways the initiatives have become institutionalized and embedded in the universities involved.

Meanwhile, the more systematic adoption of the activities became reinforced within a growing range of universities. Administrative groups were established to put their commercial relationships on a more professional footing, to manage knowledge assets, to establish patents where appropriate, and to expand the flow of funding from non-traditional sources. An example of these changes can be seen in the University of Cambridge, which started from a rather different position but was subject to the same direction of change. The difference in the starting point was that the university did not claim the intellectual property (IP) from research as its own by right. Academics had the freedom, within socially acceptable limits,[11] to use the findings to establish businesses if they so chose. A small unit was established in the 1980s with funding from a charitable donation from the Wolfson Cambridge Industrial Unit to offer advice on a voluntary basis and usually without charge to academics who chose to consult it.

Now the university does exert its default legal right through a mainstream university group, Cambridge Enterprise, which has more than 40 staff and in the 2008 annual report identified 116 new patent disclosures, made 83 patent applications, and managed over 450 active IP and license agreements. Cambridge Enterprise holds equity in 68 companies and makes a significant return for the university each year.

Another aspect of the institutional change, which applies to only a minority of the UK's universities, is the formal recognition of working with enterprises as a factor in the promotion of academic staff. The University of Ulster was one of the early adopters of such a provision, and the recently merged University of Manchester (from the previous Victoria University of Manchester and University of Manchester Institute for Science and Technology) has a similar provision that sets such activities alongside the usual academic factors or research and publications. By the creation of such direct incentives the culture of the new academic roles is becoming mainstream.

Research Quality and Selectivity

In line with global trends, the United Kingdom has followed three main policy thrusts in research quality and selectivity:

- first, the encouragement of higher-quality standards and higher productivity in research execution among publicly funded programs;
- second, a change in balance from a largely academically defined agenda to one where a purpose orientation dominates with a concentration on national priority topics; and
- third, the encouragement of internationalization of links between the UK research community and other centers of excellence outside the United Kingdom that is dealt with in the next subsection.

In terms of quality and productivity, the underlying drive has been toward scientific excellence and a productive, publicly funded research community particularly in the case of publicly funded universities. The main instrument has been a periodic Research Assessment Exercise (RAE), which is a peer assessment tool that looks at research work in each subject grouping at each university. Each team is given a ranking on a multipoint scale that at the top level recognizes research work that is judged to be at a world-class level. The categories have changed over successive rounds as has the scoring method, but in essence they have used measures such as publications in prestigious, internationally refereed journals, recognition and contributions in international fora, and awards and measures of citations to assess impact on the field. The carrot for excellence has been the allocation of additional research budgets to those academic teams that have achieved the higher scores with the corollary of reduced funding for those whose scores were below standard.

Inevitably there have been intense debates as to the validity of the methodology and the adequacy and accuracy of the judgments. But the consequence has undoubtedly been much greater attention given to measuring research quality and outputs at the institutional level of individual universities and on the allocation of discretionary budgets to competing teams within each institution. The latter factor has been crucial to individual university strategies as the resources from the higher education funding council are provided as block grants to be passed on to the individual teams at the discretion of the university's administration. That is, the global total for each university is determined by the scores of the research teams within the university but the university retains the right to distribute the moneys according to its own policies as they are independent, decision-making bodies who guard their independence.

In relation to purpose-oriented funding, there has been within the overarching strategy of funding being distributed to those doing excellent work a shift from classic academic criteria of research driven by an interest in knowledge for its own sake to a more clear practical purpose orientation. In part, this has resulted from a deliberate push to encourage more private sector funding of national R&D including that carried out in universities. In part it is also a result of the changed rules and processes that the EU has adopted in its framework programs where a much more explicit competitiveness logic underpins the allocation of funds, and in part it is a change in the underlying paradigm for publicly funded research budgets.

Some of the changes have also been responding to a perception that the United Kingdom needs to increase incentives to utilize the results of R&D rather than just doing more academic research. But also change has been spurred by a recognition that the traditional bodies of research, universities and research council centers, no longer have a monopoly of excellence even in the pure research field as seen in the path-breaking work on materials in the aerospace industries, in the advances in genetics in the biotechnology field, and in electronics and related information technologies in the ICT sector. So building strategic alliances across research-performing institutions and sectors to combine the advantages of each in the search for solutions in priority topics has become the order of the day.

International Orientation

In relation to the internationalization of links, the United Kingdom is proud that it regularly ranks among the leading four or five nations when it comes to research quality and output when measured through the classic academic output indicators, such as the number of contributions to international refereed journals, success in international academic prizes, and citations of papers in other literature. However, in spite of this there has been a major shift in thinking relating to the sources of new technological ideas that will contribute to competitiveness. We now recognize that in spite of our own contribution and its quality, our research work is only a small part of all the R&D that is being carried out in any field at any time. Therefore, to stay abreast of advancing knowledge we have to be able to access and tap into the findings that are being created elsewhere, thereby justifying strong links with the international R&D community. It has also led to a scouting program funded by the public budget to bring back information about developments elsewhere and the dissemination of this new knowledge to corporate users.

While this international orientation has been taken forward at a national level it has also informed and been reinforced by the rules and procedures of the competitively allocated European Framework Programme.[12] Substantial additional discretionary funding can be accessed where universities and businesses join a targeted research program with at least two member states (preferably more) involved in the consortium bidding for funds. This encourages an international approach as well as the construction of enduring consortia of R&D interests among universities and businesses.

One of the consequences of these requirements has been an increase in international research alliances, but until recently this has also led to a distortion that potentially undermines the quality objective. The best research is not necessarily spread through different member states of the EU or associates who qualify for the EU Framework Programme (such as Norway) or is not even necessarily being done anywhere in Europe. So funding availability does not necessarily encourage international networks that link to the world's best researchers who often are outside the EU. In the current round of the R&D programs this limitation has been recognized and some funding is available to build connections with research centers and programs outside the EU. This will take some time to bear fruit as the experience of building research consortia within the EU is that it takes at least a few years to create the right conditions for effective collaboration.

Regional Policy and Diversity

As with many national innovation systems there exists within the UK both a number of rigidities and a persistent level of heterogeneity when viewed from a regional perspective. Within a geographic triangle of the cities of Oxford, Cambridge, and London as its points, a disproportionately large share of national R&D in both private and public sectors is conducted. Additionally, the proportion of corporate headquarters in this area is very high as is the venture capital and early-stage financing sectors with the result that the area has been dubbed the 'golden triangle' The corollary being that the other regions of the UK suffer a relative deficit of R&D activity, of corporate headquarters, and of seed and venture funds to sustain new technology entrepreneurship. Also, there is a long-term persistent drift of talented population moving to the golden triangle, further reinforcing the regional disparities.

Regional policy has tried concurrently to achieve two goals that have not necessarily been easy to reconcile: the first being more equitable development opportunities across the whole UK, and the second being a concentration of effort on successful regions to manage growth and foster international competitiveness.

The more equitable opportunities strand has led to investment in specialist infrastructure, such as science and technology parks and new business incubators, usually with some form of public–private partnership in both investment and operating stages. Moreover, regional financial incentives attract mobile private investment including that coming from international sources into the United Kingdom. Some of these initiatives have been stimulated by long-established regional development agencies, Scottish and Welsh development agencies, for example, while in the English regions the agencies are significantly younger and both less resourced and less experienced. Some of the initiatives have made a difference, especially when building on more dynamic cities within their regions with a sufficient critical mass of resources, but many have merely reduced the pace of relative decline and have not changed the fundamental dynamic.

The regional policies of the EU have also had an impact, although not consistently in one direction. The EU regional policy framework seeks to reduce regional disparities across the member states in order to stabilize communities and reduce migration from less developed to more developed regions within a single European integrated labor market. Specific regions are given distinct policy designations that indicate the level of their priority for financial incentives and the nature of their disadvantage, rural underdeveloped and restructuring of old industrial activities being two of the categories. One lesson learned from strategies that initially emphasized investment in capital infrastructure, science parks, and incubators again being the elements of infrastructure of most relevance to R&D and commercialization, was that the infrastructure is not enough and that sustained long-term programs are needed to ensure that desired activities are embedded to utilize the new infrastructure.

One relevant area where the policy conflict has been significant in the United Kingdom has been in respect of public contributions to early-stage venture funding that is now provided across the UK on a regional basis. An analysis showed that even in relatively successful regions there was a funding gap that was particularly constraining of the formation and growth of new technology-based firms. This persistent and general market failure did not fit into EU regional categorization and when the UK government tried to put in place in all the regions of the United Kingdom some publicly sponsored funds, the initiative was delayed in implementation for years. The issues were mainly raised under the competition or anti-trust framework where only under specific policy frameworks in particular regions or particular sectors are such publicly sponsored initiatives allowed. A fuller analysis of this and other programs is in the section on the commercialization cycle below.

Applications and Mature Industries

One of the persistent problems in the United Kingdom has been poor performance in mature industries in R&D either conducted in-house or acquired through linkages to universities or industrial R&D institutes. The predominant business strategies have been oriented to cost reductions in what are treated as established products, and so R&D is deemed to be an unaffordable luxury. Some larger firms have retained R&D activities, but not enough. There has also been a compounding factor in the large number of small and medium-sized enterprises (SMEs) that make up the bulk of the UK economy that have as a whole been minimal users of new technologies let alone undertaking R&D. The R&D intensity in newer knowledge-intensive sectors is thought to be satisfactory though more could be done. However, for the lower-technology, more-mature industries there is a much weaker relationship that is troubling. Much of the economic activity in these sectors has moved offshore to take advantage of lower labor cost production locations, but that which does remain does little in-house R&D and has only the weakest linkages with publicly funded research institutes and universities.

There has been a range of initiatives taken to stimulate interest among these traditional sectors with schemes that promote both cost saving and productivity improvements and new product developments. A particular effort has consistently been made to promote this type of work among SMEs that are infrequent users of innovation-related services and so need both expertise and financial inducements to get more involved. These types of schemes were managed by the government's Manufacturing Advisory Service and included widely used tools such as shared cost grant schemes and registers of accredited private sector advisors whose service quality would be assured.

Programs have sometimes taken a supply chain approach with the involvement of sectoral associations and own equipment manufacturers, and in some there have been alliances encouraged with universities to improve the linkages. A relevant example is the advanced manufacturing program at the University of Warwick with the motor industry that was geared to impact the automation in production lines, the adoption of more flexible manufacturing strategies, and the shift from electro-mechanical to electronics components. A long-term alliance with resource contributions from both sides was created that included exchanges of academic and professional staff between the university and companies and a systematic program of retraining mature, qualified, and experienced engineers to take on board the new technologies. New information technologies were developed to improve product flows and optimize manufacturing lines, and adaptive work was done with the machinery suppliers to develop new tools and integrate them into production lines.

Summary

The picture that emerges from this brief review is based on the recognition of the multifaceted nature of technology upgrading and commercialization strategies that underpin the knowledge economy and of the need for significant improvement in performance in many areas. Over the last two decades, the climate and culture has changed significantly but there has also been recognition that however much has been achieved there is always more to do. The challenges of the international competitive environment mean that today's approaches will not do for tomorrow and change is a permanent part of the landscape. In the rest of this chapter more experiences relating specifically to technology transfer and commercialization are highlighted as a complement to this broader review of the innovation climate in the United Kingdom.

3   TECHNOLOGY TRANSFER STRATEGIES

It is worth noting that there are only four main strategies for transferring knowledge about advanced science and technology into productive use. All have been used widely in the United Kingdom and practice has become much more sophisticated over the last decades. The four strategies are:

- managing intellectual property assets;
- developing strategic partnerships;
- creating new technology-based businesses; and
- providing specialist technology advice.

Managing Intellectual Property Assets

The first, and most frequently used strategy is the use of the IP and patenting system to create ownership of a knowledge asset that is then offered to the commercial sector for licensing. Use of the IP system is a central and ever-growing aspect of the knowledge economy in advanced OECD countries and almost all research performing groups pay careful attention to the potential of their results for commercialization.

The IP process grants a legal monopoly in the use of a novel idea for a significant time to enable inventors to gain a sufficient reward for their prior work in developing the novel idea. These processes have two distinct parts, the first of which is a legal process to establish the IP asset. This is an area of very specialist expertise but one that is easily compatible with the legal/administrative cultures of public universities and R&D institutes that have been set up largely as an internal management function within the university's central management team.

Once the IP asset has been established, the second phase begins which is when the IP is utilized and so creates value and return to the inventor. This phase has a completely different culture: that of a commercial entity, which is not compatible with the legal/administrative cultures of public universities and R&D institutes. Thus new approaches are required for this phase to be undertaken successfully. In spite of this, the majority of universities undertake the second phase with the same team that has responsibility for the first. The consequence has been a position where the IP management department is a cost center for the university rather than a profit center, as establishing and defending patents is an expensive business. In some universities there has emerged a collaborative strategy to deal with the cost issue. For example, four of the independent colleges within the federated University of London have merged their interests, and one team carries out the IP work for all the academics of the four colleges.

However, the different culture and its demands for a different approach at the second IP commercialization stage has been recognized by a growing number of universities, and different arrangements have been put in place by individual universities. The main change has been in the appointment of partners from the commercial world who are given, for example, a first refusal right to all IP emerging from the university's research in return for a share in the revenue stream and for the investment of early-stage equity funds. The University of Leeds has done this through a part-owner joint venture that included the transfer of all its staff previously engaged in the first phase and the introduction of a new fund to invest in the proof of concept and early-venture stages. Creation of a proof of concept fund and early-stage investment funds have also been practiced in several universities, Cambridge and Manchester among others, with a variety of arrangements to ensure that there are professional management teams, although in all cases the university retains a strong position of ownership of the outcomes.

Developing Strategic Partnerships

The second approach that is becoming a much more common practice in the United Kingdom is the creation of a strategic alliance between the research and business communities where through the pursuit of medium- to long-term research new knowledge is created with a specific application in mind. In this relationship, the knowledge relies on the advanced research capabilities of the research community and thus has what has previously been called 'pure research' elements, but because of its focus on specific areas of application it also has 'applied research' elements. An example is the University of Sheffield whose advanced materials group formed a specialist research program with Boeing to work on titanium and other difficult-to-handle materials that are important in aeronautics. This was established as a separate organization with its own staff and own research program. In the case of the University of Cambridge there is a whole family of alliances across many of the science and technology subjects. One of the most visible is with Microsoft, which has its European research center on the university campus in a separate building adjacent to the university's computing department. This alliance is distinctive as it also has a significant venture fund attached to commercialize the outcomes of the joint research programs.

This area is best suited to alliances between significant concentrations of knowledge creators and users who have a scale of resources and level of sophistication to plan new products and process development over several years. It also aligns well with a focused cluster-based development strategy or geographically concentrated approach similar to that which has been one of the central planks of UK industrial development strategy for some time.

Creating New Technology Firms

The third strategy, and one that overlaps with the related areas of entrepreneurship, is the creation of new knowledge-based firms by means of an incubation process. Here the new entrepreneur takes forward the innovation into the business world by solving all the problems of application and commercialization within the new firm. This is a crucial area that has received lots of attention in advanced knowledge economies, and best-practice approaches have been accumulated through many years of experience.

A more detailed exposition of the commercialization strategy is set out in Section 4, but here it is worth noting that a number of universities have developed a specialist facility where incubation takes place for their faculty and students. Some of these are called innovation centers where a service-rich offer is provided and linked to short-term accommodation for the new firm. Some are specialist facilities, such as the University of Manchester Biotechnology Incubator which also provides space for firms that graduate from the incubator in its core building, which is a mixed-use research/teaching and business facility. Others are focused on students, for instance, the Innospace facility at the Manchester Metropolitan University, although it also offers accommodation to business ideas that come from the local community where the university is based.

The second strategy that has become widespread has been the provision of specialist start-up advice and training. Sometimes this is orchestrated through a business plan competition (most UK universities have one for student entrepreneurs), where the winning teams get advice and sometimes funding to take their business idea into practice. Sometimes it is through an entrepreneurship module using a business plan framework to take the embryo business to the point of being ready to start. Another strategy is to develop a cadre of mentors who have experience with technology start-ups and to make them available to potential new enterprises that are emerging from the research base.

The third significant strategy in this area has been the growing number of universities that have established a proof of concept fund and have some form of participation in an early-stage equity investment fund. The proof of concept stage has proved frustrating for many new technology ideas where some non-research funds are needed to prove that a theoretical breakthrough is sufficiently valid to be able to be built into a new product or process with commercial merit. This will only rarely attract commercial funds and falls outside the traditional research funding domain, so research-based universities have increasingly established such funds for their own research outputs. Most of these are still at an early stage so experience and results with successes and failures have not yet been published and are awaited with interest.

Providing Specialist Technical Advice

The fourth and final strategy is through the extensive linkages between academics and businesses operating in their fields through advisory positions taken in specific firms or in associations of firms. In this instance, the knowledge is embodied in the specialist and the dissemination method is through personal transfer. Again this is a well-established practice, particularly in practical areas such as engineering as well as in vocational subjects such as law and medicine.

Being essentially personal it has fewer implications for technology transfer and commercialization policy other than ensuring that the practice is managed to avoid detriment to the core academic work and that a suitable balance of rewards and responsibilities is set for those who participate.

Summary

Of the four technology transfer strategies, the one that has been given most attention has been the creation of new technology enterprises, but this is increasingly seen as the most complex and risky of the four strategies from the point of view of the research-performing institutions. Additionally, it is the strategy with the biggest cultural mismatch with the traditional academic culture and in practice has provided smaller returns than the other two main strategies. Subsequent to the Lambert review,[13] a greater reliance is being put on the IP strategy as one that is more compatible with the underlying cultures of the research performing universities.

4   VENTURE FUNDS AND THE COMMERCIALIZATION CYCLE

The United Kingdom has long been a center of financial services and so it is no surprise that it has the second largest formal venture funding industry after that found in the United States. In spite of this availability of funds and associated expertise, there are still systemic problems with the availability of finance for new technology-based businesses, especially those spinning out from a research base with promoters who have little business or commercial experience. It has been generally agreed that the lack of availability of early-stage risk finance has been a constraint on technology commercialization and that there are underlying theoretical reasons for this constraint as well as particular regions of the United Kingdom in which the constraint has been particularly strong.

In this section we shall discuss:

- a representation of an articulate supply of venture funds and the challenges faced in the United Kingdom, especially in relation to early-stage finance for new technology firms; and
- a trio of hypotheses that indicate that there are other weaknesses and some tools that have been used to tackle the identified weaknesses.

An Articulate Supply of Venture Funds

New ventures require funds to take them from the first stage in the identification of a technology-based product or service to the time when it is a fully established company listed on a formal stock exchange.

The various stages of the commercialization cycle are shown in Figure 3.1 and include:

- *Tier 0*: the proof of concept stage, usually funded by grants, has proven a difficult stage in the United Kingdom because it has historically fallen outside the research grant-giving bodies' activities but occurs well before a project becomes suitable for commercial funds.

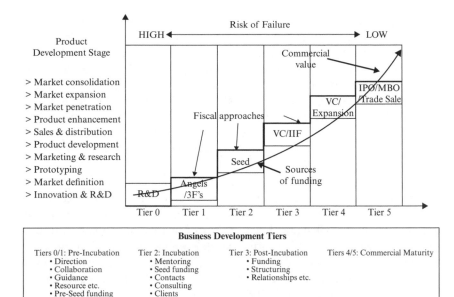

Source: Author.

Figure 3.1 The commercialization cycle

- *Tier 1*: the first informal but external funding stage, from the three Fs (friends, family, and fools) or more appropriately named 'business angels'. Groups of business angels have mushroomed across the United Kingdom over the last couple of decades, and this stage is judged to be working pretty well for most types of new technology-based firms.
- *Tier 2*: the first formal external stage of investment, the seed and start-up level, where usually small capital injections are made to meet the immediate company needs for additional capital and to build the business to a stage of initial profitability.
- *Tier 3*: when early venture capital begins to play its role for those businesses that have already introduced their product into the market and have achieved a positive trading position so an injection of new capital can quickly take them to a higher level of success.
- *Tier 4*: when larger development capital investments are made to accelerate the company growth and realize its full potential.
- *Tier 5*: the initial public offering (IPO) on a formal stock exchange so enabling the company to raise capital as it is needed to expand further.

At each stage of the injection of new capital there are associated business service needs that are also referred to in Figure 3.1. Their provision assists enterprises in maintaining their growth momentum and helps ensure a good return from the venture funding activity by mitigating some of the risks inherent in setting up and growing a new business. The challenge for policy is to provide this assistance to the fledgling businesses at a stage in their development where they are unlikely to be able to pay a full market price for the services but not to build a subsidy dependency or to spoil the market from developing long-term viable solutions from high-quality, private service firms.

As suggested earlier, there has been a persistent weakness in the United Kingdom at the early stage of the venture finance provision because of four particular challenges that new technology-based firms face. These are not absolute challenges; they are always relative in terms of alternative uses to which available venture capital can be put. This in large part explains the strong market provision of later-stage development finance and the predominance in the UK venture finance industry of management buy-out and merger and acquisition activities.

To return to the earlier stage funding dilemmas, the four areas of challenge relate to:

- *Information asymmetries and gaps*: while the researchers know the capacities of the new technology, potential investors have little expertise in this area and are unable to evaluate accurately the potential market relevance of the new ideas, so investors perceive a disproportionate risk and consequently reduce the level of their offer even when they are prepared to engage with the risk.
- *Pure technology risks associated with new developments*: potential investors want to know if the technology really works in practice and if it can be manufactured reliably and in sufficient scale to make a worthwhile return for the potential investor. Taking theoretical advances from a bench-level demonstration through a prototyping stage to large-scale production is often fraught with new technological challenges as well as taking considerable time and capital to achieve.
- *Commercial risks*: which derive from two sources: the first is essentially the lack of experience of technologists in enterprises and the commercial world, making them a more risky bet for investors, and the second is the level of uncertainty about the potential scale of market penetration that can be expected for the new technology, either to replace the current dominant technology if it is a disruptive development or to capture a reasonable share of the current market if it is an improved version of an established technology.

- *Disproportionately high transaction costs*: it costs a similar amount of time and analytic resources to go through the due diligence exercise for an investment of £0.5 million as it does for an investment of £50 million, so the economics of doing business pushes funds toward larger-scale transactions and discourages funds from investing in small early-stage investments.

Hypotheses Pointing to Other Weaknesses and Policy Responses

A simple statement of the underlying thinking behind a range of policy initiatives is summarized in the following three hypotheses, all of which apply to the United Kingdom to varying degrees. These have been tackled within the broad policy climate described earlier in this chapter and within a macroeconomic strategy that has encouraged participation in venture funding through the provision of targeted fiscal incentives.

The first hypothesis is that nationally there is a good science base from which ideas are being generated but the fully articulated range of funding needed to enable good ideas to be commercialized is missing. The policy response to this characterization has been to seek to develop particular venture funding initiatives that fill the gaps to foster new firms based on the emerging new ideas.

For example, there have been a number of universities that have put in place a proof of concept fund to take discoveries through the proof of concept stage. In the area of early-stage funding there has been an approach that stimulates a partnership approach to the provision of early-stage venture funds in all the UK regions. Each regional development agency was charged with undertaking an analysis to identify the most constraining gap where venture funds were not coming forward from the private market and to design a fund that would fill that gap. Usually these were offered on a competitive basis in the form of a public/private partnership with the public funds sitting alongside private funds and managed by the private risk-taking agent to offer venture funding that matches the gap that had been identified through the regional analysis. The volume of private finance that was raised to match the public funds, usually a multiple of three or four times the public funds, was one of the main criteria in deciding the winning competitor as well as the team of investment analysts.

The second hypothesis is that nationally there is a weak or inappropriately focused science base so too few commercializable ideas arise even though there is plenty of money to fund new ventures. So if good ideas can be generated, then they would be able to be commercialized. The policy response here is to reorient the science base to priority areas of relevance to national development and to ensure that the skill base of advanced human capital is refreshed and where possible further upgraded.

In previous sections the sort of initiatives in terms of selectivity of funding of R&D aligned to national priorities that have been taken in the United Kingdom have been described. In addition, incentives have been put in place to encourage collaborative research within strategic partnerships where the commercial partners have an interest and responsibility to identify the ideas with commercial potential and to take them forward. More effort has also been made by research-performing bodies to inform the investment and business community of the range of research being performed and the interest in principle in taking findings into the commercial domain.

The third hypothesis is that nationally there is a good science base generating good ideas and there is also plenty of money and venture funding to enable good ideas to be commercialized, but because there is no tradition of doing so, the two communities, research and financial, are unable to communicate and so are unable to bring the good ideas in a form that is suitable to those with the money to invest.

Here the response in the United Kingdom has been to put in place programs of technology transfer, building capabilities in the research base through technology transfer offices or industrial liaison units, introducing specialist services to prepare deals and specialist infrastructure to encourage incubation of new business ideas as outlined in the earlier sections. Some of the national research councils have introduced courses for their grant recipients, introducing them to the ideas of new business formation and IP strategies to ensure that they are sensitized and alert to opportunities that their research might generate. Additionally, there have been efforts to educate the investing community in the new technologies and to alert them to areas of potential. Within this general effort there have been specific schemes that relate to differential challenges faced by different technologies, as what works for biotechnology is different from what is needed for ICT.

There is, of course, a fourth hypothesis where there is neither money nor science and technology and the starting point is much further back, but this fortunately does not apply to the United Kingdom.

5   SUMMARY

The United Kingdom has come a considerable distance in its efforts to improve its performance in technology commercialization and entrepreneurship through a broad-ranging assault on related areas of national policy as well as through bottom-up initiatives from particular institutions. It is a topic that continues to receive attention and where the consequences of changes are still being worked through even as new initiatives are being introduced before the last set of changes have bedded down. The pace of change is accelerating even though the more thoughtful commentators and policy makers have recognized that change of this nature is a long-term challenge with today's decisions and initiatives likely to really bear fruit in decades to come rather than the short number of months or years that interest politicians.

NOTES

1. The Lisbon agenda, agreed in Lisbon in 2000 when Portugal was holding the rotating chair of the EU, relates to the objective of Europe becoming the most competitive and dynamic knowledge-based economy in the world by 2010. It has been very influential in S&T policy in the intervening years but has fallen far short of targets in implementation.
2. The National innovation system concept became popular during the 1980s with the realization that a systemic approach could be used to link the different aspects of traditional policy areas – higher education and S&T, for example – that are central to a fully functioning innovation system.
3. Chaos models characterize systems into non-stochastic equations that while individually simple when acting together result in predictable but complex outcomes. The insights for innovation are: first, that the relationships are systematic and not necessarily random; second, that the starting conditions of any system are crucial in determining the path the dynamic system follows; and, third, that being entropic they need continuing injections of energy to maintain and then change the trajectory. Put more simply: where you start from is important and you can make a difference through the efforts you make to the outcome achieved.
4. Cambridge, UK, emerged during the 1960s and later decades to establish itself as one of the main high-technology hubs of Europe in terms of the number and quality of both new technology-based businesses being created from the academic base of a world-class university. Initially the momentum was led by ICT applications that remain important but more recently biotechnology has become equally important and now the region is the largest concentration of commercial biotech companies in Europe.
5. Over the last decade, trust in the scientist as an advisor and guide to scientifically complex subjects has been seriously damaged in the United Kingdom. Examples include scientists asserting certainty when they were proved by subsequent events to be wrong (the transmission of BSE, mad cow disease, to humans being a celebrated case), presenting conflicting views and evidence (particularly in the area of genetic modification where the media were at least as culpable by suggesting equivalence for maverick views alongside serious research), doing research that apparently provided support for corporations that sponsored their research activities, so compromising their apparent independence, and communicating with incomprehensible jargon so being characterized as having nothing relevant to say.
6. The Royal Society is the UK academy of science and the oldest such body still in existence having been created in 1660 with members elected on the basis of the excellence of their contribution to science.
7. Named after Wilhelm von Humbolt, the Prussian Minister for Education in the midnineteenth century, who set out a blueprint for research-based universities that has subsequently been much followed throughout Europe and wider afield. It emphasized the

value of their independence and pursuit of higher-level teaching informed by leading academic research within a single entity.

8. This program at the University of Nottingham (University of Nottingham Institute for Entrepreneurship and Innovation (UNIEI) was established with funding from the first round of competitive allocations as an institute of the Business School at the university. It also created a network of faculty in each of the university's departments who were trained to look for potential commercializable research findings, assist them to establish IP and be brought to the market.

9. The White Rose Consortium was a partnership among the three leading research universities in Yorkshire – Leeds, Sheffield and York – to establish a proof of concept/early-stage investment fund that would invest in research outcomes with a focus on biotech applications in which the three universities have complementary areas of excellence. The consortium appointed professional fund managers to administer the fund and set up joint governance arrangements to ensure that all three universities' interests were respected.

10. Here a second round of competitive funding was provided and in some cases allocated to universities that had been successful in the first round to enable them to deepen and extend their practices. An example is the University of Nottingham which led a region-wide initiative to include all the universities of their region in a network that would share the good practice established during the first round when it had established UNIEI (see note 8).

11. Provided that individual faculty members fulfilled their duties – allocated teaching roles, high-quality research that was regularly published in world leading journals – the university adopted what was described as a policy of 'benign neglect' to other activities pursued by faculty. An additional set of duties relates to the colleges of which faculty are members – pastoral duties to students and frequency of dining in hall during term time being the main areas. So together with the practice of disregarding its ownership of intellectual property generated through research work this proved a conducive environment to the creating of many technology-based businesses led by faculty.

12. Currently the EU is on its 7th Framework Programme for Research and Technological Development that between 2006 and 2011 is planned to fund in excess of €50 billion of research. Its purpose is to contribute to the development of the Community and while primarily focused on EU-based research teams is open in some of its parts to all researchers globally. The majority of projects funded are carried out by consortia with members from more than one EU country and from both academic organizations and businesses.

13. The Lambert Review of Business–University Collaboration was prepared for the UK government and published in December 2003. It particularly focused on the economic impacts and commercialization of research findings and concluded that there was some good practice but that much more could be done.

REFERENCE

Nelson, Richard R. (ed.) (1993), *National Innovation Systems: A Comparative Analysis*, Oxford: Oxford University Press.

4. A stress test for creative and innovative management: entrepreneurship in a war zone

Corey P. Carbonara, Michael F. Korpi and Marc LeGare

1 INTRODUCTION

This chapter describes the growth and success of an Iraqi telecommunications start-up, Advanced Technologies for Communications (ATC), which was 'incubated' by a Texas company, Proactive Communications, Inc. (PCI). In 2003, Iraq was an extremely dynamic and dangerous environment – not only militarily, but also in terms of every other function and institution of a modern society, including communication and commerce. The current situation is improved, but Iraq remains a difficult and tumultuous place. Because of the inherent and embedded struggles there, any successful entrepreneurial efforts in this setting are worth examining. To look at the experience of PCI and ATC in Iraq, we employ the Creative and Innovative Management framework created by the IC² Institute founder Dr George Kozmetsky.

2 CREATIVE AND INNOVATIVE MANAGEMENT FRAMEWORK

The IC² Institute at the University of Texas at Austin has been regularly creating and developing constructs for better understanding how to stimulate wealth creation globally for shared prosperity. At the heart of these efforts has been the work of numerous IC² Fellows. IC²'s ability to take unstructured problems and find novel and workable solutions has created a series of blueprints for success for nations and firms around the world. IC²'s solid research on Technopolis construction, Zero Time Strategy, Diffusion of Innovations, and Fluid Learning are just a few examples.

The flagship example of a construct for creating and sustaining successful firms around the globe can be seen in the Creative and Innovative Management framework (CIM). CIM is unique in its approach to creativity, innovation, and the creation of capital, and how all of these factors relate to management practices. CIM is particularly applicable to this current case study on entrepreneurship in Iraq, and therefore a brief summary of CIM is useful before examining the experiences of PCI and ATC.

Historically, management theory has focused on efficiency or effectiveness. CIM is unique in that it adds two new important elements: flexibility and adaptability. In his book, *Transformational Management* (1985), Kozmetsky adds flexibility and adaptability as key components for expanding management theory because given the nature of disruption in a marketplace these two attributes might be even more important than efficiency and effectiveness. In *Transformational Management*, Kozmetsky highlights disruptions in a marketplace as an example of unstructured problems that need novel solutions.

According to Kozmetsky (1986), creativity is defined as a novel approach toward problems and innovation is defined as the successful implementation of creative ideas. The CIM framework encourages the creation of successful acts of management applied as solutions to specific problems. These acts of management cover the areas of organizational structure, strategy, motivation, incentives, culture and environment, alliances, mergers and acquisitions – to name a few. Also, according to Kozmetsky (ibid.), the emphasis in creative and innovative management is 'on evaluating novel ideas in management and making them more responsive to the needs of society' (xxiv). Considering the impact of what PCI has already achieved in Iraq (as outlined in this study), the CIM framework applied to this specific case study can provide valuable insight useful for future technopolis-building efforts in the Middle East and other regions.

CIM is about managing change. Kozmetsky describes this management task as 'the creation and application of knowledge in the development of policy' (xxii). In his view, policy is the key tool that management employs to direct innovation in a specific manner. Innovation is key, especially in the case of building start-up companies because it can be the opportunity generator that propels ideas forward (Kuhn, 1986, xxix). If innovation is not carefully nurtured, then there is risk of increasing vulnerability to competition and external pressures from the public sector, which can stifle growth and even cause the demise of a young company altogether. This risk will become even more heightened as firms come in to reconstruct a post-war Iraq.

CIM as a management framework is a very useful tool for guiding the study of entrepreneurial and innovative entities, especially those that try to create new enterprises from new technologies. The framework is also

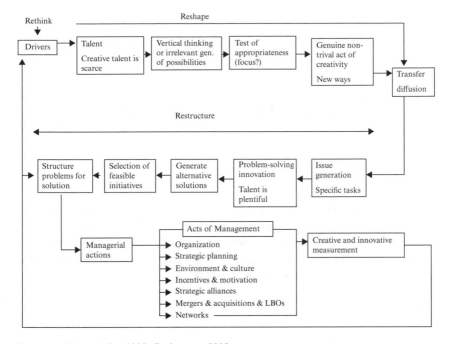

Sources: Kozmetsky, 1988; Carbonara, 2008.

Figure 4.1   *Creative and innovative management process*

useful for evaluating the myriad issues surrounding the creation of successful technopoleis around the globe.

As illustrated in Figure 4.1, the CIM framework represents management by focusing on management acts that serve as solutions to specific business problems. The CIM framework is composed of elements that cover various aspects of creativity, innovation, and the management cycle. For the purposes of this study, selected key elements most relevant to the activities of technology start-ups are analyzed. The elements highlighted are Drivers and Talent, Issues, Problem Solving, Acts of Management as Solutions, and Feedback (Carbonara, 2008).

Drivers and Talent

The first element, Drivers, focuses on the needs and problems in markets and how those are related to existing or future trends and opportunities. This element also takes a look at crises in markets. Drivers act as the navigational compass for the CIM process. Talent is the second key element.

This Talent can be identified as people within the organization (that is, key players) or external partners (that is, consultants, partners, and so on) who can play a vital role in contributing to corporate goals and identifying novel solutions to specific business problems. PCI and the start-up company, ATC, represent both internal and external talent working harmoniously to foster growth in a partnership of strategic alliance. Both Drivers and Talent are vital to creative rethinking about the direction of an organization, which will begin to reshape the company's strategies and policies.

Issues

Another key element in the CIM process is the understanding of how to identify key issues that management faces. Linking these issues to appropriate challenges and opportunities for the firm is the first step toward becoming an innovative organization. The issues are contextual by nature and fall within the following classifications:

- economic;
- technological;
- legal/regulatory; and
- socio-cultural.

Acts of Management as Solutions

Another crucial element in the CIM process is the creation of a series of Acts of Management (AOM). These are actions a firm takes to respond to change in markets and technology. In successful companies, these actions are the manifestations of being both creative and innovative. According to Kozmetsky (1988, 15–30), the AOM can be identified as:

- organizational structure;
- strategy;
- motivation and incentives;
- culture and environment;
- key strategic relationships; and
- mergers and acquisitions.

Feedback

Inherent to the CIM process is a feedback loop that allows a company to revisit key drivers, key issues, and the changing nature of problems affecting management. According to Carbonara (2008), an organization must have fluid communication and feedback to stay effective and efficient. Without proper feedback, an organization can suffer from variation in execution of the tactics and strategy set forth by the executive team. Furthermore, without appropriate feedback, an innovative and creative organization cannot succeed (ibid.). To be a successful learning organization, two types of feedback are needed: tactical and strategic.

To elicit tactical feedback, the emphasis is on answering the following questions:

1. How are we doing?
2. Are we doing things right?

To elicit strategic feedback the emphasis is on answering three different questions:

1. What do you need from us that we are not giving you now?
2. Are we doing the right thing?
3. What do you think you will need 5, 10, or 20 years from now?

It is this feedback and the cyclical nature of the process that generates the utility and value of the CIM schema. It also allows a firm to become what Kozmetsky (1988) and Carbonara (2008) call a 'learning organization' – a company that uses feedback to continuously improve. As PCI became more familiar with the CIM process, it realized that many of its intuitive management actions were in line with CIM, pairing issues to actions in solving the novel problems faced in Iraq. Figure 4.2 illustrates this dynamic CIM feedback loop.

3   PCI AND ATC

The Iraqi start-up, ATC, is currently led by two brothers of Shia/Southern Iraq lineage. The company grew to over 40 employees and has supported projects as large as the Iraqi Ministry of the Interior's Command and Control Network, which among other things, was used to support the Iraqi elections. The employees of ATC represent Iraq's religious and educational diversity. Within the company, Shia, Sunni, and Christians work together, and there are high school, trade school, and university graduates as well as a wide range of previous military, government, commercial, and medical personnel. These diverse Iraqis have become experts in the deployment, operation, and maintenance of satellite telecommunications,

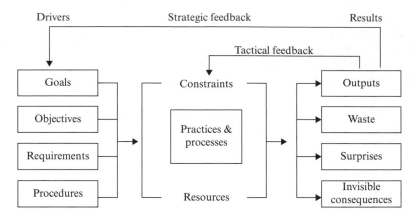

Sources: Carbonara, 1989, 2008.

Figure 4.2   The CIM feedback loop

networks, and a wide range of other information technology (IT) hardware and software. The company has operated successfully across every province in Iraq from 2004 to the present in one of the most challenging business environments.

By grounding the case study of PCI and ATC in CIM theory, the inquiry goes beyond looking at serendipitous impacts of decision making in an organization and focuses on the dynamic interplay among the disruptions that occur in technology and markets. This is particularly relevant given the dynamic and dangerous nature of Iraq for business in general and specifically for PCI and ATC because communication infrastructure is a target for those opposing the government. The relationships among management, technology, and markets necessitate a solid theoretical framework taking into account the dynamic nature of these essential components and their roles in successful technopolis construction. The experience of PCI and ATC in Iraq includes a range of successes, failures, surprises, and invisible consequences that become valuable for future entrepreneurial efforts in this and other challenging environments.

Drivers and Goals

PCI began operating satellite networks in Iraq in June 2003 in support of US military units that required an additional means of communication outside of their tactical radio system. The inability of US military radio systems to handle large volumes of data traffic is well known. In addition, the fastest way to gain connectivity (and also the safest given the insurgents' ability to target microwave and cell telephone towers) was to install Very Small Aperture Terminal (VSAT) nodes for internet access. Through 2003–04, PCI gained a wealth of unique experience as one of the few satellite telecommunications providers actually residing in Iraq. The initial PCI workforce consisted of three VSAT engineers – two Americans and one Iraqi – who supported satellite telecommunications projects ranging from individual sites to networks as large as 18 nodes.

Communication Infrastructure for Governance

In 2003, the Coalition Provisional Authority (CPA) issued 'orders' forming the basis for Iraqi law (CPA, 2009). In some cases the orders merely restated current Iraqi law or government procedures under Ambassador Paul Bremer's signature. However, in most cases, new laws or procedures were being established. Iraqi government procurement policies are just one example. The rules were often new, and the actual implementation of these rules was an unknown.

By mid-2003, communication needs began to appear in Iraq that went far beyond simply supplementing the US military's connectivity and bandwidth. PCI executives saw an emerging business environment in Iraq that was very complex and dynamic. Rebuilding Iraq was becoming a primary focus but going about this in an environment lacking the necessary infrastructure presented a formidable challenge.

Security Costs

Another factor contributing to the challenge was security costs. The General Accounting Office (GAO) reports that a significant amount of money is required to secure western contractors in Iraq. In some cases, 25 percent of project costs were security related. The short-term nature of US participation in the reconstruction strategy also had to be acknowledged. The implication of the high-dollar reconstruction programs was that successful projects would be handed over to the Iraqi government for continuation. Therefore these projects would have to operate with 100 percent Iraqi infrastructure.

Additionally, in 2004, PCI began to see that safe and secure movement could be conducted without guns, armored vehicles, or interruption to the local populace. Together with safe and secure communication capability, this could be leveraged to great advantage for development efforts.

Need for an Iraqi IT Company

From both a sovereignty point of view and a practical business point of view, any future continuation of PCI-supplied services in support of the Iraqi government would be best supported by an Iraqi partner. PCI executives concluded that they needed an Iraqi company or companies to work with because:

1. US expatriate engineers were very costly to maintain in the combat theater of Iraq.
2. Any large-scale project that PCI designed/built might be eligible for handover to the Iraqi government for long-term operations and maintenance. In this case, having a trusted Iraqi partner would likely prove beneficial.
3. PCI leaders envisaged that at some point, the US military might stimulate the economy by allowing Iraqi companies to directly bid for US projects.
4. The desired political end state – a thriving democracy and free market economy – would have to be supported from the ground up. In other words, changed attitudes and actions would only occur at the level of the average Iraqi citizen through close personal interaction.

For these reasons, PCI developed a course of action to line up an Iraqi-owned IT company that could be a strategic partner in future projects. This company could use internal relationships to secure movement, business intelligence, and react to business opportunities well ahead of US or non-Iraqi IT companies. The right kind of Iraqi partner could be matured into a leading provider of IT services in Iraq and could leverage this dynamic environment and evolve as the environment evolved. However, in early 2004, no Iraqi IT company with the necessary capabilities existed. Therefore, PCI chose to start one, offering the opportunity to the Iraqi VSAT engineer who was part of the PCI team. Advanced Technology for Communications was born.

4   TIMELINE AND ACCOMPLISHMENTS

The start-up investment required for ATC was minimal. PCI invested $5,000 to cover business registration, legal, and other fees required for an IT business in Iraq. A PCI employee, Ali Sahib, was selected as the initial ATC president. Sahib spoke excellent English as his pre-PCI employment included being a translator. PCI held a number of 'mentorship' sessions

Table 4.1   PCI and ATC milestones, 2003–2007

Date	Event
March 2003	PCI into Iraq with US ground forces supporting collaboration systems
June 2003	First VSAT systems deployed in support of 4th Infantry Division, supported by PCI
Aug. 2003	PCI invests in VSAT equipment and Kuwait facility for Iraqi VSAT projects
Sept.–Dec. 2003	Small VSAT projects; transfer PCI HQ from Kuwait to new location in Baghdad
Jan.–March 2004	Decision to start up Iraqi IT company; medium VSAT projects awarded to PCI
April–May 2004	Insurgency swells
Nov. 2004–Feb. 2005	Large VSAT project awarded to PCI; ATC scales from 1 to 20 men; PCI CEO deploys to Iraq; initial 42 nodes installed; interim elections supported by network; develop secure VOIP over satellite capability
July 2005	ATC scales to 30 personnel and takes over on-site engineering support requirement across Iraq; ATC 'Red Zone' office closed down due to insurgent attacks
Oct. 2005–March 2006	Network supports constitutional referendum; PCI CEO deploys to Iraq for contract negotiations, business development, installation methodology revision, project transition planning and mentoring; ATC at 40 personnel and larger than PCI (30 personnel); mission to Dahuk
June 2006	IC2N is world's largest, fully-meshed, secure VOIP network over satellite
Nov. 2006–Jan. 2007	IC2N at 258 nodes; PCI networks comprise over 300 nodes in Iraq alone; IC2N selected by GOI for transition; begin negotiation process
May 2007	IC2N is first successful IT project transitioned to GOI for funding through new contract; 258 nodes, 1000+ computers, 600+ phones and associated services
July–Oct. 2007	ATC trains for fiber optic installation, Cisco and Microsoft support; ATC awarded other transition projects; conducts other business development with Ministry of Communications and Defense; smaller PCI projects transitioned to ATC

with Sahib that were focused on basic business processes such as hiring personnel, business development exploration, contract terms and clauses, and business models. ATC added employees as PCI gradually increased its dependency on ATC for network implementation in Iraq. Table 4.1

presents a summary of the milestones achieved by the PCI and ATC collaboration.

Security Challenges

Until May 2004, PCI and ATC enjoyed unfettered access to most towns in the provinces. Customers provided security and transportation. Movement was rapid, expeditious, and trouble free. This situation changed dramatically in May 2004, when the insurgency began to swell and movement was severely restricted. From June to August 2004, ground movement out of the Green Zone (aka International Zone) was restricted except for high-speed drives along Route Irish (also known as the Highway of Death), the entry point to Camp Victory and Baghdad International Airport. This period of forced inactivity proved to be advantageous as Sahib began to formulate his own version of business practices based on coaching received from PCI.

Supporting Iraqi Elections

In November 2004, the next stage of the relationship between the two companies began. PCI was awarded a large-scale indefinite delivery indefinite quantity (IDIQ) contract with the Multinational Security Transition Command-Iraq (MNSTC-I) through its subordinate unit Civilian Police Assistance Training Team (CPATT). The project called for the design, deployment, and support for a large satellite telecommunications network across each province and major city in Iraq. The initial quantity called for 42 nodes in various locations across Iraq in advance of the initial Iraqi elections scheduled for January 2005. Through very difficult circumstances, the PCI and ATC team succeeded in this initial phase. All 42 nodes were in place one week prior to the elections and ready for a nationwide communications exercise. The network performed as designed – every province and major city could converse via voice over internet protocol (VOIP) and transmit data. This had never been achieved in Iraq, even before the war. At this point, ATC had grown to 20 engineers and Sahib was grooming his management team.

Growth and Development

By December 2005, as the last of the initial elections was held, ATC had grown to 40 employees, exceeding PCI by 10 people. ATC had an executive team, a management team that was functionally organized, and had matured enough in terms of business development that PCI had started to use ATC as a sole source of IT labor in Iraq. By this time, the PCI–ATC team had weathered death, kidnappings, threats, near-misses, as well as happier events like weddings and births. At the beginning of December 2004, all the employees were bachelors. While most had discussed caution about marriage and family in such a dangerous environment, the opportunity with ATC changed the outlook of many. They had hope for a better future and despite the continuing difficulties, could see that building a more positive future was possible for them, their families, and Iraq.

The large-scale network was recognized in June 2006 as the world's largest fully-meshed secure VOIP network over satellite (Furnai, 2006). This was quite an accomplishment for both companies. On the technical side, PCI engineered a one-of-a-kind network to minimize satellite latency effects on voice transport and Common Internet File System (CIFS) dependent protocols. PCI's ground-breaking engineering received priority support from brand-name IT companies such as Cisco and Blue Ridge Networks. The value of the network at end state was estimated at $52 million (hardware and services). The ATC personnel installed and maintained more than 75 percent of the nodes and associated local area networks (LANs). In fact, in late 2006, just months before the US military 'surged' with additional forces to quell the increasing violence, they installed 65 nodes in 45 days.

Challenges and Obstacles

The large-scale network supporting the Iraqi elections was not the only project that both companies worked on together. Other joint projects caused the partners to experience both success and failure and uncovered interesting obstacles for ATC. Interestingly enough, the first obstacle was a US military acquisition policy, 'Iraq First', which was intended to support broader Iraqi entrepreneurship, but which resulted in fraud and abuse. This policy originated in April 2006 and was supposed to spur Iraqi economic expansion, entrepreneurship, and individual development. The program removed specific barriers that prevented Iraqi-owned businesses from competing on a level playing field for US reconstruction business, but a complex gauntlet of requirements and procedures remained.

PCI assisted ATC with registering for this program. In early summer 2006, the leadership of both companies designed template proposals in both Arabic and English, ground rules (based on equipment types desired by the US government contracting officer, suspense timelines, and so on), and internal communication schemes that took time zone differences into consideration. Despite very close cooperation, both PCI's and ATC's efforts were frustrated by unscrupulous companies that sold grey market

IT hardware and software to unwitting contracting officers, resulting in frustrated military customers.

Another issue was the lack of ministerial mid-level managers trained for program management as well as an evolving Iraqi government acquisition process. This complex set of issues might be enough to dissuade all but the most intrepid and experienced businesses from investing in Iraq. It remains a major obstacle for PCI–ATC to overcome.

For example, the government of Iraq (GOI) Ministry of the Interior nominated the Iraqi Command and Control Network (IC2N) for transition/ project handover and subsequent GOI funding. PCI corporate leadership spent almost six months in Baghdad working the process for this project transition. Each day the PCI leaders would discuss the objectives and the progress towards meeting these goals. English and Arabic conversations could be parsed and interpreted. Often, the US team would find newly released Iraqi law and position papers guiding the evolving GOI acquisition process. These legal, financial, and operational milestones were then discussed and interpreted within the team and then within the negotiation process. To make this even more complex, the Ministry of the Interior 'customer' had a set of US military advisors (the former paying customers of IC2N and PCI–ATC) ready to assist them.

The intersection of outdated Coalition Provisional Authority (the CPA of Ambassador Bremer) orders and amendments, Interim Iraqi Parliamentary law (Foreign Investment Law of 2006 and Ministry of Planning Law on Implementing Government Contracts 2007), Iraqi and international banking procedures, and the US DoD/DoS Total Asset Recognition Program (the program for handing over reconstruction assets to a foreign government), made for a complex problem-solving environment. Through information sharing on emerging acquisition processes, collaboration on international banking standards, personal relationships established over the previous years' work in Iraq, and bonds of trust – the first large-scale US IT reconstruction project was effectively handed over for GOI funding in 2007. The contribution of ATC managers cannot be understated. The team of PCI–ATC succeeded in this transition where three other Fortune 100 companies failed with their own IT reconstruction projects.

Another area that reaped benefits for ATC was the handover in smaller projects. In the reconstruction concept, some service-based projects would be turned over to the Iraqi end client for 'ownership'. This normally implied continued funding. In cases where PCI was the service provider, ATC was positioned as the logical transition entity. PCI and ATC supported the task force in Al Anbar and Diyala provinces in 2006–07, and ATC won the transition business in those provinces.

ATC knows the Iraqi gatekeepers and key players and has built a trusted relationship with them in all key government agencies. It also has the ability to recruit specific types of people with trusted backgrounds of Sunni, Shia, and Christian faiths. For example, PCI Iraqi partners operate in every Provincial Joint Coordination Center (PJCC) in Iraq, including Dahuk, Sulaymaniyah, Tikrit, Kirkuk, Ramadi, Baquba, Baghdad, Hilla, Amarah, Kut, Diwaniyah, Nasiriyah, and Basra. These locations are usually collocated with the provincial governor or adjacent to his work location. A far larger number of nodes are located in smaller towns and cities such as Mandali, Tal Afar, Ar Ar, Kor Zabayr, Trebil, Al Qayam, and the various suburbs of Baghdad.

5 TALENT

Mentorship Goes Both Ways

As mentioned earlier, the initial ATC president and owner was Ali Sahib, who was a young man from the Sadr City suburb of Baghdad. In the earliest stages of ATC the mentoring sessions focused on acquainting Sahib with basic business operations but the sessions quickly transitioned to problem-solving conversations focused on the contrast between the general 'doctrine' of business and the particular realities of the Iraqi post-war business environment. For instance, the US government's habit of 'clause flow down' to subcontractors necessitated the ability to obtain workmen's compensation insurance, Defense Base Act (DBA) insurance, and to meet Occupational Safety and Health Act (OSHA) standards. For his part, Sahib would discuss what was possible and what was too dangerous. For instance, in 2004, there was no medical insurance of any kind. There was some form of professional and general liability insurance, but Sahib advised staying away from procuring or even asking about it because of the risk of the information getting to criminals or insurgents and inviting kidnapping or attack. In some cases PCI could manufacture a work-around solution. For example, in all US government contracts PCI was able to cover ATC's insurance requirements through its US DBA insurance coverage.

Employee Recruitment

It is interesting to note the background of the men who were employees of ATC. Since security was a primary concern for all PCI and ATC team members, vetting new employees was very important. A normal hiring process might involve media and website announcements of job openings, followed by resumé review, interviews, and skills tests. In contrast, the ATC procedure was to invite each potential employee on the basis of a previous relationship with Sahib. The relationship was based on one or more of the following: family or tribe blood lines, neighborhood affiliation, educational association established at Baghdad University, or recommendation from a trusted friend. The bottom line is that security and loyalty are much more significant factors in hiring in Iraq than any type of skill or related experience. It is also interesting to note that this approach resulted naturally in a heterogeneous religious composition. Although Sahib was Shia, the employees were a mixture of Sunni, Christian, and Shia. From a PCI point of view, there did not appear to be any religious animosity among groups at any time. This fact was discussed many times in public conversation, and the employees were always emphatic that the sectarian violence was artificial in nature and not endemic to Iraq. This peaceful coexistence of the religions in ATC remains to this day.

Training

Since security concerns trumped skills in the hiring process, training the essential skills became an important task. PCI and ATC developed a two-week training program for VSAT engineers. Tasks included satellite telecommunications theory, assembling the VSAT system, finding the satellite, commissioning the system, constructing the LAN, programming VOIP phones, and troubleshooting.

Another reason that training was so essential had to do with gaps in the Iraqi education system. Despite the fact that most ATC employees had academic or technical degrees, their education had been theory-only with little or no practical application, and the theory was based on outdated materials due to the embargoes after *Desert Storm*. In addition, the state of the university system was fragile at best due to the levels of violence aimed directly at universities, faculty, and students. By some accounts, more than 80 percent of the university capacity for education was shut down in 2006–07.

A training program had to be developed to span the gap in technical understanding. The training gave the potential VSAT engineers a basis in theory and extensive hands-on training on the equipment set that was state of the art.

Employee Turnover and a Positive Company Culture

Over the course of time, ATC employed more than 120 men. At the time this chapter was written (Spring 2009), ATC had 41 employees, some of whom had been in the company since 2004–05. The employees who left took their skills and marketed them successfully with other emerging Iraqi IT firms as well as brand-name international firms. How the team handled its first 'loss' of employees exercising their newfound freedoms is worth discussing.

In early 2005, just after the first set of elections, two of the better VSAT engineers accepted positions with Alcatel. The loss came at a time when the PCI–ATC team was consolidating the network and establishing the onsite support required by the contract. The two engineers had been selected to work at the Ministry of the Interior's National Command Center. The loss was a setback. However, from a strategic point of view it was not lost on the PCI leadership that this migration was part of the management challenge of working in the IT field in the United States as well as in Iraq. It was a key teaching moment that could be framed in terms of personal freedoms. In the particular case of these two employees, both men were Christian and were excited by the opportunity for international travel to France for training. Travel outside of their country had never been an option for them prior to the war. PCI management saw a responsibility to highlight this point and show the value of staying with the PCI–ATC team for each individual's future benefit. The general discussion ran along these points:

1. The training and skills gained from staying with PCI–ATC is very valuable and can shape a person's destiny.
2. Employees can choose where they work and how hard they work.
3. Each time a friend leaves he is exercising his freedom, and we can wish him the best.

Those first two men have remained in contact with their ATC friends and PCI leadership. Others who left also remain in contact and rely on their ATC network of friends for references and referrals.

Changed Attitudes and Actions

In December 2005, the PCI team was tasked to conduct a series of installations in Dahuk, Kurdistan. This was a very politically sensitive mission that had been delayed many times for security and other concerns. The team asked ATC engineers Nawaf and Wisam to fly via US military aircraft from Baghdad to Mosul, move by ground transport with the equipment, and complete the installation in Dahuk. A PCI site manager accompanied them to ensure appropriate support from the US military. The team completed the mission rapidly, received a general officer letter of recognition, and returned to base station in Baghdad. The team was met by shouts of joy and yells of recognition by PCI and ATC employees. Engineer Nawaf said, 'I will go anywhere and do anything for this company. Please let me do this!'. He stated this emphatically many times that afternoon, which puzzled the PCI employees, especially because of the intensity of his emotion, and made them suspect that perhaps something was being 'lost in translation'. Asking for clarification from one of the better English-speaking employees, they learned that Engineer Nawaf, a Shia, had never traveled beyond the southern parts of Iraq. His trip to Dahuk was one of the highlights of his life, and he was overcome by seeing the effects of newly embraced democratic principles and the role the company was playing in supporting them. Therefore, he would do anything for his country. 'Please let me do more work for my country!' was the reality of his sentiment.

Engineer Nawaf is emblematic of changing attitudes and actions in Iraq. He had been hired in late 2004 as a day laborer hauling VSAT system ballast and tools. He had taken the training courses offered by PCI and had been promoted to engineer in 2005. By the next year he was the installation manager for what became the world's largest secure, fully-meshed VOIP over satellite network. In 2008, he succeeded Sahib as the president of ATC.

Language

Almost all ATC employees speak some English. In most cases, English is understandable. However, the preferred means of communication over the internet was instant messenger (IM). Every PCI employee who worked with the ATC team carried all the Iraqi engineers' 'call signs'. On login to the laptop, managers could track who was available, and likewise, they could see which managers were working by the presence icons. Each man could type in English reasonably well or at least make themselves understood enough so that management called IM the 'universal translator'. Additionally, the team could exchange daily pleasantries and greetings to those engineers in distant locations.

Despite the fact that everyone could communicate using English, doing so in some cases can significantly increase the risks for Iraqis. In order to alleviate this danger, by 2005 PCI and ATC had established communication rules that protected the onsite engineers so they never had to talk or type in English. This practice remains as an overall risk mitigation measure to protect the local workforce.

Weekly business development video teleconferences (VTCs) have helped maintain the personal relationships established and fostered by PCI's corporate presence in Iraq. Presently, PCI is deploying a unified communications platform that supports presence, instant messenger, VOIP, video, and web collaboration. This will make an even greater level of communication with ATC personnel possible.

6 ISSUES

Security

The very nature of doing business in Iraq, compounded by this project's support for the elections, made the entire team targets for various anti-Iraqi forces. In the face of this challenge, ATC's management team used local information to develop a detailed and refined view of the risks and then established a course of mitigation. Often, solutions such as a delay of two or three days, entering the area by an alternative route, or installing at night or in bad weather proved to be sufficient for reducing risks to an acceptable level.

Overcoming Fatalism

Another hurdle PCI–ATC had to overcome was the cultural philosophy or attitude of 'as God wills it'. This rather common Iraqi reaction to a difficulty or challenge can stymie even the best-laid-out plan. In Iraq, where 'friction' can occur as soon as the first task is executed, PCI found understanding this attitude to be an absolute imperative. Finding ways to avoid or compensate for this problem consumed a good bit of time early on. Unforeseen circumstances often generated this task-ending statement. One effective approach PCI found was to teach why yielding to circumstance might not be the best course of action. As the ATC team's technical abilities matured, and as managers began to depend on group problem solving (rather than minimizing or overlooking problems), individuals adopted a less fatalistic position and began to assume that people working together could solve problems.

PCI used an inexpensive tool to acknowledge the success of this mind shift. As difficult problems were identified, the most dangerous or difficult ones resulted in a joint problem-solving session. This group usually consisted of the PCI operations manager and two or more of the ATC managers. The problem, conditions affecting the problem, possible solutions, and timelines were discussed. If the situation arose whereby the remote engineer was able to implement the solution (offered by the team or developed individually) rapidly, the team was allowed to hit the 'easy button' (available at a well-known office supply chain in the United States). The shift toward a teamwork-based problem-solving orientation was consistently reinforced and the change in cultural viewpoint from the 'as God wills it' fatalism is one that is consistently remembered inside the core team.

Counterproductive Government Procedures

An issue making commercial competition more complex involved US government methods of making contracts. Government Wide Acquisitions Contracts (GWACs) are an established way of procuring goods and services by the US government. However, GWACs limit competition to only those companies who competed for and won the GWAC, even to the exclusion of the in-country/incumbent provider. For example, PCI and ATC watched numerous satellite telecommunications projects disappear from visibility, even those for which both companies were providing services, and even though service continuation was required. Some of these projects were definitely within the scope of the 'Iraq First' program but simply vanished. It was not until a couple of years later that PCI found that projects in Iraq were bundled together and competed inside GWACs.

A good example of the bundled project is the Defense Information Systems Agency (DISA) Satellite Telecommunications Services–Global (DSTS-G) contract. This contract took over a number of small satellite telecommunications projects in Iraq that ultimately disappeared from visibility and were won by large companies such as DRS, ARTEL, and Arrowhead (DSTS-G primes). It was not until late 2008 that PCI gained enough visibility across these three 'primes' that its Iraqi partner could get any notice. Even then, some projects were unilaterally screened from bidding. From the outside, this contracting path appeared be used solely for the benefit of the contracting officer by reducing his workload and shifting to large-scale GWACs that had greater capacity to manage the procurement. This was an understandable course of action given the criticism laid on overworked and undersupervised contracting officers in Iraq. However, it was counterproductive to the intent of the Iraqi First concept. This particular issue remains a problem as this chapter is being written in spring 2009.

Iraq Government Inability to Spend

Competing for GOI IT projects as a team remains an ongoing effort. Numerous obstacles still remain that prevent successfully doing business with the GOI. First is funding. There are several GAO and Special Inspector General for Iraqi Reconstruction (SIGR) reports on the inability of the GOI to spend their annual budget (Bowen, 2007). This inability to spend money was attributable to many issues, among those being the high turnover in ministerial leaders and managers. PCI and ATC had firsthand experience with the turbulence in the Ministry of Communications (MoC) in 2006. Despite having known satellite telecommunication requirements and a number of qualified vendor teams that could meet the requirements, MoC managers changed so frequently that no progress could be made to refine projects and commit the money. In one case, the PCI–ATC team was told that over $50 million remained unobligated each year from Japanese communications grants because the money could not be linked to refined projects. This is not to say that no progress was ever made in this ministry. Several large-scale cellular contracts were executed in 2007–08. These were probably the most pressing communications issues facing the ministry. Yet numerous other smaller projects remained moribund for lack of funding and leadership.

Corruption

Iraq has been cited as one of the most corrupt countries in the world (Iraq, 2008). Early on, the joint commitment between Sahib and the PCI CEO was to not get involved in corrupt deals. This understanding arose from two different perspectives. First, PCI corporate management felt it was important to maintain a high moral standard in the mentor relationship. Second, Sahib's insight was that all GOI officials eventually would be under scrutiny, if they were not already, and any business dealings tainted with the appearance or even suggestion of corruption would be subject to revocation.

7   ENTREPRENEURSHIP AND TECHNOPOLY IN IRAQ

Survey of Conditions and Resources

As part of the combined business development activities among the IC^2 Institute, PCI, and ATC, a focused set of opportunities was developed. Among these was the opportunity to support USAID in its deployment of the Iraqi Community Action Program (CAP), Phase III. Briefly, USAID was looking for entities that could assist local communities in setting up organizations that would assist municipal governments in project funding, prioritization, and implementation. Phase III in Iraq meant wider utilization of local governance principles and techniques across more provinces and towns. In partnership with the IC² Institute, PCI, and ATC prepared for the proposal by conducting provincial site surveys throughout Iraq.

First, based upon publications gained from the USAID (and translated into Arabic), ATC developed a checklist of survey information that could guide the teams. This was especially significant because it demonstrated that ATC could operate outside of the 'normal' IT environment its personnel had been trained for and extend its problem solving to a broader domain. The survey information requirements were wide-ranging:

- local security conditions;
- housing conditions;
- local acceptance of a US-funded governance program;
- status of schools (primary, secondary, and undergraduate);
- status of the local state-owned enterprises (SOEs: over 150 SOEs employed 500,000 Iraqis prior to the 2003 invasion);
- condition of IT infrastructure;
- initial ideas of infrastructure projects;
- access to resources (labor, raw materials, and so on); and
- local acceptance of a projected IC² telecommunications network designed to strengthen citizen confidence in transparent government.

Second, the ATC management team did some strategic condition setting. Before any survey team was dispatched, the President of ATC gained an appointment with the senior counselors of Grand Ayatollah Al-Sistani. Since the focused provinces for this project were south of Baghdad, ATC management reasoned that all political organizational efforts would need to be coordinated with the religious leaders affiliated with the Shia-predominant south. The ATC management team briefed the senior advisors on the USAID desired goals, the project's scope (provinces and allotted funds), and intent of empowering local people to interact with greater confidence and fidelity with their elected governmental officials. The coordination meeting was successful and the ATC management team gained the blessing of the Grand Ayatollah to proceed to gather information in the provinces and conduct further coordination with his council in the event of award. This was a very significant development and completely arrived at unbidden by the US partners.

The third and most important aspect of the site surveys was the 'human dimension'. The management team was able to contact and identify the informal influence brokers of each area and gain their confidence. The measure of confidence gained by ATC can be discerned by the large number of names, cell phone numbers, and pictures they were allowed to assemble of these people of influence.

Unfortunately, the survey information and the IC^2/PCI/ATC proposal effort did not result in an award. However, when placed in the framework of the CIM process, the survey information clearly (although somewhat surprisingly) indicated that significant changes had occurred in the southern areas of Iraq, specifically the southern city and province of Basra, to the degree that this region of Iraq appears to be ripe for technopoly development and entrepreneurship.

Basra: A Future Technopolis?

Basra is a city of over 1,000,000 people and one of the four largest cities in Iraq. It has the country's only seaport (a former SOE) and an airport. Basra is also within 130 kilometers of Kuwait City, itself an oasis of international business. The province is one of the major oil-producing areas of the country and shares part of its border with Iran and Kuwait. PCI–ATC had long done business in Basra and had a reputation for integrity, loyalty, and value in conducting IT projects in the area.

The survey results for this province and the area in and around Basra showed the following:

- The seaport open and functioning to a greater degree than the past (no small feat as some PCI–ATC projects had been delayed due to transmodal operations at the port in 2006–07).
- The iron and steel, paper, and petrochemical SOEs were now working, but not optimally.
- The University of Basra was open and functioning, and ATC had established contact with the leaders of the university.
- The major tribes comprise a functioning and effective local influence structure that is working with the Basra governorate, Shat Al-Arab, and Nahiya/Gada (district and sub-district).
- Few means of public communication, beyond cell phone, exist outside of the city center.
- The local populace and influential leaders were in favor of broader means of public communications and its application to local governance.
- The local populace assessed the Iraqi government (read Baghdad) as poor in following through in proposed infrastructure projects.
- Security conditions were assessed as good. Guards would be needed at any local office to guard property.

The missing resource/capability in the list above is a robust communication infrastructure, but supplying the additional and necessary communication capabilities is PCI–ATC's core competency.

In summary, the Basra site survey indicates that the local geography, its natural resource base, its proximity to a major international business hub, its functioning sea/air/ground lines of transportation, its functioning education system, its proven cadre of IT-trained engineers, the approval from champions of similar communication and technology projects, and an ever-growing international investment stream show this city as having the preconditions for a nascent technopolis.

8   CONCLUSION

The PCI–ATC case study serves as a model for how and why a CMI approach can be fruitful not only in building individual companies but also in building technopoleis worldwide. CIM theory is an effective method to obtain relevant information and understanding of the key drivers affecting a particular market. Working through the CIM process takes the information about the drivers and translates these into concrete knowledge about specific market problems and creative institutional opportunities to solve these problems. In addition, as the drivers are more clearly understood via the CIM process, the contextual issues surrounding them foster creative solutions grounded in the needs of both the market and the company. CIM goes beyond this, however, to focus on managerial strategies that are based on a relationship among its organizational structure, strategic planning process, culture and environment (including various motivations and incentives), and strategic alliances that allow a company to establish creative and innovative management focused on flexibility and adaptability to a changing and sometimes disruptive marketplace.

CIM can also yield key insights into the effectiveness of the strategies and tactics employed by an organization. CIM proved useful in explaining PCI–ATC successes as well as its shortcomings. The PCI–ATC case study reiterates the importance of aligning management decision making to market drivers and issues, and it underscores the importance of feedback loops to continually assess the effectiveness of these same management acts. Perhaps one of the greatest contributions of the CIM process as applied to this case study is in emphasizing the importance of communication and trust.

There is no doubt that the lessons from Iraq draw from the dynamic between capacity and capabilities. Technology capacity alone was not enough for PCI and ATC to create trusted and secure communications.

Successful communication (and entrepreneurship) required the capacity to mentor and nurture fledgling ventures, new institutional development, and the ability to grow the business capabilities and enlarge the body of shared knowledge. The relationship between these two companies demonstrates technology prowess not only physically connecting a communication network, but also connecting a social network of cooperation and mentorship essential for successful commercialization (or in Kozmetskian terms, 'true innovation'). The relationship between PCI and ATC in Iraq provides an embodiment of a relationship that can be thought of as the six Cs for successful entrepreneurship:

- capability;
- capacity;
- connections;
- communications;
- cooperation; and
- commercialization.

The six Cs represent the fact that once a solid path of trusted and secure technology connections is established, the focus can be placed on establishing the social and cultural connections. In essence, the technology can be relegated to the background as a given. The main focus is on building the foundation for the relationship of the six Cs – capability, capacity, connections, communication, cooperation, and finally, commercialization.

The interrelationship of the six Cs (Figure 4.3) represents a convergence of three significant areas: the importance of secure ubiquitous communication, the importance of trusted relationships, and the importance of mutual cultural respect. The combination of these elements creates an environment for successful commercialization and entrepreneurship as an outcome – the very embodiment of creative and innovative management.

As a tool, CIM offers a comprehensive approach to studying the impact of new technologies and provides an empirical approach to the study of organizational communication. Lessons from Iraq are not enough. Further research is necessary to test the hypothesis that application of the CIM theory in a prescriptive mode is useful (in contrast to the descriptive and analytical mode of this case study). The IC^2 Institute has had much experience in successfully applying Kozmetsky's concepts in global technopoleis. Our opinion is that this success can be enhanced by an even more rigorous focus on the power of CIM and especially the feedback loop. The capture of strategic and tactical knowledge at regular intervals allows for an even greater ability for a company to be flexible and adaptable and to

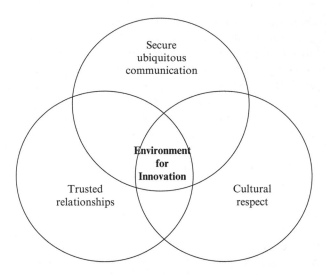

Figure 4.3   The interrelationship of the six Cs

successfully innovate in a rapidly changing world. We believe that CIM can be a proactive blueprint for global technopolis building.

REFERENCES

Bowen, Jr., S.W. (Special Inspector General for Iraqi Reconstruction) (2007), 'Can Iraq pay for its own reconstruction?', US House of Representatives Committee on Foreign Affairs Subcommittee on International Relations, Human Rights, and Oversight and the Subcommittee on the Middle East and South Asia, US House of Representatives, Washington, DC, March 27.

Carbonara, C.P. (1989), 'A historical perspective of management, technology and innovation in the American television industry', University of Texas at Austin, *Dissertation Abstract International*, **51** (2), 330, available at: http://proquest. umi.com.ezproxy.baylor.edu/pqdweb?did=746099751&Fmt=7&clientId=45950 &RQT=309&VName=PQD (accessed October 11, 2008).

Carbonara, C.P. (2008), *Creativity and Innovation: The Creative and Innovative Management Theory*, PowerPoint slides.

CPA Iraq – CPA Official Documents (n.d.), available at: http://www.cpa-iraq.org/ regulations/index.html (accessed January 15, 2009).

Furnai, M. (2006), Blue Ridge Networks™ and Proactive Communications Build Secure Communications Infrastructure for Iraqi Government, available at: http://www.blueridgenetworks.com/news/releases/2006/2006-06-13.php (accessed 6 January, 2009).

Iraq: World's Third Most Corrupt Country (2008), Alsumari News (Television broadcast), Iraq and Lebanon: Alsumari Iraq Satellite TV Network, November, 20.

Kozmetsky, G. (1985), *Transformational Management*, Cambridge, MA: Ballinger.
Kozmetsky, G. (1986), 'Frontiers of creative and innovative management: the development of a research agenda', in *Frontiers of Creative and Innovative Management*, Cambridge, MA: Ballinger, pp. xxxii–xxiv.
Kozmetsky, G. (1988), 'Why new directions for research in creative and innovate management?', in *New Directions in Creative and Innovative Management: Bridging Theory and Practice*, Cambridge, MA: Ballinger, pp. 15–30.
Kuhn, R. (1986), *Handbook for Creative and Innovative Management*, New York: McGraw-Hill.

5. The land of milk, honey and ideas: what makes Israel a hotbed for entrepreneurship and innovation?

Uzi De Haan and Boaz Golany

1 INTRODUCTION

A recent article in *The Economist* (2009) calls Israel, Singapore, and Denmark the 'lands of opportunity' and refers to them as role models to show how entrepreneurship can thrive and flourish in different cultures. The article lists some of the factors that helped make Israel a hotbed for innovation and entrepreneurship: the massive entrance of large multinational corporations (many of which are US based) that have established R&D centers in Israel; investments and actions taken by the Israeli government to educate scientists and engineers; the special role played by the universities in general and the Technion in particular; and the influx of many well-educated Jews who left the former USSR after the fall of the Berlin Wall. But the main reason for Israel's flourishing innovation and entrepreneurial activities in the eyes of *The Economist*'s editors is the fact that Israel is an embattled state located in the middle of a sea of Arab hostility. Hence, innovation is perhaps the only way for the state to compensate for its constant inferiority in population, land, and other natural resources (except the human resource).

Columnist Thomas Friedman addresses the same issue in a thought-provoking article (2008) entitled 'People vs. dinosaurs.' Friedman compares the differences among Israel, which has been investing in its people, and some of its neighbors (notably, Iran), which rely largely on oil made of fossil bones. Friedman poses the same question – what makes Israel so special – and provides answers that are rather similar to the ones listed in *The Economist*'s article mentioned earlier.

In this chapter we shall try to provide some details about the unusual climate of innovation and entrepreneurship that has become synonymous with the state of Israel as well as some insights into the driving forces behind this phenomenon. We start by providing a brief account of the major milestones in the odyssey of Israel from a poor, underdeveloped economy in 1948 to its current leading position as one of the world's centers of technological development. We then employ the models suggested by Audretsch (1995, 2005, 2006), Baum et al. (2001) and Trajtenberg (2006), and discuss the five main components of capital that fuel growth in modern economies (knowledge, financial, human, social, and entrepreneurship) in the context of the Israeli high-tech sector. Finally, we provide a summary with some concluding remarks.

2   A BRIEF HISTORY OF TECHNOLOGY DEVELOPMENT IN ISRAEL

At the end of its War of Independence in 1948, Israel was a poor country. Its economy was badly hurt by the war expenditures, the damage inflicted on its transportation infrastructure (roads, railways, bridges), the departure of the British engineers who operated many of the country's vital assets (oil refineries, sea and airports, and so on) and faced the huge challenge of absorbing millions of Jewish refugees fleeing Europe and the Arab states. At this defining moment of its history, David Ben-Gurion, the first prime minister, set the course for the country's future development by deciding to put science and technology at the top of his government priorities. Two of his decisions deserve special attention. Immediately after the war he ordered the newly formed army to establish a 'Science Command' that would be in charge of maintaining a technological edge in favor of Israel over its enemies. This science command later became an agency with the Israeli Department of Defense known as Rafael. This agency was converted into a government-owned corporation (Rafael – Advanced Defense Systems Ltd) in the early 2000s. Technological spillover from Rafael started to occur as early as the 1960s when the engineers and scientists who were trained in Rafael left the agency and established new businesses, mainly in the information and communications technology (ICT) sector and other defense areas. Some of the most successful Israeli firms operating in these areas today (for example, Elbit Systems) can be traced to this early spillover.

Another important decision made by Ben-Gurion in 1950 was to move the Technion-Israel Institute of Technology (Israel's oldest university, established in 1923) from its historic site in downtown Haifa to the outskirts of the city where it was given land and resources that enabled it to transform itself from an old-style technology school into a modern university modeled after the successful pattern of the Massachusetts Institute of Technology (MIT). In the decades that followed, the Technion has been the main source of well-educated engineers and scientists who played a major role in driving Israeli technological know-how and capabilities to its current leading position.

Not all of Ben-Gurion's initiatives aimed at promoting science and technology were successful. One of his failures was the attempt to convince Nobel Laureate Albert Einstein to move to Israel and become its second president (following President Haim Weitzman, himself a renowned chemist). But even this failure was important as it helped cement the concept that science and technology would become a core competency for the young nation.

During its first decades the Israeli economy grew rapidly through targeted, export-oriented sectors. Export orientation included agriculture, which benefited from applied agricultural research. A dominant element in developing the industrial sector was the defense need. A well-developed higher education system that had already been founded in the 1920s produced the skilled labor necessary for a local military industry. The French arms embargo imposed after the Six Day War in 1967 accelerated the development of the local defense industry because France had been Israel's major arms supplier. As a result, the nation's military industry grew into a technologically sophisticated industrial complex, involved largely in electronics, communication equipment, and aeronautics. Israel's defense expenditures grew as a percentage of GNP from 10.4 percent in 1966 to 25.2 percent in 1980. At its height, around 1984, the military industrial sector employed 65,000 individuals, including 25,000 scientists, engineers and technicians. Its output amounted to 50 percent of the electronics and aeronautics industry (Gradus et al., 1993). During the 1960s and beyond, the defense sector started spawning civilian high-technology companies like Elbit, Elscint and Scitex, supported by a strategic decision by the Israeli government to create a 'science-based' sector.

In 1969, the Office of the Chief Scientist (OCS) was established as part of the Ministry of Trade and Industry. The OCS's main objective was to provide grants to civilian research and development (R&D) projects with export potential. More programs were added later, and the OCS became a major source of funding for technology transfer from universities to industry aimed at rapid commercialization of new technologies that were developed in labs and at research institutes.

In the 1970s, the first (US-based) multinational companies established R&D and manufacturing facilities in Israel, attracted by the stable and relatively cheap top-quality scientific labor. The migration path of foreign direct investment (FDI) in Israel shows a different pattern from that in other regions, such as Ireland, Eastern Europe, and Asia. In those regions FDI is attracted by a combination of low-cost labor and local market potential. In time, with the development of a local supply base and engineering education, FDI migrates toward local development and in rare cases, local research. The industries in these regions developed through foreign investment, and ownership remained to a large degree with the foreign companies.

In Israel, the technology sector developed from indigenously initiated R&D operations for military and later civilian applications, and the resulting scientific-engineering labor base attracted FDI. Even as late as 1998, 82 percent of employment in the electronics sector in Ireland was in the hands of foreign-owned companies, compared to 25 percent in Israel. In the same year, there were only two multinational companies among the top 20 companies in the electronics sector in Israel (Roper and Frenkel, 2000). The period of rapid growth ended in 1985 as result of a worldwide downturn in the electronics market and severe cuts in the defense budget following a drop in defense spending as a portion of GNP from 21.1 percent in 1985 to 13.8 percent in 1990. At the same time, Israel gave in to American pressure and cancelled its ambitious Lavi project – a modern fighter aircraft that threatened to compete with the American F-16 fighter. As a result, the military industry laid off thousands of technically skilled workers. Simultaneously, the lack of capital influx hampered growth in the civilian sector. Moreover, despite abundant technological opportunities and support from the OCS, there was a shortage of technological entrepreneurship and of people willing to take risks (Breznitz, 2006).

The year 1991 marked the beginning of the rapid high-tech growth in Israel brought about by the concurrence and convergence of several factors. During the 1990s almost one million Jews from the former Soviet Union immigrated to Israel. Among them were many highly skilled engineers and scientists looking for employment. In 1991 the OCS created a network of technological incubators to offer employment possibilities to immigrants and to breed entrepreneurial skills and experience in a protected environment. In 1992, the government launched Yozma, a program designed to create a vibrant venture capital (VC) industry in Israel. The Yozma investment fund with $100 million in government money initiated and invested in VC funds, with the condition that any Yozma investment in a VC fund would be matched by at least one foreign and one local financial partner (ibid.). This program, initiated at the same time that entrepreneurship and venture capital began their rapid rise in the United States, proved to be a great success: Israel has become the most VC-intensive country in the world in terms of venture capital available per citizen. In 1993, the signing of the Oslo peace accords led to high expectations of a peaceful Middle East economy in which Israel could play a key role, similar to that of Singapore in Asia. The prevailing optimism in those

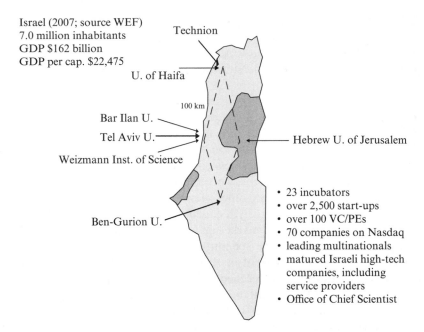

Israel (2007; source WEF)
7.0 million inhabitants
GDP $162 billion
GDP per cap. $22,475

Technion

U. of Haifa

100 km

Bar Ilan U.

Tel Aviv U.

Weizmann Inst. of Science

Hebrew U. of Jerusalem

Ben-Gurion U.

- 23 incubators
- over 2,500 start-ups
- over 100 VC/PEs
- 70 companies on Nasdaq
- leading multinationals
- matured Israeli high-tech companies, including service providers
- Office of Chief Scientist

Figure 5.1   The Israeli diamond

years brought in additional investments from multinational companies. The main components of the current Israeli entrepreneurial scene are depicted in Figure 5.1.

The convergence of all these factors produced a critical mass that propelled the high-tech sector onto a rapid-growth track, and it managed to cope well even with the dip that followed the burst of the internet bubble in 2001. The share of the high-tech in industry grew from 26 percent in 1994 to 34 percent in 2004. In 2005, FDI (mainly in high-tech) amounted to $4.5 billion, and 68 Israeli companies were traded at the NASDAQ, the second largest foreign presence after Canada (IEICI, 2005). It was estimated that 2,600 young technology companies currently provide employment to 120,000 people (Haour, 2005). Companies such as Amdocs, Comverse, Orbotech, and Checkpoint are world leaders in their industry. Microsoft, Oracle, SAP, Google, Cisco, Philips, Siemens, and Motorola, to name a few multinational companies, have R&D operations in Israel. Cisco has spent $1 billion to acquire nine Israeli companies ('The stars of David', 2006). On the World Economic Forum Global Competitiveness Index of 2008, Israel ranked 23 out of 134 countries, mainly thanks to its very high scores on technological readiness and innovation. The factors that led to the growth of the high-tech sector in Israel are depicted in Table 5.1.

Table 5.1   Converging factors acting as tipping points for high-tech growth

	New high-tech companies average per year	VC/PE raised in millions of dollars average per year
1969–1992	19	7
1993–2005	307	1,214

Source: Avnimelech and Teubal (2006).

3   KEY SUCCESS FACTORS

In this section we adopt the models developed by Audretsch (1995, 2005, 2006), Baum et al. (2001) and Trajtenberg (2006) to explain the growth of knowledge-based economies by focusing on five key components of capital (knowledge, financial, human, social, and entrepreneurship) at the firm and national levels in the Israeli context.

Knowledge Capital

Knowledge capital has been defined as consisting of R&D, innovation, and their spillovers. Israel spends nearly 5 percent of its GDP on civilian R&D, the highest relative national R&D expenditure in the world, compared to 2.6 percent in the United States and 2.4 percent in the European Union (OECD, 2005). There is a strong correlation between the number of patents published in the United States and national expenditure on R&D (per capita), supporting the approach that considers patent registration in the United States a good measure of the output of the innovation process. Given the high rates of obsolescence of knowledge capital in the high-tech sector, a steady stream of innovations (as represented by patents) is required to maintain current levels. In a comparative analysis using patent data from 1968 to 1997, Trajtenberg (2001a) has shown that Israel ranks very high in terms of the number of patents per capita. Only the United States and Japan score higher. Like most countries, Israel has four sources of knowledge creation and spillover: universities and other public research organizations (PROs), the defense establishment, multinational corporations, and start-up companies.

Universities and PROs
The Technion, a science and technology oriented research university, was established in 1923. It was followed in 1925 by the Hebrew University and in 1934 by the Weizmann Institute of Science. Israel now has seven

research universities and many more colleges. The Israeli government recognizes that the market (the private sector) cannot be fully counted on to invest in basic research where risks and potential spillovers (leaks) are very high and consequently, the level of ownership of research results is low. Therefore, the government uses grants and programs to support university research and pre-competitive research cooperation with industry. The Technion is an active member in the MAGNET program, consisting of government-sponsored research projects by industry and university consortia. The Technion is also active in the EU research programs and is second in number of grants in the FT7 program after Cambridge University. All Israeli research universities have technology transfer offices and are actively engaged in transferring research results to the private sector. Given the historical role of the Technion in the foundation of the Israeli industry, spin-offs have been the preferred option for research commercialization. The average annual number of Technion spin-offs is four versus three license agreements.

Given the characteristics of the life sciences and their commercialization, university research plays a major role in commercialization of life-sciences inventions. Fifty-one percent of all US VC-backed bio-pharma ventures are university spin-offs versus 10 percent for software ventures (Zhang, 2005). This is also the case in the Technion and is further enhanced by the Medical School at the Technion and the newly established Lokey Interdisciplinary Center for Life Sciences and Engineering involving 12 Technion faculties.

Through specific research grants, the Technion encourages applied research aimed at commercialization. The Technion Technology Transfer Office employs a proactive, hands-on approach through ongoing communication with researchers before invention disclosures, by business development assistance, and an entrepreneur-in-residence program through which experienced entrepreneurs work in tandem with Technion researchers to commercialize their inventions and in which ownership is shared between researcher, entrepreneur, and Technion (one-third each).

The Technion is well-aware that technology transfer through licensing and spin-offs represents only a fraction of knowledge transfer from universities, with the majority being transferred though its students and in the public domain. Hence the Technion encourages entrepreneurship among its students through a number of activities facilitated by the Bronica Entrepreneurship and Innovation Center and the Faculty of Industrial Engineering and Management. Some of these activities are:

● credited courses in entrepreneurship;
● an annual business plan competition;

- an innovation lab for undergraduate students;
- an entrepreneurship club; and
- the Technion-for-Life program aimed at budding alumni entrepreneurs.

Defense establishment

During the 1980s, 65 percent of total national R&D expenditure was estimated to be defense related (Peled, 2001). This percentage has been reduced drastically. Civilian R&D, consuming nearly 5 percent of GDP, is now the major R&D investor. Nevertheless, contribution by the defense industry remains significant as it spills over to the private sector in four ways. First, spillover takes place through the infusion into the private sector of about 1,000 highly trained engineers annually who finish their compulsory military service and enter the job market. High-potential high school students have the opportunity to study science and engineering before their military service with financial support from the army. After graduation, they serve for an extended period in the R&D and technology-intensive support units of the military. After completing their military service, they enter the private sector equipped with non-classified tacit know-how ready to be applied to business opportunities in the private sector. MAMRAM, the computer unit of the Israel Defense Forces (IDF), has been one of the main sources of software innovation diffusion to the private software sector (Breznitz, 2006). Many Israeli entrepreneurs in the ICT sector have served in the MAMRAM unit. Such spillovers were also reported in the biotechnology and healthcare industries (Becker, 2005). Drafting high-potential engineering graduates into the army not only resulted in knowledge spillovers but also increased human, social, and entrepreneurial capital. The young engineers gained specific high-tech experience and skills and became part of a tightly knit social network. This facilitated their entry into high-tech entrepreneurship and exposed them to teamwork, risks, and an ability to operate under conditions of uncertainty, all of which enhanced their entrepreneurial capital.

Second, defense research contracts to universities create defense-related spillovers. In the United States, approximately 70 percent of basic research funded by the Department of Defense is carried out by universities, accounting for about 40 percent of all R&D activities in engineering at US universities. Spillovers of this research created the internet and the Global Positioning System (ibid.). Although no similar data are available with regard to Israel, there are substantial spillovers, mostly indirect ones, through faculty and graduate students working on defense-contracted research and applying their know-how to civilian projects.

Third, defense-related spillovers are produced through the customer relations of the military with its suppliers leading to tightly knit networks (Vekstein, 1999). The Israeli defense industry is one of the world's top-five arms suppliers. The French weapons embargo of 1967, coupled with the British refusal to sell Chieftain tanks to Israel in the wake of the Six Day War, emphasized the need for an independent military industry. Companies like Rafael, Elbit, IAI, and El-Op specialize in complex electronic-based weapon systems. They are leaders in their fields because of their close cooperation with demanding customers such as the IDF. Spin-offs by the military industry are a fourth path for defense-related knowledge spillovers. A few of the many examples were Scitex (computerized print systems), Elscint (medical imaging), and Orbotech (a world leader in electric-optical inspection equipment). In sum, knowledge spillovers from defense-related research and industry have been and remain a major source of knowledge input to the civilian high-tech sector, as is the case in other countries with a large defense outlay.

Multinational corporations
Through FDI and joint ventures, multinational companies are major contributors to national innovation systems and reinforce other trends in the internationalization of science and technology. However, there are considerable differences in the impact of multinational companies on national innovation systems (Nelson, 1993). Unlike Japan and Korea, Israel has always been open to FDI. As early as the 1970s, Israel succeeded in attracting R&D and manufacturing investment from US-based companies such as Intel and Motorola. However, until the 1990s the influx of multinationals remained limited because of the political situation and because of the strong dominance of local (mostly defense-related) companies that generated a strong demand for scientific labor. Since the end of the 1990s, many multinational companies acquired Israeli start-ups as their local bridgehead. During 2000–09, 41 new ventures made an IPO, while 673 were acquired (IVC Research Center, 2010). Most of the acquisitions were by foreign firms. Companies like IBM, Microsoft, and Cisco made a double-digit number of start-up acquisitions. Acquisitions of high-tech companies have become the dominant mode of FDI in Israel.

Although the integration of these acquisitions by the acquiring multinational companies into their R&D function might have tended to lead to an outbound technology spillover rather than an inbound one, Israel's high tech has benefited greatly from the management know-how spillover from the multinational companies. Multinational companies trained the human capital necessary to complement the entrepreneurial capital in order to start and grow new companies.

National innovation systems need the exploration skills of both innovators and entrepreneurs and of start-up companies to create new business opportunities, and the skills of managers and incumbent companies to exploit and grow these opportunities.

Start-up companies
The turnover of scientists and engineers at start-up companies is one of the main mechanisms of knowledge spillover in clusters of knowledge-intensive industries.

A recent report made at Babson College (GEM, 2007) ranks Israel as 17th out of 53 countries in friendliness to start-ups. This is not a very high position but a careful reading of the report reveals observations such as 'of high income countries, the United States, Israel, Iceland, and Canada exhibit the highest adult population prevalence rates of high-expectation entrepreneurship' and 'in addition to Singapore, Israel stands out for its high relative prevalence of high expectation and high-growth entrepreneurs' indicating that the collective group and community culture in Israel makes company and team loyalty stronger than in other countries with strong high-tech industries. However, many founders and engineers leave their company after it exits and join another start-up. The preference to work in a small, entrepreneurial company, the technical challenge and high demand (and remuneration) make moving on to the next start-up after an exit a common phenomenon.

Financial Capital

After two decades of rapid growth, the Israeli economy reached an impasse in the early 1970s. The economy had outgrown the centralist mold that had worked well initially. Israel has few natural resources but plenty of highly skilled labor, as well as scientific capital. The question was how to mobilize these assets for economic growth. The Israeli government made a crucial decision to breed a science-based sector by providing broad financial support for commercial R&D and making up for market failures (Trajtenberg, 2006). Infant industries might need temporary protection and support because of the hazards of two types of market failure: (i) positive externalities, such as external economies of scale and knowledge spillovers, and (ii) inefficient markets in which young firms find it difficult to borrow against potential future earnings because of information asymmetries between inventors and external agents (Avnimelech and Teubal, 2006).

Although the OCS was established in 1969, it began its work in earnest in 1973 by launching a program to subsidize 50 percent of the costs of R&D projects aimed at exportable products. Successful projects were required to repay the grant by paying 3 percent royalties on annual sales.

In 1975, a bi-national industrial R&D foundation (BIRD) was established. The BIRD foundation funds projects for which the R&D is carried out in Israel and which target the US market (Breznitz, 2006). BIRD has been successful in helping Israeli companies enter the US market and attracting US multinationals to invest in Israel. In 1985, the Law for the Encouragement of Industrial R&D was passed by the Knesset; implementation was assigned to the OCS. The stated goals of this legislation were to develop science-based, export-oriented industries. Between 1969 and 1987 industrial R&D expenditures grew by 14 percent per year, and high-tech exports grew from $422 million in 1969 (in 1987 dollars) to $3,316 million in 1987 (Trajtenberg, 2001b). This was a reconstruction period of the institutional base of Israel's political economy. The old centralized socialist economy, with state- and union-owned industries and an ideology of full employment had lost ground.

With the decline of the defense industry and the influx of a large wave of well-educated immigrants, new initiatives were needed. In the early 1990s, new programs were introduced by the OCS, the most important of which were MAGNET, the incubators, and Yozma. MAGNET, which was founded in 1993, supports the formation of consortia consisting of industrial firms and research universities in order to develop generic, pre-competitive technologies. Grants constitute up to two-thirds of the approved R&D budget, with no repayment requirement.

Incubators are designed to supply the basic needs of fledgling new ventures to help them develop their innovative ideas and set up new businesses. Incubators provide financial support, plug-and-play facilities, and advisory services. The main difference among Israeli incubator programs and those in the United States and the European Union is the high level of up-front grant support that Israeli incubators receive (two-thirds of the budget, with a maximum of $500,000 for the two-year incubator period to be paid back through royalties on actual sales). Twenty-eight incubators were established in Israel during 1990–93. Twenty-three are still operating. In recent years most incubators have been privatized, with VCs acquiring shares in the incubators and using them as a vehicle for subsidized, high-risk, very early-stage investment. To date, approximately 1,000 Israeli companies have started in an incubator and 45 percent have managed to raise follow-up financing. According to the OCS, of the 369 incubator projects that completed their two-year incubator stay between 2001 and 2005, 65 percent are still operating. Questions have been raised about the impact of the incubator program on the employment of scientists, in particular immigrants, and about its cost-effectiveness (Roper, 1999). However, the effect of the well-funded and well-designed incubator program has not only been economic. The program has also served to

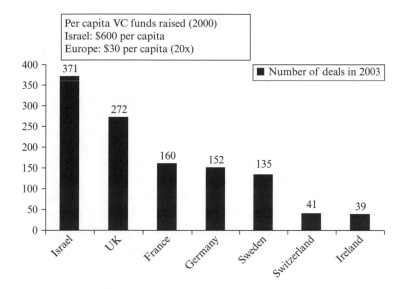

Source: IVC(2005).

Figure 5.2 Israel is the most active VC fund-raising country

legitimate early-stage technology entrepreneurship, and it has lowered the psychological entry barrier for fledgling entrepreneurs by providing the funds and expert managerial support needed to overcome market failures.

Yozma jump-started the venture capital sector in the early 1990s. Because of its great success, Yozma has led to path-dependence in the financial-capital component of the high-tech growth model in Israel, which has since been dominated by the VC investment model. With a government investment fund of $100 million, Yozma established 10 VC funds and raised $200 million by attracting foreign and local investors and offering them options to buy out government shares five years later at a predetermined price. Because of its success, the investment portfolio was privatized in 1997 and Yozma's mission came to an end. In the course of its operation Yozma brought in not only financial resources of VC funds, but also the management expertise of experienced VC managers who served as board members in start-ups. This program seems to have triggered the take-off of the high-tech sector. Between 1993 and 2000 close to $10 billion was raised by about 80 VCs, and between 2001 and 2005 another $3.2 billion (see Figure 5.2). A consolidation is currently under way in the VC market, with 23 VCs managing about 94 percent of the total capital raised (IVA, 2006). In absolute terms, high-tech VC investments in Israel are higher than in any EU country. Israel has the highest VC capital investment as a percentage of GDP in the world (IVA, 2002). Ernst & Young recently reported that in 2006, VC investments were highest in California ($12.4 billion), Massachusetts ($2.8 billion), and Israel in third place ($1.4 billion) (Ha'aretz, 2007).

The success of VCs in Israel has led to path-dependence and lock-in in the financing of the high-tech growth. As a result, other financial capital sources, such as business angels and private investors, are not well represented. The success of VC-backed funding made it possible for the government to confine itself to bridging the gap between social and private rates of return covering for market failures in the very early stage of new ventures. The defining character of government policy has been its neutrality (refraining from picking winners) and its dynamism in creating new and varied programs responsive to the needs of the 'market' (Trajtenberg, 2006).

Human Capital

The abundance of scientists and engineers in Israel prompted the government's decision to create a science-based sector. Led mostly by defense-related high-tech industries, the number of scientists and engineers in the industry grew by 460 percent between 1968 and 1984. At the same time, the overall number of employees in the industry grew by only 50 percent (Gradus et al., 1993). The experience part of human capital is self-reinforcing through the growth and failure of new ventures and the re-entry of entrepreneurs and engineers into the system. However, the formal education part of human capital with respect to science and engineering education is not self-generated by the system, but must be provided at the national policy level. To keep up with demands from the high-tech sector, new colleges were established and existing engineering and science faculties expanded. The number of science and engineering graduates from universities grew from 3,963 in 1994 to 9,458 in 2004, accounting for 26 percent of all university graduates. A technically educated human-resource base remains the main competitive advantage needed to create a high-tech sector (see Figure 5.3). Israel employs 1.68 percent of all employees in the business sector in R&D functions, compared to 0.89 percent in Japan and 0.59 percent in the European Union (Trajtenberg, 2006).

Social Capital

The Israeli culture facilitates building social capital and consequently networking. In Hofstede's study (1984) on national cultures, in which he measured cultures on five factors, he found that Israel scored 54 on

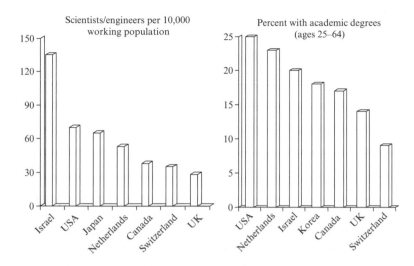

Source: Ministry of Finance.

Figure 5.3   Human capital: Israel's biggest asset

the scale of individualism versus collectivism, whereas the United States scored 91, and France scored 71. Moreover, the Israeli culture is informal and non-hierarchical, which makes personal access easy. During the three-year military service extensive networking evolves that carries over into professional careers. Honig et al. (2006) have shown that social capital accrued in the military leads to greater investment and better performance of new ventures. There is relatively easy and institutionalized availability of expertise and access to advisory boards in incubators. The same is true for events organized by the Israeli Venture Association and by professional service providers to the high-tech sector.

VC investment in companies and board membership by VCs provides companies with access to extensive VC networks, locally and abroad. VC investment in the social capital of a firm is as important as the financial capital, which is what differentiates VCs from one another when firms select them. The phenomenon of repeat entrepreneurs and engineers who remain in the start-up sector also leads to an increase in social capital. A common way of recruiting in Israel is by encouraging employees to bring in their friends.

Entrepreneurship Capital

Entrepreneurial capital at the individual level is the endowment with entrepreneurial traits such as a need for achievement, risk-taking, overconfidence, self-efficacy, and personal initiative. We are not aware of research data on individual entrepreneurial capital in Israel or of comparisons with other countries. Anecdotal evidence describes typical Israelis as improvisers, self-confident, assertive, and energetic, which implies the presence of a positive stock of entrepreneurial capital. At the organizational or regional level entrepreneurial capital is the accumulation of individual capital and the legitimacy and social desirability of entrepreneurship. Aldrich and Fiol (1994) have argued that from an institutional perspective founders of high-risk new ventures appear to be fools, unless entrepreneurship acquires cognitive and socio-political legitimacy and becomes part of the accepted norms and even of the culture.

The legitimacy of entrepreneurship and personal wealth creation took longer to develop in Israel than in many Western countries. The Israeli political–economic system was not receptive to entrepreneurs due to a historical labor–socialist tradition that was deeply antagonistic with regard to the self-employed sector, making Israel one of the few non-Communist countries where Jews did not gravitate to small businesses (Gradus et al., 1993). There was a long incubation period from the establishment of the OCS in the late 1960s to the take-off of the high-tech sector in the 1990s. Establishing the legitimacy of free capitalism and entrepreneurship took time. However, the presence of individual entrepreneurial traits among the population caused a rapid shift after the legitimacy was accepted and entrepreneurs became role models. Zilber (2006) conducted a longitudinal analysis of newspaper articles and want-ads for high-tech personnel and showed the development of collective meanings and myths that institutionalized the acceptance of social practices in the high-tech sector.

4   GOAL-SETTING AND PERFORMANCE FEEDBACK

The five multilevel capital components described above, and their interactions, comprise a static model that explains the origin and sources for entrepreneurship in Israel. Adding a feedback loop of goal-setting and performance transforms it into a dynamic model. High performance at the firm level increases the accumulated capital factors at the regional/national level, which then makes it possible to start and grow additional firms and thereby create a sustainable high-tech ecosystem. Applying the goal-setting theory by Locke and Latham (2002) on the firm level, one could argue that entrepreneurial firms outperform incumbent ones because of the focused, ambitious, and risk-taking way they set their goals. The specific character of the Israeli high-tech sector, with its limited domestic market, makes this point even more salient. In general, the reasons for specific and high goal-setting in entrepreneurial firms are:

- self-efficacy and overconfidence on the part of the entrepreneurs;
- low initial complexity and clear business vision of the new venture;
- initial performance below strategic reference points (which increases high-risk choices); and
- specific goals for results and timing set by investors.

Consequently, *ceteris paribus*, economic systems with high entrepreneurial capital will show superior performance. Although anecdotal evidence appears to confirm this proposition, systematic research is needed. In addition to the four factors leading to specific and difficult goal-setting by new ventures in general, in the Israeli case an additional factor in high goal-setting was the internationalization of new ventures, which was a strategic goal from their inception. The success of the Israeli high-tech sector challenges traditional theories of international competition. Porter (1990) has claimed that firms and countries need large local markets in order to grow and compete in international ones. Israel does not have significant domestic markets for the advanced products it develops, and therefore new ventures must begin internationalization from the outset.

Sapienza et al. (2006) have argued that an early internationalization of new firms, although risky, increases their probability for growth. The earlier a firm internationalizes, the more deeply its dynamic capabilities will be imprinted for exploiting foreign markets. By exposing firms to multiple and diverse requirements, early internationalization builds capabilities and processes in organizations oriented toward continual change. Choosing an incremental path from domestic to international markets poses a lower risk and increases the chances of survival, but it also lowers the chances of growth because it allows inertia to develop, making it more difficult to refigure capabilities. Internationalization from inception of new ventures lowers the probability of their survival but increases the probability of their growth. Israeli companies must decide whether or not to internationalize at the outset, and they must attract sufficient and appropriate human and social capital to accomplish their goals in this respect. About 50 percent of Israel high-tech firms have offices abroad (Khavul, 2001). It is mostly the marketing function that is established in their main market from a very early stage. A multilingual society, extensive overseas networks, and increasingly international repeat entrepreneurs give Israeli high tech an edge in early internationalization and affect the growth of young technology firms.

5   CONCLUDING REMARKS

In this chapter we have drawn on theories and research in economics, strategic management, organizational behavior, and entrepreneurship to propose a model of economic growth through innovation and entrepreneurship. We highlighted the five capital factors that drive economic growth in Israel: knowledge capital, financial capital, human capital, social capital, and entrepreneurship capital. These factors are crucially important both at the firm level and at the regional, national, and industry levels.

A goal-setting performance feedback loop makes the model dynamic and sustainable. The model was illustrated using the example of the Israeli high-tech sector. In its current form, this is an explorative framework; much research remains to be done to turn it into a predictive model. Although most of the variables have been described in different research areas, and some of the relationships we have hypothesized have been confirmed by research, the multivariable and multilevel characteristic of the model creates multiple indirect relations and embeddings.

Literature on high-tech growth areas, such as Silicon Valley, Route 128 in the Boston area, and Israel, has been descriptive in nature and is based on historical and anecdotal evidence. The framework we use here might contribute to the research literature by providing a better understanding of the underlying factors that explain the entrepreneurship phenomenon in Israel and its impact on the nation's economic growth. The chapter also provides policy makers with an integrative and eclectic framework for the changes required to support economic growth. Finally, the chapter provides a bridge to academic research in other disciplines, as it reflects and incorporates research constructs and findings on economic growth and entrepreneurship from different fields of research.

REFERENCES

Aldrich, H.E. and C.M. Fiol (1994), 'Fools rush in? The institutional context of industry creation', *Academy of Management Review*, **19** (4): 645–70.

Audretsch, D.B. (1995), *Innovation and Industry Evolution*, Cambridge, MA: MIT Press.

Audretsch, D.B. (2005), 'The knowledge spillover theory of entrepreneurship and economic growth', in G.T. Vinig and R.C.W. Van der Voort (eds), *The Emergence of Entrepreneurial Economics*, Research on Technological Innovation, Management and Policy, vol. 9, Amsterdam: Elsevier, pp. 37–54.

Audretsch, D.B. (2006), *Entrepreneurship, Innovation and Economic Growth*, Cheltenham, UK and Northampton, MA, USA: Edward Elgar.

Avnimelech, G. and M. Teubal (2006), 'Creating venture capital industries that co-evolve with high tech: insights from an extended industry life cycle perspective of the Israeli experience', *Research Policy*, **35** (10): 1477–98.

Baum, J.R., E.A. Locke and K.G. Smith (2001), 'A multidimensional model of venture growth', *Academy of Management Journal*, **44** (2): 292–303.

Becker, C. (2005), 'Armed with innovation. Israel has become a prolific developer of new medical technologies and the nation's dominant defense industry is often the incubator', *Modern Healthcare*, **35** (14): 26–9.

Breznitz, D. (2006), 'Innovation and the state–development strategies for high technology industries in a world of fragmented production: Israel, Ireland, and Taiwan', *Enterprise & Society*, **7** (4): 675–85.

Economist, The (2009). 'Land of opportunity: Israel, Denmark and Singapore show how entrepreneurialism can thrive in different climates', March 12.

Friedman, T. (2008), 'People vs. dinosaurs', *New York Times*, June 8.

GEM, (2007) 'High-growth entrepreneurship report', Babson College, Wellesley, MA.

Gradus, Y., E. Razin and S. Krakover (1993), *The Industrial Geography of Israel*, London: Routledge.

Ha'aretz newspaper (2007), English edition, 23 January.

Haour, G. (2005), 'Israel, a powerhouse for networked entrepreneurship', *International Journal of Entrepreneurship and Innovation Management*, **5** (1/2): 39–48.

Hofstede, G. (1984), *Culture's Consequences: International Differences in Work-related Values*, Beverly Hills, CA: Sage.

Honig, B., M. Lerner and Y. Raban, (2006), 'Social capital and the linkages of high-tech companies to the military defense system: is there a signaling mechanism?', *Small Business Economics*, **27** (4): 419–37.

Israel Export and International Cooperation Institute (IEICI) (2005), 'Your gateway to business in Israel', Israel Export and International Cooperation Institute, available at http://www.export.gov.il (accessed February 2005).

Israel Venture Association (IVA) (2002), OECD Venture capital Database.

Israel Venture Association (IVA) (2006), *IVA Yearbook* 2006.

Israeli Venture Capital (IVC) Research Center (2005), 'IVC High-Tech Survey Q3 2005'.

Israeli Venture Captial (IVC) Research Center (2010), *Israel High-tech and Venture Capital Directory*.

Khavul, S. (2001), 'Money and knowledge: sources of such capital and the performance of high-technology start-ups' PhD diss., Boston University.

Locke, E.A. and G.P. Latham (2002), 'Building a practically useful theory of goal setting and task motivation', *American Psychologist*, **57** (4): 705–17.

Nelson, R.R. (1993), *National Innovation Systems: A Comparative Analysis*, New York: Oxford University Press.

Organisation for Economic Co-operation and Development (OECD) (2005), *Science, Technology and Industry Scoreboard 2005: Towards a Knowledge-based Economy*, Paris: OECD, available at: http://caliban.sourceoecd.org/vl=3788419/cl=27/nw=1/rpsv/scoreboard/.

Peled, D. (2001), 'Defense R&D and economic growth in Israel: a research agenda', Working Paper Series no. STP-4, The Samuel Neaman Institute, Technion City, available at: http://econ.haifa.ac.il/~dpeled/papers/ste-wp4.pdf.

Porter, M.E. (1990), *The Competitive Advantage of Nations*, New York: Free Press.

Roper, S. (1999), 'Israel's technology incubators: repeatable success or costly failure', *Regional Studies*, **33** (2): 175–84.

Roper, S. and A. Frenkel (2000), 'Different paths to success: the growth of the electronics sector in Ireland and Israel', *Environment and Planning C: Government and Policy*, **18** (6): 651–65.

Sapienza, H.J., E. Autio, G. George and S.A. Zahra (2006), 'A capabilities perspective on the effects of early internationalization on firm survival and growth', *Academy of Management Review*, **31** (4): 914–33.

'The stars of David' (2006), *Red Herring*, **3** (23): 34–43.

Trajtenberg, M. (2001a), 'Innovation in Israel 1968–1997: a comparative analysis using patent data', *Research Policy*, **30**: 363–89.

Trajtenberg, M. (2001b), 'R&D policy in Israel: an overview and re-assessment', Working Paper Series no. STE-WP-2, Samuel Neaman Institute, Technion City.

Trajtenberg, M. (2006), 'Innovation policy for development: an overview', Working Paper Series no. STE-WP-34, Samuel Neaman Institute, Technion City.

Vekstein, D. (1999), 'Defense conversion, technology policy and R&D networks in the innovation system of Israel', *Technovation*, **19** (10): 615–29.

Zhang, J. (2005), 'The performance of university spin-offs. Evidence from venture capital data', paper presented at Technology Transfer Conference, Kansas City, September.

Zilber, T.B. (2006), 'The work of the symbolic in institutional processes: translations of rational myths in Israeli high tech', *Academy of Management Journal*, **49** (2): 281–303.

6. Disclosing activities by inventors and technology commercialization: a case study of a Japanese company

Michi Fukushima*

1 INTRODUCTION

Research and development (R&D) activities are not necessarily started with a clear idea of what products the technology can produce or develop. When companies implement a technology-push strategy, newly created technologies occasionally have difficulty finding appropriate applications due to their newness. As a result, some technologies cannot survive. This is especially true when the projects begin with inventors' initiatives, as many companies do not carry out a formal decision-making process to find the applications that are critical to a technology-push strategy. Therefore, the inventors have to discover the applications themselves. In order to locate appropriate applications and successfully commercialize technologies, the inventors are assumed to play an important role (Murray, 2004; Agrawal, 2006) as they are most familiar with, and tend to have an attachment to, the technology they created. In this chapter, we focus on the inventors' activities of disclosing technologies and highlight the disclosing activities that are effective in winning approval.

2 REVIEWS

Finding Application Fields in Commercialization and Disclosure Activities

Many technologies lie unused in company laboratories although the companies have allocated a considerable budget for their development. The main reason for this is the inability to find appropriate applications for the new technologies. Newly developed technologies do not always have built-in applications. Even researchers are sometimes unaware of the kind of field in which the technology that they developed can be applied. For the successful commercialization of these technologies, their appropriate fields of application need to be clearly defined.

Historically, there are a number of examples of a failure to define appropriate applications for new technologies. For example, Xerox has a famous research institute, Palo Alto Research Center (PARC), in California. PARC gave birth to epoch-making technologies. However, researchers failed to recognize the potential of the technologies and find applications for them. Instead, rival companies or newly created enterprises, such as Sun Microsystems and Apple Computer, recognized the potential of the technologies and succeeded in commercializing them (Smith and Alexander, 1999). On the other hand, nylon, invented by Wallace Carothers, a researcher from DuPont, was successfully commercialized and brought in huge profits because Carothers and his colleagues could find appropriate fields of application for nylon, such as 'stockings' or 'hose'.

In order to find appropriate applications, some researchers insist that it is helpful to disclose the technologies to others who have nothing to do with the development process in order to obtain feedback (Lichtenthaler and Ernst, 2007). Insisting on the importance of 'open innovation', Chesbrough (2003) and Lichtenthaler and Ernst (2007) claim that if firms do not apply their technology internally, they have to exploit it externally to avoid a loss of value. It is true that disclosing technology to outsiders could be a key to finding fields of application and establishing the technology's value.

Disclosing Behaviors as Politics

Disclosing activities also contribute to getting approval of the projects within the organization. When new technologies do not have clear applications, it is often difficult for the researchers to get support for that technology in the organization. However, if champions of the technologies negotiate with and convince others that these technologies have significant promise, the survival potential of technologies would be increased (see Figure 6.1). For technologies with uncertain application, in order to get approval from others, some political negotiation is needed. However, the existing research has not examined these dynamics thoroughly and there are no concrete suggestions about how and to whom the inventors should disclose their technologies.

The Role of Inventors and Their Disclosing Behaviors

Inventors can play an important role in the process of new technology development by initiating the process of finding fields of application and securing approval. Research indicates the importance of inventors in the

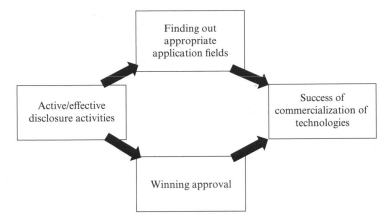

Figure 6.1   Disclosing activities and their effects

process of technology commercialization. For example, Agrawal (2006) states that only inventors have the 'latent knowledge' of technology in the development of newly created technologies on campus. Also, as inventors tend to be familiar with the technology, they are indispensable in the process of its development. Murray (2004) focuses on different aspects and insists on the contribution of inventors as not only 'human capital' but also 'social capital'. He states that the networks that inventors have are very useful when finding new application fields throughout all the stages of commercialization. Indeed, the larger the inventors' networks are, the more opportunities they have to gather information about potential applications for the new technology if they are willing to disclose information about the technology. As a result, the possibility of commercialization would increase. Takeda and Senoo (2007) shed light on inventors' disclosing activities to find applications. They conducted a survey with 314 randomly chosen researchers. Based on the survey results, they found that 94 percent of the respondents considered their communication with external/unknown people to be most important when they tried to find fields of application for their new technologies. We shall develop their line of research further by conducting surveys with more specific subjects.

The Projects and Research Questions

Although our research is along the same lines as Takeda and Senoo's, we sought some enhancement as they did not consider the nature of the projects with which the respondents engaged. Sometimes the nature of the project has strong effects on researchers' disclosing activities.

Generally speaking, projects are started on the basis of the following two research types: contract or spontaneous research. Contract research starts with client requests. In most cases, such requests are clear, and the projects are approved by upper-level employees of the companies and are formalized at the first stage. Hence, researchers do not have to explore the fields of application of their technologies themselves. On the other hand, due to the nature of their creation, spontaneous research projects are usually not approved during the first stage. Therefore, inventors not only have to invent technologies but also identify their fields of application, explain their technologies, and convince others in the company to support them. Without such efforts by inventors, it is difficult for spontaneous research projects to survive.

Disclosure activities are affected by the purpose of the projects. If projects are started on the basis of requests from other companies, inventors have to report the progress to their clients on a regular basis. However, in spontaneous research, we can observe inventors' activities as they pursue their research without any interference. Hence, we focus on the spontaneous projects.

Research that is started on the basis of researchers' initiatives is called 'skunk works' or 'underground research' (Abetti, 2004). These research activities can be observed in the stories of successful innovations in big companies, such as HP, 3M, and Toshiba (Kanter et al., 1997). These inventions are conducted 'under the table', hidden from the bosses, and not legitimized in the companies. In this kind of project, inventors must themselves find appropriate applications for their technology, gather resources, and convince others to commercialize them. Although there is some research on 'skunk works' available in the field of management, most are case studies or remain anecdotal.

In this chapter, our research questions are as follows:

- What are the success factors for the inventors to find application fields for spontaneous research projects?
- To whom and how should the inventors disclose their technology in order to win approval for spontaneous research projects?

3   RESEARCH METHODS

Data and Sample

We conducted a questionnaire survey from December 2007 to February 2008. Our research was carried out with the help of the research institute of company A. Company A is an electronics manufacturer and has a research institute as its group company. The institute employs about 1,450 researchers.

As the first step, we sent questionnaires to the senior researchers who had been working for the research institute for an average of 19.5 years. Their specialties are various and the distribution is almost equal. We asked them to recall two projects in which they had been involved, including one where they succeeded in the commercialization of their research result. Then we asked them the nature of the projects, what happened in the development process, and if and how they disclosed the projects to others. For example, whether they actively disclosed their technologies to others and how, and to whom did they disclose them. We used a 5-point Likert scale in the questionnaire. Dummy variables (1–0 data) are used for the question regarding the parties that the inventors contact. Some questions asked for actual numbers. In all, we were able to obtain responses from 106 researchers working on 181 projects.

During the next step, we divided all these projects into 'contract research' (142 cases) and 'spontaneous research' (39 cases). The results of the spontaneous research projects revealed that 21 projects succeeded in the commercialization process and implementation of the technology, while 18 spontaneous research projects failed at some point during the commercialization process.

Using these data, we compared the averages of the two types of project and tested them with the Mann–Whitney U test and Student's *t*-test. Moreover, we investigated the factors that distinguished them. On the basis of these tests, we conducted a multi-regression analysis and specified which factors have an influence on the 'approval of projects'. The model in our research is represented in Figure 6.2.

Independent Variables

In this chapter, 'researchers' disclosing activities' and 'departments to which inventors disclose their technologies' are independent variables. The indicators of these activities are as follows: (i) the number of people who engaged in seeking application fields; (ii) the timing of disclosure to inside/outside organizations; and (iii) the variety of people to whom inventors disclose their technologies. With regard to the departments, we chose seven functional departments of inside/outside companies: (i) R&D; (ii) R&D of business unit; (iii) new product development and marketing; (iv) sales; (v) production; (vi) intellectual property; and (vii) upper level of business unit. Dummy variables were used to analyze them.

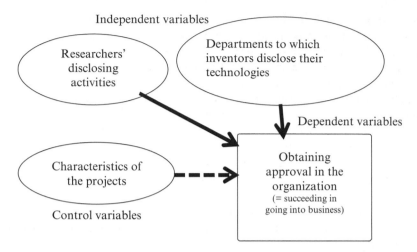

Figure 6.2   Research model

Control Variables

We considered the following as control variables: (i) the number of members who worked on the projects; (ii) the inventors' successful experiences; (iii) the variety of members' backgrounds; (iv) the degree of uncertainty on application fields of the technology; (v) the attractiveness of technology from the standpoint of rival companies; and (vi) the satisfaction with the budgets that they receive, both formally and informally. The first control variable is an actual number, while the rest are given on a 5-point Likert scale.

Dependent Variable

The dependent variable was the degree of approval of the project, which was tested on a 5-point Likert scale. Obtaining approval from the people inside the companies is an indispensable condition for the development and commercialization of technologies. Based on their judgment of the amount of approval they received, the subjects selected a number on a 5-point Likert scale.

4   RESULTS

Our survey results (see Tables 6.1 and 6.2) reveal the following points:

1. Projects that have a larger number of members tend to succeed in getting approval. However, in terms of the number of people who engage in exploring fields of application and disclose their technologies, it is preferable to have fewer people working on the project.
2. Inventors should disclose their technologies to a variety of people within their company. However, the departments to which they make their disclosure should be limited to a few, such as the R&D department, new product development and marketing department, production, and upper level of business unit.
3. Inventors should not disclose their new technologies to the upper-level employees of their companies' R&D departments.
4. Disclosing technologies to outside organizations could sometimes be effective in acquiring approval within the company. When the inventors disclosed their technologies to 'departments of new product development and marketing of outside companies', the success rate increased.

5 DISCUSSION

Inventors working on spontaneous research projects should consider the parties to whom they disclose their technologies in order to gain approval in the organization. One disclosure strategy to be found in the survey data is called a 'detour strategy'. This strategy should be adopted by a small number of people in that they should disclose their technologies to various people inside the organization from the early stage. However, they should not disclose technologies to upper-level employees of their organization's R&D department because such employees might destroy their projects. Instead, the inventors could show their technologies to the department of new products and the marketing divisions of other companies, but not to the sales department of outside companies. This could help reveal their potential and armed with the new interpretation of their technologies, the inventors can take the technologies back to the organization and seek approval to take the projects forward.

6 CONCLUSION AND FUTURE ISSUES

According to the survey, it is evident that disclosing activities by inventors are important when they are looking for application fields for their technologies and attempting to commercialize them. The survey research reveals that inventors have to choose carefully the parties to whom they disclose their technologies; moreover, they must pay attention to the timing

Table 6.2 Multiple regression analysis

	Variable	Model 1 (n = 39)	Model 2 (n = 39)	Model 3 (n = 39)
Characteristics of projects	No. of project members[#]	0.545**	0.612*	0.618**
	Successful experiences of the inventors	0.003	0.070	0.038
	Various members who engaged in the project	0.068	0.041	-0.073
	Certainty of application field of technology	-0.126	-0.065	0.169
	Attractiveness of the technology from the standpoint of other companies	0.221	0.086	0.102
	Satisfaction with budgets	-0.176	-0.115	-0.050
Characteristics of the activities for seeking application fields	No. of persons who engage in seeking application fields[#]		-0.417**	-0.379**
	Timing of disclosure, inside		-0.116	-0.252
	Timing of disclosure, outside		-0.155	-0.195
	Various members to whom it is disclosed, inside		0.532**	0.357**
	Various members to whom it is disclosed, outside		0.096	-0.040
Parties to whom inventors disclose their technology	R&D, inside[+]			0.244
	R&D of business unit, inside[+]			-0.101
	New product development and marketing, inside[+]			0.030
	Sales, inside[+]			-0.040
	Intellectual property and law, inside[+]			-0.067
	Production, inside[+]			0.058

	Model 1	Model 2	Model 3
Upper level of R&D, inside[+]			-0.325*
Upper level of R&D of business unit, inside[+]			0.148
R&D, outside[+]			-0.038
R&D of business unit, outside[+]			-0.102
New product development and marketing, outside[+]			0.489**
Sales, outside[+]			-0.202
Intellectual property and law, outside[+]			0.100
Production, outside[+]			0.238
Upper level of R&D, outside[+]			0.209
Upper level of R&D of business unit, outside[+]			0.004
R	0.644	0.753	0.834
R^2	0.414	0.568	0.695
Adjusted R^2	0.357	0.523	0.638

Note: # Real number, + Dummy variable. Dependent variable is 'Obtainig approval for going into business', *$p < 0.05$, **$p < 0.01$.

159

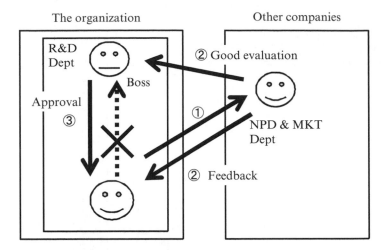

Figure 6.3   Image of 'detour strategy'

of disclosure, particularly disclosure within the organization. Parties such as product development and marketing departments outside the organization could provide inventors with inspiration and ideas for application fields of technologies. With a favorable reputation, the technologies could offer significant opportunities for their original organizations.

The causal relation between disclosing activities and obtaining approval is still debatable. In this chapter, we assume that active disclosing activities contribute to obtaining approval. However, we can assume the opposite causal relation as well: obtaining approval induces inventors to engage in active disclosing activities. However, at this point we would need further examination to verify that assumption.

The results of this research contribute to the people who cooperated with the researchers conducting 'skunk works' and also the technology transfer managers. As technology transfer managers occasionally have to sell technologies that possess uncertain characteristics and have unknown fields of application, greater awareness of how to sell these technologies to others, including to whom they should be disclosed, increases the possibility of commercialization and reduces the amount of unused technologies.

NOTE

*   This research is supported by KAKENHI: Grant-in Aid for Scientific Research (B) 21330085. This chapter owes much to the thoughtful comments and great help of Toshiya

Watanabe (Tokyo University), Yoko Takeda (Yokohama National University), Shigemi Yoneyama (Musashi University), and Dai Senoo (Tokyo Institute of Technology).

REFERENCES

Abetti, P.A. (2004), 'Informal corporate entrepreneurship: implications from the failure of the Concorde alloy foundry and the success of the Toshiba laptop', *International Journal of Entrepreneurship and Innovation Management*, **4** (6): 529–45.

Agrawal, A. (2006), 'Engaging the inventor: exploring licensing strategies for university inventions and the role of latent knowledge', *Strategic Management Journal*, **27**(1): 63–79.

Chesbrough, H.W. (2003), 'The era of open innovation', *Sloan Management Review*, **44** (3): 35–41.

Kanter, R.M., J. Kao and F. Wiersema (eds) (1997), *Innovation: Breakthrough Thinking at 3M, GE, DuPont, Pfizer, and Rubbermaid*, New York: HarperCollins.

Lichtenthaler, U. and H. Ernst (2007), 'External technology commercialization in large firms: results of a quantitative benchmarking study', *R&D Management*, **37** (5): 383–97.

Murray, F. (2004), 'The role of academic inventors in entrepreneurial firms: sharing the laboratory life', *Research Policy*, **33**: 643–59.

Smith, D.K. and R.C. Alexander (1999), *Fumbling the Future: How Xerox Invented, then Ignored, the First Personal Computer*, Lincoln, NE: iUniverse, Inc.

Takeda, Y. and D. Senoo (2007), *How Technology Is Made Visible When Exploring Its Application Fields*, PICMET Conference Proceedings, Portland, Or, August 6.

7. Creative model of science park development: case study on Daedeok Innopolis, Korea

Deog-Seong Oh and Byung-Joo Kang

1 INTRODUCTION

In today's knowledge-based economy, the development of science parks is a regional innovation strategy that generates sustained and propulsive economic activity through the creation and commercialization of new knowledge. These science parks are critical ingredients for a successful knowledge-based economy as well as instruments for innovation-oriented regional policy. The emphasis on the stimulation of high-tech industry through science parks and other initiatives by so many countries around the world is based on the assumption that technological innovation leads to economic growth (Grayson, 1993).

In the Republic of Korea, science park development began to gain momentum in the 1970s when the Daedeok Science Town (Daedeok Innopolis since 2004) was established as a national research and development (R&D) center. In particular, Daedeok Innopolis was intentionally created as an engine for enhancing national competitiveness of high technology and economic prosperity through the agglomeration of research institutes in a planned science city. Daedeok Innopolis brings together many national and regional development policy efforts from the last 40 years to achieve technology-based economic growth and regional innovation. In addition, the regional innovation policy targeting the innovative cluster is one of many critical instruments designed to achieve sustainable development through networked collaboration among higher education institutes (HEIs), research institutes, industries, and government. It is believed that Daedeok Innopolis is playing a crucial role as a regional platform for a comprehensive approach toward technology-based regional development in a sustainable context (Oh, 2006).

This chapter reviews the creative model of science park development in the case of Daedeok Innopolis over the last 30 years. In particular, the functional structure of science park development will be analyzed in terms of three different stages of development: science park, technopolis, and regional innovation cluster.

2 SCIENCE PARK: CONCEPT AND DEVELOPMENT TYPES

Definition

A science park is an organization managed by specialized professionals, whose main aim is to increase the wealth of a community by promoting a culture of innovation and the competitiveness of its associated businesses and knowledge-based institutions. To enable these goals to be met, a science park stimulates and manages the flow of knowledge and technology among universities, R&D institutions, companies, and markets; it facilitates the creation and growth of innovation-based companies through incubation and spin-off processes while providing other value-added services together with high-quality space and facilities. Malcolm Parry (2006) states that a science park is a business support initiative whose main aim is to encourage and support the start-up and incubation of innovative, high-growth, technology-based businesses through the provision of: infrastructure and support services including collaborative links with economic development agencies; formal and operational links with centers of excellence such as universities, HEIs, and research establishments; and management support actively engaged in the transfer of technology and business skills to small and medium-sized enterprises (SMEs). There are several similar terms used to describe similar developments, such as 'research park', 'technology park', 'business park', 'innovation center', and so on.

Although definitions of science park or technopolis development vary considerably around the world and significant variations occur even within individual countries, the essential concept is one of spatial development where the interface of research with commerce and industry is encouraged for the better exploitation of advanced technology. We use the terms 'science park' or 'technopolis' in the broadest sense to denote property-based development, sometimes related to urban redevelopment, which has the objective of facilitating and promoting the growth of high-tech firms through technology transfer and cross-fertilization in association with HEIs or research centers. Since the 1990s, technopolis policy, a land and property-led technology policy concept that aims at spatially clustering high-tech firms and R&D organizations, has been very popular among local, regional, and national policy makers to boost regional economic growth. In addition, it has given hope to policy makers in many countries to boost regional technology transfer, innovation, and hence competitiveness.

Broadly speaking, a science park, technopolis, or innovative cluster aims at achieving three goals. First, the most obvious goal is to foster economic development. High-tech and innovation-led growth is regarded as an absolute necessity for maintaining and increasing competitiveness of firms, regions, and nations. Second, in some countries, particularly those with overpopulated and congested urban areas, building an out-of-the-way technopolis in the countryside is often seen as a way to reduce regional economic inequalities. Economic planners hope to draw R&D out of the overburdened capital cities by relocating national research facilities and universities to new sites in the country and by luring firms with incentives to follow them there. Third, they aim at creating synergy among HEIs, public research enterprises, and firms in order to foster technology transfer, innovation, and hence, competitiveness. In the end, this should lead to creating an environment geared toward innovation. Capital and resources are naturally drawn to such a 'milieu of innovation' rather than having to be relocated through central planning (Castells and Hall, 1994).

Types of Development: Science Park, Technopolis, and Regional Innovation Cluster

Three broad categories of science park development have emerged: the science park, the technopolis, and the regional innovation cluster. The science park and the technopolis are property-based initiatives that have formal links with a university or other higher educational and research institution, are designed to encourage the formation and growth of knowledge-based businesses and other organizations normally resident on site, and have a management function that is actively engaged in the transfer of technology and business skills to the organizations on site. The technopolis emphasizes the need for a balanced approach to high-technology development (Tatsuno, 1986). Instead of only focusing on technology, it involves the creation of new settlements, complete with research parks, new universities, technology centers, housing, and cultural facilities. Masser (1991) has pointed out that technopoleis are larger in scale and often linked to the development of infrastructure and facilities in the new town model, whereas science parks are more limited in scope. Technopoleis also tend to be more production oriented than science parks and have both national and regional objectives. The national and technological objectives are to offer to high-tech industries adequate industrial land and an environment suitable for creative research. These resources have become scarce in the major metropolitan areas. Consequently, the regional and technological objective is to promote technological development in less developed areas. For this purpose, physical, scientific, and institutional infrastructure are developed in a decentralized pattern by a combination of measures taken at the local and regional levels and by national government.

The regional innovation cluster can be defined as a specific area(s) with networked location(s) where innovating actors are concentrated and interacting and functions as the source of innovative activities for the surrounding region while superseding other areas in terms of innovation competitiveness. The regional innovation cluster is a system for innovation composed of actors, processes, interaction mechanisms, and culture. The regional innovation cluster becomes the unit of competition and has various advantages in science and technology knowledge production, transfer, and utilization.

Within this definition of three basic development types, it is also possible to identify several subforms that complement other initiatives designed to stimulate a more productive relationship between industry and academia. Table 7.1 summarizes the key features of the science park, the technopolis, and the innovation cluster with respect to their nature and physical characteristics. Also, the development aspects are summarized with the structure in relationship and linkage, the activity in R&D, and the network among heterogeneous R&D activities.

Regional innovation clusters have various advantages over science parks and technopoleis in science and technology knowledge production, transfer, and utilization. Aggregation of R&D centers, entrepreneurs, and HEIs in a technopolis can exhibit a certain level of innovation, but it is not until interpersonal communication networks among researchers and entrepreneurs are established that a synergy of innovation will characterize the community as exemplified by Silicon Valley.

3 ANALYSIS FRAMEWORK OF CREATIVE MODEL OF SCIENCE PARKS: STRUCTURE AND FRAMEWORK

Functions and Components of Science Park Development

The main functions of science parks can be categorized into four primary areas: R&D, business and networked entrepreneurship, management and

Table 7.1   Types of development

Types	Features	Model
Science park: property-based initiative	Formal links with a university or other higher educational and research institution(HEI) Designed to encourage the formation and growth of knowledge-based businesses and other organizations normally resident on site Management function that is actively engaged in the transfer of technology and business skills to the organizations on site	
Technopolis: urban development	Emphasizes the need for a balanced approach Instead of only focusing on technology it involves the creation of new settlement, complete with research park, new universities, technology centers, housing and cultural facilities (Tatsuno, 1986) Larger in scale and often linked to the development of infrastructure and facilities on the new town model ⇒ whereas science parks are more limited in scope (Masser, 1991) More production oriented than science parks; has both national and regional objectives	
Innovation cluster: regional networking	To develop a network building of available intellectual, innovative and entrepreneurial resources To use these resources effectively an innovation cluster, that is, a favorable business, social, and political environment, is necessary to utilize the intellectual, innovative, and entrepreneurial resources To provide an applicability for development policy and insight into regional competitiveness Regional and national competitiveness is often decided by the innovation clusters	

Table 7.2 Functions and components

Function	Components
R&D	HEI, public R&D, private R&D, collaborative R&D, technology commercialization
Business & networked entrepreneurship	Entrepreneurship, Incubating, Venture Capital, Networking
Management & globalization	Training program, financial aid, marketing, property for rent, globalization
Infrastructure	Land use, R&D facilities, business facilities, management facilities, housing & settlement

globalization, and infrastructure (Table 7.2). R&D refers to creative work undertaken on a systematic basis in order to increase the stock of knowledge, including knowledge of people, culture and society, and the use of this stock of knowledge to devise new applications. R&D also includes the activities to create new products and technologies based on results from universities, research labs, and R&D-oriented firms.[1]

Business and networked entrepreneurship activities are important components of the value chain, which is the chain that connects markets with innovation. Business activities and networks are related to practical activities such as manufacturing products, which is the process of utilizing research results from science parks. The power source of business activities is active entrepreneurship.[2]

The function of management and globalization focuses on four components: training, financial, marketing, and property rent. Financial support in science parks should be focused on core technology fields and promote future oriented technology. The establishment of venture capital systems such as LLCs (limited liability corporations) is necessary to promote the settlement and development of investment culture.[3]

Infrastructure is the general social capital for specific activities. Infrastructure in science parks is the general social capital used by institutions in the science parks in order to generate regional innovation and to enhance regional economic activities. It includes the physical environment that is managed and operated in science parks.[4]

To identify these kinds of structure, case analysis of a successful science park, technopolis, and innovation cluster development is necessary. For our case analysis, Daedeok Innopolis in Korea was selected. Daedeok contains the component of R&D (HEIs, public, and private institutions, and so on), business and networked entrepreneurship (service activities

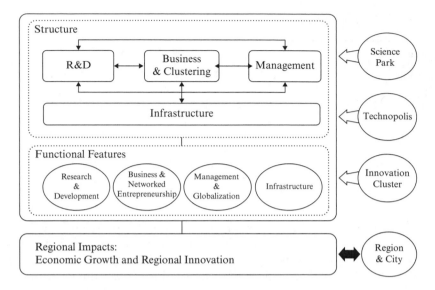

Figure 7.1   Analysis of Daedeok Innopolis in accordance with each development stage

for entrepreneurship and business incubation), management and globalization (property for rent), and infrastructure (management and business facilities). It also has the components to support technology transfer, spinoffs and capacity building.

Analysis Framework

In this chapter, we suggest a creative model for a science park based on the experience of Daedeok Innopolis. A conceptual framework is necessary to identify the development features of a science park (Figure 7.1). Daedeok Innopolis has been developed over the last 40 years by functional features in accordance with three different development steps: science park, technopolis, and regional innovation cluster. With this consideration in mind, we analyze the functional structure and regional impact in Daedeok Innopolis that is a creative model of science park development in the Republic of Korea.

The analysis follows four steps: first, an overview and historical background of science park development in Daedeok is presented. Second, a functional structure that is characterized with each science park model is identified: science park, technopolis, or innovation cluster. Third, functional relationships and linkages among functions and components as well as functional features are analyzed in accordance with each developmental stage of a science park. In particular, we find out how to work together with its own functions and components as well as how to play a vital role for successful science park development and regional innovation. Fourth, the regional impacts on economic growth and innovation of Daedeok Innopolis are identified based on the growth pattern in the time sequence of science park development.

4 CASE STUDY: DAEDEOK INNOPOLIS IN DAEJEON METROPOLITAN CITY, KOREA

Historical Review

Initiated in 1970 and designed in 1973 as Daedeok Science Town (hereafter referred to as DST), Daedeok Innopolis (new name) has undergone continuous self-renewal over the past 30 years to better respond to the economic demands of the nation. Today, Daedeok Innopolis is reorganized as a global cluster that signifies the retrenchment and renewed commitment to placing Korea's high-tech prowess in the global spotlight.

In 1973, on a site covering 27.8 square kilometers, the Korean government began the construction of DST. The cost of the development was one trillion Korean won, which was provided by the national government and private businesses. Keeping step with the growing size of the science park in Daejeon, the name has twice been changed, from Daedeok Science Town (1972–99) to Daedeok Valley (1999–2004) and finally to Daedeok Innopolis (2005–present). Daedeok Innopolis is located in the center of the nation's territory, approximately 167.3 km from Seoul, the capital of South Korea. At a distance of about one hour from major cities including Seoul, Daegu, and Gwangju, exchanges with other regional government officials, industry leaders, and researchers are convenient. In total, there are 70 R&D institutes, six universities, and 800 high-tech companies situated on this site, which is regarded as one of the best areas in which to live and work in Korea. For operational purposes, the grounds have been organized into five distinctive zones.

There were three distinct processes in the development of Daedeok Innopolis (see Table 7.3 and Figure 7.2). At the initial stage, DST in 1973 (within Daedeok Innopolis) was the sole science town in South Korea that had been developed as a mecca for science and technology with a strong research workforce. DST was intentionally created as an engine to enhance national competitiveness in high technology and economic prosperity through the agglomeration of research institutes, bringing

Table 7.3   History of Daedeok Innopolis

Stage	Period		Features
Initial stage	1972–74: infrastructure construction	May 1972:	Elementary plans for town construction decided
		March 1974:	Construction of facilities and institutes commences
	1978–89: R&D capacity expansion	April 1978:	Research institutes start moving in (Standards and Science /Chemical Technology/Shipping Institute)
		Aug. 1981:	'Fundamental Construction Plan for Daedeok Industrial Base'
	1990–99: innovative creation	Nov. 1992:	Daedeok Science Town completed, private research institutes moved in
		Dec. 1993:	Daedeok Science Town Administration Law enacted
		Jan. 1997:	'Daedeok Science Town Management Plan' announced
Middle stage	2000–04: cluster formation	March 2000:	High-tech start-ups started moving in, DST renamed as Daedeok Valley (DV)
		Nov. 2004:	Daedeok Special R&D Zone Law enacted
Mature stage	2005–: innovation cluster launched (Daedeok Innopolis)	Jan. 2005:	Daedeok Science Town/ Daedeok Valley/Special Zone redesigned as 'Daedeok Innopolis'
		Sep. 2005:	Daedeok Innopolis HQ founded
		Nov. 2005:	Creation of Brand Identity logo

together many national and regional development policy efforts from the last 30 years. The DST research complex has been built with the investment of US$3.16 billion over the past three decades to better respond to the economic demands of the nation. It also possesses a vibrant mixture of next-generation technologies such as information technology (IT), biotechnology (BT), and nanotechnology (NT). It has been well developed with a healthy balance among research institutes, academic institutes, industries, and the public sectors, following the model of 'the next Silicon Valley'. Recently, venture parks are being actively developed in order to cover the huge number of high-tech SMEs produced through DST's development.

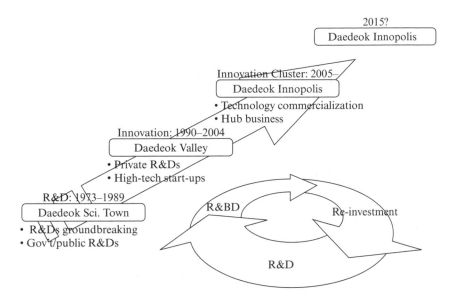

Figure 7.2   Evolution of Daedeok

Analysis of Structural Change: Science Park, Technopolis, and Innovation Cluster

Science park model

DST's development features (see Figure 7.3) at the initial stage illustrate the model of a science park. As a national hub for development of science and technology, the main objectives in the initial stage of the science park are:

- *Constructing infrastructure*: Designing, developing, and managing the science park. Also includes forging connections with other cities and regulating development of the science park (regulating green areas, building-to-land ratio, floor space index, and so on).
- *Managing and operating the science park*: Harmonizing R&D facilities, amenities, and welfare facilities. Also includes maintaining the balance between supply and demand in the science park.
- *Constructing institutional infrastructure*: Establishing institutional structures to regulate environmental pollution, to activate business and R&D activities, and to enhance the environment for residents.

This science park model contains three main functions: R&D, business, and infrastructure (Table 7.4). Management is only limited to

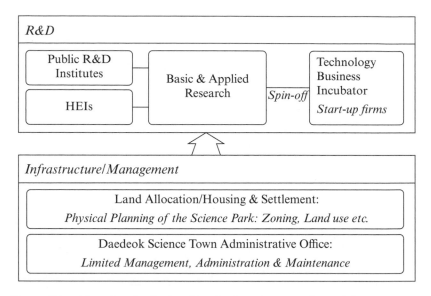

Figure 7.3   Functional relationships in the science park model

infrastructure-related services. In terms of R&D, research and education were led by research-centered HEIs. The training of experts in basic science was improved. Public research institutes focused on conducting national R&D projects and constructing national R&D infrastructure. They also focused on the construction of a national framework of science and the development of strategic industries with a long-range vision. Private R&D institutes formed a hierarchical relationship with their mother firms and concentrated on R&D related to those firms. They focused on building R&D infrastructure and R&D activities. In this stage, the commercial potential of R&D results in basic science or engineering from research-centered HEIs promoted the construction of the science park: business incubation centers and technology exchange centers were built in HEI and R&D institutes to support technology commercialization. Collaborative R&D also began. R&D experts trained in research concentrated HEI led technology commercialization activities.

In terms of business and networked entrepreneurship, the Daedeok Science Park focused on non-industrial basic science activities during the initial stage. Thus entrepreneurship activities were barely present at this stage; nor were business incubation activities supported. The only business incubation space provided were labs in HEIs. In order to support business start-ups, a systemized business incubation system

Table 7.4   Functional features of the science park model

Function	Main features	Key role
R&D	HEIs that lead advanced science technology R&D.	HEIs, National R&D Center
	Government-affiliated research institutes*	
Business activities/ technology commercialization	Firms that originated from research institutes in advanced science fields	Spin-offs of R&D labs
	Venture firms that originated from labs in HEIs or research institutes (research-centered HEIs)	
Infrastructure	Management departments in HEIs or research institutes	Management office
	A special management institute, which is established by the central government, managed, and operated the science park	
	→ An independent management institute is established	
	The science park should be managed, designed, and developed by the central government	

Note: *In order to increase national science and technology capacity, major R&D projects were supported by the government (government-affiliated institutes).

is required. For example, pre-incubation systems and TBI (technology business incubator) projects in HEIs. The venture capital methods at this stage were mainly Angel Funds, which is a type of risk financing. Funds were mainly provided to venture firms by individual investors. Only lab business start-ups in research-concentrated HEIs were supported at this stage. Administrative networks among public research institutes were formed, and R&D activities were mostly conducted with government aid. As a result, independent networks among institutes were barely existed. More networks needed to be formed among firms, HEIs, and research institutes to promote R&D activities and to support business incubation. At this stage, however, technology commercialization and venture activities were mainly conducted in labs located inside research institutes and HEIs.

During the initial stage, the infrastructure of the science park was limited to R&D-related facilities such as the R&D center, HEIs, and so on, which did not have industrial functions. Since the Daedeok Science Park was initially designed as a research and education city and was built as a

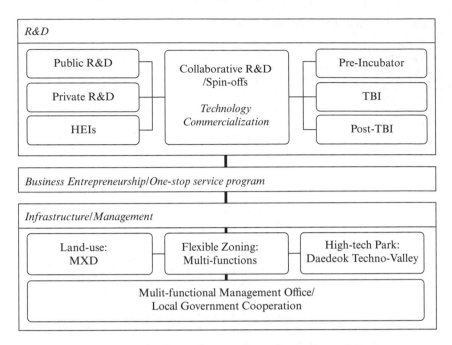

Figure 7.4   Functional relationships in the technopolis model

national science and technology city, business activities were not recognized in the initial stage; nor did legal structures or institutes that manage business facilities exist. The function of the Science Park's Management Office included designing the science park, selecting occupying institutes for the park, and other management functions. Education, research, and residential facilities were harmonized in the DST.

Technopolis model
The middle stage of Daedeok Innopolis's development shows the technopolis model in action (see Figure 7.4). The model is a total system for innovation and technology commercialization. During this stage, HEIs and research institutes actively supported business incubation activities through continuing legal support and constructing infrastructure (for example, a business incubation center). Cooperation between the science park and the local government is important for collaborative activities. In order to expand R&D activities into technology commercialization activities, the R&D capacity of the science park was enhanced. In addition, industrial areas were expanded next to the science park. At the same time, as various infrastructures were expanded within the park, a legal structure

Table 7.5   Functional features of the technopolis model

Function	Main features	Key role
R&D	Active collaborative research programs among industries, HEIs, and research institutes Enhancing local R&D support capacity	Collaboration among firms, HEIs, and research institutes
Business activities/ technology commercialization	Various business incubation centers were promoted by active technology commercialization and sound entrepreneurship Venture activities and technology commercialization activities of venture firms or medium sized firms are supported by local government	Various business incubation centers
Management	A multi-functional office creates jobs to cope with the expansion of the science park. To control the surrounding area of the science park, the institute collaborated with the local government to connect the activities of the science park with local innovation	Local government support in business activities, R&D activities, management activities/ multi- functional management institute
Infrastructure	The role of the local government was expanded to develop venture firm areas, establish various support institutes and etc for local economic prosperity, to encourage private firm investment and participation	

to efficiently manage and operate the infrastructures was established. Venture firms were created and the role of HEIs became more important in this stage. All HEIs, including research-centered and local engineering HEIs, conducted technology commercialization and collaborative research with firms, research institutes and HEIs.

The main features of technopolis development at the initial stage are as follows (Table 7.5). In terms of R&D, HEIs became more important since they are the source of venture firm start-ups. Various local HEIs moved into the science park and engaged in collaborative R&D activities with other firms and research institutes. HEIs mainly conducted research projects offered by the government with help from the public research institutes. With research-centered and local HEIs participating actively, R&D activities in the science park were enhanced; the groundwork for venture firm start-ups was established. Research projects assigned by the government were conducted by HEIs. Public research institutes led collaborative research projects with industries and HEIs, conducted research projects offered by private firms, and so on. As HEIs' and firms' R&D activities increased and expanded, the public research institutes' functions also increased and expanded. Public research institutes supported the creation of venture firms by establishing business incubation centers. In government-affiliated research institutes, national and collaborative R&D projects were conducted. In the process, technology commercialization, technology transfer, and spin-off activities occurred. In order to support these activities, support systems such as business incubation systems were established.

In terms of business and networked entrepreneurship in a developing technopolis, a system to utilize research results from research institutes and HEIs in order to support potential entrepreneurs and venture firms is necessary. Business incubation activities should be expanded from a small number of public institutes and HEIs to various local institutes. Also, business incubation activities should be integrated and diversified to promote regional development. There should be an integrated support system for venture firms, which includes customized business incubation, specialized collaborative networks, venture communities, and venture capital programs in order to support venture firms efficiently and flexibly.

In terms of management and globalization, the management and operation of the technopolis become more professional. The management and operation services include education programs that are developed by public institutes and financial aid for venture firms, marketing services, institutional support, various equipment, facilities, and so on. Technology commercialization was the core topic of education programs: technology marketing, technology management, advertisement of products, and so on. Financial aid was provided to venture firms in order to help venture firms settle down and make progress. A financial aid system that focuses on supporting venture firms was established by the central government. Local governments also adhered to the central government's policy of supporting venture firms and their growth, plus the function of business incubation centers established by local governments was enhanced by the provision of financial aid. An integrated operation and management office was established and integrated a system that synthesized the governance of the science park including management and infrastructure maintenance. The cooperation with local government was taken for the sustainable development of technopolis.

As a function of the infrastructure for the technopolis, industrial space for venture firms and R&D facilities was increased in order to expand early R&D activities into technology commercialization. As various infrastructures in the science park developed, legal structures became necessary to efficiently manage and operate the facilities. A structured division of roles in R&D facilities, business facilities, and management facilities was established. The integration of culture and society with local residents was emphasized in order to make best use of the mother town's infrastructure.

Regional innovation cluster model
At the mature stage of development, Daedeok Innpolis shifted into the innovation cluster model: a center of high-tech industry and business excellence. In order to establish an innovative cluster, the collaborative system among firms, HEIs, and research institutes has been further developed and refined. A regional innovation cluster like Daedeok aimed to maximize science and technology innovation through network building. Global marketing strategies were enhanced as Daedeok Innopolis tried to attract foreign institutes and investment into the science park. In particular, a cooperative system among firms, HEIs, and research institutes was strengthened in strategic industrial fields such as IT, BT, and NT. As a result, an innovative cluster was built, and collaborative R&D is actively pursued in order to conduct technology commercialization. Numerous networks among firms have been created in order to support technology commercialization and business activities (see Figure 7.5).

Experts in science and technology and integrated professional training programs are required to build an innovation cluster as it is important to create clusters of related institutes to promote the growth of strategic industries. Financial aid and support of specific technologies are also important. Cooperation with international innovative clusters and global marketing strategies induces synergy effects in the development of science and technology.

In the innovation cluster model, pleasant residential areas and strategic high-tech industries should be harmonized. In addition, the innovative cluster should encourage local innovation. Land use should be improved to activate high-tech R&D activities. A systematic and integrated structure of R&D, business and management facilities is required in order to promote the development of high-tech strategic industries (Table 7.6). A multi-purpose site was established in Daedeok Innopolis to attract strategic industries, foreign advanced research institutes, and foreign research-centered firms. An international support infrastructure was established to enhance global competitiveness while maintaining a local awareness.

R&D/Business

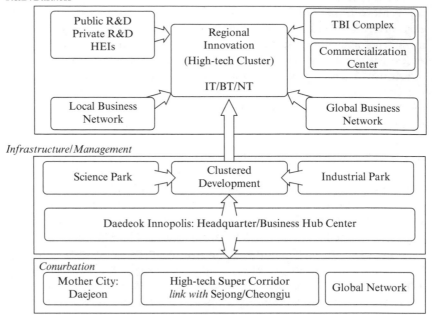

Figure 7.5   Functional relationships in the innovation cluster model

The main features of the science park development at the mature stage of regional innovative cluster were as follows: the R&D function was focused on research-centered HEIs leading R&D activities in national strategic industries. Core science fields such as IT, BT, and NT were the main areas of research in order to increase national competitiveness. Through collaborative research among HEIs' research institutes, and industries, technology commercialization was pursued. HEIs' roles and functions were diversified, and in order to maximize the efficiency of technology commercialization activities, public research institutes supported R&D activities in specific fields. By creating clusters of strategic industries, technology can be accumulated. Continuous R&D activities and the formation of strategic industry clusters are required for sustained technology innovation.

In terms of business and networked entrepreneurship, an institutional system and infrastructure were established to support entrepreneurship activities. This led to the construction of an innovative cluster. Potential entrepreneurs in strategic industries were discovered and supported with the aim of establishing an industrial cluster and a regional innovative system. Business incubation services, including the provision of space and

Table 7.6   Functional features of the regional innovation cluster model

Function	Main Features	Key Role
R&D	An innovative cluster to be created to promote the growth of strategic industries The collaborative network among firms, HEIs and research institutes is enhanced Local governments should actively support the creation of innovative clusters Regional innovative projects are conducted by central and local governments	Collaboration among firms, HEIs, and research institutes
Business activities/ technology commercialization	A support system for business incubation activities: in addition to providing business incubation space, technology support, marketing support and other professional support was provided Clusters of strategic industries are created by the cooperation between science park and local governments Business activities such as technology marketing, technology commercialization, and technology transaction are managed by specific centers of regional innovation The Techno-park was established as the core of regional platform The Strategic Industry Planning Team prepared future-oriented strategy	Strategic industrial projects led by local governments
Management	Integrated education programs to train R&D experts and to support professionals: specialized education programs, customized education programs etc.	Global business infrastructure (management facilities, local governments, and international organizations)
Infrastructure	Land-use system to promote business activities and R&D activities in the innovation cluster: clusters of strategic industries, multi-purpose sites etc.	

facilities and institutional structures, were improved. As a result, venture firms became more active. Professional support services such as business consulting and technology marketing were provided as part of business incubation programs. Such programs were customized and divided into three stages. These systemized programs supported the establishment of venture firms. Business incubation programs then supported the stabilization of venture firms, and ultimately, the venture firms contributed to the establishment of an innovative cluster.

In terms of management and globalization, a regional innovation system was established by cooperation between the HEIs and local government. The customized education programs were focused on technology commercialization and business incubation. Education programs in specific fields or retraining programs were also diversified. For example, consistent education programs were offered by education institutes such as the University of Science and Technology, the Technology Management Graduate School, and the Patent and Law Graduate School. During the stage of establishing an innovative cluster, a financial aid system is necessary in high-tech fields. Financial aid was provided to specialized or advanced technologies. To encourage cooperation among different technology clusters, cooperation networks were created among related institutes in the science park.

In terms of infrastructure, land use was more specialized to attract high-tech firms to the park, and mixed-use development was harmonized in the development of Daedok Innopolis. Amenities and education facilities were also built next to residential areas in the park. Daedok Innopolis tried a flexible system approach to contain the rapid expansion of tenant space needs of developing high-tech firms. Sustainable strategies, including pre-incubator, technology business incubator, and post-incubator comprised the main elements of business.

5   DAEDEOK INNOPOLIS'S IMPACT ON ECONOMIC GROWTH AND REGIONAL INNOVATION

Regional Impacts: Outline of Growth Patterns and Trends

The volume of employment created by Daedeok Innopolis is relatively small by global standards. However, taking into account that Daedeok Innopolis's employment consists of a professional workforce that is the center of knowledge and technology, its employment rate is meaningful in terms of future-oriented development. A highly trained research workforce in public and private R&D centers has been concentrated

Table 7.7 Institutions and employment in Daedeok Innopolis

		Year					
		1979	1985	1990	1995	2000	2005
	Total	9	13	33	52	68	86
Rearch institutes	Number of researchers	3,879	6,129	6,920	7,640	14,913	22,395
	Govt-contributed institutes	5	8	19	17	20	20
	Private institutes	3	3	8	21	25	33
	Investment organizations				6	10	10
	Higher education institutes	1	2	3	3	4	6
	Number of foreign scientists					85	252
Other organizations	Public organizations					9	11
	Supporting organizations						6

Sources: Korea Bank, *Statistical Yearbook*, Authority of SMEs (Daejeon·Chungnam Branch), Statistical Yearbook.

in Daedeok Innopolis for the last 40 years. About 86 institutes are currently located there. Private research institutes are now dominant, but government-subsidized research institutes still have a presence. The latter held sway until 1990 when private research institutes took over. Investment organizations began to appear from the mid-1990s, about 20 years after the initiation of Daedeok Innopolis (Daedeok Science Park was established in 1973), and their number grew very slowly from 2000. Daedeok is a good place to transfer technology and science to nearby firms but it does not have a sizable population. Therefore, investment organizations in Daedeok Innopolis do not exceed a certain number.

There are about 22,000 researchers, including 6,000 PhD holders who work in private and public research institutes and universities (see Table 7.7). It can be argued that there is a high possibility of commercialization of research results or high-tech commodities from high-tech research activities in Daedeok Innopolis because no other place in Korea has as many high-powered researchers. Foreign scientists began to settle in Daedeok Innopolis from 1999, and there are now about 260 researchers working there.

Table 7.8   Number and volume of sales by venture firms in Daedeok Innopolis (unit: firm, thousand US$)

	1999	2000	2001	2002	2003	2004
Total	250	300	500	776	811	824
Identified	150	170	340	503	413	425
Unidentified	100	130	160	273	398	399
Amount of annual sales	2,095	3,637	3,676	3,646	4,800	7,773

Source: Authority of SMEs (Daejeon·Chungnam Branch), *Statistical Yearbook.*

The Growth of Hi-tech Venture Business

The economic impact of Daedeok Innopolis is apparent through a rapidly growing number of venture businesses. Since the late 1990s, active spin-offs from research institutes and universities have been facilitated through Daedeok Innopolis. Although several previous assessments indicated that the mere concentration of public and private research organizations in one location could not generate a high incidence of high-technology spin-offs, similar types of organization in Daedeok Innopolis have been a significant source of technology-oriented new ventures; Daedeok Innopolis's fervor for venture start-ups has been spreading into the whole Daejeon area from the late 1990s and currently about 824 firms are under operation.

The growth of venture business is also shown in sales increases. According to a study by Daejeon Metropolitan City, the amount of turnover by venture business was US$7,773 in 2004. Over the last 15 years, venture firms in Daedeok Innopolis have made outstanding progress. The growth rate of venture firms increased exponentially. The economic impact from venture firms on the regional economy is not significant but the growth rate is very high. The volume of sales from venture firms located in Daedeok Innopolis in 2004 was nearly four times that of 1999 (see Table 7.8).

Start-up venture firms were initiated at the end of the 1980s and grew slowly until the International Monetary Fund (IMF) crisis in Korea. They then grew very rapidly from 1999 due to the central government's support policy for venture firms to achieve economic prosperity to mitigate losses from the IMF crisis. The benefits of job creation from venture firms were realized by the citizens of Daejeon Metropolitan City from the year 2000 (see Table 7.9).

Table 7.9   *Growth of venture firms' start-ups at major R&D center in
Daedeok Innopolis*

Year	1990	1992	1994	1996	1999	2002	2004
No. of firms	2	6	7	20	154	130	219
No. of jobs created	35	84	96	187	924	2,212	3,237

Source: Daedeok Innopolis, 2008, *Guideline and Manual of Science Park Development.*

Table 7.10   *Trends in business incubation centers in Daedeok Innopolis*

Year	Incubating institute	No. of occupants (firms)	No. of occupants (persons)
1998	1	140	893
2000	16	350	2,523
2002	18	310	2,943
2004	18	287	2,601
2007	20	322	2,994

Source: MOST, 2008, *Synthesized Development Plan for Daedeok Innopolis.*

Business incubation plays the role of connecting science and technology to real markets and economic development. Key functions for successful business incubation are proper planning, management, location
selection, connecting with universities, positive marketing, establishing
global networks, and providing financial aid. Since the establishment
of an incubation center in the Korea Advanced Institute of Science and
Technology (KAIST) in 1994, about 20 business-incubating organizations
have begun in Daedeok Innopolis. They are connected to universities,
research institutes, government institutes, and private firms. Currently,
about 322 venture firms are under incubation, and some 3,000 employees are working with the funds from the government or out of Daedeok
Innopolis (see Table 7.10).

Intellectual property accumulated in Daedeok Innopolis is growing
rapidly. Table 7.11 shows that the number of domestic patents in 2004
was nearly five times that of 1997. However, in the case of international
patents, the number of patents in 2004 was about nine times that of 1997.
These statistics indicate that Daedeok Innopolis is a hub of knowledge
innovation and a center for future growth in this knowledge-driven era in
Korea.

Table 7.11   Trends in intellectual property in Daedeok Innopolis

Year	Domestic patents	Domestic patent on a new device	Computer programs	International patents
1997	4,125	201	8,142	623
2000	12,289	609	14,379	2,026
2002	14,221	778	19,488	2,687
2004	19,787	1,304	26,767	5,597

Source: MOST, 2008, *Synthesized Development Plan for Daedeok Innopolis.*

6   CONCLUSION

In this chapter, we discussed the Daedeok model of science park development based on the experience of Daedeok Innopolis over the last 30 years.
In particular, we aimed to establish a model for science park development
based on the strategies and know-how that have accumulated in Daedeok
Innopolis since the 1970s. Before proceeding to the case study, the types of
science park development and their functional structures were reviewed.
We explored the main issues of science park development by focusing on
the main functions and detailed components. The three steps of science
park development – science park, technopolis, and regional innovation
cluster – are identified, and the four main functions (R&D, business, management, and infrastructure) and their detailed components are suggested
through an analysis of Daedeok Innopolis.

With these considerations in mind, we looked closely at the case of the
Daedeok Innopolis development based on the conceptual framework,
including the functional structure of creative science park developement.
Three clear phases were identified as follows:

- science park at the initial stage: a national hub for development of
science and technology;
- technopolis at the middle stage: a synthesized system for innovation
and technology commercialization; and
- regional innovation cluster at the mature stage: a center for business
excellence for high-tech industry in the global market.

The detailed analysis according to the four main functions and supporting components explains how science parks work together with their own
functional structure and which components can play a vital role for successful science park development and regional innovation. The growth

Table 7.12   Growth pattern and regional impact in Daedeok Innopolis

Development stage	Growth pattern	Regional impact
Initial stage	Leading the national R&D capacity through government research institutes	Since Daedeok Innopolis was established by the central government initiative, there has been weak linkage between the science park and surrounding region, – therefore impact from job creation and regional economic growth was meager
Middle stage	Venture firms were created to take advantage of research results from Daedeok Innopolis. Spin-offs and start-ups were strongly supported by the central government	Emphasis was given to the development of advanced technologies Linkage among HEIs, industries, and research institutes was strengthened
Mature stage	Number of foreign R&D institutes is expected to rise dramatically and international patent registration will grow rapidly. Science and technology output will be more extensively utilized	Daedeok Innopolis is expected to play a role as a worldwide regional innovation cluster

patterns of Daedok Innopolis and their regional impact are summarized in Table 7.12.

We suggest here five strategies from the findings of our research for organizations that are planning to build science parks in developing countries:

1. To commercialize research results from R&D institutes and HEIs in the science park, business incubation activities and potential entrepreneurs should be actively supported. In order to support technology commercialization, the construction of infrastructure, the securing of adequate funding, and the building of venture firm networks are important factors.
2. To support entrepreneurial activities, a multi-dimensional support system that includes education, support, and cooperation among institutes is required. Support should be given in various fields such as education, policies, and funding by various institutions.

3. In science parks, a financial aid system that builds trust between firms and markets is necessary. Venture firms in their initial stage have low financial credit and have difficulty in securing funds. Thus, financial aid should be provided to these firms so that they can utilize financial aid to build credit.
4. Government support is necessary to help venture firms to secure venture capital funds, especially in the initial stages. After the start-up phase, consistent funding should be provided by private investment firms to help venture firms become stable.
5. Venture capital programs should be customized to individual venture firms, and diverse venture capital programs should be created. Depending on the venture firm's condition, loan and investment methods should vary.

We hope that this chapter will provide guidelines for technical assistance and act as a stepping-stone for policy makers in developing countries when they plan to establish a science park.

NOTES

1. The basic function of R&D is located within universities and research institutes. These are the core of innovation in science parks and promote technology commercialization through collaborative research among universities, industries, and research institutes. Furthermore, they contribute to the success of science parks, the innovation of technology, and the industrial growth and economic development of the region.
2. Business activities such as discovering potential entrepreneurs, supporting high-tech venture firms, commercializing technology, and forming clusters of innovative organizations connect R&D results of research institutes directly to the economy. The key point of science business is establishing systems to support high-tech venture firms and to help them settle down in the area. The process is done by providing funding, consultation, and facilities. Thereby, commercialization of science and technology in science parks can flourish. At the same time, cooperative systems among universities, public research institutes, and private research institutes can be developed to utilize the outcomes of high-tech industries. The creation of cooperative systems can provide more than innovative products and technologies; it can also provide opportunities to exchange human resources, ideas, research facilities, and tools.
3. There are two different types of marketing strategy in science parks: the first focuses on the marketing of individual firms; and the second strategy focuses on the marketing of the science park as a whole. The use of both strategies is encouraged in order to maximize a synergy effect. Rental services in science parks can be divided into two different categories: rental of facilities and rental of space. An integrated rental system to diversify rental options and simplify rental processes should be built to maximize efficiency.
4. The principle of infrastructure in science parks is a rational regulation between supply and demand. Infrastructure includes land, facilities, and environment.

BIBLIOGRAPHY

Castells, M. and Peter Hall (1994), *Technopolis of the World*, London: Routledge.

Cooke, P. (2004), *Regional Innovation Systems: The Role of Governances in a Globalized World*, in M. Heidenreich, and H. Braczyk (eds), London, New York: Routledge.

Cooke, P. (2005), 'Regional innovation, entrepreneurship and talent systems', *Manuscript prepared for special issue of International Journal of Entrepreneurship & Innovation*.

Cooke, P. and Uranga et al. (1998), *Regional Innovation System*, Oxford: Oxford University Press.

Daedeok Techno Valley (2002), *Masterplan of DTV*, Daejeon: Daejeon Metropolitan City.

Daedeok Innopolis (2009), available at: http://www.ddi.or.kr/

Daejeon Metropolitan City (1997), *Daejeon High-Tech Industrial Estate Development Bebauungsplan*, Daejeon: Daejeon Metropolitan City.

Grayson, L. (1993), *Science Park: An Experiment in High Technology Transfer*, London: The British Library.

Hassink, R. 2005. 'Regional innovation support systems and science cities', UNESCO-WTA International Training Workshop on Science City Governance, Daejon, Korea World Technopolis Association (WTA), pp. 133–56.

Kang, B.S. (2004a), 'The process of developing a regional innovation system and its path for growth focusing on the empirical research of Daedeok Valley', Korea Association of Local Government Studies.

Kang, B.S. (2004b). 'A study on the establishing development model for research parks', *Journal of Technology Transfer*, **29**: 203–10.

Ko, S.C. and I.H. Kim (1998), *The incidence of high technology spin-offs and innovative milieu: the case of Daedeok Science Town, Korea*, in Proceedings of WTA Conference, Daejeon, Korea, pp. 167–89.

Korea Land and Housing Corporation (2010), available at: http://world.lh.or.kr.

KOSEF (Korea Science and Engineering Foundation) (1992), *Development strategies for the future: Taedok Science Town*, Daejeon, Korea (in Korean).

Lowe, E.A. (2001), 'Eco-industrial Park Handbook for Asian Developing Countries: A Report to Asian Development Bank', Environment Development, RPP International, Emeryville. CA, available at: http://www.indigodev.com/Handbook.html (accessed October 18, 2002).

Malecki, E.J. (1997), *Technology and Economic Development: The Dynamics of Local, Regional and National Competitiveness*, Harlow: Addison Wesley Longman.

Masser, I. (1991), 'By accident or design: some lessons from technology led local economic development initiatives', *Review of Urban and Regional Development Studies*, **3**: 78–93.

Massey, K., P. Quintas and D. Wield. (1992), *High-Tech Fantasies*, London: Routledge.

MKE (Ministry of Knowledge and Economy), Republic of Korea (2008), available at: http://www.mke.go.kr/.

Monck, C., R.B. Porter, P. Quintas, S. Storey and P. Wynarczyk (1988), *Science Parks and the Growth of High Technology Firms*. London: Croom Helm.

MEST (Ministry of Education Park and Technology), (1989), *The Basic Plan of Technobelt in Korea*, Seoul: MOST (in Korean).

Oh, D.S. (1993), 'High-technology and regional development policy: an evaluation of Korea's Technopolis Programme', *Town and Regional Planning* (TRP), **118**.

Oh, D.S. (1995), 'High-technology and regional development policy: an evaluation of Korea's technopolis programme', *Habitat International*, **19**: 213–28.

Oh, D.S. (2002), 'Technology-based regional development policy: case study Daedeok Science Town, Daejeon Metropolitan City, Korea', *Habitat International*, 26: 213–28.

Oh, D.S. (2006), 'Sustainable development of technopolis: Case study of Daedeok Valley in Korea', 2006 UNESCO-WTA International Training Workshop, Daejon, Korea: World Technopolis Association (WTA).

Oh, D.S. and S.K. Jeong (2002), *Eco-Industrial Park Development Plan*, Daejeon, Korea: Hanwha Co. (in Korean).

Oh, D.S. and B.J. Kang (1998), 'Networking the technology sources and technology transfer infrastructure with reference to Taejon Metropolitan city', *Journal of the Korean Regional Development Association*, **13** (2): 183–98.

Oh, D.S. and I. Masser (1995), 'High-tech centers and regional innovation: some case studies in the U.K, Germany, Japan and Korea', in C.S. Bertuglia (ed.), *Technological Change, Economic Development and Space*, Berlin: Springer, pp. 295–333.

Oh, D.S., K.B. Kim and S.Y. Jeong (2005), 'Eco-industrial park design: a Daedeok Technovalley case study', *Habitat International*, **29**: 269–84.

Parry, Malcolm (2006), *The Planning, Development and Operation of Science Parks*, Cambridge, UK: UK Science Park Association, (UKSPA).

Porter, M.E. (1997), *On Competition*, Boston: Harvard Business School Press.

Simmie, J., J. Cohen and D. Hart (1993), 'Technopole planning in Britain, Ireland and France', Working Paper 6, Planning and Development Research Centre, University College London.

Tatsuno, S. (1986), *The Technopolis Strategy: Japan, High-Technology and Control of the Twenty-first Century*, New York: Prentice Hall.

TSO (Ministry of Science and Technology) (1996), 'Daedeok Science Town', Information Paper, Daejon, Korea.

TSO (Ministry of Science and Technology) (2002), 'Daedeok Science Town', Masterplan, Daejon, Korea.

8. Malta: a Mediterranean island state, its university, and its future

Juanito Camilleri and Albert Caruana

1 INTRODUCTION

Malta is the largest of the three small islands that make up the Maltese archipelago. It is centrally located in the Mediterranean and given this strategic location, Malta has been a melting pot of civilizations that go back to around 5200 BC. The islands have belonged to all the main powers that controlled the region, including: Phoenicians, Carthaginians, Romans, Byzantines, Arabs, the Holy Roman Emperor, the Order of the Knights of St John (Knights of Malta), the French, and the British Empire.

The Maltese Islands have a total land area of 316 km² (122 miles²) and a population of just over 400,000, making it one of the most densely populated countries in the world. Malta's population is predominantly Catholic and there are two official languages: Maltese and English. It has a Mediterranean climate: mild with rainy winters and hot, dry summers. Malta is a parliamentary democracy fashioned on the UK Westminster model. It gained independence from Britain in 1964, became a Republic in 1974, and joined the European Union in 2004. Malta adopted the euro currency (€) on 1 January 2008. In 2007, GDP per head was €13,158, which in purchasing power standard terms comes to 77.7 compared to the EU27 average of 100. In January 2009, inflation stood at 3.1 percent and unemployment at 6.0 percent.

Malta is a microstate. Given its size, its industry is not extensive, social networking is quite effortless, state institutions are within easy reach, and it has one university. This chapter outlines the evolving role of the University of Malta in tandem with Malta becoming an independent state, and projects a vision for Malta and its Alma Mater. This is done with reference to the main models of knowledge and technology transfer illustrating different perspectives ranging from 'Mode 2' (Gibbons et al., 1994) to 'National System of Innovation' (Freeman, 1987, 1995; Lundvall, 1992) to various 'Triple Helix' models (Etkowiz and Leydesdorff, 2000). Moreover, this is projected from a historical perspective of the situation prior to independence in 1964 and the drive towards economic sustainability after independence and since membership in the European Union. The role of Malta's only university is intricately and symbiotically embedded within this progression. The relevance of the Triple Helix models to the local situation is considered and a matrix depicting the characterizing features of modern-day universities of different orientation is employed. This matrix is used to identify the current orientation of the University of Malta and to provide direction for the future. Finally, a vision is projected for the role of the University of Malta in effectively fostering innovation and nurturing Malta's drive toward a knowledge-based society. This vision will necessitate new legal and operational frameworks that will make for effective state–university–industry collaboration.

2   MODELS OF TECHNOLOGY TRANSFER

The literature is replete with definitions of knowledge and technology transfer that emphasize different aspects (for example, Hoffman, 1985; Williams and Gibson, 1990). In the context of country development, technology transfer can be seen as a process where by countries seeking development pursue the acquisition of proprietary know-how from foreign sources. Malecki (1991) holds that if a nation has been unable to develop its indigenous technological capability sufficiently to compete, it can obtain technology through transfers from other sources. This inflow of foreign technology can be either in the form of investments or in the form of direct technology flows (Janszewski, 1981). Cohen (2004) has argued that technology transfer can have transformational potential at the national level only if it is adapted, modified, improved, assimilated, and diffused in a cumulative way into the national system of the host country. Within the nation state, at least three main theoretical models of knowledge development have been put forward in the literature: Mode 2, National System of Innovation, and Triple Helix models.

Mode 2

Mode 2 represents the perspective put forward by Gibbons et al. (1994) in their book *The New Production of Knowledge: The Dynamics of Science and Research in Contemporary Societies*. Mode 1 represented the old model of scientific discovery characterized by the dominance of theoretical and experimental science within clearly defined disciplines and subdisciplines undertaken by independent scientists employed by autonomous universities. The authors saw Mode 2, which they claim took hold in the mid-twentieth century, as representing a paradigm shift where knowledge is said to have the following main characteristics:

- Knowledge is problem focused and generated in an application context. Knowledge is no longer seen as generated via 'pure' science but as using an 'objective' research process whose results might possibly have relevant applications and where any resultant practical aspects could act as the basis of technology transfer and management.
- Knowledge is 'trans-disciplinary', resident in individual research-ers, and generated from the employment and interaction of various individuals from different disciplines that together seek to solve a problem. Knowledge is therefore less likely to be found in patents and in the leading journals of individual disciplines.
- Knowledge is socially distributed and not limited to universities. It includes such others as consultants and think-tanks, and interaction is facilitated by the straightforward methods of communication that are available today.
- Knowledge is not subject to one standard but necessitates multiple accountabilities.

Knowledge that encompassed the above characteristics was considered in four main contexts. First, in the context of research commercialization such a perspective allowed for significant leeway when pitted against the view that characterized commercialization of research as a threat to sci-entific autonomy. The second context considered looks at mass university education. Here it is recognized that limits to funding coupled by a drive to expand student numbers and concurrently expand quality research might create conflicting objectives. It is argued that this tension results from the remnants of Mode 1 perspectives of research and that Mode 2 can facili-tate both mass education and the wider social dissemination of research undertaken. A third context considers the role of the humanities in making knowledge available. It is argued that in a Mode 2 perspective, the human-ities' role is recognized as it highlights the social role that is often distrusted by the natural sciences. A further context considered the globalization reality where it is also argued that a Mode 2 perspective of knowledge can unlock some of the contradictions that globalization produces.

Not surprisingly the reaction to Mode 2 has by no means been over-whelmingly positive (for example, Etzkowitz and Leydesdorff, 2000; Shinn, 2002). Moreover, Ziman (1996) has argued, not without justifica-tion, that governments are increasingly 'putting strict financial ceilings on their patronage' and that the interface being demanded of universities with industry precludes immediate publication of findings by identifying it 'as "intellectual" property, which may be kept secret for commercial reasons' (p. 752). The debate in this stream of research is ongoing and has been followed by the book *Re-thinking Science: Knowledge and the Public in an Age of Uncertainty* (Nowotny et al., 2001 – three of the original six authors) and by further reactions.

National System of Innovation

A National System of Innovation (NSI) (Freeman, 1987, 1995; Lundvall, 1992) has been defined as the network of institutions in the public and private sectors whose activities and interactions initiate, import, modify, and diffuse new technologies (Freeman, 1987, 1). The author focused on the situation of Japan whose strongly nationalistic strategy gave much importance to the pursuit of innovation. A main focus of the study was to understand the variety of actors, including government, education, firms, and research centers, that go to make the underlying NSI 'system'. The NSI concept emphasizes the role of various institutions in the innovation system. For example, Freeman describes Japanese education and notes that many engineers in Japan had a formal basic science background, received practical training and frequent upgrading within their industry together with across firm experiences that provided each with some understanding of the relationship among various operations so that 'the "system" approach is inculcated at all levels of the work force and not only at top management' (Freeman, 1987, 46).

Lundvall (1992), who focused primarily on North European countries, uses the NSI model to argue that the most fundamental resource in the modern economy is knowledge, necessitating that the process of learning should be taken into consideration in the context of interactions among institutions. Freeman (1995) highlights a major institutional innovation by the German dyestuffs industry when in 1870 they introduced on a regular, systematic, and professional basis, an in-house industry research and development (R&D) department. However, he observes that technical change does not depend only on R&D but also on many other related activities such as education, training, production, engineering, design, quality control, and so on. In emerging industries, R&D is often seen as the source of continuous innovation. To promote economic growth in developing countries, the government needs to strengthen technological capability to support the transition to a knowledge-based economy or a learning economy (Lundvall and Borras, 1999). However, it is clear that a 'systems' thinking approach is required if success is to be achieved.

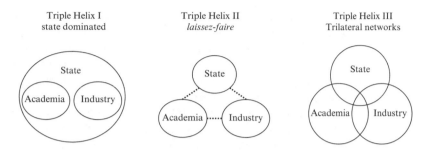

Figure 8.1   Modes of relationship among state, industry, and academia

Triple Helix Models

The Triple Helix model proposed by Etkowiz and Leydesdorff (2000) makes use of a biological DNA analogy to seek to describe the interlinked role of state–university–industry interaction. The model gives considerable importance to the role of universities as agents for innovation and suggests this as a 'natural' progression from a Mode 2 and an NSI approach. The authors describe three Triple Helix model arrangements that they number sequentially and evolutionarily as I, II, and III (ibid.).

Triple Helix I is that encountered in the former Soviet Union and many of its then satellite states. Here the nation state encompassed academia and industry and controlled and directed the relations among them (see Figure 8.1). Triple Helix I is considered a failed model, and its structure impedes bottom-up initiatives. A number of Latin American countries have maintained aspects of this model where the state is expected to coordinate industry and academia toward a common development goal. For example, in Argentina, Sábato's triangle concept provided government with a rationale to coordinate university and industry in order to develop new technologies and industries (Sábato and Botana, 1968; Sábato, 1997).

An alternative model of industry–state–university relations, Triple Helix II, represents the *laissez-faire* model of relations where the three entities have clear and separate institutional spheres with minimal interaction among the different entities (see Figure 8.1). This can be underlined by a political philosophy that gives prominence to minimal state intervention and can be a first reaction for a system moving out from a Triple Helix I structure. MacLane (1996) has opposed close industry–university interaction, arguing that the bottom line of universities is not and should not be measured in dollars or technological advances but rather on ideas and intellectual creativity. He saw the university as needing to take the long view. If it did not, it would compromise its value. He believed that universities were one of the best ways society had devised to accomplish the difficult task of discovering and evaluating ideas and transmitting them to new generations. He also argues that academic technology transfer mechanisms such as encapsulating knowledge in patents might bring about unnecessary costs. He does not view these patents as enabling mechanisms, and points out that knowledge can be transferred more easily without them. In Sweden, the Research 2000 Report takes a similar stance and argues that the role of the university should be research and teaching. It recommends withdrawal from any envisaged direct contribution to industry (Etzkowitz and Leydesdorff, 2000). In these perspectives universities should pursue basic research funded as an end in itself that might provide only long-term practical results.

Triple Helix III involves the development of trilateral networks and hybrid organizations and is put forward as the ultimate progression that can provide an alternative dynamic for innovation in national economies (see Figure 8.1). Triple Helix III is seen as being able to generate a knowledge infrastructure in terms of the three overlapping spheres of state, academia, and industry, with each taking the role of the other and with hybrid organizations emerging at the interfaces. It acknowledges that while a 'hands-off' posture might have been successful in the past, today's circumstances require a more intensive interrelationship (ibid.). Etzkowitz and Leydesdorff claim,

> The common objective is to realize an innovative environment consisting of university spin-off firms, tri-lateral initiatives for knowledge based economic development, and strategic alliances among firms (large and small, operating in different areas, and with different levels of technology), government laboratories, and academic research groups. Such arrangements are often encouraged, but not controlled, by government. (112)

3 THE UNIVERSITY OF MALTA UNTIL INDEPENDENCE

A historical perspective that looks at the role of the University of Malta since its origin in 1592 until independence in 1964 shows that international developments that occurred from the nineteenth century until independence seem largely not to have penetrated the insularity of Malta. Before independence, Malta had little industry and what evolved was largely an elite 'professional university' that catered primarily to sustaining the then established professions. The epoch up to independence can be conveniently split into the period of the Knights of Malta from 1592 to 1798, followed by the British period from 1800 to independence in 1964.

Malta under the Knights of St John and the University of Malta

The arrival of the Order of St John in 1530 was an important milestone in Malta's development. The Knights came from some of the best families in Europe. They brought considerable wealth to the islands and built Valletta, together with many other buildings and fortifications. They also improved much of the infrastructure. Malta could never provide enough wheat for its population and with increased prosperity the population also grew. Ensuring supply was a constant concern. With the Knights came also the fleet of the Order and the Knights, together with the locals, were very much involved in corsairing against the Ottoman Turks. These activities, which brought considerable wealth, required facilities for vessels to be built and serviced. Although a dockyard is first mentioned in November 1374 (Wettinger, 1993, 66), given the important maritime component of the Order, it was natural for them to expand and improve this sector. The Order saw to the development of the Arsenal and of fully fledged dockyard facilities.

During the time of the Knights there existed two other powers in Malta, that of the Roman Catholic Church and of the Holy Inquisition. The Church dominated everyday life but was one of the main movers in the development of education. As early as 1578, the Jesuits were empowered by papal decree to confer the degrees of *Magister Philosophiae* and *Doctor Divinitas*. Indeed, the university traces its origin to the founding of the *Collegium Melitense* by the Jesuits, which was set up through direct papal intervention in 1592. The foundation deed specified that besides philosophy and theology, other subjects such as grammar and the humanities should be taught. This college was run by the Jesuits similar to their other colleges established elsewhere and also provided higher education (Leaver, 2001). 'In 1727, the Jesuit College was enhanced with the faculty to confer academic degrees on its students' (Borg, 1974, 230).

The wave of opposition to the Jesuits that swept Europe in the mid-eighteenth century also reached Malta, and the Jesuits were banished from Malta in 1768. Grand Master Pinto appropriated all the revenue accruing from their property on the island with the aim of establishing a *Pubblica Università di Studi Generali*. Pinto signed the decree constituting the University on 22 November 1769. The three founding faculties were those of theology, law, and medicine. At the time a number of other foreign professors were brought over to help establish the university. However, both the Chancellor and the Rector were appointed by the Grand Master not by the university itself (Leaver, 2001).

Until the British period, the university had three faculties – theology, law, and medicine – that were very much concerned with creating professionals. The state controlled the top appointments and provided funding, while the Church continued to have significant influence as many of the academics were prelates. The Faculty of Theology provided a flow of trained ecclesiastics who helped ensure continuity. The same can be said of the Faculty of Law, which provided the legal professionals that enabled the functioning of the courts and legal system very much in the tradition that had developed over the centuries. The roots of the Faculty of Medicine are intertwined with the fact that the Knights of the Order of St John were Knights Hospitallers and as part of their *raison d'être*, ran the *Sacra Infermeria*. This was the principal hospital on the island and reputed at the time to be among the best hospitals in Europe. The provision and running of a hospital and medical facilities brought to Malta an important technological transfer. It was Grand Master Cotoner who in 1676 appointed Giuseppe Zammit as '*lettore*' in Anatomy and Surgery and took charge of courses in these areas conducted at the *Sacra Infermeria*. This attempt at formalizing medical teaching at the Order's hospital is considered the beginning of the medical faculty of the university. The Faculty of Medicine was very much tied to providing the medical practitioners and the staff required to enable the functioning of the *Sacra Infermeria*.

Malta under the British and the University of Malta

The Order of St John had been weakened by the French revolution when much of the Order's estates in France were confiscated and revenues consequently dried up. In Malta the Order had grown despotic and when, in June 1798, Napoleon appeared outside Malta's Grand Harbour, many French knights were not willing to offer any resistance. The Napoleonic forces came ashore and after some skirmishes the Order quickly capitulated. However, French rule was short-lived. By early September the Maltese population had taken up arms against the excesses undertaken by the French administration. The Maltese, with eventual assistance from the British, sustained the blockade of the French in Valletta until the French surrendered in September 1800. Malta passed from under the Knights to the French and on to the British as a protectorate and later a colony.

Malta's location and its fine harbors have been both its attraction and its curse. It has been an attraction because it has made it a coveted location that could provide a military naval base to anyone who wished to dominate the Mediterranean. This fact brought to Malta a certain degree of overseas investment and development. Yet this has also been Malta's curse because it has inevitably meant political domination. The dockyard of the Knights evolved into a Royal Navy Dockyard with further expansion and the later addition of dry docking facilities. The use of Malta by the Royal Navy as their main naval base in the Mediterranean had a direct effect on the island. Malta would suffer depression during times of peace and boom during times of tension and rumors of war.

During the brief French interlude, formal university teaching came to an end as Napoleon abolished the university. Fortunately, a few weeks after the French were forced to leave, the British reinstituted the university. In 1836 a Royal Commission that looked at the workings of the university put forward suggestions that resulted in a statute that 'vested control of the University of Malta in the Rector who was responsible only to the Head of Government. The courses were to be divided into four faculties: Philosophy and Arts; Medicine; Law; and Theology, with each of these Faculties having its own special Council' (Leaver, 2001, 24). In 1915 the university increased its faculties from four to six, by separating literature and science and raising the course of engineering and architecture to faculty status. A seventh, the Faculty of Dental Surgery, was added in 1954 (Savona-Ventura, 1996). During the British period the university underwent a series of changes in its statutes and regulations, sometimes gaining and sometimes losing autonomy. Full autonomy occurred in 1947 when the university came in line with other universities in the United Kingdom.

The addition of the Faculty of Engineering and Architecture in 1915 was very much in line with the earlier faculties of theology, law, and medicine. The engineering aspect was building, not industrial engineering. During their stay in Malta the British continued to strengthen and add to the fortifications and installations built by the Knights. Malta has no mineral resources but its rock layer includes Globigerina limestone that is used extensively in all buildings and characterizes Malta's own unique built environment. Mallia (2001) notes that the building technology employed is based on third-century Nabatean technology imported into Malta during the Early Middle Ages. The professionally trained architects, engineers, or town planners brought in by the Order of St John in 1566 to advise them on their building programs very often learned from the vigorous building tradition that already existed on the islands. Although the resulting buildings display a classical façade and plan, the construction techniques employed are traditional Maltese (Mahoney, 1988, 80). The Faculty of Engineering and Architecture like those of theology, law, and medicine produced enough graduates to sustain their respective profession in a very limited market.

Until the end of the Second World War, it was not possible to talk of industry in Malta as there was practically none. Fenech (2005, 249–56) who researched Malta between the First and Second World Wars describes it as follows:

Malta's fundamental problem was its particular form of underdevelopment. The island was overpopulated, had no natural resources, little agricultural land, and next to no manufacturing bar a couple of small factories and cottage industries such as lace, tobacco products, and residual cotton spinning and weaving. Agriculture rendered about a third of Malta's wheat requirement, fresh vegetables and fruit for local consumption, and a few cash crops for export . . . Otherwise, the chief civilian economic sector was commerce . . . Then there were the activities relating to defense, which by the turn of the century had come to rule Malta's urban economic life . . . The Services retained such a crucial place in the economy that for many people the erratic movements of the [British] fleet could make all the difference between coping and hardship. . . . The Office of Charitable Institutions administered the State hospitals, asylums and orphanages, government dispensaries, the poorhouse, and the *Monte di Pietà* (pawning office) . . . Otherwise State and society relied heavily on the wide-ranging parallel network of charitable institutions run by the church and religious orders.

During the Second World War Malta fought alongside the British and the Allies, and British fighter bombers and submarines from Malta were instrumental in sinking many of the supplies leaving Italy and destined for Rommel's forces in North Africa. Malta was in turn very heavily bombed and blockaded. The population faced starvation and Malta had the questionable distinction of being the most heavily bombed place during the Second World War – even more than Stalingrad. The university building in Valletta was among those hit. Malta after the war was in ruins, employment was in short supply, and many people emigrated. After the war, the British government pursued a policy of military expenditure reduction with major consequences on those employed with the services and at the Naval Dockyard. The Maltese-elected representatives sought to slow down this process and extract as much development support as possible, while arguing among themselves whether to seek integration with Britain or independence and later what form of independence.

The decline of the British Empire and the cutbacks in the Royal Navy saw the dockyard become a commercial dockyard in 1959 and it was nationalized in 1968. There can be little doubt that the dockyards provided an important foundation for Malta's industrialization. The technological challenge provided by building and repairing what has always been the largest piece of equipment of its time inevitably led to a technological culture among the people involved in this work and a familiarity with the most important technologies (Ghirlando, 1993, 537). The Dockyard School that was created in 1858 together with the Dockyard Apprenticeship Scheme was responsible for producing some of Malta's first engineers (Ellul Galea, 1973). Ghirlando (1993, 545) observes that when a new degree course in engineering was started in 1963, it was

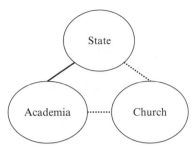

Figure 8.2   Pre-industrial Triple Helix model

initially held at the former Dockyard School and included dockyard apprentices who were sponsored to pursue degrees.

Malta's size and its colonial history make the circumstances of its university rather atypical. The Knights of Malta and later the British colonial administration preferred to keep strong and direct control over the university. Up to independence there was practically no industry of any size with the exception of the dockyard. It is therefore difficult to speak of any Triple Helix arrangement that included industry, and it was perhaps the Church rather than industry that continued to wield considerable influence and constituted a third element into what can be proposed as a pre-industrial Triple Helix model (see Figure 8.2).

All universities are focused on teaching but it is argued that what provides them with their stance is the degree to which they undertake research and to what extent they are involved with industry in their research. Use is therefore made of the dimensions of 'Research Focus' and 'Industry Focus' to suggest a matrix that describes the emerging university characteristics arising from the adoption of particular state–academia–industry configurations or alternatives. Ever since its inception until at least independence, the University of Malta operated in the pre-industrial Triple Helix model as depicted in Figure 8.2. By the end of the British period the original faculties of theology, law, and medicine that existed until the times of the Order were augmented by literature and science, engineering, architecture, and dental surgery. This array of faculties underlined the university's focus on professional training that necessitated high industry involvement in terms of considerable teaching input by trained proficient practitioners in the different professions. Almost inevitably, the research output of such an institution was limited. A university characterized by these properties can be described as a Professional University (see lower left-hand quadrant of the matrix in Figure 8.3). The late-nineteenth-century development that added research as an integral mission of the university in many parts of the

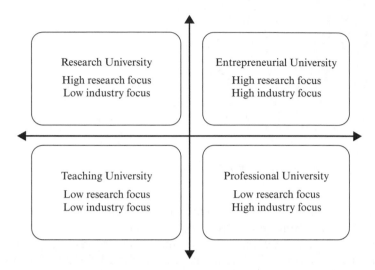

Figure 8.3   Stance in university evolution

world mostly passed Malta by. There are exceptions: an example is Temi Zammit, who had specialized in bacteriology in London and Paris and who in 1905 discovered that brucellosis was transmitted by goats' milk. Sir Temi Zammit (he was subsequently knighted in 1930) contributed significantly to the elimination of undulant fever in Malta.

4 MALTA AFTER INDEPENDENCE, INDUSTRIALIZATION, AND THE UNIVERSITY OF MALTA

Malta became independent in 1964, and the British military base came to an end in 1979. Much of the rapid growth achieved in Malta's economy has taken place since independence. It has also been a period that has witnessed a gradual erosion of the influence of the Church. The major challenge faced by subsequent Maltese governments has been to ensure employment. The 1960s were characterized by two main industrialization thrusts involving the development of tourism and manufacturing, primarily of textiles and clothing.

Tourism was identified as a potential source of jobs and source of foreign revenue. Its growth mirrored what was happening in other parts of the Mediterranean with a growing number of arrivals and construction projects aimed at meeting demand. Investors were provided with various prime sites often at nominal cost. Initially most of the tourists were British and this remained so for a number of years. Numbers grew steadily to reach 725,580 tourists in 1980 with 76.24 percent being British.

From 1981 the local currency appreciated against the sterling, and the number of tourist arrivals dropped, reaching a low point of 477,626 in 1984. The introduction of an exchange rate support mechanism started a reversal while later marketing repositioning activities that followed a strategic review by Horwath & Horwath (1989) involved activities aimed at diversification to other European markets. An emphasis on special interest products enabled growth that saw tourist arrivals reach 1.2 million in 2008. When tourism started, Malta had few hotels and minimal infrastructure. Some facilities that catered to the British military base existed but hotels needed to be built. Many of the hotels that came to Malta in the early period brought along practices of hotel management and operations that did not previously exist.

Today tourism has become very much a local industry. Most of the hotels are locally owned as many who made money from the construction booms that took place have invested in hotels often running franchises of international brands. The setting up of Air Malta in 1974 with support from Pakistan International Airlines was an important infrastructural development as it enabled greater diversification of the local product and represented an important transfer of technology.

Manufacturing was primarily in the textiles and clothing sector. The growth of this sector in Malta came about as the industry moved ever farther south in the 1960s and 1970s and eventually east around the turn of the century in its pursuit of cheaper manufacturing cost. By 1985 there were 165 firms in the textiles and clothing sector employing 8,835 employees who represented 33 percent of all employment in manufacturing. Foreign investors typically transferred their manufacturing technology to the different countries of operation but key functions and control rested with the central office where the firm was based. Any transfer of technology was a means to an end; that end being profit but the technology that was transferred enabled the start of an important integration of Malta within the global economy. Moreover, once outputs had to be sold in a competitive market, it no longer was just a question of substituting labor with cheaper labor but a recognition that innovations that improved quality in production needed to be developed and incorporated. Yet power rested with the owner who knew the market and processed information as to how to make the technology work. Owners had an interest in transferring technology but could not afford to risk creating new competitors (Grech, 1978).

Transfer of technology was instrumental in fostering an industrial

Table 8.1   Students at the University of Malta, 1964–2008

Academic year	1964–65	1974–75	1984–85	1994–95	2004–05	2008–09
Students	547	1,042	1,408	5,805	9,530	9,665
Males	447	740	984	3,011	4,152	4,114
Females	100	302	424	2,794	5,378	5,551

Source: NSO, Education Statistics, Malta.

mentality and the required attitude to work. The first-generation factory workers were mostly young unmarried females employed on the factory floor in line production processes. This was a significant social step as for the first time Maltese society with a strong Catholic ethic accepted that women could work outside the home in industry – a situation that was previously not socially accepted as it was believed that a woman's place was in the home. Eventually it became acceptable that women continue in employment until they got married; later, until they had their first child and even later to have children and return to work. The new factories also fostered management roles that did not previously exist. Middle-management positions became available and in these roles of organizer, the people involved learned to ensure how the production process could be supported to continue to function. Senior management positions were initially occupied by overseas nationals but over time were replaced by locals.

Four years after independence, in 1968, the new campus of the University of Malta outside Valletta was inaugurated and all six faculties were relocated there, with the exception of the Medical School which moved near St Luke's Hospital, the islands' main general hospital. The gradual rise of industry and the slow but sure decline in the influence of the Church together with a growing university student population (see Table 8.1) could have eventually given rise to a Triple Helix II arrangement. Instead, a situation that more closely resembled Triple Helix I resulted.

The Labour government elected in the period from 1971 to 1986 took an increasingly interventionist approach to the Maltese economy. This involved the nationalization of various industries including the two major banks, the telecommunications company, and the port and airport operations. In addition, the state also undertook a range of direct industrial investment and followed a policy of import substitution so that by 1985 there were 709 firms employing just over 4,000 people in the food and furniture industries – two industries composed of small local firms that were heavily protected. Nevertheless, the state also continued to seek to attract foreign direct investment with some notable successes like ST Thompson as well as various German manufacturing firms.

It was in the pursuit of this policy that the university witnessed significant turmoil. The Education Amendment Act of 1978 restructured the style and pattern of higher education in Malta. It saw the amalgamation of parts of the 'Polytechnic' that ran mostly vocational type courses with the university to create two universities. On one hand, the Faculty of Engineering and Architecture together with the new Faculty of Education and that of Economics and Management studies were to form what was termed the 'New University'. On the other hand, the arts, science, and law faculties remained at the University of Malta, which was restyled the 'Old University'. The Faculty of Theology was withdrawn from the University of Malta and came under the auspices of the Church. A further amendment to the Education Act in 1980 changed the title 'New University' to 'University of Malta' and transferred to it the Faculty of Law while suppressing the arts and science faculty together with the 'Old University' (Savona-Ventura, 1996). The underlying premise was utilitarian with a desire to promote courses that were seen to be directly relevant to Malta's development. Research was officially frowned upon. Somewhat ironically for all the talk of change, with the suppression of the Faculties of Arts and Science, the university had become more of a Professional University; all the faculties now were about developing professionals who would have practical skills that it was believed industry required.

Change came with the enactment of the Education Act of 1988 that refounded the University of Malta. The reform sought to build a university that provided a broader range of courses that were complemented by a considerable growth in student numbers (see Table 8.1). As part of this process, three more faculties were added to the six that had remained. This involved the re-establishment of the arts and science faculties together with the reorganization of the Faculty of Engineering and Architecture, which was split into two separate faculties, namely the Faculty of Architecture and Civil Engineering (now the Faculty of Built Environment) and the Faculty of Mechanical and Electrical Engineering (now Faculty of Engineering). The Faculty of Theology was reunited with the university as its tenth faculty. With the addition of the new Faculty of Information and Communication Technology in 2008, there are now 11 faculties together with a number of centers and institutes that together in the academic year 2008–09 support 9,655 students of which 57.5 percent are women.

From a Professional University to a Teaching University

The last 20 years has seen the successful transformation of the University of Malta. The variety of courses available has increased considerably and significant academic effort has gone into course development. In spite of the very limited investment in research by both government and local industry, and the weak research milieu engendered in the university until the late 1990s, there have been some noteworthy individual success stories. These have stimulated the development of various sectors of the economy and society including: medicine, aquaculture and fish pathology, physiology and biochemistry, and various engineering disciplines, including information and communication technologies (ICTs).

To date, the University of Malta can be said to be operating as a Triple Helix II where although the university enjoys relative autonomy it still relies on the state for its annual budget while relations with industry are at an individual rather than at an institutional level. This position underscores a teaching university character with a portfolio of research and industry collaboration that is still embryonic (see Figure 8.3).

Malta in the EU, the University of Malta, and Research Commercialization

Malta became a member of the European Union in 2004 and adopted the euro on 1 January 2008. The island is undergoing rapid and radical socio-economic change, catalyzed and at the same time cushioned by EU membership. The European Union, and indeed the adoption of the euro, not only exposes Malta and furnishes it with access to a seamless European market space, but also provides the backbone of the operational and reference framework that will condition, and to a large extent enhance, Malta's future socio-economic development.

Having established its credentials as a mainstream European state, it is now crucial, perhaps more so than ever, that Malta projects a clear medium-term vision, as it is precisely this vision that should brand the country. As a member state at the southern frontier of the European Union, Malta can continue to play a significant role as a crossroad between the EU and North Africa. Moreover, as it has the hallmarks and the economic infrastructure of a strategic location for interregional and intercultural trade in a global economy, Malta's role in the Mediterranean invites it also to look beyond to North America, the Middle East, and the Far East.

In 1992, the government of the time commissioned the Malta Council for Science and Technology to compile its first national vision document, *Vision 2000* (MCST, 1992). *Vision 2000* projects Malta as a regional hub and identified information technology as a key economic driver: as a revenue-generating sector in its own right, but more importantly, as an indispensable revenue-support sector enhancing all other sectors of the economy.

Having started the process of civil service reform based on the introduction of information technology and modern-day management systems (MSU, 1998), in 1993 the government commissioned a broader study to formulate a National Strategy for Information Technology. Published in 1994 by the Malta Council for Science and Technology (see Camilleri, 1998), it laid the foundation for subsequent strategy reviews to the present day. Although much groundwork was laid for certain aspects in the interim period, it was the establishment in the late 1990s of a ministry dedicated to the formulation and implementation of the evolving national ICT strategy (MIIIT, 2007) that cut through the rhetoric, placed Malta on the international ICT map, and concretely attracted significant foreign direct investment into the country.

Today, some 10 years later, we witness the ICT vision unfolding into reality with the initiation of Smart City (http://www.smartcity.ae/malta/) that has become an inextricable part of brand Malta. The construction of Smart City is underway, and the quest to attract companies to build in or transfer their operations to this modern-day township has begun albeit dampened somewhat in the wake of the devastating economic recession that is setting in across the globe.

5   VISION 2015

In 2007, the Prime Minister of Malta made the following Vision statement (Gonzi, 2007): 'Our vision is of an intelligent European, Mediterranean island nation, promoting peace, security, justice and well-being, a smart hub generating wealth and prosperity and an incubator fostering expertise, innovation and entrepreneurship.' This statement inspired the formulation of *Vision 2015* that more concretely invites Malta to continue building on past success achieved in the following revenue-generating services sectors of the economy and to aspire to attain excellence thereto:

- *hospitality services*: destination, cultural, thematic, transit, conference tourism;
- *health and care services*: foreign patient care, retirement destination;
- *maritime services*: flag, trans-shipment, port, ship/boat/rigs, leisure, security;
- *business and financial services*: back-office, legal, banking and insurance, transaction processing, data warehousing, call-centers; and
- *educational services*: language schools, executive training, postgraduate schools, educational tourism.

Moreover it is reasonable to envisage that Malta's manufacturing and software development industries will depend more and more on the island's ability to move up the value chain in specific niches, which in turn, will require such industries to be backed by cost-efficiency, creative product development, and readily available expertise.

In short, Malta's future depends on the quality of its human capital; it depends on the aptitude, but, perhaps more so, on the attitude of its human resources. The strategic thrusts set in *Vision 2015* are no less than the initial steps in a quest to transform Malta into a knowledge and creative economy and society on a sector-by-sector basis. This said, not all of the sectors mentioned are at the same stage of development, and excellence will not be achieved unless the country engenders a culture of innovation and entrepreneurship.

From a Teaching University to an Entrepreneurial University

For Malta to attain the goals put forward in *Vision 2015* there is no doubt that the University of Malta must make the transition from a Teaching University to an Entrepreneurial University, but it must do so without compromising the quality and expansion of its teaching output. At present, the University of Malta is laying the legal foundations to strengthen its governance, to protect its intellectual property, and to build an institutional research portfolio. Moreover, the university is forging strategic alliances with leading international counterparts in a bid to create a portfolio of International Masters Programs and ancillary research collaborations. It is envisaged that the Old University Building in Valletta will be gradually transformed into an International Graduate School. The first programs were launched in September 2009.

In the wake of the rapid expansion of the university's teaching portfolio in the past two decades, many doctoral students who were sent abroad to pursue their studies have returned to a teaching post at the University of Malta. Unfortunately, a significant number, particularly those earning doctorates in the fields of engineering and science and technology, have not returned to Malta simply because, to date, the country has failed to create a milieu that is conducive to research, technological development, and innovation (RTDI). As the university is still building its teaching portfolio and capacity, most of those who return to the University of Malta on completion of their doctoral research have to immediately immerse themselves in a grueling teaching load that effectively stunts the growth of their research potential just as they are starting to become international currency.

The recent revision of the conditions of work for academic staff and the creation of alternative paths of career progression has marked a major

Policy and Identity		
Understanding and projecting the Maltese identity and refining the system of public and social policy formulation in Malta: • as an island and small state • *vis-à-vis* Europe and the Mediterranean region and • *vis-à-vis* global governance		
Technologies and systems to enhance the quality of services • Hospitality services • Health services • Financial services • Transportation services • Educational services • Communications services	**Technologies and systems to enhance high-value manufacturing** • Food • Electronics • Software development • Pharmaceutics • Other consumables	**Technologies and systems to enhance sustainable development** • Water • Alternative energy • Waste management • Coastal management • Marine • Agriculture
Fundamental science and technology • Digital technology and media • Biotechnology and pharmacology • Earth sciences	**Design and aesthetics** • Artistic and content design • Architectural and engineering design • Product design	

Figure 8.4   An institutional research framework for the University of Malta

milestone that will allow the university not only to enhance the quality of its teaching but also to expand its research portfolio and collaboration with industry: this, on the assumption that adequate financing will be available for more academic positions to be staffed. At present, the University of Malta lacks the crucial stratum of post-doctoral research fellows, and this is the principal reason why it has so far failed to project a significant and coordinated institutional RTDI portfolio. This is also one of the main reasons why Malta continues to lag behind *vis-à-vis* the Lisbon benchmarks with respect to RTDI.

Now that the collective agreement for academic staff provides the right enabling framework, the University of Malta needs to establish a post-doctorate research fellowship scheme that will support young outstanding researchers to dedicate their full-time effort to research initiatives that are essential to the socio-economic development of the islands. Among the targeted areas of priority are those identified in the National Strategic Plan for Research and Innovation 2007–2010 (MCST, 2006), namely: ICT, health-biotech, environment and energy resources, and value-added manufacturing and services.

Figure 8.4 illustrates an institutional research framework that the University of Malta can adopt as a reference framework to prioritize its medium- to long-term research projects. This framework identifies six overarching themes under which specific projects or research clusters can be developed in response to identified national socio-economic needs or opportunities, namely:

- policy formulation with an eye to the development of Maltese identity;
- technologies and systems to enhance the quality of services;
- technologies and systems to enhance high-value manufacturing;
- technologies and systems to enhance sustainable development;
- fundamental science and technology in priority niches; and
- design and aesthetics.

Notwithstanding the above, unless the university finds a way of sustaining a significant number of researchers working on coordinated projects within this framework, it will not be able to fulfill its potential as a leading driver of the development of the economy and society. The costs involved in building and sustaining research of international caliber in just one of the areas identified in Figure 8.4 suggests that the government must significantly increase its investment in RTDI at the university and thus come in line with the Lisbon targets. Moreover, the financing of the university must be seriously rethought: the university must be allowed to accrue assets; investment in infrastructure and equipment for teaching and research should be tax exempt; and government allocations should reflect the true cost basis of the teaching and research programs. Moreover, the setting up of a University of Malta Trust Fund for Research, Development, and Innovation and the updating of legislation to allow tax incentives for donors is a crucial step forward.

If the University of Malta is to continue to build on its legacy of excellence, and if it is to contribute fully to the implementation of Malta's Vision 2015 and beyond, then the Education Act, the law that regulates the governance of the university, must be revised. At present, the governing structures of the university are not conducive to modern management practice and academic auditing and accountability need to be improved. In tandem, the university's autonomy also needs to be strengthened: today government funding comes at the price of cumbersome procurement procedures, bureaucracy, and procrastination. Finally, the university must be given broader latitude to generate and accrue its own funds.

Discussions between the government and the university have started to address the concerns outlined above. The target is clear: the national vision expressed by the prime minister can only be achieved if the university is empowered to become an Entrepreneurial University, and this in turn can only be achieved via trilateral initiatives where government, academia, and industry work in cooperation towards a Triple Helix III mode of operation.

REFERENCES

Borg, V. (1974), 'Developments in education outside the Jesuit "*Collegium Melitense*"', *Melita Historica*, **6** (3): 215–54.
Camilleri, J. (1998), 'A national strategy for information technology', in R. Mansell and U. When (eds), *Knowledge Societies: Information Technology for Sustainable Development*, Oxford: United Nations Publication, Oxford University Press, pp. 152–66.
Cohen, G. (2004), *Technology Transfer: Strategic Management in Developing Countries*, New Delhi: Sage.
Ellul Galea, K. (1973), *L-istorja tat-Tarzna: Studju, Tagħrif, Analiżi*, Pieta, Malta: Ħajja Printing Press.
Etzkowitz, H. and L. Leydesdorff (2000), 'The dynamics of innovation: from national systems and Mode 2 to Triple Helix of university–industry–government relations', *Research Policy*, **29**: 109–23.
Fenech, D. (2005), *Responsibility and Power in Inter-war Malta: Book 1*, San Gwann, Malta: Peg Publishing.
Freeman, C. (1987), *Technology and Economic Performance: Lessons from Japan*, London: Pinter.
Freeman, C. (1995), 'The national system of innovation in historical perspective', *Cambridge Journal of Economics*, **19**: 5–24.
Ghirlando, R. (1993), 'Birgu – birthplace of Malta's technological society', in L. Bugeja, M. Buhagiar and S. Fiorini (eds), *Birgu: A Maltese Maritime City*, Vol. II Msida, Malta: Malta University Press, pp. 535–46.
Gibbons, M., C. Limoges, H. Nowotny, S. Schwartzman, P. Scott and M. Trow (1994), *The New Production of Knowledge: The Dynamics of Science and Research in Contemporary Societies*, London: Sage.
Gonzi, L. (2007), 'Growing stronger, talking point', *The Times*, April 25.
Grech, J.C. (1978), *Threads of Dependence*, Msida, Malta: Malta University Press.
Hoffman, L. (1985), 'The transfer of technology to developing countries', *Intereconomics*, **20** (3): 263–72.
Horwath & Horwath (UK) Ltd (1989), *The Maltese Islands Tourism Development Plan*, London: Horwath & Horwath.
Jansizewski, H.A. (1981), 'Technology – importing: national perspectives', in T. Sagafi-Nejad, H.V. Perlmutter, and R.W. Moxon (eds), *Controlling International Technology Transfer*, New York: Pergamon, pp. 321–5.
Leaver, A.J. (2001), *Malta's Ancient Seat of Learning: A Guide to the Old University of Malta*, San Gwann, Malta: Peg Publishing.
Lundvall, B.-Å. (ed.) (1992), *National Innovation Systems: Towards a Theory of Innovation and Interactive Learning*, London: Pinter.
Lundvall, B.-Å. and S. Borras (1999), *The Globalising Learning Economy:*

Implications for Innovation Policy, Luxembourg: Office for Official Publications of the European Communities.

MacLane, S. (1996), 'Should universities imitate industry?', *American Scientist*, **84** (6): 520–21.

Mahoney, L. (1988), *A History of Maltese Architecture from Ancient Times to 1800*, Zabbar, Malta: Veritas Press.

Malecki, E.J. (1991), *Technology and Economic Development*, London: Longman.

Mallia, D. (2001), 'Building technology transfer between Malta and the Middle East: a two way process', International Millennium Congress – Archi 2000 ICOMOS Proceedings UNESCO, Paris, 10–12 September, available at: http://www.unesco.org/archi2000/pdf/mallia.pdf (accessed March 2009).

MCST (1992), *Vision 2000: Malta a Mediterranean Hub Based on Information Technology*, Valletta, Malta: Malta Council for Science and Technology.

MCST (2006), *The National Strategic Plan for Research and Innovation 2007–2010: Building and Sustaining the R&I Enabling Framework*, Valletta, Malta: Malta Council for Science and Technology.

MIIIT (2007), *The Smart Island: The National ICT Strategy for Malta 2008–2010*, Valletta, Malta: Ministry for Investment, Industry, and Information Technology.

MSU (1998), *Information Systems Strategic Plan (ISSP) for the Public Service (1999–2001)*, Valletta, Malta: Management Systems Unit.

National Office of Statistics (NSO) (annual) 'Education Statistics, 1964–2008', National Statistics Office, available at: http://www.nso.gov.mt/site.page.aspx.

Nowotny, H., P. Scott and M. Gibbons (2001), *Re-thinking Science: Knowledge and the Public in an Age of Uncertainty*, Cambridge: Polity Press.

Sábato, J.A. (1997), 'Bases para un régimen de tecnología', *Redes*, **4** (10): 119–37.

Sábato J. and N. Botana (1968), 'La Ciencia y la Tecnología en el Desarrollo Futuro de America Latina', paper presented at the World Order Models conference, Bellagio, Italy, 25–30 September.

Savona-Ventura, C. (1996), 'The health of the Maltese population', Internet Home Page at: http://www.geocities.com/savona.geo/index.html (accessed March 2009).

Shinn, T. (2002), 'The Triple Helix and new production of knowledge: prepackaged thinking on science and technology', *Social Studies of Science*, **32**: 599–614.

Wettinger, G. (1993), 'The Castrum Maris and its suburb of Birgu during the Middle Ages', in L. Bugeja, M. Buhagiar and S. Fiorini (eds), *Birgu: A Maltese Maritime City*, Vol. I, Msida: Malta: Malta University Press, pp. 31–71.

Williams, F. and D.V. Gibson (eds) (1990), *Technology Transfer: A Communication Perspective*, Newbury Park, CA: Sage.

Ziman, J. (1996), 'Is science losing its objectivity?', *Nature*, **382**, August, 751–4.

9. Technology transfer in Mexico: trends in public policies and the program at Monterrey International City of Knowledge

Jaime Parada Ávila

1 INTRODUCTION: OVERVIEW OF FRAMEWORK CONDITIONS FOR INNOVATION AND TECHNOLOGY TRANSFER IN MEXICO

Technology transfer (TT) is a very important element for the economic development of a country or region. It can be defined as the transfer of new technologies across international borders, generally from developed countries to others still in development, or, at a local level, from universities or research institutes to third parties capable of commercializing the technology as new services or products.

In Mexico, the Foundation for the National Award in Technology, in its glossary, defines technology transfer as the ordered and systematic flow of technologies in an organization, either done internally or externally. In the latter case, it is normally regulated by a commercial agreement that involves economic remuneration. Although there is already an official norm for terminology in technology management (NMXGT001IMNC2007), which defines technology transfer, the process itself is not established as a systematic transfer of technologies among Mexico's national research centers and universities to the industrial sector, which might explain the minimal impact of the national science and technology policies in the economic development of the country.

If one compares the gross domestic expenditures on R&D (GERD) financed by the productive sector in some of the main Organisation for Economic Co-operation and Development (OECD) countries with the situation in Mexico (see Table 9.1), one sees that the level of expenditure is significantly lower in Mexico (Dutrénit et al., 2008, 18).

In the current context of liberalization and economic deregulation,

Table 9.1   Mexico: R&D intensity, selected sectors

Classification by technological intensity	R&D / Value added		
	OECD	Mexico	Gap Mexico/ OECD%
High-tech industries			
Pharmaceuticals	22.3	0.35	1.56
Office equipment, accounting and computing machinery	25.8	0.11	0.41
Radio, TV and communications equipment	17.9	0.04	0.20
Medical, precision and optical devices	24.6	0.15	0.60
Upper medium-tech industries			
Machinery and electrical appliances	9.1	0.49	5.38
Motor vehicles	13.3	0.44	3.31
Chemical products (except pharmaceutical)	8.3	0.79	9.50
Other transport equipment	8.7	0.18	2.11
Other machinery and equipment	5.8	0.02	0.26
Low medium-tech industries			
Rubber and plastic products	3.1	1.04	33.68
Carbon, petroleum derivates and nuclear energy	2.7	0.18	6.77
Fabricated metal products (except machinery)	1.9	0.29	15.30
Basic metal and metallic products	1.9	1.10	57.92
Low tech industries			
Other manufacturing	1.3	1.29	99.59
Good, paper, printing and publishing	1	1.37	137.03
Food, beverages and tobacco	1.1	0.11	10.43
Textiles, textile products, leather	0.8	0.21	26.18
Total manufacturing	7.20	0.45	6.30

Note: Based on data from 12 OECD countries: US, Canada, Japan, Denmark, Finland, France, Germany, Ireland, Italy, Spain, Sweden, and UK.

Source: OECD: At-JBERD and STAN databases, May 2003.

the lack of science, technology and innovation (STI) capability has led to specialization in market segments characterized by low-technology-based value-added industries in local and globalized productive processes. Today, although there is a trend toward manufacturing high-value-added, high-technology products in the Mexican industry, the industrial manufacturing is still dominated by the low-value commodities (Figure 9.1).

Over time, not only has the Mexican government created programs, tools, and mechanisms to promote STI capabilities but also at the state level, local governments have established institutions and agencies to

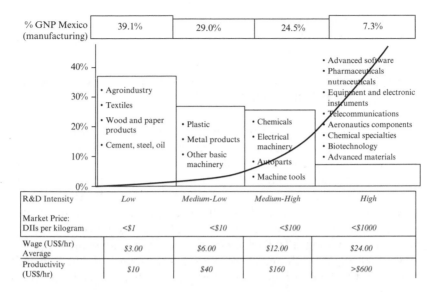

% GNP Mexico (manufacturing)	39.1%	29.0%	24.5%	7.3%

R&D Intensity	Low	Medium-Low	Medium-High	High
Market Price: DIIs per kilogram	<$1	<$10	<$100	<$1000
Wage (US$/hr) Average	$3.00	$6.00	$12.00	$24.00
Productivity (US$/hr)	$10	$40	$160	>$600

Note: Most of Mexico's industrial production is in low-value commodities.

Figure 9.1 Composition of Mexican industrial production

help with the task. The National Council for Science and Technology (CONACYT) is perhaps the best-known institution created by the federal government to foster STI, and it may well be considered the core of the national innovation system (NIS). In a broad sense, NIS represents an innovation ecosystem, which for Mexico's purposes is defined as the set of elements (agents, organizations, or institutions) from the academic, business, and government sectors, whose activities and interactions result in the production, dissemination, assimilation, and conversion of technological knowledge into new products or services or advanced manufacturing technologies. It is within this ecosystem, that in Mexico, as in any other country, TT is done under a legal framework.

Since 2001, the NIS has undergone a series of transformations and reforms promoted mainly by structural reforms in the federal government and legislation, which has resulted in the industrial sector's growing awareness of the long-term benefits that a close relationship with the universities and research centers might bring.

The main features of the Mexican NIS and the key actors and its interactions are also reflected at a regional level. In this context, the role of CONACYT is virtually the same across the country, but it depends on the local actors (academia, enterprises, and state and local governments) for how well the policies, tools, and instruments are used and complemented at the state level to attain an effective regional innovation ecosystem (RIS).

2 THE ROLE OF CONACYT AS STI POLICY MAKER AND ITS PROGRAMS

The role of the federal government in the NIS is mainly carried out by CONACYT, which regulates the framework to support and promote STI. Accordingly, the Council establishes the policies, legal framework, programs, instruments, and evaluation mechanisms to modify the performance of the other key actors in STI activities. CONACYT is the entity responsible for dictating STI policies for the federal government and disposes of an important portion of the total federal budget reserved for science and technology (S&T). Programs such as the scholarship program, the National System of Researchers (NSR), the System of Public Research Centers, and the fund programs for fostering S&T are directly under its administration.

In 2006, the total budget administrated by CONACYT amounted to US$508 million, which represented 17 percent of the total federal expenditures in science and technology. The resources were distributed in the main programs as follows: scientific and technological research (26.6 percent); scholarship program (37.6 percent); and NSR (26.6 percent). These resources allowed CONACYT to support around 20,111 postgraduate students (44.8 percent PhDs and 55.2 percent Masters), 900 scientific and technological projects, and 13,485 researchers with a membership in the NRS program (Dutrénit et al., 2008, 35).

Mexico must emphasize the STI policy to direct the NIS towards more experimental development, so understanding the need to produce more relevant research products to be transferred to the industry and generate a healthy TT practice, CONACYT has designated a larger budget to encourage project proposals in this area. Since 2001, it has implemented new subprograms for technology development and for the creation of new technology businesses under the shelter of the Special Program of Science and Technology (PECyT). The PECyT defines strategic sector and regional programs, based on the strategic knowledge fields, and consists of a proactive policy mix for the promotion of:

- public/private research and development (R&D);
- consortia and research networks of excellence;
- private investment in S&T activities;
- university–enterprise linkages;

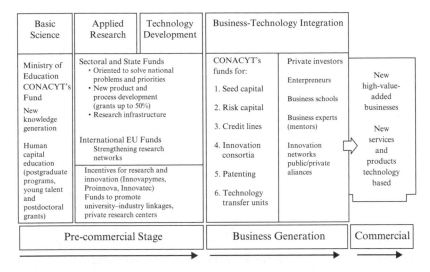

Basic Science	Applied Research	Technology Development	Business-Technology Integration		
Ministry of Education CONACYT's Fund

New knowledge generation

Human capital education (postgraduate programs, young talent and postdoctoral grants) | Sectoral and State Funds
• Oriented to solve national problems and priorities
• New product and process development (grants up to 50%)
• Research infrastructure

International EU Funds
Strengthening research networks

Incentives for research and innovation (Innovapymes, Proinnova, Innovatec)
Funds to promote university–industry linkages, private research centers | | CONACYT's funds for:

1. Seed capital

2. Risk capital

3. Credit lines

4. Innovation consortia

5. Patenting

6. Technology transfer units | Private investors

Enterpreneurs

Business schools

Business experts (mentors)

Innovation networks public/private aliances | New high-value-added businesses

New services and products technology based |
| Pre-commercial Stage | | | Business Generation | | Commercial |

Note: CONACYT's science and technology policy mix of programs and instruments tries to advance the productive sector towards the new economy.

Figure 9.2 CONACYT's main programs and instruments, 2001–2008

- innovation and competitiveness; and
- intellectual property (IP).

CONACYT's Main Programs and Instruments

More than 60 funds or programs have come to life following the objectives of the PECyT. They are oriented to promoting and funding basic and problem-oriented research, the regionalization of the innovation system, R&D in private companies, innovative projects from entrepreneurs, and the formation of highly specialized human resources. The most important programs and subprograms of the current Mexican STI policy mix are shown in Figure 9.2, and we shall discuss briefly the ones considered most important to promote innovation and TT practices.

Sector funds

With concurrent resources provided 50:50 CONACYT: state ministries or government agencies, the funds aim to promote the development and consolidation of STI capabilities according to the strategic goals of the ministry. To date, there are 18 sector funds that open at least once a year for proposals' reception. The two funds considered the most important are:

- *Sector Fund Public Education Ministry–CONACYT*: Promotes the development of scientific and technological research of the highest quality in the strategic areas needed to strengthen the NIS and the NSR.
- *Sector Fund for Economic Development based on Science and Technology*: The Ministry of Economy and CONACYT's resources combine in this fund to encourage innovation and technological development projects in the industry. Technology transfer is given a boost in this fund, as the project selection and evaluation gives better scores to proposals presenting evidence of a company's linkage with universities or public research centers. Companies must present the proposals, and up to 50 percent of the project expenses are covered by the fund.

Mix funds
CONACYT created these funds in partnerships with state or municipal governments, providing 50:50 concurrent resources for a trust, intending to translate the PECyT to motivate regional STI capabilities and develop scientific and technological projects according to local demands. In 2008, there were 32 mix funds.

Institutional funds
CONACYT reserves a large portion of its budget for programs that are deemed strategic and where the institution is solely responsible for its good performance (AVANCE, scientists' repatriation, researchers' incentives, and formation of human resources in science and technology).

AVANCE (high value added in businesses with knowledge and entrepreneurship)
The objective of this subprogram is to foster new companies that are based on innovative products and processes resulting from technology and scientific research projects. Established companies can participate in the program as long as they are developing a new line of products or services. The fund furnishes resources to be employed during the phase of transition between research and prototype (Last Mile), as well as provide leverage in the phase of capitalization of the company.

AVANCE is a program that includes: Last Mile, Entrepreneurship Fund, Credit Lines, Fund for Technology Transfer Units, and School of Business. AVANCE explicitly calls for proposals in the strategic areas of: information and communications, biotechnology, materials, advanced manufacturing processes, and urban and rural development infrastructure. Public research centers (PRCs) and higher education institutions

(HEIs) can participate if the proposal involves technology transfer to a company or plans for the establishment of a spin-off company belonging to the researcher or the institution.

In the first two calls for proposals, 2003 and 2005, AVANCE received 580 applications, more than 65 percent coming from companies and the rest largely from PRCs and HEIs. One hundred and forty projects were approved. According to the CONACYT's Work Report 2008 published on its website, by the end of 2008, the subprogram had awarded funds for approximately US$59 million to 218 proposals in the five years since its inception in the following modalities:

- new business based on innovation: 140 proposals;
- technology and business feasibility studies: 44 proposals;
- entrepreneurship fund CONACYT-NAFIN: 25 projects;
- credit lines: 6 projects; and
- strategic alliances and innovation networks (AERIs): 19 proposals. This is a new instrument to promote the links among HEIs, PRCs and companies to construct networks that will work in the 'coopetence' scheme, and to elevate the competitiveness of the productive sectors of the country.

National System of Researchers (NSR)
This program maintains a network of the most highly productive scholars and researchers across the disciplines who are given remuneration supplements in recognition for their work. Although most of its members work for HEIs or PRCs, only a small proportion of Mexican academics are part of the NSR system. Selection occurs through a peer review system, and maintaining membership is based on continuing productivity. In 2008, the NSR accounted for more than 14,000 researchers in widespread S&T activities.

The Graduate Scholarship program
This program constitutes the most important source of funding for Mexican students to pursue graduate education in Mexico or abroad. In 2008, there were around 27,000 active scholarships funded by the program.

IDEA (Incorporation of Mexican Scientists and Technologists to the Social and Productive Sectors of the Country)
This instrument works under the proposal of a research project that incorporates master or doctorate degree professionals to a company. CONACYT pays full salary for one year and supports the second year of the project with funds with the understanding that the company will

hire the professional after that time. In 2007, there were 39 masters or doctors carrying on research activities in industry supported by this instrument.

R&D Fiscal Incentives program and other instruments to promote companies' innovation activities
These incentives worked as a fiscal credit until 2008. The scheme was successful in promoting R&D investment in companies as hundreds of research projects were approved where the criteria applied were innovative products and services, existing linkages among universities and industries, and evidence of the effect in the competitiveness of the company. It returned as a fiscal credit 30 percent of the R&D expenditure. In 2006, the program awarded more than $390 million to 3,155 approved projects, benefiting 561 companies ranging from micro, to small, to medium size, and 326 large or corporate enterprises, according to CONACYT. For 2009, the Fiscal Incentives program has been transformed into three new subprograms to provide better accountability of the resources and financing directly R&D in companies:

- *Technology-based innovation for the competitiveness of the enterprise (INNOVATEC)*: Its objective is to incentivize big companies or corporations to invest in STI, fund private research centers, help with intellectual capital portfolio management, and fund technology projects involving new processes, products, and services.
- *Technology-based innovation for high-value-added businesses (INNOVAPYMES)*: Its main goal is to promote STI in SMEs and fund research projects of innovative products or processes.
- *Innovation and research development in precursor technologies (PROINNOVA)*: This fund is exclusively to promote linkage between industry, HEIs, and research centers.

Monterrey's companies (158) are the leading applicants (387 projects) for CONACYT's Incentive Funds for Technology Research and Innovation (2,500 million MXP). The results of the call, recently published, show that for the first time Monterrey has taken the uppermost position in awarded funds and projects, exchanging its second place position with Mexico City.

Finally, there is another instrument created in 2009 by CONACYT, the Institutional Fund for the Regional Development of Capabilities in Innovation, Scientific and Technology Research (FORDECyT). This fund seeks to promote the development of technology poles at the regional level, helping with the creation of infrastructure and formation of specialized human resources. Nuevo León is participating alongside the northeast states of Tamaulipas and Coahuila with a project for the integration of a biotechnology incubator to be installed at the Research and Technology Innovation Park (PIIT) in Monterrey.

The Ministry of Economy has incorporated a new program to add to the set of instruments that promote industrial development. The Program for the Development of High Technology Industry (PRODIAT) is another strategy to promote the transfer and adoption of cutting-edge technologies and to enhance the competitiveness of the high-tech sector and its precursors.

Notwithstanding the efforts of the federal government, there are still areas of opportunity that must be resolved at regional, state, or city levels to achieve greater TT among companies and research centers or universities. One of them is the creation of intermediary institutions or organizations with very definite roles and resources to be used in promoting funds and mechanisms that accelerate the formation of a critical mass of new innovative companies that will catapult the economy of a region. In 2004, the state of Nuevo León initiated a concerted effort to create a systematic approach to attract and create new high-technology-based companies into its productive sector. The tradition of Monterrey and its metropolitan area as a pioneer and spearhead in the rational management of resources and industrialization processes needs to move to the logical next step: to take advantage of the regional entrepreneurship and the national STI policies and create an efficient innovation ecosystem.

3 PROGRAM: MONTERREY INTERNATIONAL CITY OF KNOWLEDGE (MICK)

In 2003 the government of the state of Nuevo León started a program to endow and articulate an innovation ecosystem in Monterrey and its metropolitan area that would accelerate the inclusion of Monterrey into the new knowledge economy. National policies and programs developed under the PECyT by CONACYT were used to tailor the local government's instruments and to obtain funds for the promotion of the innovation in the region.

According to the study published by PricewaterhouseCoopers (Hawksworth et al., 2007) detailing the largest city economies in the world and how this might change by 2020, Monterrey is predicted to be placed 54th of the largest urban economies for 2020. With the implementation of the MICK program, this position will be surpassed, in agreement with the vision of the state government:

Nuevo León will be a region leader at worldwide level because of its high and balanced economic development, in regard to the best use of its competitive advantages and of the development of its human capital, the technological innovation, the sustainability, the consolidation of the traditional economic activity, the fortification of strategic sectors and the synergy between the academic, enterprise and public sectors of the society. (González-Parás, 2007)

The successful MICK model is based on a knowledge culture, the establishment of a state policy and the sufficient allocation of resources, the clear and defined roles of its participants and the way they interact, the definition of the strategic areas of knowledge in which the program focuses, the creation of the organizations and structure needed to boost them and to implement the key initiatives, the statement of the strategy and the key activities, the evaluation of the advance and the results, and its impact on the creation of value for citizens, institutions, and companies (Figure 9.3).

Structure of the MICK Model

An analysis of the structure of the MICK model will illustrate the key components as defined in Figure 9.3.

Foundations

Among the most relevant characteristics of the society that thinks of itself as *regiomontana* (of the city of Monterrey), we can highlight the following, which are related to the culture of knowledge:

* long-term vision;
* participative leadership;
* entrepreneurship and creativity;
* science, technology, and innovation;
* digital culture;
* appreciation of knowledge;
* sustainability and social responsibility; and
* teamwork.

A legal framework has been put in place to ensure the long-term continuity of the program. The state policy includes laws, regulations, mechanisms, and the creation of legal instruments and the accountability of the resources allocated to the program. MICK is one of the five strategic programs defined within the State Plan of Development 2004–2009 to promote and consolidate Nuevo León as a worthy global competitor in the new economy. It is considered as a long-term plan, 25 years, with review of goals and advances every three years.

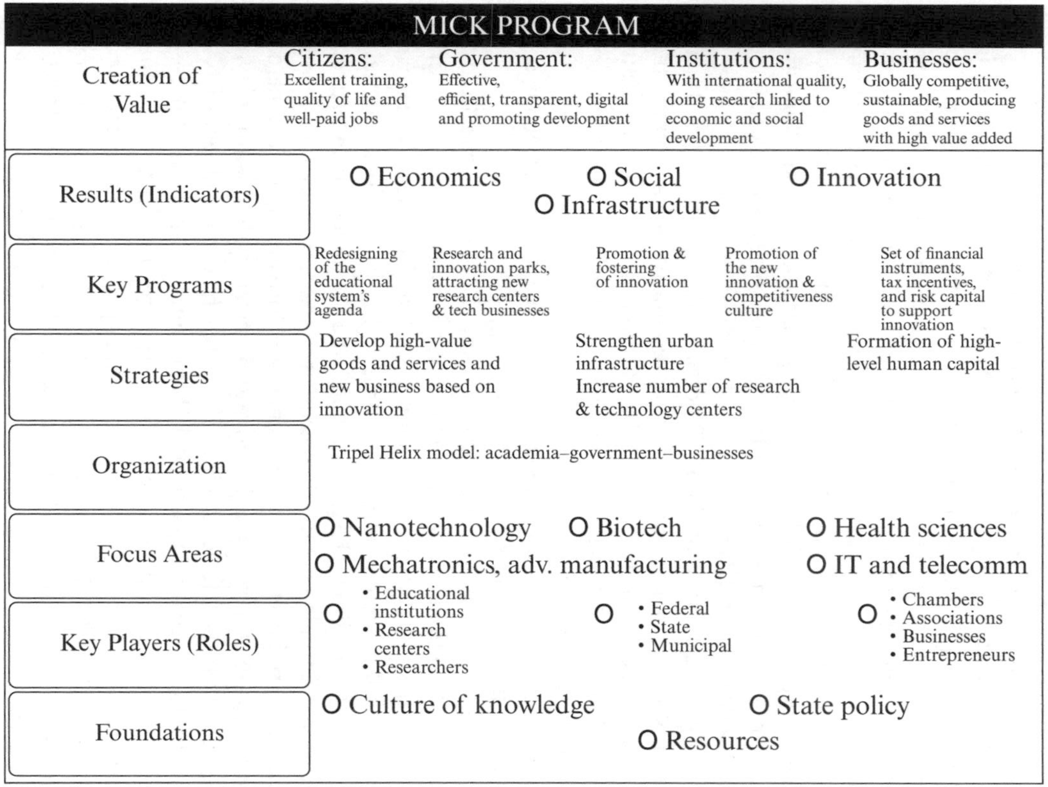

MICK PROGRAM

	Citizens:	Government:	Institutions:	Businesses:
Creation of Value	Excellent training, quality of life and well-paid jobs	Effective, efficient, transparent, digital and promoting development	With international quality, doing research linked to economic and social development	Globally competitive, sustainable, producing goods and services with high value added
Results (Indicators)	O Economics	O Social O Infrastructure	O Innovation	
Key Programs	Redesigning of the educational system's agenda	Research and innovation parks, attracting new research centers & tech businesses	Promotion & fostering of innovation	Promotion of the new innovation & competitiveness culture	Set of financial instruments, tax incentives, and risk capital to support innovation
Strategies	Develop high-value goods and services and new business based on innovation	Strengthen urban infrastructure Increase number of research & technology centers		Formation of high-level human capital
Organization	Tripel Helix model: academia–government–businesses			
Focus Areas	O Nanotechnology O Mechatronics, adv. manufacturing	O Biotech	O Health sciences O IT and telecomm	
Key Players (Roles)	• Educational institutions • Research centers • Researchers	• Federal • State • Municipal	• Chambers • Associations • Businesses • Entrepreneurs	
Foundations	O Culture of knowledge	O State policy O Resources		

Figure 9.3 Model developed for Monterrey International City of Knowledge program

In March 2004 the Law for the Promotion of Development Based on Knowledge became effective. From that date, the MICK program began to take on an institutional life. The law was modified in 2005 to allow the creation of a new organism, the Institute of Innovation and Technology Transfer of Nuevo León (I2T2), which would assume the leadership of the program, taking full responsibility for its execution.

One of the primary targets of I2T2 is to foment the formation of intellectual capital by means of linking programs between academia and companies, and by promoting and transferring the applied research and the technological development toward the necessities of the market in order to accelerate the economic growth in the state. It does so by establishing the coordination of actions among the public, private, and academic sectors, administering the resources and ensuring that there are mechanisms to induce innovation and technology transfer to ensure a successful regional innovation ecosystem (RIS).

The organic structure of the I2T2 consists of a governing body and a citizen advisory council composed of representatives of academia, industry and other government partners. In addition, the state government has implemented viable financial instruments to sustain the innovation ecosystem, and has agreed to allocate economic resources, concurring with funds from the federal, state, and municipal governments, the academic sector and private initiative (Figure 9.4).

The generation and the granting of capital seed and risk funds for projects and companies with a technological base are essential for the knowledge-based development economy. In Mexico, the venture capital market is still underdeveloped. According to the National Survey on Innovation Capabilities (ESIDET, 2006), the resources for investment in innovation are fundamentally financed with the enterprises' own resources (64 percent), public funds (19 percent), and private funds (12 percent). These data also confirm that the private financial system is not playing a vital role within the Mexican NIS. Therefore, the establishment of Nuevo León's Fund for Innovation (FONLIN) is fundamental, since it ensures local access to seed and risk capital, necessary to connect the investments in science and technology with commercial applications that generate new businesses. The FONLIN is generated from the resources contributed by the Inter-American Development Bank (IADB), I2T2, CONACYT, and other investors. The initial amount of 100 million MXP annually will support the incubation and development of businesses based on innovation.

Nuevo León has managed to fully seize CONACYT's mix funds, providing resources for the development of science and technology that responds to the needs of the state. Nuevo León's mix fund is the highest in the country: more than $840 million from 2003 to 2008, including

State budget

- Prioritization in the budget for science and technology, allocating fiscal resources to this area for more than 2,000 million pesos from 2004 to April 2008

Mixed funds (Consejo Nacional de Ciencia y Technología (CONACYT) y Nuevo León state government)

- 50:50 state government:federal government contributions. More than 840 million pesos in technological and scientific infrastructure from 2003 to 2008. (includes concurring academia and private sector investments)

Impetus to the investment of more than 1% of GDP in science and technology over the next five years

- Encourage private sector participation by creating tools to support innovation and maximizing the portfolio of supporting tools by diverse federal, state and municipal government entities

Programs to support investment in innovation, research and technological development in the enterprise (CONACYT)

- Technological innovation for high-value-added businesses (INNOVAPYME) $600 m
- Technological innovation for the competitiveness of enterprises (INNOVATEC) $700 m
- Development and innovation technology precursors (Proinnova) $1200 m
- It is estimated that companies in Nuevo León will get 20% of resources ($500 m in 2009)

Seed capital funds and venture capital

- Fund to support the creation and start-up businesses based on innovation of Nuevo León
- Nuevo León Fund for innovation (FONLIN) (2009) with an initial contribution of $95 m (T2T2 $20 m, CONACYT $30 m, $30 m IDB, $15 m FUNTEC)

Figure 9.4   Resources for innovation activities available in Nuevo León and their use

resources channeled from the federal government, state, and those contributed by companies and academia to the approved projects. Nuevo León's mix fund supports the strategic areas defined in the MICK program, such as nanotechnology, biotechnology, biomedical devices, electronics and telecommunications, information technology (IT), mechanical engineering, design and advanced manufacturing, advanced materials, and chemical engineering.

The federal and the state governments also plan to support micro, small, and medium-sized enterprises in the development of projects involving technology and innovation, as well as the development of infrastructure in R&D of private enterprises, research networks, and public and private research centers.

Additional funding comes from PROSOFT, a support tool for the development of the software industry and related services under information and communication technologies (ICTs). This fund is administered by the Ministry of Economy through an agreement with the different states. The Ministry of Economy contributed to the development of the IT cluster in Monterrey, financing the initiative of 40 small and medium-sized software development companies to form an association, and that are grouped together as the Monterrey IT cluster.

Furthermore, it is recognized that communication and dissemination of the knowledge produced and needed to create a new economy must be available to all the interested parties. To promote a better interaction among the bidders and applicants of technology, the I2T2 created the State System of Interaction and Information Science and Technology (SEIICYT), which began operation in 2008. It is an online system that promotes TT, networks of collaboration among scientists, technologists, representatives of private industry, and postgraduates. Since the start of operations the system has cataloged more than 600 players in S&T in Nuevo León.

Key players, roles and the Triple Helix model
Whereas a major part in the process of innovation and TT interactions is among the actors involved, usually HEIs, or research centers and companies, it is important to consider the environment that surrounds them for the interactions to be effective. In this regard, it is important to create structures that act as intermediaries, translating the language of the university to the language of the company and vice versa. The state government of Nuevo León has embraced the task of creating an adequate environment and infrastructure to make these interactions flourish in the MICK program.

The Triple Helix model has been selected by the program because it fits the innovation ecosystem model, allowing for non-linear interactions and feedback among industry, academia, and government while working together and integrating other actors as required. The Triple Helix model facilitates the identification of policy instruments for industrial development to attain the benefits of the innovation. The three main stars in the development of the region became strategic partners under this model.

At the national level, Mexican companies, the productive sector, have maintained a low profile in the innovation system until recently.

CONACYT's instruments for promotion of business R&D, TT, and technological innovation were reformed in 2002, and since then there has been a growing involvement of Mexican and multinational companies based in Mexico in STI activities. According to the results in the two Encuesta Sobre Investigación y Desarrollo de Tecnología (ESIDET) surveys conducted by CONACYT in 2001 and 2005, between 2004 and 2005, 23 percent of a total of 16,398 firms surveyed made some innovation either in product or in process. The survey also gives evidence on the investment in R&D carried out by innovative firms. In 2001 their expenditures in R&D as a percentage of their total expenditures in innovation were only 8.6 percent, while acquisition of machinery and equipment absorbed 66.5 percent. However, in 2006, the composition of the expenditures changed dramatically: R&D grew fivefold (up to 42.5 percent) since 2001 and the resources allocated for acquisition of machinery were reduced (down to 39.7 percent) (ESIDET, 2001, 2006; Dutrénit et al., 2008, 58).

In terms of the role of industry in the Triple Helix model, industry in Nuevo León has taken very seriously the challenge to improve its competitiveness and enter the knowledge economy. The participation of the productive sector includes representation by industrial companies, industrial chambers, and associations. Their commitment to the MICK program is shown in the formation of strategic clusters, which are working according to the concept of 'coopetency', understood as collaboration in competition. In agreement with the coopetency concept, local, national, and global companies within the same productive sector work jointly and in collaboration with the HEIs, research centers, and the government to develop greater synergies, economies of scale, and networks of suppliers. This joint effort propels the productivity and competitiveness of its sector, transforming scientific research into new products and services, and accelerates the TT to the companies in the sector.

The second actor in the Triple Helix model, academia, has been a player on the national level for quite some time. Mexico's higher education system consists of universities, technological institutes, state educational institutions, and normal schools (training of primary and secondary teachers). In 2006 there were around 2,171 HEIs, of which 33 percent are public and 67 percent private, located all over the country. In 2006, public HEIs attracted nearly 64 percent of the total students. The most important public and private HEIs, such as the National University of Mexico (UNAM), the National Polytechnic Institute (IPN), the Technological Institute of Higher Studies of Monterrey (ITESM), the Metropolitan Autonomous University (UAM), the State University of Nuevo León, as well as other state universities were established between 1930 and 1980.

Since 2002, the most prestigious research universities in the country have started to deploy several strategies for commercializing their research, such as providing incubators for their own researchers to start up new businesses and offering the research to entrepreneurs to be transformed into new products or technologies. Some examples of these efforts are detailed in Appendix 9A1.

With increasing frequency, but not as often as one would like to see in Mexico, the research papers are picked up by the industry and converted into new products and services with the help of the original owners of the knowledge. Usually, collaboration between academia and industry takes the form of providing well-developed human resources to the companies, joint agreements with universities for graduate programs for the companies' technicians, or specific improvements of processes and solutions for problems that impact the company through cost reductions and higher product quality.

The role of Nuevo León HEIs in the Triple Helix is twofold: first, they are in charge of producing highly capable human resources in strategic knowledge areas and second, they create and disseminate new knowledge that in the long or short term might be converted into new technologies that bring benefits to society. The most important universities in Nuevo León signed an agreement with the state government to participate actively in the MICK program: Universidad Autónoma de Nuevo León (UANL) State University, Instituto Tecnológico de Estudios Superiores de Monterrey (ITESM) Private University, Universidad de Monterrey (UDEM) Private University, and Universidad Regiomontana (UR) Private University.

The UANL State University is the third largest university in Mexico and the institution with the greatest number of researchers (325) in the NSR in the northeast of the country. It has modified its bachelor and graduate programs to include topics on entrepreneurship and technology management, as well as preparing continuing education programs for its researchers about patents, copyright, and entrepreneurship (see Appendix 9A2 for details).

In 2008 the ITESM Private University consolidated as an educative system of excellence at the national level with 33 campuses in the Mexican Republic. Since 2005, the institution has grown substantially in the field of research. One hundred and twenty-two research chairs have been created, 65 of which are at Monterrey campus. This research chair scheme brings together experienced teachers, young teachers, and students engaged in a line of research (see Appendix 9A2 for details).

UDEM Private University is the third most important university in the city-region of Monterrey, and the UR Private University directs its efforts and resources towards the continuous improvement of excellence.

The role of the state government in the Triple Helix, besides the commitment of resources to the program and the construction of educational, telecommunications, urban and scientific–technological infrastructure according to the program goals, has been to organize the structure for public participation in support of the tasks and strategies of the MICK program through the creation of citizens' councils and the coordination of citizen participation in Nuevo León. These councils increase the interaction among citizens and seek the active participation of civil society. In addition to the creation of I2T2, there are a number of decentralized and citizen participation organisms that contribute to the development of the program.

Definition of strategic knowledge areas and focus on industrial sectors
Ten strategic economic sectors through five technological areas were defined through company and university consensus. The five technological areas in which the MICK program set out to concentrate the efforts on innovation in existing companies and to attract new ones are: biotechnology, mechatronics and advanced manufacturing, nanotechnology, information technologies and telecommunications, and health sciences.

Organization and government of the industry–academia innovation groups
With support from the Ministry of Economic Development of the state of Nuevo León and the participation of I2T2, citizens' advisory councils were created. Their function is to foster synergies and support the development of strategic industries such as software, aerospace, medical and biotechnology, automotive, electronics and appliances, among others.

The citizens' advisory councils are defined as groups that include multiple participants from various sectors such as business chambers, professional associations, universities, trade unions, and political parties. The council members have organized into strategic clusters integrated by companies, universities, governmental research centers, and institutions. To date, there are eight clusters integrated in the sectors of: aerospace, automotive and auto parts, electro-domestic appliances, agro-alimentary, IT and software, health services, biotechnology, and nanotechnology.

Strategy of the MICK program
The MICK program centers its strategy on achieving its vision by 2025, as expressed by the state government: 'Monterrey will be placed among the top 25 cities competing internationally, able to attract and retain capital and human talent, to produce goods and services with high added value through knowledge and innovation, and providing the best quality of life

for its citizens' (González-Parás, 2007). The program seeks to foster an innovation culture among the inhabitants of the state, increase GDP per capita by attracting knowledge-intensive, high-tech industries, and engaging in activities that create knowledge for economic benefits.

The core strategic actions identified to achieve these goals are:

- to promote the development of high-value goods;
- to promote innovation in the productive sector;
- to increase the formation of high-level human capital;
- to promote the culture of an innovation society;
- to increase investments in technological R&D;
- to promote new businesses based on innovation;
- to strengthen urban infrastructure and cultural options; and
- to increase the number of research and technology centers.

MICK's key programs and the progress of strategic projects
Deployment of the strategy of the MICK model has resulted in the implementation of strategic projects (key programs in Figure 9.3) to achieve:

- a model of high-quality education in line with the vocation of the city with comprehensive and strict evaluation parameters, transparent selection and training of teachers, and use of ITs and communication leading to a greater percentage of the population undertaking a tertiary education while staying connected to activities that allow for a high level of employment and entrepreneurship;
- a higher investment of public and private resources in science, technology, and innovation capabilities with the objective of generating knowledge, technology transfer practices and intellectual capital; and
- an urban infrastructure of the highest quality with high human capital formation and investment in the best projects to be competitive and to offer citizens and visitors the best living conditions.

Notwithstanding the importance of all the projects, for the purpose of this chapter we shall focus on some of the programs that contribute directly to the establishment of new businesses based on innovation and foster technology transfer in the regional innovation system, such as the installation of the research park and the technology business incubators and the commercialization of technologies through the INVITE program. However, the progress and the most important activities carried out in all the programs and projects are reported, along with the results and benefits of the MICK program so far (see Figure 9.5).

Figure 9.5 Progress of the MICK program, 2004–2009

	ECONOMIC ⊕	SOCIAL ⊕		INNOVATION ⊕	
RESULTS (INDICATORS)	2008 income per capita = US$18,465 High-tech exports = US$802.1 million 2008 direct foreign investment = US$4.2 billion	Income distribution 2004 Gini coefficient = 0.4329 Level of education Average years of education = 9.75 years 2008 higher education coverage = 35.5%	Educational quality indexes, PISA Score in Science, Reading & Math = $ 435 R 455 M 432 Assigning value to knowledge % of persons who value knowledge, based on the 2008 survey = 86%	Graduate studies 2008 enrollment/graduates = 1,839 / 3,726 2009 seed and risk capital = US$ 10 million Number of researchers in the SNI in 2008 = 548	Patents = 30 2008 state expenditure in Science, Technology, and Innovation, public and private, % of state's GDP = 0.8 %

KEY PROGRAMS	REDESIGNING AND UPDATING OF THE EDUCATIONAL SYSTEM'S AGENDA • Science and technology for children • Encyclomedia • Redesigning the universities' curriculum RESEARCH AND INNOVTION PARKS, ATTRACTING NEW RESEARCH CENTRES AND TECHNOLOGY BUSINESSES • Creation of the first Research and Technology Innovation Park (PIIT) • New research centers in Monterrey:54 • Institute for the Development of IT Talent (IDETI) • Centers at the Research and Technology Innovation Park (PIIT):27 PROMOTION & FOSTERING OF INNOVATION IN BUSINESSES UNIVERSITIES, AND RESEARCH INSTITUTIONS • Decentralization of the Incorporation of Mexican Scientists and Technologists (IDEA) program, and CONACYT's Scholarship program • New CINVESTAV Master's Degree programs and CONACYT centers established in the PIIT • Instrument to innovate 'TRIZ'	CREATION AND ATTRACTION OF NEW STRATEGIC BUSINESSES • Creation of 8 strategic clusters • Center for Business Networking • INVITE / IC² program • Business incubators: 3 high-tech, and 6 medium-tech • 100% of the energy for the metro is produced from garbage biogas TECHNOLOGY AGREEMENTS WITH FRANCE, CANADA AND THE EUROPEAN COMMUNITY EXPANSION OF URBAN INFRASTRUCTURE AND CULTURAL OPTIONS • 2007 Culture Forum • Santa Lucia Riverwalk • Expansion of the metro transport system • Creation of museums: North East Museum, Government Palace Museum, and the Steel Museum, Furnace 3 • Free internet covering 296 acres (120 ha.) • One fourth of the population have a new home	PROMOTION OF THE NEW INNOVATION & GLOBAL COMPETITIVENESS CULTURE • 12 radio capsules • Innovation page published in Monterrey's newspapers • Creation of the Integral Information system, International City of Knowledge • Science, Knowledge & Technology Magazine • Biographical Dictionary with 600 researchers CREATION OF A SET OF FINANCIAL INSTRUMENTS, TAX INCENTIVES, AND RISK CAPITAL TO SUPPORT INNOVATION • Mixed funds • Tax incentives • Fund for the promotion of SMEs • Creation of the Nuevo León Fund (FONLIN)

ORGANIZATION	Citizens Councils (2008) 32 (Federal Government, Public Sector, and Specialized Programs)	Consulting Citizens Councils (Businesses, Universities, Government)	8 Councils for the Development of Strategic Clusters (Strategic Production Groups)

FOUNDATIONS	Definition of Monterrey International City of Knowledge (MICK) MICK (MTYCIC), Strategic Program for the Transformation of Nuevo León (2003)/ Promotion of Knowledge-Based Development (2004) Creation of the Innovation and Technology Transfer Institute (I²T²), (2005)	Agreement between the Nuevo León state government and educational institutions to promote the MICK (MTYCIC) (2004) Agreement for the creation of the first technology park in the state (2005)

229

Selected MICK Projects

Project Park of Research and Technology Innovation (PIIT)

The first Integral Park for Innovation and Technological Development in Mexico and Latin America (PIIT), was born under the Triple Helix model, based on an agreement among the government of the state of Nuevo León, the National Council for Science and Technology, UANL, ITESM and UDEM in June of 2005, and it is a landmark of the MICK program.

Before PIIT, Monterrey had an excellent network of industrial parks (more than 2,212 hectares), and the existing research centers pertaining to the local universities were isolated within its corresponding campuses. The PIIT houses research centers of diverse local, national, and foreign universities, with possibilities of synergy in the use of the infrastructure and equipment. Accomplishments include joint postgraduate programs, reinforcement of the formation of human resources, and innovation in the strategic industry clusters in which they participate.

The model of a fourth-generation research park designed for PIIT has also attracted global and local companies and public research centers. The park facilities take advantage of world-class technology infrastructure for research and telecommunication, such as telepresence, virtual networks, and multiple meeting points for work or recreation, to encourage teamwork and the realization of multidisciplinary projects. The membership of the park in international associations such as the Association of Universities Research Parks (AURP) and the International Association of Science Parks (IASP), as well as the international network of the established centers has already positioned the PIIT as an important player in the research park arena. The PIIT recently housed two international congresses: NanoMonterrey 2009 and the IASP Latin American Branch conference.

One important feature of the park was the establishment of two high-technology incubators for the creation of new high-tech businesses: one in nanotechnology and another in biotechnology. The incubator spaces were designed in collaboration with Arizona State University and the IC^2 Institute of the University of Texas at Austin.

The PIIT is classified as a semi-specialized park, since it favors the high-priority sectors of science and technology for the MICK program but does not refuse to admit companies or start-ups working in other technology areas if their strategy and objectives are aligned to the program. The areas of major interest are those established by the MICK program.

A trust has been created for the operation of the PIIT (FOPIIT), in which it is indicated that the park will operate under a condominium regime. The trust is governed by an Advisory Council of Institutions composed of tenants who have fulfilled to date the requirements necessary to settle in the park. The I2T2 acts as the trustee and grantor from the state.

The PIIT is located in the municipality of Apodaca, Nuevo León, 10 km from the new freeway to the Mariano Escobedo airport. Its proximity to the international airport and the location of a great number of important industries in numerous industrial parks nearby makes it especially attractive and promises to be an advantage for facilitating TT and establishing linkages among the research centers, universities, and the industry.

Some data related to the park are as follows:

- total area: 195 acres (70 ha);
- investment in infrastructure (first-level and sustainable services): US$100 million;
- investment in R&D buildings and equipment: US$200 million;
- other support services: hotels (100 rooms), meeting rooms, restaurants, and service businesses;
- nine research facilities of seven universities: UANL, ITESM, UT, Texas A&M, UDEM, UNAM, and University of Arizona;
- nine public centers for R&D, incorporating mechatronics, advanced materials, nanotechnology, product design, water technology, food technology, biotechnology, IT & software, renewable energy technology, optics, applied math, and health sciences;
- 12 private R&D and technology centers (global and local companies), including Motorola, Pepsico, Sigma Alimentos, Viakable, and Qualtia Prolec-GE;
- three business incubators in nanotechnology; biotechnology; and sustainable housing and renewable energy; and
- 3,500 new jobs: researchers, engineers, and support personnel in the next five years.

Program creation and attraction of new strategic companies

The Regional Program of Competitiveness and Innovation of Nuevo León identified the regions and local strategies for the regional integration of the northeast of Mexico with the south of United States: Nuevo León, Tamaulipas, Coahuila, Chihuahua, and Texas.

In 2004, Nuevo León signed an agreement of collaboration with the IC^2 Institute of the University of Texas at Austin to incorporate the research done in the northeast of Mexico in a program of commercialization in the international markets, since it is of high priority to the state government to bring forward the research as technological innovations in the international market: the Regional Commercialization of Technologies program (INVITE).

Within INVITE, researchers learn to formulate business plans for attracting financing for their technology developments and receive tutoring and valuation of the technology by experts participating in the program. To date, INVITE has worked with 41 chosen projects from Nuevo León, Tamaulipas, Coahuila, and Chihuahua, resulting from three calls for proposals. The achievements of the INVITE program so far are:

Projects from the 2nd program: 2006 to date   The selected technologies received 18 letters of interest by one or more companies:

- six of 20 cooperation agreements signed;
- one technology achieved a commercial contract and licensing;
- two technologies continue with the possibility of success to reach a trade agreement; and
- 20 technologies were provided with market studies that generated marketing strategies and recommendations for business strategy.

Projects from the 3rd program: 2008 to date   Seven of the 15 technologies received letters of interest by one or more companies:

- six of 15 cooperation agreements signed;
- one technology has achieved a partnership and distribution of its product;
- five technologies are in the process of negotiation to achieve a trade agreement; and
- 15 technologies were provided with market studies that generated marketing strategies and recommendations for business strategy.

Program of business accelerator and incubators
Driven strongly since 2004 by the concerted efforts of the state, federal, and municipal governments, universities, and the local enterprise sector, the program has inaugurated 13 business incubators, a number that has contributed to strengthen the MICK program. To these facilities, two new businesses incubators for firms based on nanotechnology and biotechnology will be added by the PIIT at the end of 2010.

Notwithstanding the short time since the formal beginning of the program, there are some benefits and profits that demonstrate that its approach and the sum of efforts, strategies, actions from the private, academia and government sectors are paying off. The annual average income of the workforce has grown by 8.5 percent, an increment higher than inflation which in these five years has averaged 3.3 percent. Nuevo León has grown at an annual rate near 5 percent, when the national average is 3.3 percent, and in the US is 2.9 percent. This growth rate, which has increased in the last four years, will continue upwards in the medium and long term with the MICK program. The GDP per capita of the state, US$18,465 per inhabitant per annum is almost twice as large as the national average in 2008.

The leadership of Nuevo León in the international market is corroborated by the dynamics of its exports. In 2004 these represented 19 percent of the local GDP. By 2007, the proportion reached 30.3 percent, which means that state exports grew from US$10,400 million in 2004 to US$20,620 million in 2007 with an annual growth average of 26.0 percent in that time. Data that also reflect the real advances of Nuevo León in transforming the industry sector towards higher use for innovation and technology are the composition of the exports of the companies located in the state. According to the classification established by the OECD for the sectors of knowledge and with data from the Ministry of Economic Development of Nuevo León, (Data NL), it is proven that in 2007 the exports of high and upper-middle technology represented 72.0 percent of the total state exports and were equivalent to almost US$15,000,000.

4 CONCLUSIONS

There is plenty of evidence that supports the claim that the Mexican NIS is incomplete and that at the regional level there have been successful efforts to correct these deficiencies. One such is the MICK program in Nuevo León, which is transforming the local innovation ecosystem, making non-linear interactions succeed under a Triple Helix model and by taking advantage of the federal tools and incentives coupled with a state government strategy that includes allocation of resources, a legal framework, and the creation of support infrastructure strengthened under the assurance of long-term planning and continuation of the program.

The state government has deployed a series of subprograms and policies to promote the development of the knowledge society. The results are expressed in the unfolding of science, technology, innovation culture, and modern productive activities that jointly develop the intellectual capital, incite more and better uses of knowledge, help traditional enterprises to succeed as well as promote the new knowledge-based businesses, thus galvanizing the traditionally marginalized regions and communities.

Intermediary organizations, such as I2T2 or specialized tech transfer units, are needed to provide linkage services among research centers, universities, and companies, not only to promote transfer ownership of existing technologies, but also to ensure that more research is aimed at the strategic areas jointly defined by the private sector and academia. An important recommendation is the definition of relevant indicators that will track the progress of the programs. In the case of the MICK program, there are several indicators that will be measured in the next stages of the project with the goals projected to year 2025 as follows:

1. Economic:
    a. income per capita = US$50,000;
    b. direct foreign investment = US$8.65 billion;
    c. high-tech exports = US$6.5 billion.
2. Innovation:
    a. graduate studies enrollment/graduates = 50,500/17,000;
    b. number of researchers in the SNI = 3,500;
    c. state expenditure in STI, public and private, % state's GDP = 2.0 %;
    d. patents = 950;
    e. seed and risk capital = US$500 million.
3. Social income distribution:
    a. Gini coefficient = 0.30;
    b. level of education: average years of education = more than 12 years;
    c. higher education coverage = more than 50%;
    d. educational quality indexes, PISA Score in Science, Reading, and Math = S 520; R 520; M 520;
    e. assigning value to knowledge % of persons who value knowledge, survey = 90%.
4. Infrastructure; research and technology innovation parks = 740 acres (300 ha):
    a. educational infrastructure (investment in infrastructure and equipment) = US$70 million per year;
    b. internet users for every 1,000 inhabitants (2008) = 80;
    c. cultural and recreational infrastructure (no. of museums in metropolitan area) = 35.

REFERENCES

Carreño, Luis Antonio (2009), Personal Communication to the author.
Dutrénit, Gabriela, Mario Capdevielle, Juan Manuel Corona Alcántar, Martín Puchet Anyul, Fernando Santiago and Alexandre O. Vera-Cruz (2008), 'The Mexican National System of Innovation: Structures, Policies, Performance and

Challenges: Background Report to the OECD Country Review of Mexico's National System of Innovation', México: CONACYT.
Encuesta sobre Investigatión y Desarrolo Experimental (ESIDET) (2001), INEGI-CONACYT.
Encuesta sobre Investigatión y Desarrolo Experimental (ESIDET) (2006), INEGI-CONACYT.
García-Gardea, Eugenio (2009), Personal Interview (Division Director, Technology Based Enterprise Development, ITESM), available at: http://www.itesm.edu/wps/portal/.
Gomez, Ricardo (2009), Personal Interview, March (Director of CIETT).
González-Parás, Natividad (2007), Speech given by the Governor with reference to the MICK program, Nuevo León Government.
Hawksworth, John, Thomas Hoehn and Meinon Gyles (2007), *Which are the largest city economies in the world and how might this change by 2020?*, UK Economic Outlook, PrincewaterhouseCoopers.
Lizardi, Víctor, Fernando Baquero, Guillermo Estrada, Hilda Hernández, Héctor Chagoya, Scott Belser, Teresa de León, Fernando Guillén, Guillermo Frades and Enrico Martínez (2008), *Propuesta de un modelo de transferencia de tecnología para México, Comisión de Transferencia de Tecnología de ADIAT*, México: CONACYT.

APPENDIX 9A1   SOME HIGHER EDUCATION INSTITUTIONS IN MEXICO AND THEIR TECHNOLOGY TRANSFER EFFORTS

Universidad Nacional Autónoma de México (UNAM)

Formally established in 1910, the UNAM is the oldest, largest, and most important university in Mexico. Research at the UNAM is organized in two subsystems: humanities research and scientific research. Both subsystems comprise research centers and research institutes distributed across the country, though most university centers and institutes concentrate their activities in Mexico City. Monterrey will house three research units of the UNAM in the PIIT research park to be inaugurated in 2010. In 2007, the two subsystems employed 2,337 researchers and 1,693 technicians. The scientific production was as follows: 3,084 articles, 1,283 reports in internal yearbooks, 397 books, and 948 chapters in books (Dutrénit et al., 2008, 43).

In May 2008 on the initiative of the Rector, the Coordination of Research and Development of the UNAM (CID) was established in response to one of the lines governing its work program – to increase the linking of research with the priority issues for national development. Its aim is to support the transfer of knowledge, technologies, and products developed at the university to agencies and companies from the public, social, and private sectors and to enhance their use by society. The UNAM's conviction is that with the CID, the problem of the low number of patents (approximately 150 patents over the past 20 years) will disappear, as it was a result rather of cultural aspects (not valuing patents from the researchers' point of view), than of low merit scientific and technological research results. The CID will disseminate IP culture and will promote the writing of patents of the R&D results.

Instituto Politécnico Nacional (IPN)

The IPN has two entities associated with TT: (i) the Polytechnic Unit for Business Development and Competitiveness (UPDCE) which includes the Office for Corporative Attention and Subdirección de Atención Empresarial (SAE) and (ii) the Center for Technology Based Business Incubation (CIEBT).

The role of the SAE in TT is to promote, arrange, and monitor transfers of technology or technological services that are developed at the institute for the productive sector, in particular micro, small and medium-sized enterprises (MSMEs). In addition, since 2005, SAE has administered the UPDCE Patent Center through an agreement with the Mexican Institute of Industrial Property (IMPI) with a focus on creating a culture of IP among students, teachers, and researchers. The center is the only one in the country closely linked to an entity with IMPI technology (Lizardi et al., 2008, 69).

Centro de Investigación y Estudios Avanzados (CINVESTAV)

Established in 1961, CINVESTAV's main goal is the formation of highly qualified human resources both for research and teaching. CINVESTAV integrates 28 academic departments organized within nine centers, two of which are located in Mexico City and seven of which are located in different states.

In 2008, the 550 researchers (senior and assistant) produced 904 scientific articles in international journals. CINVESTAV is the leading national academic institution in patenting and in transferring technologies to the private sector. It holds 122 national patents and 55 international patents. Thirty technologies developed by CINVESTAV's researchers have been transferred to companies or agencies. CINVESTAV has a strong tradition of collaboration both with national and international academic institutions. Two of the star companies that commercialize research from CINVESTAV are Bioskinco, which developed the first living human skin grown to cover skin lesions, and Lapis, which commercializes veterinary vaccines and products (Carreño, 2009, personal communication).

APPENDIX 9A2   TWO EXAMPLES OF TECHNOLOGY TRANSFER PRACTICES AT MEXICAN UNIVERSITIES

Technology Transfer Practices at the Universidad Autónoma de Nuevo León (UANL)

UANL has over 50 patent applications, 15 patents granted, and myriad copyrighted material. University patents are diversified in application areas such as: agriculture, engineering, environment, genomics, health, biotechnology, food science, and nanotechnology. To help the university with the innovation and technology transfer processes, the Center for Business Incubation and Technology Transfer (CIETT) was created in 2005. Even though the university has recently begun the task of achieving a systematic TT process, it has a long story of success linking with regional industries, such as the relationship between the doctorate program in materials science at the Faculty of Mechanical and Electric Engineering and VITRO, CEMEX, NEMAK and TERNIUM, which has resulted in joint scientific publications and patents, and more than 20 doctoral students whose theses were done working directly with the industry.

Recent successes include three new companies, commercializing products such as biological agents for veterinary medicine: PRONABIVE (National Program for Veterinary and Biological Agents), an immune-transfer factor, and NUTRIS, a software program used by nutritionists to help them design specialized diets (Gomez, 2009).

Instituto Tecnológico de Estudios Superiores de Monterrey (ITESM)

ITESM has 114 patent applications, of which 77 are routed through IMPI and the others are applications at an international level in diverse countries. The institution already has two international patents, one for an opto-electrical device for detecting cervical cancer, and the other for the production of invert syrup from sugarcane juice. The areas where the technology developed national patents issued to ITESM have been applied are as diverse as economics, biotechnology, IT, and nanotechnology, among others.

The increase in the number of patent applications is in part due to the establishment of research chairs in 2003, and the opening of the business incubator at ITESM for environmental care and ecology-related technological companies. The research strategy includes concepts such as research chairs, research centers, doctoral programs, entrepreneurial technology parks, IP management, and the marketing of such developments to have commercial impact. Another driver to encourage the researcher to seek a patent is that the researcher receives 30 percent of the revenue generated when the innovative products are developed and marketed.

Examples of successful cases of companies or spin-offs of the technology-based ITESM incubators include Optima Energy, IDTEC, a company that designs and implements integration tools for automation of production and packaging, handling technology, with sales of more than one million dollars annually, and PESS, a company that uses technology to ensure the operation of gas turbines for CFE, in predictive maintenance strategies.

To date, 12 companies in the areas of biotechnology, medicine or engineering, of which five involve new technologies or technology-based products from students or researchers of the institution, are in business accelerators or incubators belonging to the ITESM (Gardea, 2009).

10. Technology transfer and the development of new technology-based firms: Polish perspectives and a case study on nanotechnology

Dariusz Trzmielak

1 INTRODUCTION

The issue of innovation and science and technology management represents the nature of the free market economy. The creation of knowledge is one of the main tasks of higher education; however, knowledge needs to be transformed. During this time of globalization and integration of the Polish economy with the European Union, the tempo of knowledge creation, technology transfer, and the implementation of innovation are one of a company's competitive advantages. The main focus of this chapter is on technology transfer from universities to enterprises, new technology firm developments, and barriers and stimulators for innovative industry enterprises. The purpose of this chapter is to provide scientists and entrepreneurs with comprehensive information that will aid in understanding the changes within the Polish high-tech markets, and present a case study from the nanotechnology sector focusing on knowledge and technology transfer components.

The chapter is organized as follows. Sections 2 and 3 begin by outlining the essential aspects of European and Polish innovation markets. Section 4 focuses on the Polish nanotechnology road map and is aimed at analyzing future perspectives for high-tech companies. Section 5 presents the case study of a spin-off company operating in the nanotechnology sector by providing an example of management of technology development and transfer. Examples of scientists who have become successful entrepreneurs are also provided. The chapter allows readers to draw important insights into the development mechanism by which Polish scientists and entrepreneurs strengthen their competencies and enter into high-tech international markets. Section 6 concludes.

2   INNOVATIONS, NEW TECHNOLOGIES, AND ORGANIZATIONS FOCUSED ON THE DEVELOPMENT OF IDEAS

Achievement of a sustainable competitiveness on a global scale by the European Union will require a dynamically developing economy based on knowledge. The development of research and new technologies has become a basic element of the EU strategy (Lisbon Strategy). The initiative to create a common European Research Area (ERA) accelerated the integration of resources. The creation of common technologies and their development have become a priority in research programs, such as framework programs. Research and development (R&D) expenditure in Europe remains at a level of 1.6 percent of GNP, which is lower than in the United States (2.8 percent) and Japan (3.1 percent). The prognosis for China indicates that in as early as 2010, R&D expenditure for the country will reach the EU average (Siemaszko and Supel, 2006).

The European R&D goals as set by the Lisbon Strategy, are to achieve by 2010 R&D intensity of at least 3 percent. In 2005, only two member states exceeded the EU goal of achieving R&D intensity of 3 percent of GDP: Sweden and Finland. The average EU member R&D intensity is lower than in the United States (Eurostat Pocketbooks, 2008). The new members of the European Union have lowered the EU R&D intensity average because only three countries, the Czech Republic, Slovenia, and Estonia, have higher R&D expenditures than 1 percent (Figure 10.1). Most countries, including Poland, have an R&D intensity at 0.5 percent of GDP, which makes technology transfer and innovation policy the national strategy for the next few years.

Some programs are successfully addressing the need to increase R&D intensity. The Sixth Framework Program for 2004–2006 was successful in increasing industry participation in academic research. The CRAFT program, aimed at small and medium-sized businesses, was of particular significance. However, structural changes in the external environment pushing for a more proactive role of universities in technology transfer only started in Europe in the early 1990s (Baldini, 2006). The transfer of technology from academia to commerce is key to the commercialization of academic research results. Analyzing results achieved in Europe and the United States shows that Europe is ahead of the United States in terms of licenses and new companies produced, whereas Europe trails the

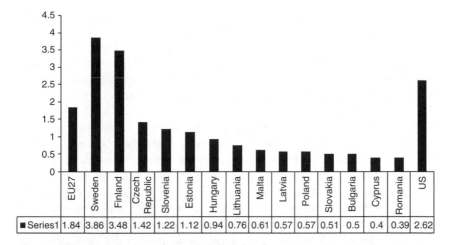

■ Series1	EU27	Sweden	Finland	Czech Republic	Slovenia	Estonia	Hungary	Lithuania	Malta	Latvia	Poland	Slovakia	Bulgaria	Cyprus	Romania	US
	1.84	3.86	3.48	1.42	1.22	1.12	0.94	0.76	0.61	0.57	0.57	0.51	0.5	0.4	0.39	2.62

Source: Based on Eurostat Pocketbooks (2008, p. 10).

Figure 10.1 R&D intensity in the EU27 and the US

United States in terms of income from licenses participating in research ('European technology transfer operates better than believed', 2006).

Innovation and new technologies have always been under development in Poland, which has many inventors and entrepreneurs who have made names for themselves through their ideas and undertakings. In the 1980s, the idea arose to create a technological park in Poznan. Undoubtedly, it was the system reforms following 1989 that laid the foundation for comparatively free infrastructure development for the development of innovation, technology transfer, and commercialization of research results. Matusiak (2006) notes five periods of commercial innovation development in Poland: the pioneers (from the Solidarity revolution to 1993); the solution of labor market problems (1993–96); the stabilization of the system and new ideas (1998–2000); the pre-accession period (1997–2004); and the first experience in the EU (following 1 May 2004). A sixth period can surely be added: the dynamic development and inclusion of Polish institutions in European and global networks for innovation and development of new technologies. At present a significant commercial competitive advantage of Poland and Eastern European countries is low labor costs coupled with a large consumer market. This situation will not continue indefinitely and therefore an essential element of continued company development must be the building of company competencies in innovative operations, including operations in the field of R&D (Ministry of Regional Development, 2007).

Poland is among the group of catch-up countries to the EU level of development (along with Bulgaria, Croatia, Hungary, Latvia, Lithuania, Malta, Romania, Slovakia, and Turkey) but has an above EU27 average rate of improvement. Relative strengths, compared to the EU countries' average performance, are in human resources, firm investments, and economic effects. The relative weaknesses are in finance and support, linkages and entrepreneurship, and throughputs (European Innovation Scoreboard, 2009).

A further indication of institutional development supporting development of innovation and technology transfer is the fact that the survival rate for companies in Poland in their first year of operations for the years 2001–04 was 63 percent. This means that an average of 40 percent of companies ceased operations in this period. A decisive majority of companies financed innovative operations with their own resources (94 percent). Two out of five companies financed innovative operations with external funding. Polish companies utilize academic and developmental body resources to a limited extent. Only every thirtieth company during 2001–03 had R&D cooperation agreements with academic and developmental institutions engaged in the development of new technologies. Companies tend not to engage in R&D as a source of new technological solutions or products as such activities are deemed highly risky and bring no competitive advantage. Nine out of 10 companies introduce all product innovations, and almost three-quarters manufacture new technologies based on their own resources. Sources of an external nature are of little significance to companies. In this case technology transfer leads to the copying of foreign solutions without legal or financial consequence. In the case of a quarter of companies, technology transfer leads to the purchase of research results, whereas one in a hundred companies declares the purchase licenses allowing for use of patents, or consumer and industrial designs (Życiński and Żołnierski, 2007).

The development of new technologies in Poland is becoming more and more dynamic. As recently as 2002–03, software accounted for the largest share in investment expenditure. The second investment group was new production lines. It is particularly worth noting that the level of investment in new technologies was highest in the 'gazelle' segment. Almost every second company invested in new technologies in 2002–03, which is a result twice as high as that noted in the small and medium-sized enterprise (SME) sector of companies not belonging to gazelle. The main new technology investments were directed at the production industry. These companies were in good financial condition owing to steady growth in GNP in Poland from the beginning of the 1990s. The increase of GDP per capita was one of the highest in Europe and significant worldwide. Indices of GDP between 1995 and 2007 were 72.6 percent.

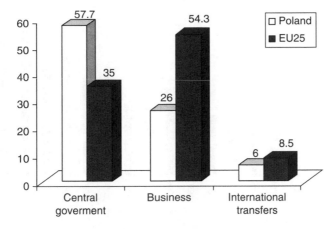

Source: Ministry of Regional Development (2007).

Figure 10.2   Financing of R&D in Poland and the EU25

On the other hand, there is a visible relationship between investment and increased long-term debt. This indicates that a necessary condition for investment in new technologies was external funding in the form of bank loans. Bank loans are a more restrictive form of financing and the restricted financial covenants can hamper a firm's ability to operate independently of the loan sources. Long-term debt usually costs more, since it is more risky. As a consequence, long-term debt was not easy to obtain by SMEs, unless they could be secured with long-term assets (Berger et al., 2004).

A strategic aim of Polish innovation policy for the years 2007–13 is to increase company innovation for the maintenance of an economy on a path of rapid development and to increase financing of R&D results by business (see the finance structure of R&D work in the European Union and Poland presented in Figure 10.2). A condition for the effective implementation of innovation policy is the creation of an efficient institutional system and the development of mechanisms to coordinate activity at the central and local levels. A significant potential conditioning company innovation is R&D potential (Gulda, 2006).

The problems with commercialization result from many factors such as: the minimal cooperation among SMEs and the research sector, low awareness of the opportunities to make use of academic and developmental institution resources for company development, the domination of the purchase of new machines and equipment (Mazurek, 2008) and the low effectiveness of patents. The dominant model for knowledge transfer in

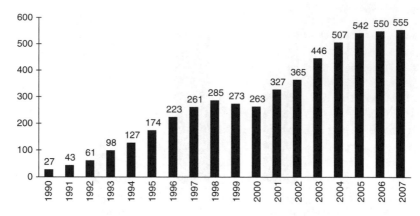

Source: Matusiak (2006).

Figure 10.3   Growth in the number of innovation and business development organizations in Poland

Poland is personnel development, consulting service systems, access to information, and knowledge transfer system organization. This allows for increased scale of the transfers of technical and experimental achievements to national and global circulation. As Jasiński (2005) claims, Polish companies show too little interest in technology transfer and the scale of the diffusion process for technology is too small. From this the models for technology transfer account for changes in innovation infrastructure, know-how, and best-practices transfer.

In recent years, centers supporting transfer and commercialization of research results and technologies, such as technological parks, technology transfer centers, and technology incubators, have become particularly popular (see Figure 10.3).

In Europe, academic-technological parks are seen as entities creating places of employment and the intellectual property market. The concept of a crossbreed as proposed by Pierre Laffitte is very much alive: gather in one place the operations characterized by advanced technologies and financial institutions (Isaak, 2009). The structures supporting the development of technological commerce (centers of innovation, technology transfer, and technology incubators) have the task of caring for the company. A significant element in Poland are the special economic sectors (SSEs), as companies located in SSEs are exempt from income tax for 10 years and pay only half for an additional five (Jaśkiewicz, 1999). One-third of parks are actually projects, that is, at the market entry stage. One-fifth of parks are at a very early stage in development. In 2008, Polish academic-technological parks guaranteed funds, such as raised risk capital funds, were not in operation (Fabrowska et al., 2008).

3 TECHNOLOGY ACCESS KEYS AND LIMITATIONS IN TECHNOLOGY TRANSFER AND COMMERCIALIZATION AND POLISH PERSPECTIVES

Stawasz (2006) highlights that the realization of resource allocations by SMEs is more significant in more economically developed nations. The SME sector is not only a source of invention but also a more effective source of invention (Simon, 2008). In Poland, SME sector companies are decidedly weaker when compared with other EU members (employment in Polish companies is 25 percent lower than the average in the European Union). Market research has indicated (Dzierżanowski et al., 2007) a limited investment of SME into new technologies. Three percent of SMEs invest in R&D, and 2 percent declare cooperation with academics and plan to purchase the results of academic activities. The SME sector invests in lower risk assets such as machinery, plant equipment, and software. Every second SME argues that machinery and plant equipment is its last activity in new technology development. Every third SME has invested in IT software in recent years. A few main factors stimulate the increase of technology transfer and R&D expenditure in Poland. The most significant are:

- competition;
- market sector: production companies have the highest expenses;
- identification of weaknesses in relation to competitors;
- quality of human resources;
- identification of development strategy in company; and
- potential for innovation, such as: the possibility to introduce new products and new production lines, production capability, the chance to enter new markets, and elasticity of production.

Technology transfer is cooperation that 'means active participation with other enterprises or non commercial institutions in innovation activities' (Eurostat Statistical Books, 2008).

Benneworth (2006) argues that there are different models of spin-off development. Some universities focus on supporting entrepreneurial professors (Newcastle University), while others encourage students to create their own businesses after graduating, providing loans, advisory services, and access to laboratories (University of Twente). Universities can have a strong impact on spin-off incubation when they persuade established companies to become involved in core research activities. Universities tend to be more supportive of their daughter companies where they have entrepreneurial infrastructure (for example, technology incubators) on campus. It is easier for them to establish new businesses exploiting their academic knowledge.

Benneworth and Charles (2005) identify the main value of spin-offs in their being high-technology firms. The most successful economies are dominated by high-tech companies, which is why spin-offs generate added value for the economy. Kondo (2007) defines spin-off companies as those commencing operations based on their relationships with the academic world. These companies use the technologies, human resources, and even capital resources of universities in their incubation phase and in later operations. With this in mind, it can be said that such companies are academic companies.

Roberts and Malone (1996) provide a wider interpretation of companies generally referred to as 'splinters', and add that such companies are formed not only on the basis of relationships with universities, but also on the basis of relationships with R&D institutes and government laboratories. Splinter companies are formed with the aim of implementing research results in industry. The industrial application of research into new technologies is therefore key in the formation of spin-off companies. Isabelle (2007) identifies three types of so-called new technological company (NTBFs: new technology-based firms) taking into consideration the type of company on the basis of whose operations the splinter company is formed from and the relationship between the new company and the organization providing know-how or know-who. The three types are: companies formed on the basis of license received from a mother company (spin-off companies); companies formed by university graduates or employees, not associated by license or patent with a mother company (spin-out companies); and companies formed on the basis of knowledge transfer (also on the basis of license received) from a public research agency (spin-in companies).

The generation and transfer of knowledge and technology is the principal goal when creating and developing innovative firms, business infrastructure, science and technology parks, R&D centers, and high-tech incubators. The national and regional strategy has to attract scientific projects, build laboratories, and strengthen the universities. University and industry must engage in appropriate coalitions and play a key role in innovation policy. The creation of new enterprises logically indicates the development of incubators and research laboratories with the support of the university or R&D organization (Bugliarello, 2000).

Technology transfer can be specified as the product- and process-oriented effects of innovations. The main innovation effects of companies in Poland improved the quality of products and services. Two out of five SMEs indicated improved quality as a high degree of importance relevant to the percentage of active innovation enterprises during 2004–06 (GUS, 2008). Enterprises employed more than 249 people focused on an increased range of products as the significant effect of innovation.

The situation in the Polish market concerning innovation, technology development, and science transfer highlights the factors hampering innovation policy in industrial enterprises: cost and market orientation. Lack of funds within the enterprise and the high cost of innovation were dominant barriers to innovation and implementation during 2004–06. These factors above all prevented SMEs from introducing innovation strategies. Polish enterprises suffer from uncertain demand for innovation and companies dominating in the sectors. One key knowledge and technology transfer was difficulty in finding cooperative partners for science and technology commercialization. These factors are important for the development of the science and technology parks and centers for technology transfers at universities. Market research on determinants that stimulate international cooperation of beneficial organizations within the National Coherent Strategy shows that organizations at science and technology parks and high-tech incubators intensively seek international partners for their clients (spin-offs, spin-outs, and other innovative firms).

Innovation policy and international cooperation have been two of the goals of science and technology park managers (ProAcademia, 2008). They work on the stimulation of cooperation between industry and academia. The formal and informal linkages among firms and science and research organizations produce information flows conducive to innovation or lead firms, universities, and R&D institutes to science and technology transfers. Technology and science transfers often depend on the organization of intellectual assets, which creates innovation and makes commercialization of innovation possible. The market value of inventions, new technologies, and new products significantly concentrates on intellectual capital components as human capital (the combination of knowledge, skills, and experience of scientists, firm managers, and employees), structural capital (an organization's ability to transfer know-how and know-why outside the organization), partner capital (the relations between partners used for exchanging knowledge and improving qualifications), and innovation capital (the creation and implementation of new technologies and products to the markets) (Mróz and Rogozińska-Mirut, 2007). Analyzing the enterprises' innovation activity we can argue that qualified personnel, a component of human capital, is one of the weaknesses of

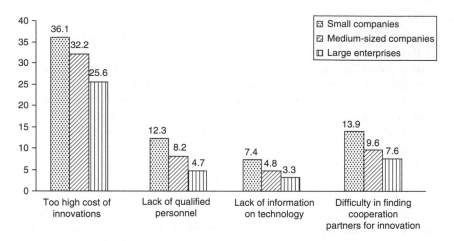

Source: Based on GUS (2008: 153).

Figure 10.4   Main barriers in industrial enterprise activities, 2004–2006

Polish innovation. The lack of qualified personnel is a factor hampering the innovation activity of industrial enterprises but the main barriers in implementing company innovation strategy are the high cost of innovations and the difficulties in finding cooperation partners for innovations (see Figure 10.4).

The facility to apply academic research in practice is possible with the stimulation of Polish academic research institutions, companies, public sector entities, and non-governmental organizations, which can benefit from transferred technologies and know-how and can also offer their own achievements in order to commence commercial operations (Gontar and Trzmielak, 2005). A network of associations is a key element in the transfer of knowledge to business. Further to Mason and Rosner (2002) we can add that the network of associations that exists in contemporary business has led to an easier than ever increase in ideas for new technological solutions external to the organization. Organizations wishing to obtain innovative knowledge place an emphasis on research development or the transfer of results.

Polish governmental organizations, such as the Polish Agency for Enterprise Development did a lot to stimulate and encourage companies, R&D institutes, and academic organizations to be active in commercialization fields. The Polish Agency for Enterprise Development under the honorary patronage of the Polish Ministry of Economy organizes an annual competition for innovative organizations called

Table 10.1   Best Polish technologies and products at International Innovation, New Technology and Products Exhibition in Geneva

2008	2007
Multi-directional recycling of sewage sludge and proteinaceous offal polluted with chromium and other heavy metals	Screening audiometer 'Kuba Mikro AS' Series of frequency converters MFC-710 of rated power up to 315 kW
Integrated 3D measurement system ScanBright	Measuring system for quality inspection of resistance welded joints
PCP – technology of polycarbonate cards personalization	SKZ-81 haulage assembly with a dual power system
Experimental complex for investigation of high temperature properties of molten metals and alloys	Ophthalmic applicators with monolithic active core for eye cancer brachytherapy
Technology for purification of crude nickel sulphate	
Personal bullet-proof suit	

Source: Polski Produkt Przyszłości (2009).

the 'Polish Product of the Future'. The competition categories include product and technology of the future at the pre-implementation stage and product and technology of the future at the implementation stage. The competition has excellent promotional goals. Several of the best technologies were exhibited and awarded with medals, cups, and financial rewards at the International Innovation, New Technology, and Products Exhibition in Geneva. The best of these technologies are presented in Table 10.1.

The effective technology transfer of the best technologies depends on the ability to transform the added value into potential partners, meeting client needs, asset turnover, and return on sales. Unfortunately the grants and awards are only a promotion tool of technology and knowledge management. Companies, R&D institutes, and universities need to improve their targets step by step with measures of technology's added value and value drivers that lead to technology transfer and commercialization.

In terms of the protection of intellectual property rights, the commercialization of research results in Poland has been burdened with the stereotype that the invention itself possesses some added value that should be implemented in the company. Polish law dictates that an invention is a

research results, might form a new academic company (spin-off), which will commercialize the results of research work.

5. A company seeks a partner for R&D activities and offers funding for research and/or cooperation.
6. The company has a team, which, based on the results of research work performed within the company, might form a new company (start-up) within the structure of the business-oriented educational institution.

In analyzing the six situations above that force the management of intellectual property, it is important to define what might be sold and what is of value to the company and academic institution. It should be emphasized here that education associated with the commercialization and transfer of technology aims to provide academics with knowledge, which allows them to differentiate academic value from market value, which Razgaitis terms 'value and price' (2003). Value is the minimum sum of costs borne in the development of technologies, which may be increased by the sum of the academic research institutions' outlay, the rate of invested capital return, the anticipated profit, and the sum of resources allowing for further research on the transaction subject. Price is the value (market value), allocated to or negotiated by the parties to the transaction.

Schuh et al. (2008) indicate four kinds of value, which we may refer to as property transaction value: historical value (costs borne by the research body), present value (costs that might presently be incurred preparing and conducting similar research), trade value (the monetary equivalent that can be received from the buyer), and future value (which comprises future income generated through the implementation or use of intellectual property rights). The last two values are dependent on the construction of the purchase phase (Simon and Fassnacht, 2009). Property transaction value may comprise:

1. patent rights and know-how;
2. technology transfer and know-why: documentation associated with technology (process descriptions, research results), access to academic research institution experts who can advise on the implementation of technology or work for the buyer;
3. rights to equipment used in the R&D phase;
4. guarantee that the patent or other intellectual property exists and is not in breach of third party rights;
5. the right to represent the research body where the research results or patents are associated with another academic activity or other technologies;
6. the right to information or first option to purchase future research

results associated with the transaction subject, which the research body might generate in other research work; and
7.   the right to sublicense.

The first and second situations are examples of the passive activity of academic institutions, which are dominant in the Polish market. This passiveness results from the isolation of patent authorities from the process of commercialization. The commercialization process might begin only when a patent has been granted, and in many cases, this might place limitations on the sales of research results and cooperation with business. However, a developing infrastructure and the entering of R&D activities into the national development program force the third and fourth activities. Scenarios five and six are a beginning of market orientation on the path of R&D product generation. Companies recognizing a strengthened position through development or purchase of research results seek partners for cooperation. This might cover only the ordering of research or participation in joint research projects, or inclusion in a technology incubator with its access to academic institute resources.

The stimulation of joint development projects between academic institutions and research development bodies is a two-way relationship. The business-oriented infrastructure in the form of technology incubators and technology transfer centers and the financing of business projects based on research results attracts business to educational institutions and simultaneously forces the academics to take an active role. They are included in business projects by the companies themselves as companies are offered public funding for cooperation with academics. Thus changes are made in what academic institutions have to offer, bringing about market benefits.

A basic problem that arises in the management of intellectual property at academic institutions are the rights and obligations resulting from intellectual property created within the institution and the share of the intellectual property stakeholders in the commercialization of research results (for example: inventors, laboratory, company, faculty, department, institution, region, business, industrial sector and so on). Each academic conducting academic projects within the scope of academic institutions who creates prototypes produces research results that might be commercialized or from which intellectual property rights (material and economic) might arise is bound by contract of employment with the institution. Thereby research results are the property of the employer. The motivation system does not always consider benefits from the creation of research results suitable for commercialization, other than academic benefit. Research institutes in which new technologies or potentially beneficial innovations are created, in their own interest and in response to market changes, are starting to clearly define the complete process of intellectual property management, including a share in the rights of research results. A significant number of intellectual property management models in academic institutions in Europe and the United States clearly highlight the share (at least in economic terms) of inventors, and the rights to intellectual property.

European countries have recently reformed their intellectual property laws to grant intellectual property rights to universities, echoing the landmark US Bayh–Dole Act. In Polish academic institutions the rising models are aimed at including patent authorities in the commercialization process for research results and transfering, in part, the economic rights to the intellectual property to academics. Changes in the intellectual property protection system have begun in all leading academic institutions. The Jagellonian University has gone furthest with such changes, giving not only economic rights (50 percent of income from commercialization) but also instituting internal university regulations that allow for the transfer of ownership rights to the invention.

The modernization of the technology transfer processes from academics to business through assistance in protecting intellectual property in potential markets is a priority in the development of science and high-tech sectors for the Polish Ministry of Science and Higher Education for the next several years. New policies will allow the university for the first time to maintain a comprehensive record of intellectual property and the commercialization of its intellectual property, which is likely to have a positive effect on the allocation of university resources. It will also facilitate the funding of patent applications with the patent authorities in accordance with the World Intellectual Property Organization and/or the European organization procedures (Santarek et al., 2008).

4   NANOTECHNOLOGIES, NANO SPIN-OFFS, AND THE EUROPEAN ROADMAP

Eloy (2008) indicates that a wide range of possible functions, easier integration, and more affordable pricing create the potential market for nanotechnologies. The nanotechnology market is very fragmented and few products have reached high volume sales. However, general investment in nanotechnology has increased significantly. The value of sales of products employing nanotechnology in 2004 reached approximately €9.5 billion, which accounts for 0.1 percent global industrial output (Wawrzyński and Karsznic, 2007). The sale of products containing elements resulting from research results in the nanotechnology sector is forecast to reach 15 percent of total industrial output by 2015 (Independent Working Group, 2005).

Nanotechnology research has experienced rapid growth in knowledge and innovation. The European Union has recognized nanotechnology as a critical research domain that allows technology transfer from science to business and an increase in a wide range of fields of application. Huang et al. (2006) indicate that by concentrating the analysis only on the rate of number of patent increases in nanoscale science and engineering, significant growth can be observed (the percentage of USPTO nanoscale science and engineering patents increased from 3.8 to 4.9 percent during 2001–04 if patents are keyword searched by 'full-text'). Europe made significant progress during 2002–06 as expenditures in science and nanotechnology R&D reached €1.9 billion in 2006. For comparison, the United States spent €2.7 billion and Japan €2.1 billion (Support of SME share, 2007).

During 2004–06 the global sum of public and private sector expenditures in nanoscience and nanotechnology was €24 billion. Europe accounted for more than a quarter of this amount (European Commission, 2008). The United States, Japan, and the European Union hold the leading places in nanotechnology research. China is also a significant player, and the Chinese government invested approximately €195 million in nanotechnology, particularly in the cities of Beijing, Hong Kong, and Shanghai, the latest of which established the Shanghai Nanotechnology Center (Michelson, 2006). In the United States, work is underway in the following areas: nanoscale forces and processes, nanostructure, nanomaterials, nanoelectronics and nanomagnetics, nanooptics, nanoscale equipment, nanoanalytics in nanoscale, nanobio, nanomedicine, and production machinery and processes. In the European Union, particular emphasis is placed upon the development of nanoelectronics and nanomagnetics, nanostructure and nanomaterials, nanobiotechnology and nanomedicine, as well as nanoscale forces and processes (see Figure 10.5). Japan is the leader in micro-electromechanical systems (MEMS). In 2005, the Japanese MEMS market reached approximately €2.9 billion, with the greatest application value in innovation processing and communication equipment, and automotive and precision equipment (the value of nanoscience and product is presented in Figure 10.6). More than 70 Japanese companies involved in MEMS development and manufacturing have their own clean room and production facilities (Eloy, 2008).

The transfer of nanotechnology research results to the market occurs in most developed and developing countries. The leading position of the United States in a number of applications of industrial products employing nanotechnology results from the commercially stimulated use of innovation. Japan and the European Union are powerful players in the implementation of research results from the area of nanotechnology. However, both regions vary in developing market trends. Japan focuses

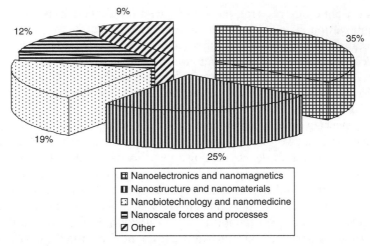

Source: European Commission (2005).

Figure 10.5   EU investment in nanotechnology sectors

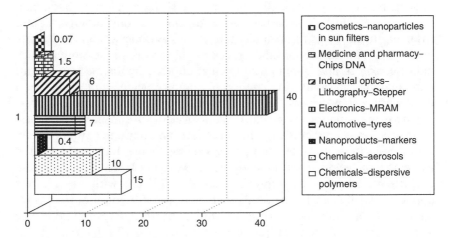

Source: Wawrzyński and Karsznic (2007) based on Luthor (2004).

Figure 10.6   Market value of nanomaterials and products based in nanotechnology (€bn)

on the commercialization of nano sector research results obtained by large companies. In the European Union, activity is concentrated on the transfer of research results to the market via the SME sector. The commercialization of nanotechnology is a dynamic process incomparable to other sectors because it concerns almost all aspects of the creation of a market product (Poteralska and Zielińska, 2007).

In Poland, nanotechnology research is conducted primarily by academic institutions, Polish Science Academy institutes, and R&D institutions. Together with the development of science, an increasing number of SMEs, including spin-offs, are created, which make use of large research institute laboratories, order research, or seek assistance in company development. There has been very significant development and progress in nanotechnology (Ministry of Science and Higher Education, 2006).

Nanoscience and nanotechnologies are the future direction for scientists and businesses but they lead to many problems named by Peterson (2006) as 'The Valley of Death'. Challenges include:

- conflicts in similar patents – broad area of science;
- huge leap from technological discovery to prototype and business plan;
- potential negative effects on health and the environment; and
- export restrictions of the country.

All these difficulties create opportunities for the best projects, scientists, and business plans. The broad area of work offers many scientists and companies the chance to find their niche for future perspectives. Nanoscience and nanotechnologies can be used to repair the damage already done by industry. Nanoscience can address issues related to the environment, biosphere, and water. It improves recycling efficiency by building sustainable systems. Nanoscience and nanotechnologies provide opportunities for SMEs and emerging and developing countries because nanoscience and nanotechnologies construct new industries, create niches in the markets, and make SMEs potential partners for large companies.

Kanama (2007) argues that the technological and economic risks involved with R&D for the nanoparticle area depend on market trends and growth. The highest risk and relative market growth, in 10 years, are in hydrogen storage, pigments, fuel cells, and medical discoveries. The smallest market growth areas are expected in cutting tool bits, antibacterial applications, automotive catalysts, rubber, and new dental composites. However, these areas of nanoscience and nanotechnologies involve relatively low levels of financial risk. Nanotechnology applications are pushing the boundaries in a number of sectors, such as research in the field of microelectronics and the manufacture of nanodevices at the molecular level based on the use of generic material ('Nanotechnology makes use of biotechnology', 2006). Nanoelectronics, nanophotonic, and nanoinstrumentation are three areas that have received the most funding based on dollar investment. They are founded by or associated with leading researchers at top-tier academic institutions (Leff, 2006).

Polish scientific and technological research is concentrated in universities and R&D public institutes. New segments such as biotechnology and nanotechnology provide strong opportunities for new companies. Present research indicates that spin-off companies and start-ups are the best prepared to stimulate innovation transfers in biotechnology and nanotechnology. Polish innovation based on patents is developed in universities and public R&D institutes; however, a change in attitude among researchers in universities is the decisive factor determining the success of technology transfer to the private sector. Polish public and EU money went to support the building of infrastructure in 2002–06. (The number of technology incubators, science and technology parks was doubled; see Figure 10.1.) The new period of financial support focuses on developing laboratories and stimulating the scientific research that would be transferred to high-tech companies.

Countinho et al.'s (2003) study based on Mexico, Costa Rica, Colombia, Brazil, and Chile problem analysis shows that additional support with economic evaluation of technology and products, and the training of researchers on basic aspects of intellectual property plays a crucial role in stimulating research institutes to carry out technology transfers and management functions. The transformation of the science and R&D sectors are the main focus of new EU member states but it is known that new members of the European Union also have a lower number of R&D employees and their enterprises have a low demand for patents (Vaněček, 2008). Other major work has to be undertaken to change companies' preferences in cooperation and innovation policy.

5   TECHNOLOGY TRANSFER AMONG UNIVERSITIES AND ENTERPRISES: THE POLISH NANOTECH START-UP APPROACH TO COMPETITIVE ADVANTAGE

Poland's story of high-tech development following the Second World War is relatively short. Step by step, Polish companies have been trying to enter international markets and compete in R&D markets. Promising high-tech ventures in biotechnology, nanotechnology, and clean energy sectors are actively seeking partners, business angels, and promising scenarios where the transfer of knowledge from high-level universities and R&D institutes to the business world occurs (Trzmielak, 2005). The University of Łódz Technology Incubator is an example of an organization carrying out innovation as an answer to changes in its external and internal surroundings. Two Polish start-ups incubated there sought a way to solve problems that consequently led to an increase in their existing processes, product productivity, and competitive advantage. They interacted with the University of Łódź, which Dalmau Porta et al. (2007) argue has led to technology transfer and enterprise development.

Amepox Ltd and Amepox Microelectronics Ltd: Strategic Challenges with Nanotechnologies

Entrepreneurial ventures in Poland formed on the basis of university knowledge and R&D activity that was demanding and challenging at the end of the twentieth century. Amepox Ltd and Amepox Microelectronics Ltd (AXMC) are typical spin-out companies formed by an academic institution but not associated by license with or patented to a mother company. Since companies use several technology transfer mechanisms and ways to commercialize research and innovations, they are forcing university researchers to seek outside funding and to find new competitive advantages in the market. Technology transfer, defined as a process of transformation of R&D resulting in marketable products (*Paxis Manual*, 2006), occured in AXMC in two dimensions: internal and external. Successful innovation was based on strong knowledge, including R&D capacity and a well-educated staff. Additionally, collaboration was a necessary element of new product development.

Company growth and development

Amepox Ltd based its development primarily on the work of former Technical University scientists. Amepox Ltd's owner had been fascinated with permanent electronic interconnections, adhesives that conduct heat, electricity, and magnetic current, and decided to establish his own firm in 1988. The fundamental assets of the new company were the scientific background and university knowledge and laboratory experience of the new company staff at Łódź Technical University. The electronics market was difficult to penetrate for microcompanies at the end of the 1980s because of Polish law and the monopoly of big electronic companies (many of which collapsed in the early 1990s when Poland entered the free market). The company examined its human resources, diagnosed the market conditions necessary for sustaining a competitive advantage, and focused its activity on manufacturing special chemical resistant materials and applications for the construction industry.

The company defined the market in three areas: customer function, technology, and customer segments. The customer function focused on satisfying the needs of the company's clients. Two needs of the market were recognized at the beginning as: (i) safe usage of plastic floors and (ii) floors and antistatic usable area due to tightened safety and fire regulations. The technology dimension recognized that the physicochemical parameters of prime coat materials should provide easy penetration into surface layers of porous concentrate ground floor, bind weaker fractions, close micropores in concentrated structures, and have high resistance to different typical chemical substances and exploitation factors. Basic technology determinants for competition were the novelty of presented solutions and their technical parameters, along with high quality and compliance with standards. The last dimensions were identified as new industry branches that demand surface charge-free environments – for example, for production of electronic elements, computers, or in computer control rooms. Analysis of the customer segments was important to understand and compare direct competitors and other participants. It provided technical staff with the knowledge of how to create added-value products for the market and for company technology. Innovation in this area required not only competence in regenerating plastics and polymers but also in the antibacterial quality of materials.

After many years of activity on the Polish market, Amepox Ltd was one of the largest manufacturers of high-quality floor materials in Poland. It had highly qualified scientists with PhD degrees, technical staff, and R&D laboratories. The several years that the company's owner worked at the Technical University of Łódź had a profound influence on the R&D activity. Motivated staff started research programs on different types of silver powder and flakes with the highest metallic and ionic purity. The implementation of Amepox R&D results laid the foundation for new a company, Amepox Microelectronics Ltd (AXMC), established in 1991.

AXMC grew to become one of the best-known and most profitable nanoscience companies in the Łódź region and indeed in Poland. The Łódź local government presented the firm with an award in the Łódź high-technology products competition in 2006, 2007, and 2008. The company's most widely known product is nano inkjet glue, which contributes to the development of newer and faster nanoelectronics. Revenues doubled each year following the technology's development in 1998. Nano inkjet glue was typically sold to the electronics industry where buyers consider the quality of the product most important. In most cases, product quality was more important than price because it allowed users to secure a competitive advantage in the sector. Because the development process was long, costly, and risky, the company applied for EU grants. A milestone was reached by AXMC in its Five Framework Program participation, which offered special incentives to encourage companies to work on new products.

R&D and competitiveness

From the beginning of the 1990s, AXMC was very attractive as a cooperative partner in scientific fields. Its intellectual potential and R&D activity made the knowledge and experience of company employees vital during the production of R&D products. AXMC's development has been based on the production of materials for electronic applications. It has unique achievements and technological solutions in electrically conductive formulations with nano silver additive, electrically conductive ink for inkjet technology, thermally activated electrical conductivity with very small particle size formulations, extremely flexible electrically conductive ink, electrically conductive formulations with very high temperature resistance, and silver powder with the highest purity and nano size particles.

AXMC promoted its research, invested in laboratories, and implemented technology for producing atomic-sized silver powder grains. Silver powder with the smallest possible dimensions (3–8 nanometers: nm) is produced by only a few companies in the world. Only two companies in the whole world were able to obtain silver powder dimensions of 3–8 nm in 2006. These achievements have been possible because of cooperation with Polish universities and within EU framework programs.

AXMC technology and knowledge transfer came from two directions: from business to academia and from academia to business. The unique scientific research pursued by AXMC and its close relationship with well-known Polish universities, such as Wrocław Technical University, Łódź Technical University, and Łódź University, created the opportunities to work on new technologies with industrial applications. AXMC and the Biochemistry Institute of Łódź Technical University focused on the research and technical data included in professional literature and evaluating the precise size of nano silver powder. AXMC and its industry implementations afforded a lot experience for scientists at both Łódź universities as they developed new projects based on the technical data gathered during the continued cooperation. The results of the cooperation made it possible to assess the requirements for silver concentration to have effective Gram-plus and Gram-minus bacterium growth inhibition. The scientific organizations that cooperated with AXMC have double results: scientific and market oriented.

Due to 10 years' experience in manufacturing and the technical university background of the company owner and his staff, AXMC successfully formulated a nanotechnology manufacturing strategy. A clear understanding of the impact of nanotechnology on the final products characterized the AXMC cooperative offer with scientists. Low material costs and having their own laboratory provided opportunities for the company to experiment with nanotechnology innovation. Key competitive advantages could be achieved based on human resources and additional cooperation with university R&D departments.

Competencies and international projects
Human resources gave AXMC the opportunity to cooperate with top-level businesses and academics. The president of AXMC knew that cooperation with the best gave them the chance to develop the company and enter new markets. European framework programs were the best way to find financial partners for scientific research. The Fifth Framework Program participation was the first stage to European markets. Poland, in association with other EU countries, began to cooperate in framework programs in 2002. AXMC had started to cooperate with Wrocław Technology University and using its network, AXMC joined an international team working on new materials and processing techniques for bonding and underfiling flip chips and bonding of heatsinks in order to realize a significant improvement in flip chip technology. The project task allowed further miniaturization of microelectronic products. The objectives were very ambitious because the small Łódź company with 15 employees had to demonstrate a top level of research and high-tech knowledge.

The partners in the first project (Nanojoining) were exclusive to AXMC. They became the bridge to international competition. Cybermetix, Boschman Group, Robert Bosch, Microdrop Gesellschaft Fuer Mikrodosier Systeme, Industrial Technology – Eindhoven, the Netherlands Organization for Applied Research, and Thales Microelectronics targeted such developments as new underfill materials containing nano size fillers with superior properties, new electrically and thermally conductive adhesives, a transfer molding process capable of underfiling flip chips in mass volume, and an inkjet dispensing technique for electrically and thermally conductive adhesives. Polish enterprise developed its own proprietary method for producing silver nanoparticles with diameters as small as 3–8 nm. It was a surprise to their partners because only one other company in the world had achieved nanoparticles with diameters of 3–5 nm. The accomplishment attracted global interest from potential customers such as Nokia and Siemens.

The lack of experience in the global market was a key factor stimulating AXMC's progress in wider implications of project discoveries. The big partners concentrated on the microelectronics market and had not recognized the added value of the bactericidal properties of silver. AXMC focused its research on domestic appliances, air conditioning system components, and floor cladding materials. It made use of its core business areas, familiarity, and past experience with hospital and food factories. Silver nanoparticles were found to be extremely effective bactericides and could be used as polymer fillers in new applications. The main benefits for AXMC in participating in the Nanojoining EU project were that new international partners shared their business and scientific know-how and best practices; that new experience was gained on the international R&D markets; and that references for new clients were obtained.

AXMC as a typical spin-off company had strong relationships with universities, including the University of Hamburg, the University of Cambridge, and University College Cork. AXMC worked with these universities on the development of novel inorganic nanostructured materials. The company was interested in novel nanophotonic devices based on an all-inorganic nanostructure with enhanced photoemission activity and thermal stability to be used in transistor light emitting. The new research marked the beginning of the implementation of a new strategy focusing on large consumer markets such as mobile telecommunications, power consumption, and the automotive industry.

The consumer markets needed not only new high-tech products but also lower prices and higher product effectiveness. The more effective product would be commercialized if producers reduced size, weight, material consumption, and power consumption. Nano research goals indicated that various producers of mobile phones, computers, monitors, printers, home appliances, or controller units for automotive applications would be the potential clients for the Łódź company. The developments of nanotechnology and products characterized AXMC's activity in the international market and demonstrated its strengths as an R&D company.

Cooperation with the High-tech Incubator at the University of Łódź
AXMC invested in R&D with an eye on future products in the nanosector. It initiated several cooperation initiatives to find innovative products. Unfortunately building technological strength and its use for a company's competitive development had to be synchronized with business management. AXMC presented novel solutions and new technical parameters of its products but strong competition forced the formulation of an implementation and development strategy for every new innovative group of products. As AXMC's experience in technology management was limited, the EU project provided money, time, and partners to develop new technology but the real market offered higher competitive pressure. Technology and market management needed to forecast the development of the nano sector and assess the market potential for future AMXC products to meet the company goal of transferring novel technologies and innovative solutions to international companies in an effective and profitable manner.

Recognizing the importance of the management role in creating a market and AXMC's technology roadmap, AXMC joined the High-tech Incubator at the University of Łódź. It was one of the first companies to enter the new incubator at the University of Łódź. The president of AXMC, assisted by the highly educated staff, was able to build a team to run a new project that helped with the implementation of the technologies and 'ideas under construction'. The incubator program was supported by Lockheed Martin Corporation, and the Polish government offset the program's costs by having the opportunity to quickly identify pre-qualified strategic partners in the United States and the European Union. AXMC developed a business strategy for high-tech technology products or services in order to bring them into the international market. The company benefited from the Mining and Matching program by establishing relations with American companies, spurring the sale of new products to the world market. AXMC, which worked in the areas of nanotechnology development and implementation in the market, additionally needed:

- assistance in assessing the market potential of its high-tech products;
- access to information: market and industry sector analysis;
- assistance in preparing the enterprise business plan;
- financing from outside sources;
- assistance in negotiating with potential partners and investors;
- help with constructing the best possible model of collaboration with a business partner;
- evaluation of intellectual property with a prediction of the value of technology development with investment of venture capital; and
- optimizing the business model of the enterprise for the coming years.

Two years of cooperation with the University of Łódź (2004–06) provided AXMC with an understanding of the financial markets. There was no doubt that increased nano product sales in the market depended on financial investment in the company. The microelectronic sector needed a larger quantity of AXMC nano silver than the company's production capacity. The new nanotechnology development and growth of sales of nano silver products versus plastic floors and smooth flooring coating indicated that AXMC required a new vision to enlarge production capabilities. It would expand the firm beyond the R&D phase. Venture capital would provide the impetus for such a transition. Those venture capitalists with whom the company met at the university were somewhat reluctant to get involved in funding a venture that was not part of a nano industry but only focused on R&D activities alone and with project partners.

The business future of AXMC

Setting up a business in the nano sector was an interesting challenge as AXMC started with very little cash, no markets, no product for international markets, and no business model for international business cooperation. The technology developed in the EU framework programs brought the company a chance for growth and venture capital investment. The experience with known world organizations, R&D practices, and its core assets affected the value of the company. As an associated client, AXMC spent two years in the High-tech Incubator at the University of Łódź building a business model for R&D generation products. However, one of the most crucial moments was the financial investment into AXMC's new nano silver businesses. The model of venture development and potential foreign clients signaled to the investors that AXMC was a business that could partake in venture capital and grow with nanotechnology.

Producing the new nano product was time consuming. Fortunately, AXMC was given two years from its potential clients for R&D on the nano silver inkjet products, which was enough to finish venture capital negotiation and to invest in new laboratory and production assets. The microelectronic industry wanted the new technology that produces silver nanoparticles with diameters as small as 3–8 nm. AXMC did not spend millions but created a world-class R&D generation product accepted by Nokia and Siemens. Long-term company strategy had to be responsible for production development and maintaining unique skills and knowledge. The firm invented ink-jet technology with nanosilver particles for the microelectronics industry and nanosilver for antibacterial actions. The nano products did not come with high production costs. Therefore, AXMC as a nano product supplier could maintain a competitive advantage over foreign product manufacturers.

6   CONCLUSION AND CAVEATS

The national strategy created by the Polish government for the 2007–13 period aimed at creating key organizational structures that would increase prosperity by focusing on firms' new technology developments. Science and technology development can be one of the company strategies to achieve a successful outcome, defined as the creation of value for new products for the market, a competitive advantage for the company, and increased wealth for the company owners and investors.

Polish high-tech companies try to find new perspectives on competitive global markets by introducing new products in the knowledge base. The new sectors are challenging for Polish scientists and entrepreneurs but are closely connected to the opportunity for international cooperation and innovation industry enterprise activity. Not only do enterprises aim at improving the quality and competitiveness of the product to help the company achieve customer satisfaction, but they also invent new methods and models to help the organization maintain the highest world standards, advance in their activities, and prepare themselves for global cooperation and competition. New sectors and cooperation with the best market players are strategic directions in organization development. Collaboration strategy, especially in the exchange of organization experiences, gives future perspectives for sales growth and revenue.

REFERENCES

Article 24 (2003), *Industrial Property Law*, Zakamycze: Zakamycze Press, 19.

Baldini, N. (2006), 'The act on inventions at public research institutions: Danish universities' patenting activity', *Scientometrics*, **69** (2): 387–407.

Benneworth, P. (2006), 'The role of university spin-off firms in strengthening regional innovation system in weaker place', paper presented at the Sixth European Urban & Regional Studies Conference, Roskilde, Denmark, September.

Benneworth, P. and D. Charles (2004), 'University spin-offs policy and economic development in less successful regions: Learning from two decades of policy practice', *European Planning Studies*, **13** (4), 537–57.

Berger, K., W. Burdecka, J. Chmiel, I. Czaja, R. Drozdowski, A. Forin, W. Ziemianowicz, A. Haber, K. Jasicki, U. Kopeć, B. Kujawa, P. Matczak, Z. Pawłowska, A. Rybińska, M. Skrzek-Lubasińska, A. Tokaj-Krzewska, A. Żołnierski and L. Zienkowski (2004), *Report on SME Sector Companies in Poland for 2002–2003*, Warsaw: Polish Agency for Commercial Development.

Bugliarello, G. (2000), 'Knowledge parks and incubators', in R. Dorf (ed.), *The Technology Management Handbook*, Florida: CRC Press, pp. 1–45.

Countinho, M., E. Balbachevsky, D.O. Holzhacker, D. da Costa Patrão, R. Vêncio, R. Da Silva, M. Lucatelli, L. Dos Reis and M. Marin (2003), 'Intellectual property and public research in biotechnology: the scientists' opinion', *Scientometrics*, **58** (3): 641–58.

Dalmau Porta, J.I., B. Pérez Castaña, I. Baixauli and J. Bauxauli (2007), 'Technology transfer between research units and enterprise: an approach to center model in the impact on territorial strategic targets', in J.J. Girardot and B. Miedes-Ugarte (eds), *Territorial Intelligence and Governance Participative Research – Action and Territorial Development*, International Conference of Territorial Intelligence, Huelve: CAENTI, 68–76, available at: http://www.territorial-intelligence.eu (accessed 15 January 2008).

Dzierżanowski, M., M. Rybacka, S. Szultka, R. Pasternak, K. Flaht, M. Woźnicka, S. Wilski, L. Bielewicz and A. Rządca (2007), *Survey Report. Investment Direction in SME Sector Companies*, Warsaw: Pentor Research International for Polish Agency for Commercial Development.

Eloy, J. (2008), 'Market analysis and growth for micro-nano products', in

D. Tolfree and M. Jackson (eds), *Commercializing Micro-Nanotechnologies Products*, London: CRS Press, pp. 106–142.

European Commission (2005), 'Some Figures about Nanotechnology R&D in Europe and Beyond', Unit G4, Nanoscience and Nanotechnologies, National Strategy for Poland, European Commission, Research DG, December.

European Commission (2008), *Commission Communication to European Parliament and* European Innovation Scoreboard 2008, Comparative Analysis of Innovation Performance, Pro Inno Europe, January, available at: http://www.proinno-europe.eu/metrics (accessed 15 January 2009).

'European technology transfer operates better than believed', (2006), *Cordis Focus*, 271, October: 22.

Eurostat Pocketbooks (2008), *Science. Technology and Innovation in Europe*, European Commission.

Eurostat Statistical Books (2008), *Science. Technology and Innovation in Europe*, European Commission.

Fabrowska, P., D. Kozdęba, M. Mackiewicz, B. Michorowska, A. Moniszka, A. Szerenos, P. Tamowicz, D. Wecławska and E. Wojnicka (2008), *Benchmarking Technological Parks in Poland. Research Results*, Warsaw: Polish Agency for Commercial Development.

Gontar, Z. and D. Trzmielak (2005), 'Knowledge transfer within the scope of an offset program as a chance for Polish companies', in *Acta Universitatis Łódźiensis*, Łódź: Folia Oeconomica, pp. 99–111.

Gulda, K. (2006), 'Innovative policy in Poland to 2013', in *Innovations in Commerce for the Future*, Łódź: SOOIPP Annual, pp. 23–32.

GUS (2008), *Innovation Activities of Enterprises in 2004–2006*, Warsaw: GUS.

Huang, Z., H. Chen, X. Li and M.C. Roco (2006), 'Connecting NSF funding to patent innovation in nanotechnology (2001–2004)', *Journal of Nanoparticle Research*, **8**: 859–79.

Independent Working Group for the Prime Minister's Science, Engineering and Innovation Council (2005), 'Nanotechnology, Enabling Technologies for Australian Innovative Industries', Australia: PMSEIC.

Isaak, R. (2009), 'From collective learning to Silicon Valley replication: the limits to synergistic entrepreneurship in Sophia Antipolis', *Research in International Business and Finance*, **23**: 134–43.

Isabelle, D.I. (2004), 'S&T commercialization strategies and practices', in F. Thérin (ed.), *Handbook of Research on Techno-Entrepreneurship*, Cheltenham, UK and Northampton, MA, USA: Edward Elgar, cited in Association of University Technology Managers and R.M. Hindle and J. Yencken (2003), 'Public research commercialization, entrepreneurship and new technology based firms: an integrated model', *Technovation*, **24** (10): 63–4.

Jasiński, A.H. (2005), *Barriers in Technical Transfer in the Investment Market*, Warsaw: University of Warsaw.

Jaśkiewicz, A. (1999), 'Model concept for technological parks', in B. Marciniec and J. Guliński (eds), *Academic and Technological Parks. A Polish Perspective*, Poznań: Poznań Press, pp. 15–29.

Kanama, D. (2007), 'EU nanoroadmap: issues and outlook for technology road-maps in the nanotechnology fields', *Quarterly Review*, **23**, April: 55–64.

Kondo, M. (2007), 'Upsurge of university spin-offs in Japan', in M.H. Sherif and T.M. Khalil (eds), *Management of Technology. New Direction in Technology Management*, Amsterdam: Elsevier, pp. 92–102.

Leff, D.V. (2006), 'Investment in nanotechnology', in L.E. Foster (eds), *Nanotechnology Science, Innovation, and Opportunity*, Englewood Ciffs, NJ: Prentice-Hall, pp. 57–62.

Lundvall, B. (2004), *Innovation, Growth and Social Cohesion: The Danish Model*, Cheltenham, UK and Northampton, MA, USA: Edward Elgar.

Luther, W. (2004), *Das Wiertschaftliche Potenzial der Nanotechnology*, Dusseldorf: VDI Technologiezentrum GmbH.

Mason, H. and T. Rosner (2002), *The Venture Imperative: A New Model for Corporate Innovation*, Boston, MA: Harvard Business School Press.

Matusiak, K.B. (2006), *Development of Commercial Support Systems: Indicators, Policy and Institutions*, Radom–Łódź: Institute for Sustainable Technologies Press.

Mazurek, B. (2008), *Knowledge and Technology Transfer Model*, Łódź: Higher School of Commerce and Management.

Michelson, E.S. (2006), 'Nanotechnology policy: an analysis of transnational governance issue fading the United States and China', National Science Foundation Young Scholar, available at: http://www.law.gmu.edu/nctl/stpp/pubs/Michelson.pdf (accessed 15.April).

Ministry for Regional Development (2007), *National Reference Framework Strategy 2007–2013*, Ministry for Regional Development, Warsaw, October.

Ministry of Science and Higher Education (2006), *Nanoscience and Nanotechnology: National Strategy for Poland Report*, Warsaw.

Mróz, M. and J. Rogozińska-Mirut (2007), 'The development of intellectual capital in contemporary organization', in J. Lewandowski, S. Kopera and J. Królikowski (eds), *Innovation and Knowledge in Innovative Enterprise*, Łódź: Technical University of Łódź, pp. 27–33.

'Nanotechnology makes use of biotechnology' (2006), *Cordis Focus*, RTD Results Supplement, 57, October: 31.

Paxis Manual for Innovation Policy Makers and Practitioners (2006), 'Analysis and Transfer of Innovation Tools, Methodology and Policy', European Commission General Enterprise & Industry Directorate.

Peterson, C. (2006), 'Perspective on policy: maximizing benefits, minimizing downsides from nanotechnology', *Foresight Nanotech Update*, **56**: 13–14.

Polski Produkt Przyszłości (Polish Agency for Enterprise Development) (2009), available at: http://ppp.parp.gov.pl/druk.php?proc=538 (accessed 30 April 2009).

Poteralska, B. and J. Zielińska (2007), 'Organization of research within the field of nanotechnology and nanoscience in the world', in A. Mazurkiewicz (ed.), *Science and Nanotechnology: State and Perspectives for Development*, Radom: Institute for Sustainable Technologies Press – State Research Institute, pp. 295–406.

ProAcademia (2008), 'Determinanty rozwoju współpracy międzynarodowej beneficjentów funduszy strukturalnych na poziomie Narodowej Strategii Spójności', Łódź : Raport końcowy dla Ministerstwa Rozwoju Regionalnego (unpublished report).

Razgaitis, R. (2003), *Valuation and Practicing of Technology-based Intellectual Property*, New York: John Wiley & Sons.

Roberts, E.B. and D.E. Malone (1996), 'Policies and structures for spinning out new companies from research and development organizations', *R&D Management*, **26** (1), 17–47.

Santarek, K., J. Bagiński, A. Buczacki, D. Sobczak and A. Szerenos, (2008), *Technology Transfer from Academic Institution to Business: Creation of Technology Transfer Mechanisms*, Warsaw: Polish Agency for Commercial Development.

Schuh, G., S. Klapser and C. Haag (2008), 'Technology balance: technology valuation according to IASB's value in use approach', in W.M.H. Sherif and T.M. Khail (eds), *Management of Technology Innovation and Value Creation*, Singapore: World Scientific, pp. 105–07.

Siemaszko, A. and J. Supel (2006), *Analysis of Polish Team Participation in Framework Research, Technology Development and Implementation Projects*, Warsaw: National Contact Point for European Union Research Projects.

Simon, H. (2008), 'Hidden champions of the 21st century: success strategies of unknown world leaders', Seminar materials, November 17, Warsaw.

Simon, H. and M. Fassnacht (2009), *Preismanagement*, Netherland: Gabler.

Stawasz, E. (2006), 'Trends and barriers in SME development in Poland', in *Innovation and Commerce for the Future*, Łódź: SOOIPP Annual, pp. 33–48.

'Support of SME share' (2007), SMEs in Framework Programs for Scientific Research, European Commission.

Trzmielak, D. (2005), 'Knowledge transfer from academia to business: experiences of the Polish university offset program', in D. Trzmielak and M. Urbaniak (eds), *Technology Policy and Innovation: Value-Added Partnering in a Changing World*, Łódź: Innovation Center at the University of Łódź, pp. 245–50.

Vaněček, J. (2008), 'Patenting propensity in the Czech Republic', *Scientometrics*, **75** (2): 381–94.

Wawrzyński, R. and W. Karsznic (2007), 'Applications of nanotechnology', in A. Mazurkiewicz (ed.), *Science and Nanotechnology: State and Perspectives for Development*, Radom: Institute for Sustainable Technologies Press – State Research Institute, pp. 251–94.

Życiński, S. and A. Żołnierski (2007), *Report on SME Sector Companies in Poland for 2005–2006*, Warsaw: Polish Agency for Commercial Development.

11. Portugal at the crossroads of change, facing the 'shock of the new': people, knowledge and ideas fostering the social fabric to facilitate the concentration of knowledge-integrated communities*

Manuel Heitor and Marco Bravo

1 INTRODUCTION

This chapter focuses on the challenges that specific world regions and small countries, like Portugal, are facing in their experience of international knowledge networks. It is factual and presented in the context of the emerging debate worldwide on patterns of innovation (OECD, 2009a) and the need for long-term growth strategies. The analysis requires us to look at competence building and the need to better understand the evolving phenomenon of 'democratizing innovation' (von Hippel, 2005); we argue that value creation requires a serious commitment to the advanced training of human resources ('Increasing human resources', 2004) and to supporting and promoting their research (basic and translational) through knowledge networks.

This is because Portugal has recently achieved the Organisation for Economic Co-operation and Development (OECD) average in terms of the number of researchers per thousand workforce (that is, about 8.2 in 2009, although this is still low compared to the United States and Japan) and it has become a commonplace that 'knowledge is increasingly important'. Commonplaces are comforting, but often sterile, both intellectually and in terms of suggesting actions to private and public decision makers, given that it is difficult to add much novelty to discussions associated with commonplaces (Conceição et al., 2003a).

Some 40 years after John Ziman launched a discussion on 'public knowledge' (1968) and 30 years after his work on 'reliable knowledge' (1978), to appreciate the significance of scientific knowledge we must understand the nature of science as a complex whole. In *Real Science* (2000), we are reminded 'science is social', meaning 'the whole network of social and epistemic practices where scientific beliefs actually emerge and are sustained'. The practical implication is that we need to maintain the expansion of the social basis for scientific and technological development. This demands strong convictions not only from the scientific and technical professions and from public and private research organizations, but also from students and from the general population. The growing appropriation of scientific and technological culture by society is thus one of the central aspects of the argument discussed in this chapter.

It is in this context that the American system is often taken as a world reference, although analysis has shown that it is of the utmost importance to understand the diversity of policies and mixture of public and private incentives (Conceição et al., 2004). Moreover, its long history of past investments and current division of labor or specialization cannot be replicated in systems of smaller scale and less complexity. The key elements of American history are those of diversity of policies and increasing institutional specialization and of the clarification of the unique roles of private and public incentives to support science and technology (S&T).

We must take up the challenge of probing deeper into the relationships between knowledge and the development of our societies. Our inspiration comes from, among others, the seminal work of Lundvall and Johnson (1994), who challenge the commonplace by introducing the simple, but powerful, idea of learning. Lundvall and Johnson speak of a 'learning economy', not of a 'knowledge economy'. The fundamental difference is the dynamic perspective. In their view, some knowledge does indeed become more important, but some also becomes less important. There is both knowledge creation and knowledge destruction. By forcing us to look at the learning process, rather than the mere accumulation of knowledge, they add a dimension that makes the discussion more complex and more uncertain, but also more interesting and intellectually fertile.

The richness of the concept of the learning economy has been demonstrated in recent years throughout the world by both leading scholars and policy makers. It has been recently addressed beyond Europe (Conceição et al., 2003b), and it is at the center of the debate in China, India, and Brazil. For example, M.G.K. Menon, former Indian Minister of Science and Technology and Member of Parliament and current President of the

India International Center in New Delhi, has recently written about the conditions necessary for innovation to thrive, which require specific local action through a process of communitization.

This closely follows the lessons that Eric von Hippel (2005), a well-known professor at MIT, has provided in recent years based on the American experience that user-centered innovation is a powerful and general phenomenon. It is based on the fact that users of products and services – both firms and individual consumers – are increasingly able to innovate for themselves. This is growing rapidly due to continuing advances in computing and communication technologies and is becoming both an important rival to and an important feedstock for manufacturer-centered innovation in many fields.

Von Hippel has also shown that the trend toward democratization of innovation applies to information products such as software and also to physical products, and is being driven by two related technical trends: first, the steadily improving design capabilities (that is, innovation toolkits) that advances in computer hardware and software give to users; and second, the steadily improving ability of individual users to combine and coordinate their innovation-related efforts via new communication media such as the internet. In other words, beyond suitable technical infrastructure, the process of democratization of innovation requires people with the ability to engage in knowledge-based environments. It is about people and knowledge, and this constant interaction has gained particular importance in recent years.

It is clear that the emerging patterns of innovation require new perspectives for public policies, which in many countries have in the past relied on supporting manufacturers and their intellectual property. Certainly we need to move on from those days and consider better ways to integrate policies, as well as to diversify across Europe (Conceição and Heitor, 2005).

The remainder of this chapter is organized as follows. Section 2 shows the recent impressive progress Portugal has made in knowledge-related indicators, especially since the second half of the 1990s, as well as the country's relatively low commitment to the knowledge economy some 20 years ago. We quantify the evolution of people, knowledge and ideas and argue for the need to understand the complex interactions between knowledge and society. This leads to Section 3 where the structure of incentives within the European context is discussed, including its differences from the US system, which is often taken as a world reference. Section 4 addresses the institutional context, focusing on higher education and the structural reform undertaken in Portugal in recent years. Our final discussion and conclusions are presented in Section 5.

2   THE CONTEXT TO FOSTER PEOPLE, KNOWLEDGE AND IDEAS

The current emerging discussion on the role of knowledge and innovation should be understood in the context of the social and economic changes in Portugal within the European Union. This is quantified in terms of the changes in people, knowledge production and the diffusion of ideas, focusing on the evolution from a period based on investment to a stage based on innovation.

Methodological Background

Bearing in mind the concept of the knowledge-based economy, it can be said that performance in competitive knowledge environments depends basically on the quality of human resources (namely their specializations, skills, educational levels, and learning capacity) and on activities and incentives that are oriented towards knowledge creation and diffusion (Conceição et al., 2003a).

This analysis is framed conceptually in a systemic view of the role of knowledge, in which the main issue concerns knowledge sharing and diffusion. Therefore, the analysis focuses on the understanding of a complex national context, considering the following factors:

- *People*: refers to the country's human capital, in particular to the levels of formal education achieved by its workforce. Portugal has a dual society (Conceição and Heitor, 2005), in which most of the mature workforce has low educational and training levels, contrasting with a younger population with similar qualifications levels to those in other OECD countries. This has resulted in new challenges for developing the workforce's qualifications and attracting new talents to science and technology in order to foster scientific employment and expand national and international knowledge networks.
- *Knowledge*: is linked to the creation of new knowledge in Portugal because the country had serious deficits in the scale and intensity of its research and development (R&D) in the recent past in comparison with other OECD countries.
- *Ideas*: refers to knowledge diffusion and therefore to the innovative capacity to which the relationship of firms with R&D centers brings new challenges and also increasing accountability of its activities.

In order to complete the analysis, other aspects are discussed that are considered in our conceptual framework, such as:

- *Incentives*: consisting of 'necessary conditions', especially in terms of the public and private efforts that are vital to develop new and disseminate existing knowledge. In this context, market conditions, competitive structures and public policies are considered, especially those associated with R&D and higher education funding.
- *Institutions*: consisting of 'sufficient conditions' for scientific development and the success of a system able to foster sustainable strengthening of scientific institutions, as well as an appropriate legal and institutional framework for higher education at international reference levels.

In this discussion we avoid the issue of infrastructure, in terms of the necessary conditions for the development of science, the functioning of scientific institutions and their relationship with society and firms in particular. The section discusses the structure of incentives by looking at Europe and the United States as a whole and identifying relevant differences between them. In addition, institutions are discussed in the particular context of higher education and the related major reforms undertaken in Portugal in recent years.

People

The number of researchers in Portugal has recently achieved the average OECD level in terms of the number of researchers per thousand workforce. In 2009, for the first time it reached about 8.2 per thousand workforce. It is thus nowadays similar (and even higher in some cases) to the levels of Spain, Ireland, Italy, Germany, the Netherlands, and the United Kingdom. Figure 11.1 shows that in recent years Portugal had the second highest percentage growth rate in terms of the total number of researchers (measured in full-time equivalent, FTE) per thousand workforce (about 34 percent), well above the European average (which grew by only 5.4 percent from 2003 to 2006), Spain (13 percent) and Ireland (7 percent).

Although the values given may have been associated with an attempt by those responsible for R&D statistics in Portugal to bring the figures closer to reality by devoting more attention to statistical inputs from particular areas of business, the data also show that the increase in overall research personnel has been matched by a significant increase in the total researchers in the business sector, which has increased by 111 percent between 2005 and 2007, and 170 percent between 2005 and 2009, from 4,014 to 10,841 FTE (Figure 11.2). Most strikingly, according to the Ministry of Foreign Affairs, in 2009 and 2010, Portugal attracted over 1,200 highly qualified

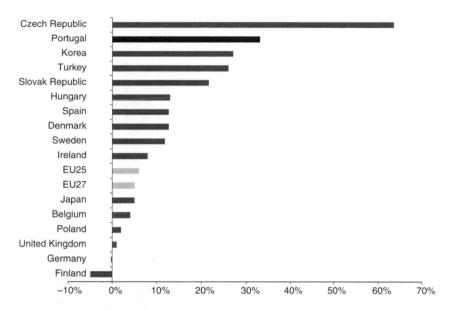

Sources: MSTI-2008, OECD; Portugal: GPEARI/MCTES: Gabinete de Planeamento, Estratégia, Avaliação e Relações Internacionais/Ministério da Ciência, Tecnologia e Ensino Superior, *Inquérito ao Potencial Científico e Tecnológico Nacional* (IPCTN).

Figure 11.1   *Variations in the number of FTE researchers per thousand working population, 2005–2007*

foreigners of more than 40 nationalities outside the European region, almost seven times the number in 2007. Of the total of 1,225 highly skilled foreigners pursuing their professions in Portugal in 2009 and 2010, 183 were researchers, while 356 were academics and the remaining 686 were mostly business professionals, medical and paramedical practitioners, computing experts, electrical engineers, chemical specialists, legal specialists, liberal professionals, and other highly trained personnel.

The proportion of R&D personnel as a percentage of total employees varies significantly between OECD countries (Figure 11.3) (OECD, 2009b). In 2005, Finland and Sweden had the highest number of people employed in R&D occupations, respectively, 32 and 28 people per thousand employed. On the other hand, Mexico had only two people employed in R&D per thousand employed, while Turkey had four. Portugal and Poland also showed levels below 10.

Regional differences within countries are the largest in the Czech Republic and Austria, where, respectively, in the regions of Prague and Vienna there are more than 40 people per thousand employed in R&D. In

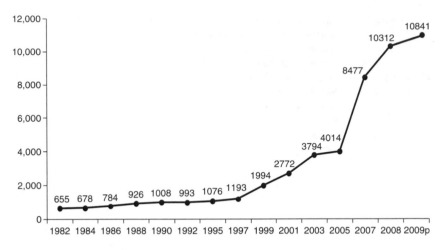

Note: (p) provisional data.

Source: GPEARI/MCTES: Gabinete de Planeamento, Estratégia, Avaliação e Relações Internacionais/Ministério da Ciência, Tecnologia e Ensino Superior, *Inquérito ao Potencial Científico e Tecnológico Nacional* (IPCTN).

Figure 11.2   Total R&D researchers in the business enterprise sector (FTE), 1982–2009(p)

the case of Portugal, there were over 20 people per thousand employed in Lisbon in R&D in 2007, more than twice the country's average.

It should be noted that for 13 out of 17 countries taken into consideration by the OECD (2009), the capital region has the highest rate of employees in R&D, in most cases with values much higher than the country average. But concentration in the capital region of R&D personnel is also seen in countries showing less regional dispersion.

Our analysis is based on the evidence that the skill level of the labor force determines a region's ability to promote and use innovation. Two additional issues should be considered, (i) the level of women's participation in science; and (ii) the number of students in tertiary education.

Regarding women in science, the latest available data show that Portugal has achieved a remarkably high rate of female researchers, particularly in academic research (Figure 11.4), with their share of the total number of researchers increasing from about 41 percent in 1997 to 44 percent in 2007.

The number of students currently in tertiary education is important because it determines, in part, a region's future competitiveness in terms of its ability to promote and use innovation. Taking students enrolled in tertiary education as a percentage of the total population in 2005, on average

Source: OECD (2009b).

Figure 11.3   Regional disparities in R&D personnel per 1,000 employees in OECD countries, 2005

of about 4 percent of the population were enrolled in tertiary educational programs in OECD countries. Portugal follows this average, but the figure varies significantly between countries (Figure 11.5). South Korea had the highest percentage of students (more than 6 percent), followed by the United States and Finland.

In 20 out of 23 OECD countries, there is a positive correlation between a skilled labor force and the number of universities and students, showing that some regions are better equipped than others in terms of current and future stock of human capital, and for dealing with technological change.

Regional differences within countries were even larger than among countries. Portugal, together with the Netherlands, Ireland, the United Kingdom, Canada, and Japan, displayed narrow differences in tertiary enrollment rates. On the other hand, Sweden, the Czech Republic, and the Slovak Republic showed the largest internal differences in enrollment in tertiary education, ranging from over 10 percent to close to zero. For

a) Per performing sector

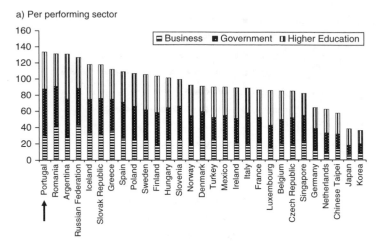

Source: OECD (2007a).

b) Evolution 1997–2003

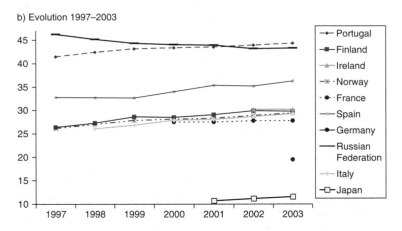

Note: Headcount, for last available year or 2003.

Source: OECD, data extracted September 29, 2010 from OECD.Stat.

Figure 11.4   Women as a percentage of all researchers, 2008

the Czech Republic and the Slovak Republic and for most of the other countries taken into consideration, the region displaying the highest rate is the capital region.

It should be noted that over the 10 years between the mid-1990s and the mid-2000s, the total student enrollment in higher education institutions

Note: On average, about 4% of the population were enrolled in tertiary educational programs in OECD countries. The capital region displays the highest rate of enrollment in advanced education in most OECD countries, with the notable exception of the USA.

Source: OECD (2009b).

Figure 11.5   Percentage ranges of students enrolled in tertiary education in OECD regions, 2005

worldwide nearly doubled. As a result, institutions are engaging in and moving toward new kinds of transnational partnerships and mergers. But in comparison to the United States, European universities must overcome a greater number of challenges in this competitive and global educational landscape. For instance, considerable differences exist between Europe and the United States in the type of student engaged in higher education and the level of performance of individual universities. European universities not only have a smaller proportion of students between the ages of 20 and 29 enrolled in tertiary education compared to the United States, but the United States has significantly more universities ranked highly by the leading university ranking references. Additionally, differences in the strength of institutional leadership are suggested by significantly fewer highly cited researchers at European institutions, and in autonomy, separate European and American universities.

It is obvious that the rise in qualification level of the young Portuguese population is associated with the fact that the Portuguese higher education system grew rapidly in the 1980s and 1990s and opened up to young people of all social classes, rising from 30,000 students in the 1960s, to nearly 400,000 students since the late 1990s. After a period of relative stagnation, the following figures quantify the current trend associated with the reform process described later in this chapter:

- Total enrollment in tertiary education of 20-year-olds has increased by 10 percent over the last three years (2005–08), reaching about 33 percent of this age-group (compared to 30 percent in 2005). In other words, one in three 20-year-olds in Portugal is enrolled in tertiary education. This is similar to the European average, although still lower than that for most industrialized regions. It has resulted mainly from an increase in non-university higher education opportunities, which grew at a considerably higher rate than that of university education.
- Total enrollment in tertiary education of adults aged 30–34 has increased by about 20 percent over the last three years (2005–08), reaching about 4.1 percent of the corresponding age group (compared to 3.5 percent in 2005).
- The total number of graduates per year increased by about 19 percent over the 2005–07 period, with graduates in S&T rising in recent years to about 18 per thousand population aged 20–29 years (well above the EU average). At the same time, the number of new PhDs in science and engineering (S&E) per thousand population aged 25–34 increased to 0.42 in 2007, compared to only about 0.3 in 2001.

Figure 11.6 quantifies annual changes in S&T higher education entrants, graduates and PhDs for 1993–2003 and clearly positions Portugal among countries that favor technical education. This is important, because according to recent findings, increases in the number of students in S&T fields appear to be correlated with increases in gross expenditure on S&T per inhabitant, whenever the annual average increase of gross expenditure on R&D (GERD) per inhabitant exceeds 3 percent.

Moreover, the need to foster public understanding of science and to improve scientific and technological culture in society at large is well accepted in Portugal as part of the national science policy, in which schools and other institutions (particularly science centers and science museums) have an important role in stimulating curiosity and desire for

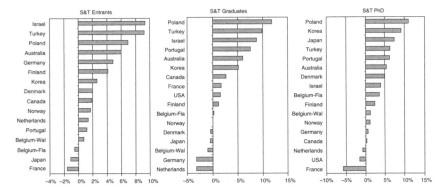

Source: OECD (2006).

Figure 11.6   *Average annual change of S&T higher education entrants,*
graduates, and PhDs, 1993–2003 (mean normalized
regression coefficient)

scientific knowledge. The European report 'Benchmarking the Promotion of RTD culture and Public Understanding of Science' (Miller et al., 2002) acknowledges the leading role of national programs such as *Ciência Viva*, implemented in Portugal since 1996.

Public funding for the promotion of scientific and technological culture has attained the indicative level of 5 percent of public S&T funding. The network of *Ciência Viva* centers has been extended throughout the country to a total of 18 centers at present. Projects to reinforce experimental teaching of the sciences in primary and secondary schools and to promote scientific and technological culture are being implemented in close cooperation with schools and research centers, corresponding to approximately €14 million of public funding in 2007–08. In addition, the *Ciência Viva* holiday program places secondary school students in research and higher education institutions, including, for the first time in 2008, an exchange between Portugal and Spain. This program has involved over 5,800 secondary school students since 1997. Also, the public involvement of children and their families in summer activities in astronomy, biology, geology, and engineering has become routine under the scope of the *Ciência Viva* centers.

Although these figures indicate clear progress, they also show that the country has a long way to go in an increasingly globalized society. Portuguese society shows dual characteristics concerning educational qualifications. There is an active workforce with low educational levels and a younger population with similar qualifications to countries with more developed economies. However, development in the educational

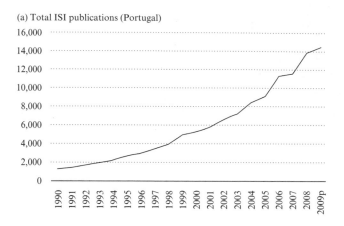

(a) Total ISI publications (Portugal)

Note: (p) provisional data.

Sources: GPEARI: Gabinete de Planeamento, Estratégia, Avaliação e Relações
Internacionais, method of global count from Thomson Reuters, National Citation Report
for Portugal 1981/2009.

Figure 11.7a   Scientific publications

structures is held back by high retention and school dropout rates in
secondary education. Until a few years ago, Portugal had the highest premature school dropout rate of the entire European Union (the premature
dropout rate is of individuals from 18 to 24 years of age, who left school
before completing secondary education – twelfth year of studies – per each
100 individuals from 18 to 24 years of age). Premature integration into the
labor market, with low qualification levels, makes this population very
vulnerable in periods of economic stagnation or slowdown occur.

Knowledge

We recognize that scientific progress is a source of development. In fact,
according to the *Frascati Manual,* R&D is defined as a 'creative work undertaken on a systematic basis in order to increase the stock of knowledge of
man, culture and society, and the use of this stock of knowledge to devise
new applications' (OECD, 2002). Thus, public resources invested under
rigorous international assessment policies lead to new knowledge, better
advanced training of new human resources for society, new ideas and processes, which increasingly result in innovation, modernization of institutions,
improved quality of life, economic productivity, and better employment.

Scientific output in Portugal has doubled since 2004 when measured in

(b) Publications per million population (2006) in relation
to public expenditure on R&D

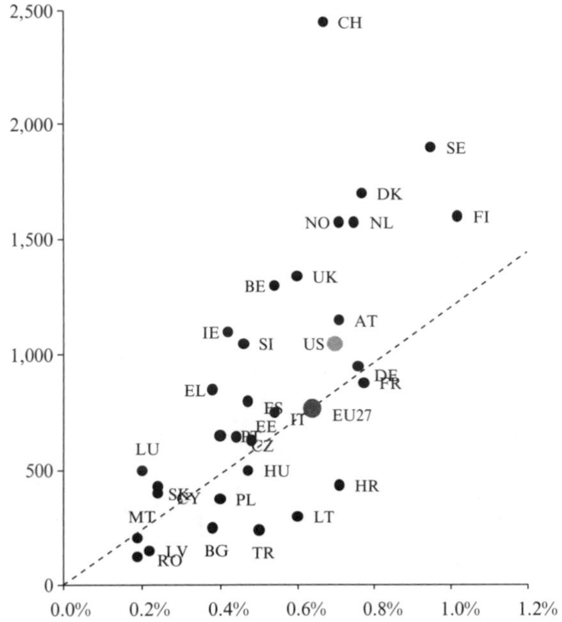

Note: The dotted line links the origin to EU27 – for the points in this line the ratio
between the two values is equal to that of EU27 average.

Source: 'A more research-intensive and integrated European Research Area – Science
Technology and Competitiveness Key Figures Report 2008/09', European Commission,
DG Research; Data from Thomson Scientific/CWTS, Leiden University, Eurostat, OECD.

Figure 11.7b   Scientific publications

terms of the number of internationally referenced scientific publications.
Figure 11.7(a) shows that scientific output in Portugal has increased by
more than 1,000 percent over the last two decades measured in terms of
the number of internationally referenced scientific publications, 1,275 in
1990; 14,460 in 2009. Figure 11.7(b) quantifies the relative scientific competitiveness of OECD countries and shows that Portugal, with about 626
scientific publications per million population in 2008, is above the EU27
average ratio between output (publications) and input (public expenditure
on R&D). This indicates that Portugal's science base is internationally
competitive, although still lacking the critical mass necessary for the concentration of knowledge-integrated communities.

The growth in Portugal's scientific production is currently based on

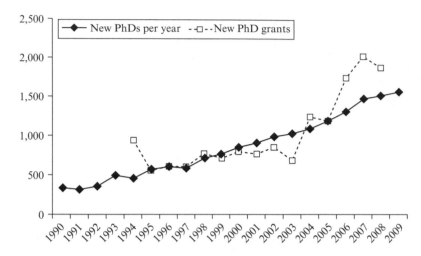

Note: * Data not available for comparative purposes in the 1990–94 period.

Sources: GPEARI: Gabinete de Planeamento, Estratégia, Avaliação e Relações Internacionais; Fundação para a Ciência e a Tecnologia (FCT): Portuguese Science and Technology Foundation.

Figure 11.8   New PhDs concluded and new grants awarded by the Portuguese Science and Technology Foundation (FCT), 1990–2007

about 12,000 PhD researchers working in academic R&D centers (measured in FTE), corresponding to an increase of 25 percent in the last two years and a doubling of the number of PhD researchers since 2000. This strong growth has had clear results in terms of the impact and visibility of the Portuguese scientific community internationally.

It should also be noted that around 20 percent of all new PhDs awarded since 1990 have been awarded or recognized in Portugal in the last two years. In 2009, Portugal had surpassed the target of 1,500 new PhDs a year (Figure 11.8). The percentage of new PhDs awarded to women recently passed the 50 percent mark, the highest percentage ever. The number of new PhDs in S&E fields currently represents around half (47 percent) of the total, while in the early 1990s they accounted for only one-third of all PhDs awarded (31 percent in 1991). This reveals the increasing capability of Portuguese universities in offering PhD programs, as well in international cooperation, but it also poses new challenges regarding the mechanisms that guarantee the quality of PhD programs, and the need to strengthen their internationalization and to establish international scientific research networks, in which PhD students can be essential links.

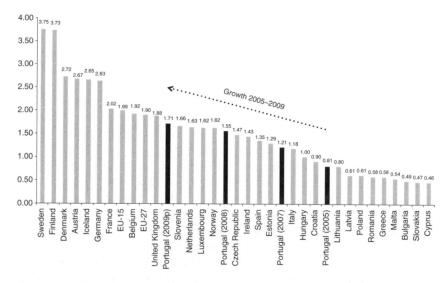

Note: Data for 2008; values for Sweden, Denmark, and Czech Republic are estimates; values for Austria, Germany, Belgium, UK, and Bulgaria are provisional; Portugal: 2005, 2008 and 2009p (p = preliminary).

Source: Eurostat, MSTI 2009, Main Science and Technology Indicators.

Figure 11.9   Total R&D expenditure as a percentage of GDP per country, 2008

The rise in PhD holders has been promoted in recent years, together with scientific employment, through a new program launched in 2007 to support contractual arrangements for researchers. Over 1,200 new PhD researchers were contracted by summer 2009. It is expected that this will stimulate major changes in the academic community and facilitate the renewal of teaching and research staff. In addition, it is clear that the national and international mobility of new PhD holders, mainly within the European area and in the context of a need to promote the internationalization of research units is particularly relevant in the current stage of development of the Portuguese S&T system.

The evolution documented in the previous paragraphs is the result of investments; Figure 11.9 illustrates that in 2009 the total R&D expenditure in Portugal (1.71 percent of GDP; it was 1.55 percent in 2008) surpassed that of Spain (1.35 percent) and that of Ireland (1.43 percent) in 2008. Portugal had the highest growth of any European country in terms of total R&D expenditure in the 2005–07 period (about 46 percent as a percentage of GDP), well above the EU15 average (only 1 percent), Spain (9 percent), and Ireland (5 percent).

Again, we should note that the values given may have been given a positive bias by the efforts of those processing R&D statistics in Portugal to bring the figures closer to reality. Nevertheless, this should not be considered as a methodological change but rather as an attempt to uncover hidden and/or underestimated R&D efforts within a stable methodology. In fact, the total public budget for R&D grew at 11 percent per year from 2004 to 2009, while it had grown at 10 percent per year from 1995 to 2002, among the highest figures in Europe. This is important, because analysis has shown that fostering and maintaining excellence of the knowledge infrastructure is the most effective way for public funding to provide and facilitate resources (including qualified human skills) to firms and to stimulate their own investment in S&T, as well as to foster an entrepreneurial environment for innovation (Conceição and Heitor, 2005).

In fact, the increase in public investment in R&D in recent years is matched by a steep rise in companies' investment in R&D. The businesses' share of the GERD grew by 71 percent from 1995 to 2005, a figure unmatched in Europe, as described below. But it was only from 2005 onwards that business expenditure on R&D exceeded that of higher education institutions, with overall figures exceeding €1 billion from 2007 onwards. These changes coincided with a review of the tax system for corporate R&D in 2005, in a way that has fostered business expenditure on R&D, as well as the employment of research personnel in private corporations.

Regional differences within countries are even larger than among countries (Figure 11.10). The United States, Sweden, Finland, and Korea show the largest regional disparities in R&D intensity across their regions. For the United States, the state of Maryland devotes 5.8 percent of its GDP to R&D, while the state of Wyoming spends only 0.45 percent. Ireland, together with Greece, the Slovak Republic, Belgium, and Portugal, displayed minor differences in R&D intensity between regions. It appears that countries in which R&D intensity is the highest are, on average, also those displaying the most internal disparities.

But our focus is on the conditions that have fostered the *concentration* of knowledge-integrated communities and, therefore, the localization of large R&D intensities (R&D expenditures as a percentage of GDP). While we continuously improve our understanding of knowledge-based economies and the processes that enable learning societies to be sustainable, analysis has systematically shown the combined and evolving role *institutions* play, together with that of *incentives* (Conceição et al., 2003b).

Over the last decade, science policy toward institutional development in Portugal has been based on two main pillars: (i) strengthening and

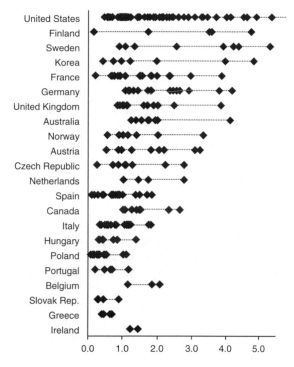

Source: OECD (2009b).

Figure 11.10 Range of regional R&D intensity (R&D expenditure as a function of GDP) in OECD countries, 2005

restructuring the network of research centers throughout the country (in universities and related private, not-for-profit institutions) through a systematic international evaluation every three years with direct impact on their funding levels, which has consistently been implemented in Portugal since 1996; and (ii) promoting critical mass across all scientific disciplines by establishing a network of selected 'Associated Laboratories' in the form of relatively large research consortia oriented towards thematic networks in a number of selected institutions after an international assessment. By 2007, the network of scientific institutions included 510 research centers (257 after the 1996 evaluation) and 25 Associated Laboratories (with the first three launched in 2001), with an overall level of institutional funding of about €71 million in 2007 (€25 million in 1999).

It is in this context that a revised approach to institutional development has recently been launched, with particular emphasis on institutional cooperation at national and international levels, as a way of encouraging scientific activity in networks that promote inter-institutional relations. As well as helping to overcome the effects of the limited size of some research units, developing such science-based networks is intended to encourage the creation and dissemination of new knowledge and stimulate scientific development in a climate of constant change and growing internationalization of the scientific base.

In this respect, one critically important and emerging institutional issue relates to the training of students and young scientists in order to provide them with the core competencies that help them become successful researchers and prepare them with the appropriate transferable skills for the job market outside research and academia (Ernst, 2003).

In addition, recognizing scientific knowledge as a public good introduces the need to consider new policy dimensions in S&T policy that are designed and implemented in a way that fosters independent scientific institutions, for which the organization of transnational institutions might provide a useful framework. It is also in this context that major efforts have been undertaken to promote the internationalization of the Portuguese scientific community.

Casual observations show that patterns of scientific strength and weakness are strongly influenced by the nature of the societal and technological problems to be solved. In any case, the current understanding of the complexities of the knowledge base that underlie future scientific and technological advances is very limited, which led Keith Pavitt (1998) to conclude many years ago that 'the aim of policy should be to create a broad and productive science base, closely linked to higher (and particularly postgraduate) education, and looking outward both to applications and to developments in other parts of the world'.

Under this broad scope, the following actions deserve special mention:

- A strategic program of international partnerships in science, technology, and higher education was initiated in 2006 and by September 2007 the first doctoral and advanced studies programs were officially launched, bringing together several Portuguese universities and leading universities worldwide, including MIT, Carnegie Mellon University, and the University of Texas at Austin. Unprecedented in Portugal, these programs in 2007 facilitated the creation of effective thematic networks involving a large number of Portuguese institutions with the objective of stimulating their internationalization through advanced studies projects and sustainable schemes to stimulate new knowledge and exploit new ideas in collaboration with companies and internationally renowned institutions, as follows:
  - The MIT–Portugal program (http://www.mitportugal.org/),

launched in October 2006 in the field of 'engineering systems', attributing special emphasis to the complex processes associated with industrial production, sustainable energy, bio-engineering, and transport systems, in which Portuguese and MIT faculty and researchers identified three main thematic areas for R&D in close cooperation with an industrial affiliation program. They include sustainable energy and transportation systems, stem cell engineering for novel therapies in regenerative medicine, and materials and design-inspired products with specific applications in electric mobility and new medical devices. Overall, the program involved over 340 master's and doctorate students at the beginning of its third year in September 2009.

- Through the joint program with MIT, cooperation with the Sloan School of Management was strengthened through an international MBA program, 'Lisbon MBA'. This involves co-funding from seven major Portuguese companies and banks in a way that will stimulate new research and the quality of education in management sciences in Portugal.

- The CMU–Portugal program (http://www.cmuportugal.org/), was launched in October 2006 with emphasis on information and communication technologies and involving dual professional master's and PhD programs by Portuguese institutions and Carnegie Mellon University. The areas covered include new generation networks, software engineering, cyber-physical systems for ambient intelligence, human-centric computing (including language technology), public policy and entrepreneurship research, and applied mathematics. Overall, the program involved about 170 master's and doctorate students at the start of its third year in September 2009.

- Under the University of Texas at Austin–Portugal program, an 'International Collaboratory for Emerging Technologies, CoLab' was launched in March 2007 (http://www.utaustin-portugal.org/), focusing on collaborative research in advanced interactive digital media and integrating advanced computing and applied mathematics. Overall, the program involved about 70 doctorate students at the start of its third year in September 2009.

- Also under joint collaboration with the University of Texas in Austin, a 'University Technology Enterprise Network: UTEN' was established in 2007 and oriented towards international technology commercialization and the professionalization of university technology managers.

- The Harvard Medical School–Portugal program on translational research and information (http://www.hmsportugal.org/), which has established a new collaborative framework, launched in May 2009, to foster translational and clinical research programs and the development of a new infrastructure for delivering medical information across academic institutions and to the general public.
- The launching of Portuguese–Spanish networks oriented towards new developments and applications of nanosciences within a boarder framework associated with the establishment of the Iberian International Nanotechnology Laboratory (INL). This was created by an international treaty between Portugal and Spain signed at the end of 2006 and is under construction in Braga (northern Portugal). It is the first international research laboratory set up in the Iberian peninsula and is expected to achieve a reputation as an international institution of excellence with 200 researchers from all over the world and an annual operating budget of around €30 million matched by a similar investment budget funded equally by both countries.
- Cooperation with the Fraunhofer Gesellschaft for the establishment in Portugal of the first Fraunhofer Institute in Europe outside Germany through the recently established Fraunhofer Portugal Research Association. This is an ambitious project focusing on emerging information and communication technologies, such as 'Ambient Assisted Living', to be complemented by the establishment of R&D consortia and cooperative projects involving several Portuguese institutions and Fraunhofer institutes in Germany.

Strengthening the internationalization of higher education and S&T is recognized as a way to stimulate the integration of national institutions in emerging scientific networks at an international level. In general, internationalization should be a full component of all higher education institutions, stimulating the mobility of students and academic staff, and strengthening scientific and academic activities in networks.

Projects of interest to Portuguese industry have been launched, and this synergy has been extended by industrial affiliation programs, especially in stem cell engineering for regenerative medicine, automotive engineering, low-energy systems (via the MIT–Portugal program), telecommunications and information systems (via the CMU–Portugal and Fraunhofer–Portugal programs) and interactive digital media (via the UT Austin–Portugal program). A network of technology transfer offices to support the development and internationalization of technology-based entrepreneurial projects has also been developed under the scope of the UTEN.

Ideas

The above analysis indicates the need to give constant priority to people and knowledge in a way that promotes networks of institutions with the necessary critical mass capable of promoting the international standing of Portuguese scientific and tertiary education institutions. We now complement this vision by looking at the diffusion of ideas. Our analysis has emphasized the following:

- First, innovation must be considered together with competence building and advanced training in individual skills through the complex interactions between formal and informal qualifications. This requires a broadening of the social basis for knowledge activities, including higher education enrollment, and strengthening the top of the research system leading to knowledge production at the highest level.
- Second, strengthening experimentation in social networks necessarily involves flows of people. It is organized cooperation among networks of knowledge workers, together with different arrays of users that will help diffuse innovation. But establishing these innovation communities requires the systematic development of routines of collaboration on the basis of sophisticated research projects, as well as the design of products and services. This requires public policies to foster 'brain circulation' among leading institutions worldwide.

In the following paragraphs we address these issues by looking at the evolution of three different and complementary measures namely: (i) private expenditure on R&D, which measures the private efforts toward innovation undertaken, mainly by medium and large companies; (ii) the capacity of Portuguese companies to successfully export knowledge-based services; and (iii) emerging technology-based start-ups, using a dedicated observation exercise.

Figure 11.11 shows that Portugal experienced the highest growth rate in Europe in private R&D expenditure in recent years, which practically doubled when measured as a percentage of GDP between 2005 and 2007 (97 percent increase). It reached 0.6 percent of GDP in 2007 and 0.8 percent of GDP in 2008 and 2009, while it was only 0.3 percent of GDP in 2005.

Figure 11.12 shows the sectors with the highest investment in R&D, and simultaneously those with the highest growth between 2005 and 2009, 3.9 times in this period: R&D investment in knowledge-intensive sectors has quadrupled since 2005, of which the financial services and insurance

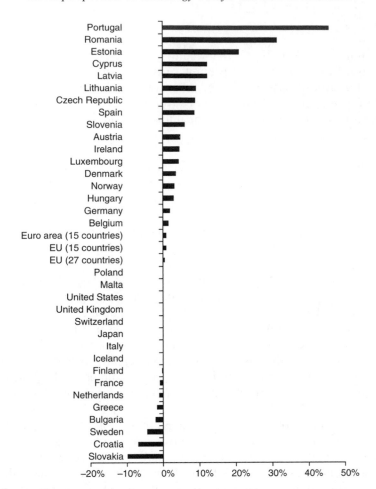

Source: GPEARI/MCTES: Gabinete de Planeamento, Estratégia, Avaliação e Relações Internacionais/Ministério da Ciência, Tecnologia e Ensino Superior, *Inquérito ao Potencial Científico e Tecnológico Nacional* (IPCTN).

Figure 11.11   Variation of private R&D expenditure as percentage of GDP, 2005–2007

sectors are responsible for the highest increase (nine-fold), while communications registered an eight-fold increase, followed by computing activities (six-fold). Private expenditure in the energy sector also increased 80-fold, while that in the automotive sector increased seven times. During the same period, R&D investment in the food industry sector increased 3.5 times and the pharmaceutical industry by only 1.5. On the other

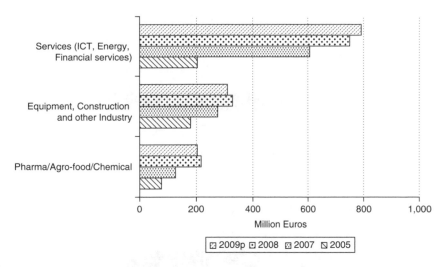

Note: (p) provisional data.

Source: GPEARI/MCTES: Gabinete de Planeamento, Estratégia, Avaliação e Relações Internacionais/Ministério da Ciência, Tecnologia e Ensino Superior, *Inquérito ao Potencial Científico e Tecnológico Nacional* (IPCTN).

Figure 11.12   *Private expenditure on R&D in the main sectors of activity, 2005 and 2009p*

hand, R&D expenditure decreased during the 2005–07 period for the electrical appliance and construction sectors, although with a relatively low absolute level overall. This is partly due to methodological issues affecting the classification of companies in the various sectors listed and also to market-related adjustments in these two sectors, which are particularly affected by the demand for construction (especially public infrastructure).

An interesting feature of the recently formed Portuguese business research landscape is that the top 100 most intensive companies in R&D represent 80 percent of the BERD, employing 5 percent of the total employment by companies in Portugal. These 100 companies represent 23 percent of the total turnover of companies in Portugal, corresponding to €84 million.

The same group of firms registered around €15 million in exports, which corresponds to 29 percent of the total national exports. In fact, data also show that the exports of this group grew four times more between 2007 and 2008 than the exports of the total of the Portuguese economy.

The top 100 most intensive firms in R&D also generated €11 million

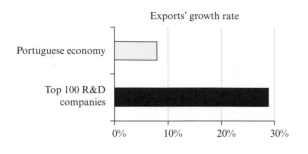

Exports' growth rate

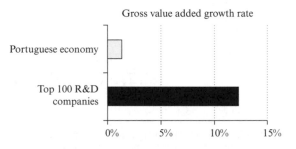

Gross value added growth rate

Source: INE, GPEARI/IPCTN.

*Figure 11.13   Exports growth rate and gross value added growth rate
between 2007 and 2008 for the Portuguese economy and the
top 100 companies with the largest R&D expenditure*

of gross value added (GVA), corresponding to 13 percent of the total
national value (Figure 11.13). The value generated in Portugal by these
100 firms, when expressed in terms of GVA, grew 12 percent between 2007
and 2008, a growth rate almost 10 times higher than the one observed for
the whole of the Portuguese economy in the same time period.

To conclude our analysis, we now turn to S&T-based entrepreneurship, which is increasingly seen as a key element of a nation's or a region's
ability to grow and prosper. Silicon Valley and Route 128 in the Boston–
Cambridge area, the most dynamic regions in the world today in terms
of growth and innovation, were propelled mainly by new technology and
the creation of start-ups such as Apple, HP, Google, and Intel, to name a
few. At the same time, start-up companies are also becoming global enterprises and engage in services, manufacturing, and research throughout
the world, with strong links to universities and research groups. Others
are going beyond their borders to procure products and services at lower
prices, often from new companies or subsidiaries in countries such as
China, India, and Brazil. Well-trained engineers and computer scientists

from Bangalore and Shanghai are competing for jobs that traditionally went to their counterparts in Europe and the United States.

At the same time, research universities worldwide are attempting to foster a range of technology transfer offices and commercialization activities, together with industrial liaison programs, mostly intended to foster entrepreneurial environments and launch technology-based start-ups. Bringing ideas to the market is their main goal.

In this section, we address this issue by looking at a thorough assessment of national inventors, entrepreneurs, and companies carried out in Portugal over the last year by the UTEN. As a result of that assessment, Table 11.1 shows a series of technology-based SMEs and related business ventures selected using the following criteria: (i) a technological capacity located in Portugal; (ii) a university–research connection; (iii) an intellectual property strategy (provisional or approved patents, copyrights, trade secrets) associated with the venture; (iv) an emerging venture, not necessarily mature; and (v) a clear commercialization interest and potential. A two-step assessment was performed for each company, including a 'Rapid-Screen' assessment with specific criteria used to determine the technology's readiness for commercialization, and a 'Market-Look' that focused on 8–12 interviews in the technology's potential markets.

From an analysis of the above sample it is clear that innovation is not a direct consequence of R&D, but it is also clear that continuous public investment in R&D has been crucial in training a large number of people over many years and in creating the necessary environment to foster new technology-based businesses. In the academic literature, the lack of validity of the linear model of innovation has been repeated *ad nauseam*, but the fact remains that it still informs much of the policy rationale for investing in R&D. There is no question that the ideas that result from formalized knowledge exploration lead, in the long run, to innovations, but to expect this to be the case in the short run is misguided for both firms and governments. Many authors, for example, have shown that venture capital is probably much more effective in promoting innovation than R&D at the firm level.

This does not mean that firms and governments should stop doing R&D, but rather that they should do it for the right reasons. And there are many right reasons, from promoting human capital to extending the frontiers of knowledge. But in terms of public policy, the realization that innovation and R&D are not as tightly correlated as commonly was thought is particularly important. This realization means that firms might lack even more incentive to perform their own R&D than previously thought, and thus require stronger intervention by the public sector,

Table 11.1 Examples of technology-based (early stage and mature) SMEs set up by university alumni

Sector	Name	Founded	Location	Technology-based products or services	Links to R&D Center/ University
Agro/Food	Cook.Lab	2007	Lisbon (PT)	Molecular gastronomy research, new food products development	Institute of Agronomy (ISA), Technical University of Lisbon
	MicoPlant	2006	Gondomar (PT)	Micogourmet, Micogest, Micogrower Produce, develop and commercialize mushrooms	University of Trás-os-Montes e Alto Douro
	Natural Concepts – Bioteknics	2007	Guimarães (PT)	Controlled production of extracts and fractions with antioxidant, anti-aging and neuroprotective activities, by in house developed techniques	University of Minho
	Prosense, Lda	2009	Lisbon (PT)	R&D in sensory analysis of food products	Institute of Agronomy (ISA), Technical University of Lisbon
	Agri-Ciência, Consultores de Engenharia, Lda.	2000	Lisbon (PT)	Decision support systems for knowledge and information management (Web-based business intelligence solutions)	Instituto Superior de Agronomia / University of de Évora / Centro Operativo e de Tecnologia de Regadio
	Castro, Pinto & Costa, Lda.	2000	Maia (PT)	OleoTest – reliable, fast and cheap method to control the food oils quality	

Bio/Pharma		Year	Location	Description	Institution
	Bioalvo SA	2005	Lisbon (PT)	Global Platform Screening for Drug Discovery (GPS D2) – drug discovery platform based on in vivo assays performed in humanized yeasts	ICAT-School of Sciences, University of Lisbon, laboratory facilities
	Biopremier	2003	Lisbon (PT)	Diagnosis methods, molecular design (agro-food, clinical)	ICAT-School of Sciences, University of Lisbon, laboratory facilities
	NZYTech Lda	2008	Lisbon (PT)	Synthetic genes, recombinant enzymes, analytical and diagnostic test kits and molecular biology products	School of Veterinary Medicine, Technical University of Lisbon
	Stemmaters	2007	Guimarães (PT)	Bone/skin regenerative medicine	3B's / University of Minho
	Alfama	2002	Boston (US)/ Lisbon (PT)	Carbon monoxide releasing molecules (CORMs)	IMM/ University of Lisbon / ITQB / New University of Lisbon
	Bioskin Molecular and Cell Therapies	2002	Maia (PT)	Biomaterials and stem cell therapies	FEUP / University of Porto
	Bioteca	2002	Lisbon (PT)	Stem cells cryopreservation	IST / Technical University of Lisbon
	Biotecnol	1997	Oeiras (PT)/ Durham (US)	Anti-HER2, Anti-Hsp90, Cardiotrophin I, anti-PTHrP	
	Biotrend	2000	Lisbon (PT)	In-house projects aiming at the production of high value biomolecules	IST / Technical University of Lisbon
	Crioestaminal	2003	Cantanhede (PT)/ SP/ IT	Cryopreservation of stem cells	IMM/IPO/IST/Biocant

Table 11.1 (continued)

Sector	Name	Founded	Location	Technology-based products or services	Links to R&D Center/ University
Energy/Environment/Sustainability	Advanced Cyclone Systems, S.A.	2008	Porto (PT)	Mechanical or electrostatic recyclone systems for high efficient particle capture	FEUP / University of Porto / New University of Lisbon
	Albatroz Engineering	2006	Lisbon (PT)	Sensors, computers and avionics hardware and software embarked in vehicles to identify automatically and in real-time potential hazards for utility and transportation assets, with emphasis on power-lines	IST / Technical University of Lisbon
	WSBP Electronics	2008	Coimbra (PT)	Energy analyzer, emissions reporting, S3 Web-based service, building performance and automation	University of Coimbra
	WS-ENERGIA	2006	Oeiras (PT)	DoubleSun® Four and Five, Heliots, Solar Trakers (WST1000/1600) Solar concentration technology which integrates precise tracking with 2 X flat reflective optics	
	SRE	2003	Torres Vedras (PT)	SRE stacks – development of portable fuel cells	IST / Technical University of Lisbon

Category	Name	Year	Location	Description	Institution
ICT/Software/Digital Media	AuditMark	2008	Porto/Lisbon (PT)	Web Campaign Auditing, Web traffic Analysis, Browser Recon – browsers' identification tool applied to web traffic analysis and auditing	FEUP / University of Porto
	Bullpharma	2008	Cascais (PT)	Web-platform Auction Arena	University of Aveiro
	ClusterMedia Labs	2008	Aveiro (PT)	LiveMeans Engine®, SoundsLike.Me	
	Critical Links	2006	New Jersey (US)/ Coimbra (PT)/ Southampton (UK)/ Castelfiorientino (IT)	EdgeBOX – Integrated system for internet and communication management, with remote control. Applied to schools and other public and private services. Specific product delivered for PMEs EdgePACKS	
	Critical Manufacturing	2009	Germany	Improve – a new method to master the efficiency of semi-conductors in European industry	
	Critical Materials	2008	Guimarães (PT)	VS2 – Virtual Structural Simulation System – intelligent system for the evaluation of the structural integrity of critical components in the aeronautics industry	PIEP / University of Minho
	Edit on web	2003	Viseu (PT)	Services on: Digital Libraries / eBookplus (Digital Book)	INESC Porto / FEUP / University of Porto
	EXVA	2008	Guimarães (PT)	HVR – High-video recorder systems allow the connection of analog and IP video cameras, in the same equipment	Avepark / University of Minho
	FoodInTech	2008	Porto (PT)	FSM-I, FSM-A, SURFACE.T	FEUP / University of Porto

Table 11.1 (continued)

Sector	Name	Founded	Location	Technology-based products or services	Links to R&D Center/University
ICT/Software/Digital Media	Keep Solutions	2008	Braga (PT)	Digital preservation and advanced solutions for digital archives and libraries	University of Minho
	Metatheke software	2007	Aveiro (PT)	Applications for digital books, E-book platforms, Digital Libraries, Digital Archives, Digital Museums	University of Aveiro
	NWC network concept	2008	Lisbon (PT)	Kelius Multiservice Platform: application on buildings, cruises, business parks; network management	IST / Inesc ID / Technical University of Lisbon
	Practical Way	2008	Porto (PT)	Civil engineering software	FEUP / University of Porto
	SpectralBlue	2008	Guimarães (PT)	Pervasive technologies: next generation in visual pattern recognition technology, delivering accurate traffic and usage data to users in a variety of fields (e.g. retailers, and municipalities)	University of Minho
	Take the Wind	2008	Coimbra (PT)	Human Body 3D – 3D models with high realistic textures from human anatomy to physiology	IPN Incubator / University of Coimbra
	Ubisign, Tecnologias de Informação, lda	2005	Braga (PT)	SituAction – Web-based Digital Signage Software platform, supporting collective wireless interaction	University of Minho
	Vectrlab, SA	2008	Lisbon (PT)	Digital gaming applications / 3D	ICAT/University of Lisbon

ICT/Software/Digital Media				
Wizi	2008	Lisbon (PT)	Mobile software for finding friends and the time to get to them	Instituto Superior Técnico (IST)
Xarevision	2007	Porto (PT)	Intelligent Digital Signage Networks – artificial intelligence based technology matching content to audience, time and location	Inesc-Porto / FEUP / University of Porto
Critical Software	1998	Coimbra (PT)/ San Jose (US)/ Southampton (UK)/ Bucharest (RO)	ISVV – Independent Software Verification & Validation Premfire, WMPI, WOW, Xception	University of Coimbra
Link Consulting	1999	Lisbon (PT)	eBanka, e-doclink, Balcão Único, e-Urban	Inesc / Instituto Superior Técnico (IST)
Maeil Consultores	1999	Lisbon (PT)	Maeil Transporter – Shipping Management Tool for Liner Agencies and Freight Forwarders MdM – Maeil doc Manager, MdM e2	Taguspark / IST / Technical University of Lisbon
MOG Solutions	2002	Maia (PT)	mxfSPEEDRAIL, TOBOGGAN, MXF DEV. TOOLS	INESC Porto / FEUP / University of Porto
WIT Software	1999	Coimbra (PT)	WIT PC/Toolbar/Web Communicator Vodafone Cube, Adidas Eye Ball,	University of Coimbra
Y-dreams	2000	Almada (PT)/ Austin (US)/ Shanghai(CN)/ Barcelona(SP) / Rio de Janeiro (BR)	Interactive MUPI Nokia N90, Virtual Sightseeing	FCT / New University of Lisbon

Table 11.1 (continued)

Sector	Name	Founded	Location	Technology-based products or services	Links to R&D Center/University
Medical/ Devices/ Diagnostics	Biodevices	2006	Aveiro (PT)	iTReport, CAPView, BioDreams, VitalJacket	University of Aveiro
	BlueWorks	2007	Coimbra (PT)	OphthalSuite (Acquisition & imageCORE), EyeDropper: Compliance Validation System; Medical Expert Diagnosis	University of Coimbra; Centro Cirúrgico de Coimbra; NEUROEYE – Electromedicina e Psicofisiologia da Visão, Lda; ISA – Intelligent Sensing Anywhere, S.A
	Critical Health	2008	Coimbra (PT)	Retmaker – automatic detection of lesions in the retina of diabetic patients suffering from diabetic retinopathy	IBILI / University of Coimbra
	GenoMed	2004	Lisbon (PT)	HCV Genotype (amplifies viral nucleic acids extracted from patient's plasma samples to determine the genotype); Detection of Hepatatis B virus genetic diversity (allows investigation of the genetic diversity of HBV in infected patients)	IMM / University of Lisbon

iSurgical 3D	2009	Guimarães (PT)	3DPectus System – system for automatic and personalized modelling/bending of surgical prosthesis for correction of pectus excavatum based on pre-surgical imagiology information (CT Scan). This technology allows a more accurate surgical intervention	University of Minho
PETsys	2008	Lisbon (PT)	PET – positron emission tomography used as a new medical imaging system for the diagnosis of breast cancer	LIP / Instituto Superior Técnico (IST)
Plux	2007	Covilhã / Lisbon (PT)	bioPlux – wireless and miniaturized signal acquisition system (great applicability in the healthcare area, particularly in physical therapy)	UBI / IST-UTL
			powerPlux – package composed of signal acquisition hardware and automated signal processing software to allow sports technicians to rapidly evaluate and diagnose the physical conditions of their athletes	
			bioPlux motion – autonomous device with an integrated xyzPlux triaxial accelerometer	

Medical/ Devices/ Diagnostics

303

Table 11.1 (continued)

Sector	Name	Founded	Location	Technology-based products or services	Links to R&D Center/University
Microelectronics/Materials/Equipment/Robotics	CustomLenda Solutions, S.A. (Super Ego)	2008	Lisbon (PT)	Healthy/ergonomic footwear	IST / Technical University of Lisbon
	Fluidinova	2005	Porto (PT)	RORpaint, NETmix, RIMcop, nanoXIM, CFDapi	FEUP / University of Porto
	idea.M, Lda	2008	Porto (PT)	Composite materials used in musical instruments	UPTec – FEUP / University of Porto
	OCEANSCAN-Marine Systems & Technology, Lda	2008	Porto (PT)	Light Autonomous Underwater Vehicle System (LAUV)	University of Porto
	Ownersmark SA	2008	Porto (PT)	Structural Composite Poles in Thermoplastic Matrix	Universities of Minho and Porto
	Ply Engenharia	2006	Oeiras (PT)	Opencell technology & multimaterial truck cargo bodies	IST / Technical University of Lisbon; FEUP / University of Porto; University of Coimbra; University of Aveiro

Category	Company	Year	Location	Description	Institution
Microelectronics/Materials/Equipment/Robotics	SelfTech	2008	Lisbon (PT)	Robotic solutions, autonomous intelligent systems as well as hardware and software for embedded systems	IST / Technical University of Lisbon
	Techsuber Lda	2008	Lisbon (PT)	Multiple-layered assemblage of wood and other natural based materials	Institute of Agronomy (ISA), Technical University of Lisbon
	Tomorrow Options	2007	Porto (PT)	WalkinSense and ChangeYourPosition are electronic, portable and wireless medical devices: The former to monitor and assess lower limbs condition and the latter to avoid bedsores or decubit ulcers	Inesc Porto / FEUP/ University of Porto
	UAVision	2005	Lisbon (PT)	Aeronautics, Mecatronics, Remote Sensing: low-cost autonomous aerial platform for agriculture, forest and surveillance applications	ISA / IST / Technical University of Lisbon
	We Adapt	2008	Braga (PT)	FashionMe – 'Haute Couture' and casual wear for disabled people with their own brand BodyMe – devices for physical reconstitution	University of Minho
	Fibersensing, Sistemas Avançados de Monitorização, S.A.	2004	Maia (PT)	Developer and manufacturer of optical fiber Bragg grating (FBG) based sensor systems for advanced monitoring applications	Inesc Porto / FEUP / University of Porto

Table 11.1 (continued)

Sector	Name	Founded	Location	Technology-based products or services	Links to R&D Center/University
Microelectronics/Materials/Equipment/Robotics	IdMind	2000	Lisbon (PT)	Robotic kits, based on microcontrollers, used in a variety of innovative projects, up to complex robots developed for varied ends, such as: search and rescue, robotic soccer, art, and publicity	IST / Technical University of Lisbon
	ISA	1990	Coimbra (PT)	iLogger –multi-purpose autonomous (GSM/GPRS based, battery powered) remote management system providing data logging, automatic reading and alarms	ISEC / FCTUC / LEI (UC) / University of Coimbra
	Multiwave	2003	Maia (PT)	Pulsed fiber lasers; optical sources	Inesc Porto /University of Porto

Source: UTEN (2009).

particularly in times of increased uncertainty in global markets. This might be particularly important for late industrializing countries such as Portugal, with scientific and technological systems that are not yet fully developed and mature. Often these countries show very low levels of private commitment to R&D, with disproportionately high government expenditures on R&D.

The notion that partnership is the solution to many current policy questions might no longer suffice. New skills requiring intense and effective direct contact among different institutional agencies are essential and increasingly utilized. Linkages among different parts of the system will now require assimilating, sharing, acquiring, and creating knowledge. Firms seek access to knowledge in labs, universities, and research centers. Universities search for collaborations, contracts, and agreements from businesses. University students are employed and trained by industry. Entrepreneurs, innovative agents, knowledge producers, researchers, academics, and students are connected in a process of knowledge producing and sharing.

The challenges for policy in order to move towards inclusive modern societies and wealth generation are really threefold. First, what can be done at the level of our science and education systems to provide the bridges across disciplines required to cope with the increased complexity of every-day issues? Second, what can be done at the regional and national level to establish and sustain learning networks and trajectories that can lead to wealth creation and the required entrepreneurial capacity allied to new scientific competencies and training needs? Third, how can the overall learning process be made more inclusive, so that fewer regions and countries are excluded, extending the global reach of learning networks?

3 THE STRUCTURE OF INCENTIVES: IS THE EUROPEAN APPROACH SUSTAINABLE?

We now turn to an analysis of the structure of incentives for people, knowledge, and ideas, as well as the social capabilities that enable the context in which knowledge networks develop. We shall focus on a European perspective because the challenges facing Portugal are, above all, those facing Europe as a whole.

How far will Europe be able to strengthen a public funding policy for R&D that is oriented, focused, and consistent? This is particularly relevant when compared with the experience in the United States, where public funding has been relatively focused and consistently oriented towards academic and basic research. Europe, in contrast, has had a diffuse and non-focused public funding policy that has attempted to fulfill a number of different objectives, varying over time to accommodate circumstances, and shifting priorities leading to inconsistent allocations. The recent successful launch of the European Research Council provides a new orientation and suggests that Europe needs to increase public funding of R&D that is consistently allocated and oriented towards academic and basic research in a way that can stimulate the development of knowledge infrastructure. Fostering and maintaining the excellence of this knowledge infrastructure are the most effective ways for public funding of R&D to provide new opportunities for all citizens and to help provide the necessary resources (including qualified human skills) for firms to increase their own investment in S&T, as well as to promote the entrepreneurial environment necessary for innovation.

Figure 11.14 shows that the EU15 has doubled its GERD over the last 25 years, but the gap in GERD between the United States and the European Union has widened, with gross American expenditure on R&D increasing by more than 2.3 times over the same period. At the same time, China has increased its GERD more than fivefold in the last decade. The strong economic performance of the US economy through the 1990s, along with the changes outlined above, has contributed to a general and widespread shift towards market-based, rather than publicly supported, incentives for S&T in most OECD countries, and especially in Europe. In fact, the conclusions of the EU intergovernmental summit held in Lisbon in 2000 (the Lisbon Summit) can be interpreted as a call for Europe to enact policies that, in part, seek to replicate and improve upon the innovation-based economic performance that has characterized US economic growth (Rodrigues,

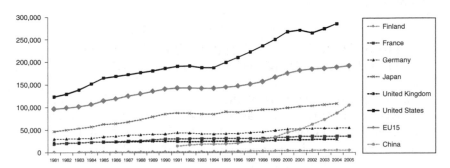

Source: OECD.

Figure 11.14   GERD in the EU15, the US, China and selected industrialized countries (million constant 2000$ and PPP)

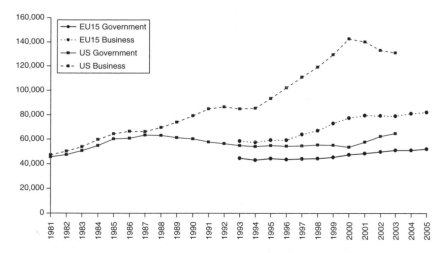

Source: Eurostat.

Figure 11.15   *Private and public spending on R&D in the EU15 and in the*
                US (million PPS at 1995 constant prices)

2002). But, overall, private spending on R&D in the EU15 has remained
stable since 2000 at around €80 billion and has not kept up with the equivalent American increase during the 1990s, as documented in Figure 11.15.
In addition, public spending in Europe has increased only slightly.

An examination of the sources of funding and expenditure on R&D
in Europe and the United States offers some insight into the reasons for
the challenges discussed above. The ratio of public expenditure to industry expenditure on R&D in Europe is low but there has been a long and
persistent downward trend in this ratio in both the EU and the United
States. Despite the growth in the amount of funding from private sources
in the United States, public expenditure on basic R&D has not gone away.
Instead, it has increased since the mid-1990s and continues to push private
spending on basic R&D.

Figure 11.16 complements the analysis first published by Conceição et
al. (2004) for the United States and compares the ratio of public versus
private R&D expenditure in the total expenditure (vertical axis) and for
basic expenditure only (horizontal axis) from the post-war period to
2006. Four stages can be identified in Figure 11.16. First, the growth of
total public funding overall through 1965, when public expenditure was
twice as large as private expenditure. Throughout this period, the ratio
in basic expenditure remained relatively stable at around 2, increasing
to 2.5 at the peak of total public/private expenditure. This is the launch

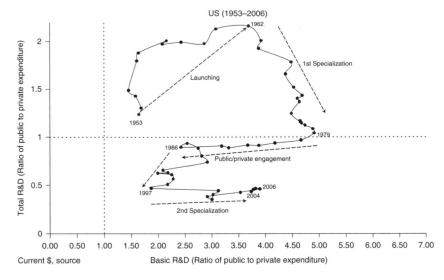

Figure 11.16   Ratio of public to private expenditure for total R&D and for basic R&D in the US

period of the US S&T system. Then, from 1966 through 1987, the total public/private ratio decreased rapidly but, at the same time, the basic R&D public/private ratio also increased sharply. This is the 'first specialization' period, as US public funding focused more on basic R&D, and applied R&D was increasingly left to the private sector. Third, through the 1990s, the trend was that both ratios decreased, although the basic science ratio is still very high, at around 3. Finally, and surprisingly, since 2000 there has been a 'second specialization' period, as US public funding again focuses more on basic R&D, with the private sector also increasing its funding of basic research, although at relatively moderate levels.

Following the analysis of Conceição et al. (2004) we note another important aspect revealed by the structural analysis mentioned above: much of the retreat in public funding in the United States is related to the pulling back of financial support to defense-related R&D. In fact, for the first time since 1980, non-defense-related R&D public expenditure in the United States is equal to defense-related expenditure. It is also important to note that the abrupt decrease in public expenditure in 1987 is related to the beginning of the decrease in defense-related expenditure. Non-defense public expenditure on R&D in the United States has been tending to increase for more than 20 years.

The growth in non-defense public R&D expenditure in the United

States has gone mostly to health and to basic science. In 1999 the US Congress committed itself to doubling the funding of the National Institutes of Health (NIH, which funds research in health-related areas) and of the National Science Foundation (NSF, which funds basic science). Preliminary budget requests of the Bush administration for 2003 complied with this commitment, putting the funding of the NIH at close to US$30 billion. But Conceição et al.'s analysis has also shown that the public allocation of R&D resources to universities has exhibited a persistent upward trend over the last half-century. While federal labs and private industry have historically received most of the federal funds (private industry with two large peaks in the mid-1960s and the mid-1980s), if current trends continue, universities will soon become the main receivers of public support for R&D in the US.

Enhancing the level of public expenditure in the EU to improve the S&T environment in Europe has several policy implications. First, the debate on increasing expenditure in R&D in Europe needs to improve understanding of the different nature of private and public incentives for S&T. For instance, making blanket recommendations to enhance property rights or to limit public resource allocation might be misguided. The US experience shows that a diversity of policies and increasing institutional specialization, in addition to clarification of the role of private and public incentives to support S&T, are needed when making R&D policy. Increasing and strengthening public funding for R&D also requires funding to be directed towards academic and basic research in a way that will foster the knowledge infrastructure, offering funding that will provide companies with the necessary resources to increase their own investment in S&T, and allow funding to foster the entrepreneurial environment and facilitate new entries in the market (Rodrigues, 2002).

In fact, analysis shows that the need to modernize funding mechanisms and to ensure a better balance between institutional and competitive funding for universities has become a key issue in meeting the global challenges of research and international competition. This certainly includes the need to preserve the institutional integrity of the university (Conceição and Heitor, 1999, 2007) as well as to create flexible financial mechanisms to attract and secure new talent in Europe. But it might also, as shown by Paul David and Sten Metcalfe (2007), increase competition and collaborative patterns among funding agencies in Europe. We need to strengthen the role of the European Research Council and to foster additional competitive funding schemes with a transnational configuration by promoting collaborative arrangements among national funding agencies in Europe.

In this regard, and following the emerging discussion in Europe about the future of S&T (Gago, 2007), it is clear that, by and large, the financing of higher education and of science and innovation has occurred in Europe along rather traditional lines. Governments, and in many cases ministries of S&T, directly undertake R&D or subsidize (directly or indirectly, through tax measures) R&D performance and technological innovation. Governments raise or forgo revenue to pay for this support. Yet, the history of science is rich with varied means of financing science and technological innovation. More importantly, developments in the size, integration, and technologies available in global capital markets present the opportunity to think about new financing possibilities and processes of societal engagement in S&T policies. These involve moving from traditional, 'one-way' (and most of the time fragmented) government policies, to integrated multi-stakeholder policies involving a wide range of public and private agents. Again, the internationalization of funding agencies and mechanisms in Europe should be discussed in this context and in a way that contributes to the diversification of funding sources.

4 WHICH INSTITUTIONS ARE FOSTERING COMPETENCE BUILDING FOR KNOWLEDGE? THE WAY TOWARDS REFORMING TERTIARY EDUCATION

A key area of institutional reform in Portugal with considerable impact on knowledge production and diffusion has been the tertiary education system, which is under pressure to meet the demands imposed by a globalized knowledge society without compromising quality deliverance. This is because, in Europe, although most institutions and their staff have recognized the need for change for many years, the way in which institutions are organized, either internally or through traditional links with society, as well as their incentive structure, have continuously delayed reforms. Consequently, it is only in recent years that reforms have emerged directly carried out by governments in many different countries and political regimes. The Portuguese system is no exception to these mounting pressures, and change has recently been introduced through governmental actions (Gago and Heitor, 2007).

In the same way that the US S&T system as a whole is taken as a worldwide reference, the US university system is also used as a role model for its rapid responsiveness to economic changes and contribution to wealth creation (NAE, 2003). For many years there has been a growing understanding, mainly by European counterparts (European Commission, 2003), that universities are important engines of economic growth and development instead of mere institutions of higher education learning (Saxenian, 1986), with increasing evidence of their importance as developers of regional industrial and technological development (Cooke and Huggins, 1996). This is a role that US universities, and especially research universities, assumed throughout the second half of the twentieth century (Rosenberg, 2002).

Here, too, as with the whole US system, there is the perception that private funding associated with a high level of industry–science relationships stimulates the dynamics of academia, with a much more direct and impactful way on socio-economic development at both the regional and national levels. The possibility of obtaining funding from private sources and incentives (such as intellectual property rights, IPR) is also appealing for European universities as they strive with increasing demands for change and for closer engagement with society.

At a time of increasing financial difficulties due to public budget constraints, there is the expectation that these links among research activity and its application in society will be reflected in more direct and immediate financial flows (Neave, 1995). However, this perception is leading to an institutional convergence among what universities do (and are supposed to do) and what firms and other agents do. In fact, more than a decade after Burton Clark launched the idea of 'entrepreneurial universities' (1998), there is still much to learn about their impact, and analysis (Conceição and Heitor, 1999) has clearly considered this convergence a potential threat to the institutional integrity of the university and the future of scientific research due to the commoditization of knowledge (Nelson, 2004). Above all, we follow Charles Vest (2007), former MIT President, in his most recent book where he says 'what is best about American higher education – we *create opportunity*. That is our mission. That is our business. That is first and foremost what society expects of us.'

The issue is *not* to 'save the university' but rather to understand who will play the fundamental and unique role that universities have played in the overall cumulative system of knowledge generation and diffusion. It appears that the United States is not willing to allow this integrity to be jeopardized. By misunderstanding US policies towards university-based research, there is a grave danger that European university policy will destroy these basic functions, which would be detrimental to the global production of knowledge and also certainly harm the development prospects of Europe itself, particularly in comparison with the United States.

It is in this context that this section attempts to deepen the emerging discussion facing the reform of tertiary education institutions (TEIs), and systems in coming years. The key role for policy makers and governments worldwide is to select priority actions and make the correct decisions regarding where and how to start the reform process.

For the purposes of this section, we shall use examples of the current Portuguese reform of tertiary education in order to illustrate our main arguments. This is because nearly three years since the OECD's Education Policy Committee met in Lisbon to review Portugal's higher education policy in December 2006, a number of steps have been taken to follow up on the Committee's recommendations and a thorough legal reform of the Portuguese tertiary education system has been completed (OECD, 2007b). This brings about significant changes in the internal system of governance of TEIs (including their management structure), as well as in their external societal relations (including internationalization, research partnerships, and business links, as well as external evaluation and accountability), which have been implemented together with an exceptionally large increase in public investment in S&T.

The remainder of this chapter focuses on two interrelated issues that are central to understanding the reform of TEIs, namely: (i) improving participation rates and fostering diversified systems for improved knowledge transmission and learning; and (ii) strengthening knowledge production and internalization for improved knowledge networks, together with strengthening institutional integrity and systems linkages.

How to Increase Participation Rates and Improve Learning?

Let us start with the need to open up tertiary education worldwide by strengthening the bottom of the pyramid. In fact, our fundamental assumption is that students matter and that the main reason for governments to increase funding for tertiary education is to increase participation rates and extend the recruitment base and the number of students in tertiary education (Barr, 2004; Barr and Crawford, 2005). At the same time, it is also clear that new opportunities are required to give students more flexible pathways across different types and levels of educational qualification, including recognition of prior learning and credit transfer, in order to reduce repetition of learning. As a result, increasingly diversified systems are required.

But it is also clear that the need to modernize funding mechanisms and ensure a better balance between institutional and competitive funding for tertiary education is leading the discussion in governments worldwide (Conceição et al., 2003b). More important than discussing the details of funding formulas for institutional funding mechanisms is to review the overall share of institutional and competitive funding sources, as well as to promote student support mechanisms. This certainly includes the need to preserve the institutions' integrity, as well as to create flexible financial mechanisms to attract and secure new talents in our institutions and to meet the global challenges of research and international competition.

Still, the key issue is how to increase and balance loans and grants for students, as well as to develop innovative loan systems and to combine them with flexible legislation to accommodate reasonable student incomes through part-time work, particularly at TEIs. Nicholas Barr (2008a) insists that the goal is to provide free education to all students by requiring that all graduates share the costs. However, the correct amount to be shared among taxpayers and graduates, as well as other private sources, is yet to be determined, which must be done on socio-political and non-scientific grounds.

Although income-contingent loan systems are becoming a common reference worldwide, as acknowledged by the OECD, it should be noted that their applicability is especially dependent on the characteristics of the existing fiscal system. This is why in the fall of 2007 an innovative system of student loans was introduced in Portugal with mutual guarantees underwritten by the state, complementing the system of public grants, thereby improving access to higher education for all students. About 6,500 loans had been contracted by summer 2009 through the banking system, which represents an important new achievement for Portugal and Portuguese families, following current practices in modern societies at the OECD level.

According to Michael Gallagher (2008),

> [T]he Portuguese initiative satisfies the key policy criteria: it is a horizontally equitable scheme; it represents good value for students; it is financially sustainable at higher volumes of student take-up; it is low risk for government and financial institutions; it avoids the need for additional administrative infrastructure. The loan facility reduces disincentives to study by covering reasonable living costs while deferring repayment obligations till after graduation.

Still regarding the new Portuguese loan system, Barr (2008b) applauded the facts that: the scheme is universal; it supplements existing grants rather than replacing them, and hence extends students' options; it has no blanket interest subsidy; and it has a highly innovative element of mutuality, which is the key that makes it possible for the scheme to make use of private finance. The loans scheme also has incidental benefits, by virtue of the requirements for progression and incentives for improving grade point averages. In particular, it should encourage students to develop their studies and complete their degrees, and to undertake courses that are more likely to lead to positive employment outcomes.

How to Foster Academic Research and Internationalization?

Let us move on to learning and teaching and the current debate in Europe. The global environment, the challenges facing higher education in Europe, and the low levels of public expenditure on R&D underscore the need to engage in further higher education reforms within Europe, to address the S&T challenges, particularly in the context of the ongoing Bologna process, which aims to create a common European higher education area by standardizing the academic degrees to be fully compatible throughout Europe. So far, reform efforts do appear to be leading to some successes. Even though the Bologna process is voluntary, most institutions recognize the great challenges and opportunities facing higher education in Europe and have made efforts to incorporate Bologna issues into their specific institutional strategies and activities. Furthermore, most institutions view the Bologna process as an opportunity to address many of the problems that have long existed in Europe. There are, however, challenges that remain in this reform movement to adapt higher education in Europe to the global environment and to improve funding for R&D. Understanding the relationship among the Bologna reforms and the social and national contexts in which they take place, and expanding the European higher education policy dialogue to include more issues, remain significant challenges in the current process. Overall, changing the patterns of teaching and learning, making students' work more active, and fostering student-centered education schemes are the ultimate goals. We need to allow students to determine their own learning paths and trajectories, particularly through education cycles, but also across institutions in different regions and countries.

The debate requires tertiary education institutions in general to better understand how people learn. It is clear that learning systems vary considerably across the full spectrum of disciplines, with arts and medicine using project-based approaches and engineering and the social sciences following a more intense academic drift. But if the ultimate goal is to increase participation rates and the recruitment base of tertiary education, we believe the debate will benefit from current knowledge of basic and secondary education levels.

The US's National Academies report 'How people learn' (National Research Council, 2000) provides clear evidence that 'designing effective learning environments includes considering the goals for learning and goals for students'. Given the many changes in student populations, tools of technology, and society's requirements, different curricula have emerged along with needs for new pedagogical approaches that are more student centered and more culturally sensitive. The requirements for teachers to meet such a diversity of challenges also illustrates why assessment needs to be a tool to help teachers determine whether they have achieved their objectives. But supportive learning environments, particularly fostering a culture of belief in science, need to focus on the characteristics of class-room environments that affect learning. In this respect, the authors were referring to the social and organizational structures in which students and teachers operate, including the environments created by teachers, but also out-of-school learning environments.

The idea that science should be considered as an open system, with diversified ways of participation, mainly derives from the fact that scientific activity is increasingly part of people's lives, so that the training of scientists should not be restricted to a specific group of people, but rather should be a broad part of today's education. In this context, it has become clear that the renewal of education systems has been particularly influenced by constructivism (Bennett, 2003). Following Piaget's (1973) view of knowledge construction by using 'active methods which require that every new truth to be learned be rediscovered or at least reconstructed by the student', Seymour Papert (1991) added the idea that knowledge construction 'happens especially felicitously in a context where the learner is consciously engaged in constructing a public entity'. And this is because 'without knowledge, practice is limited and without practice, knowledge will never be fully realized' (Reeve and Rotondi, 1997). This constructionist viewpoint facilitates the 'new milieu of discovery, learning, and sharing' mentioned above, and experience suggests that its strengths include: (i) exposing students to a multidisciplinary design experience; (ii) prompting participants to think about systems architecture; (iii) raising issues of organizational processes in a technical context; and (iv) building learning communities of students, faculty, and staff.

Following the practices, skills, attitudes and values described above, educators at all levels should take into account that learning a new practice requires moving through discovery, invention, and production not once, but many times, in different contexts and different combinations (European Commission, 2007). To achieve these objectives, we must learn from new research and foster evidence-based project and experimental work, as well as focus attention on the transferable skills students should acquire. But we also need to reduce drop-out rates in tertiary education and to involve students in research activities from the early stages. In summary, we need to go beyond the structure of tertiary education and gradually concentrate our efforts on measuring and taking stock of the diversity and evolution of specific student-centered parameters.

This type of discussion has led much of the current reform in Portugal, which promotes a 'binary system' of tertiary education, with polytechnic education concentrating on professionally oriented and vocational training, while university education should concentrate further on postgraduate education.

Non-university tertiary institutions are seen in many countries as nearer to the labor market and the more flexible arm of higher education. But, how to identify labor market needs, and how to provide the necessary skills, qualifications and technical know-how? Are non-university institutions more region specific and consequently in a better position to judge the needs of local industry and promote local and regional clusters of innovation?

To a large extent, these questions remain to be answered. We also need to increase the number of adult students in tertiary education by removing barriers to their entry and success with due attention to the socioeconomic environment. This certainly strengthens the need for diversified systems of tertiary education, with greater differences in learning and teaching systems in professionally oriented and science-driven programs.

In Portugal, full regulation that aims to bring tertiary education in line with the Bologna process was implemented very successfully, including the opening of higher education to a new public and the development of post-secondary education through the polytechnic subsystem: (i) in the 2007–08 academic year, about 87 percent of initial training courses were already organized in accordance with the principles of the Bologna process; (ii) the opening of higher education to new people through the new access regime for adults (that is, those over 23 years of age) resulted in the number of individuals entering tertiary education by this means rising to roughly 11,750 in 2007–08 and 10,850 in the 2006–07 academic year, up from around just 900 adults who first enrolled in tertiary education in the 2005–06 academic year; and (iii) in 2007, a total of 190 short, post-secondary degree programs were offered in higher education institutions, involving more than 4,000 students.

It is also clear that we need to foster institutions that pay attention not only to emerging scientific and technological developments, but also to societal changes and the constant changes in the labor market, which means looking beyond our own higher education institutions and monitoring students' employability over the various education cycles. Portugal recently launched a new observation system to monitor student demand through a biannual publication of information regarding graduate job seekers registered in employment centers. In addition, under the new Higher Education Act, tertiary education institutions are required to collect and publish annual information on their graduates' employment and career experiences up to five years after their graduation.

How to Foster Academic Research and (International) Systems Linkages, Together with Institutional Autonomy and Integrity?

Let us now turn to the issue of reinforcing the top of our tertiary education systems, by fostering the internationalization and specialization
of research universities. It has become a commonplace that we need to
encourage academic R&D and the internationalization of universities,
particularly by promoting student mobility and university networks able
to foster competitive research and learning environments and to attract
and train highly qualified human resources. The key issue is the creation
of conditions to strengthen institutions and of the necessary critical masses
to compete at the highest international level. There are two main aspects
of the discussion (Conceição and Heitor, 2005).

First, the debate has confirmed that the progress of scientific and technological knowledge is a cumulative one, depending in the long run on the
widespread disclosure of new findings. For example, Paul David (2007) has
consistently shown that 'open science is properly regarded as uniquely well
suited to the goal of maximizing the rate of growth of the stock of reliable
knowledge'. As a result, universities should behave as 'open science' institutions and provide an alternative to the intellectual property approach
of dealing with problems in the allocation of resources for the production and distribution of information. Consequently, the main challenge
for public policies is to keep a proper balance between open science and
commercially oriented R&D based on proprietary information. At what
level should governments foster cooperative exploratory research, which is
recognized as vital for the sustainability of knowledge-driven economies,
in response to the increasing demand from individuals, research units and
private firms for incentives for non-cooperative, rivalry knowledge?

Second, at the institutional level, graduate schools have been developed
progressively worldwide over the past decade in diversified ways, ranging
from interdisciplinary structures based in a single university (thus closely
resembling the US model), to subject-specific inter-university structures.
In general they aim to provide a better link between research training
and research strengths and, in a few cases, have provided flexible structures to attract and contract researchers and graduate students in a way
beyond that provided by traditional university departments. But, should
we rely on structures beyond traditional departments in order to promote
research universities? And how can we ensure that graduate schools make
their graduates more employable? Can the skills be transferable? And how
is quality assurance to be ensured?

Again, this conceptual discussion drove much of the recent reform of
Portuguese tertiary education, which was promoted in close interaction

with the government's 'Commitment to science' (Gago and Heitor, 2007), by fostering public and private investment in S&T, including the extensive program of international partnerships with leading institutions worldwide presented above. Unprecedented in Portugal, these programs have facilitated the creation of effective thematic S&T networks involving a large number of Portuguese institutions in collaboration with companies and internationally renowned institutions.

The overall goal is to facilitate a long-term strategy to strengthen the country's knowledge base, to foster economic growth, and to enhance the quality of life in Portugal, by promoting the strategic coordination of public and private investments to explore international cooperation and industry–science relationships with leading institutions worldwide, in a way that sustains strategic investments in people, knowledge, and ideas.

In this respect, and following some of the issues raised by John Ziman (1968) many years ago and also noted by Nobel Laureate Richard Ernst (2003), one critically important and emerging institutional issue relates to the training of students and young scientists in order to provide them with core competencies that help them become successful researchers and prepare them with appropriate 'transferable skills' for the job market outside research and academia.

Our final point concerns the need to preserve the institutional integrity of TEIs while promoting dynamic and responsive institutions by widening the scope of diversity and of institutional autonomy, while ensuring effective accountability (Conceição and Heitor, 2007). Many authors over the last two decades (Pavitt, 1987; Rosenberg and Nelson, 1996) have argued that whatever does not harm the institutional integrity of the university is acceptable. Companies and universities have evolved in a social context, to the point of attaining what these authors call 'institutional specialty'. Thus, whereas companies are concerned with obtaining private returns for the knowledge that they generate, universities have traditionally made knowledge public. By means of this specialization, or division of labor, knowledge has accumulated rapidly, as shown by the unprecedented levels of economic growth since the end of the Second World War.

This argument can be analyzed in detail, in the context of the knowledge-based economies (Oliveira et al., 1998). The threats to a university's institutional integrity in fact go beyond the extension of its activities to links with society, which, if excessive, could lead to resources being spread too thinly. More serious problems might arise if higher education institutions take the path of privatizing the ideas that they produce and the skills that they develop.

We may begin by analyzing the higher education function of teaching, which contributes to the accumulation of knowledge, specifically of skills, through the formal process of learning through education, or 'learning by learning'. This process is divergent (Conceição and Heitor, 1999): a university education combines the transmission of codified knowledge by the teachers with the individual characteristics of the students, in a process in which the interpretation of ideas leads to the accumulation of unique skills. Given this situation, each student can benefit from these skills in the future.

Moving on to research, it is worth noting that the great majority of the ideas that are generated in universities are of a public nature, this being the essence of the specific contribution that the university makes to the accumulation of ideas. Incentives for the production of these public ideas come from a complex system of reward and prestige within the academic community. In a well-known survey of university teachers in the late 1990s in the United States, the most satisfying factor, chosen by 86.2 percent of the sample, was autonomy and independence (UCLA, 1997). Again, the temptation to privatize university research results could threaten fundamental aspects of the way universities work and their essential contribution to the accumulation of ideas.

To summarize, our conclusion is that the institutional integrity of TEIs should be preserved, and an important point in terms of public policy is that state funding of TEIs should not be reduced. However, this measure by itself is not enough. From a more pragmatic viewpoint, TEIs should respond to the needs of society, which include rapid and unforeseeable changes in the structure of the employment market and the need to furnish their graduates with new skills beyond purely technical ones, in particular learning skills. The need to promote dynamic and responsive TEIs involves widening the scope of diversity and of institutional autonomy while ensuring effective accountability. Again, it must encompass preserving the institutional integrity of TEIs, while new forms of knowledge production (as put forward since the early 1990s by Limoges et al., 1994) should be considered in reforming TEIs and their links with society.

A diversified system presents advantages relating to research integrity. Analyzing the function of university research shows that it actually includes various subfunctions, not always clearly defined, but which should be the subject of distinct public policies and forms of management:

- *Research and development* (R&D), which aims at the accumulation of ideas through convergent learning processes that are associated with processes of knowledge codification. This is the most common form of research, particularly in the context of economic development and from the standpoint of the relationship among universities and companies.

- *Research and teaching* (R&T), in which research functions as a way of developing teaching materials, as well as improving the teaching skills of the teaching staff, and which is also associated with convergent processes of knowledge codification.
- *Research and learning* (R&L), in which the value of the research is not necessarily in the creation of ideas, but in the development of skills that enhance opportunities for learning. Research thus appears as a divergent function, associated with processes of interpretation.

According to Conceição and Heitor's (1999) analysis, R&D and R&T are more related to the creation of ideas. In this context, care is required in the choice of individuals with suitable skills for these types of activity. In turn, R&L is associated with a learning process, which seeks to develop learning skills through the experience of doing research.

In these circumstances a diversified system could respond effectively to the different demands made of it in the emerging economy, by being selective in R&D and R&T, and comprehensive in R&L. Indeed, in the context of the knowledge economy, the comprehensive nature of R&T should be extended beyond the university to cover the whole education system, as a way of promoting learning skills. In this situation, it seems essential to place renewed emphasis on education and, to a certain extent, to reinvent its social and economic role. Educational institutions must rethink their relationships with the individuals, families and communities among which they find themselves, presenting themselves as vital providers of opportunities to develop formal learning processes, while at the same time encouraging a way of life that promotes learning through social interaction.

To sum up, rather than presenting a detailed plan of public policy options and forms of management for higher education, in the above paragraphs we have addressed how the concepts developed in the literature can be used to analyze the challenges facing the integrity of university research in the knowledge-based economy, and what kind of opportunities can be discerned. Among our substantive conclusions are the importance of preserving the institutional integrity of tertiary education institutions, not only by avoiding excessive dissipation of their resources in activities related to their links with society, but most importantly by maintaining the academic character of their basic functions of teaching and research. In an environment in which education should promote learning skills, we highlight the need to identify and understand the different components of university research, so as to enhance the selectivity of the R&D and R&T subfunctions, while ensuring the widespread availability of R&L. It is argued that a diversified higher education system can free universities from many of the pressures that they are experiencing today, by helping to ensure the preservation of their institutional integrity.

The question that arises is how far universities can sustain their own independence and support integrity in research. To quote the Nobel Laureate Richard Ernst (2003),

> Universities should consider themselves as cultural centers with far-reaching radiance rather than merely serving as training grounds for academic specialists. The integration of knowledge, perception, and comprehension, as well as compassion, is at least as relevant as extreme specialization. Obviously, scientific excellence is indispensable, but insufficient in isolation.

This leads us to better understand how much effective university networks can help to further basic university goals and preserve research integrity. In fact, many research universities have developed into new and innovative institutions, both national and international in scope, organized as consortia and combining in their open structures teaching, research, business incubators, culture, and services. Challenges emerge as universities develop new institutional capacities further challenges emerge. In particular, most universities are faced with the need to increase and diversify their sources of funding, as well as with increasing leadership and management functions.

Higher education institutions are under pressure to reform as a result of increasing global challenges. The relationship between universities and governments, their main source of funding and their governing authority in most cases, remains an uneasy one and often does not reflect the realities of an evolving political, social, and economic environment. Multiple objectives should not be pursued at the cost of compromising learning and research environments for students, which also require continuous adaptation and improvements (such as in the new context of the Bologna process in Europe).

A final remark about the legal status of TEIs. We have seen, especially in continental Europe, that increasing the autonomy of TEIs has been one of the main objectives of sector reforms in different countries in recent years. Granting independent legal status to TEIs is one means of achieving this goal: it gives them greater autonomy to govern themselves and function as they see most appropriate, freely and independently, in pursuit of work that is deemed essential to society (Hasan, 2007). In addition, recognizing scientific knowledge as a public good implies the need to consider new dimensions in S&T policy that are designed and implemented in a way that fosters independent scientific institutions, among which the way in which transnational institutions are organized may provide a useful framework.

It is in this context, that the new Legal Framework of Higher Education

Institutions approved by the Portuguese Parliament in September 2007 established the organizational principles of the higher education system, the autonomy and accountability of institutions, the establishment of governing boards with external participation, diversity of organization and legal status of public institutions, particularly as private foundations, establishment of consortia, and recognition of research centers as part of the universities' management framework.

5   DISCUSSION AND CONCLUSIONS

We argue in this chapter that the innovative capacity of a country depends largely on the concentration of knowledge-integrated communities as drivers of larger communities of users. This requires a broad social basis for and commitment to science policies and institutional reforms, in a way that effectively integrates multi-stakeholders and a wide range of public and private agents. This is discussed in the context of evolving and changing patterns in Portugal.

We now discuss three major implications of our analysis. First, we need to consider innovation together with competence building and fostering individual skills through the complex interactions between formal and informal qualifications. We need to widen the social basis for knowledge activities, including higher education enrollment, and we need to strengthen the top of the research system leading to knowledge production at the highest level. The number of graduates, on the one hand, and of PhD holders, on the other, remain well below European objectives. Moreover, the European lifelong learning landscape needs to be redesigned if Europe is to succeed. Higher education institutions are key to this reform, which should take into account the revolution arising from information technologies in the internationalization and inclusion of all sectors of society in the fabric of knowledge networks.

Second, we need to consider the social shaping of technology and the emergence of 'human-centered systems'. This is because although incentives and infrastructure are essential to economic development, they do not tell the whole story of the differences across the various knowledge networks under development in Europe. Incentives and infrastructures do not operate in a vacuum, but shape and are shaped by the particular context in which they operate. In our analysis, the local context must have embedded a set of social capabilities that define the context in which knowledge networks evolve.

For example, analysis has shown that the mobilization of the information society must overcome some critical uncertainties (Mansell and

Steinmueller, 2000), including: (i) unclear expectations related to the level of dematerialization of social and economic activities; (ii) effective adoption of new technologies by citizens and customers, which is particularly influenced by accessibility, affordability and usability; and (iii) unpredictability of demand for interactive services from both localized and geographically dispersed communities. Our evidence shows the critical need for appropriate management of these uncertainties and for suitable infrastructures, incentives, and institutional frameworks to be promoted over time and across space.

Third, also we need to consider experimentation in social networks, which necessarily involves flows of people. It is organized cooperation among networks of knowledge workers together with different arrays of users that will help diffuse innovation. But establishing these innovation communities requires the systematic development of routines of collaboration on the basis of sophisticated research projects, not limited by administrative constraints and facilitating new forms of designing and using products and services. William Mitchell, from MIT, referred to these communities as 'creative communities', for which the experimentation of new ideas in 'design studios' is particularly important to provide adequate forms of interaction of users with adequate research environments (Bento et al., 2004).

But we also know today that the development of these communities depends on attractive settings that facilitate the exchange of talent among the different poles of knowledge networks. It requires us to evolve from the old paradigms of 'brain gain' to that of 'brain circulation' among our regions. Let us recall someone who was born in Rotterdam, studied in Paris and in Louvain, did research in Cambridge and London, and worked in Basel. This is not new; it happened some 500 years ago with Erasmus of Rotterdam, and our challenge is to make this same learning scenario possible for all European citizens.

To cope with such a variety of demands and with a continuously changing environment, tertiary education systems, in particular, need to diversify. But the challenge of establishing modern tertiary education systems requires effective networks and a platform of research institutions, notably to stimulate political debate among the various stakeholders and to assist in the networking of national constituencies promoting the positioning of our institutions in the emerging pathways of brain circulation worldwide. We argue that strengthening external societal links and 'system linkages' is critical in making the institutional changes required to meet the needs of global competition and the knowledge economy.

For example, the debate on the emerging reform of European universities analyzed in this chapter in terms of the allocation and future evolution of R&D expenditure in Europe must take into consideration the different nature of private and public incentives for S&T and foster the strategic collaborative involvement of both public and private stakeholders. Blanket recommendations to enhance property rights or to limit public resource allocation, based on perceptions of the US experience, may be misguided. In fact, the key message that emerges from analyses of long-term patterns of US investment in S&T is that the development of the US S&T system was based on a diversity of policies that led over time to increased opportunities for citizens, as well as to increased institutional specialization based on a clear separation of the role of private and public incentives to support S&T.

To conclude, our analysis calls for policies that consider long-term approaches to dynamic environments that need continuous monitoring, assessment, and external evaluation. We need to focus attention on fostering advanced human resources and the concentration of knowledge-integrated communities as drivers of larger communities of users. This requires a continuous public effort but also a better understanding of the effectiveness of the mix of public support mechanisms and private incentives for the development of knowledge networks.

This chapter brings together emerging worldwide issues and leads to new insights in science policy and technology commercialization. It discusses recent approaches to technical change in Portugal, based on an emerging diversity of policies and increasing institutional specialization, and clarification of the role of private and public incentives to support S&T. This process is reflected in the trend in developed economies towards increasing private investment in S&T. We argue for the need to promote and integrate public and private strategies in modern societies that foster a non-hierarchical integration of formal policies and informal system linkages leading to knowledge-driven societies. This requires us to open up science policies to multiple public and private agents and includes the continuous adaptation of systems of competence building and advanced studies, among which reform of higher education is particularly highlighted in the chapter.

NOTE

*   A version of this chapter has been published in *Technical Forecasting and Social Change*, **77** (2010), 218–47.

REFERENCES

Barr, N. (2004), 'Higher education funding', *Oxford Review of Economic Policy*, **20** (2): 264–83.
Barr, N. (2008a), 'Lessons learned from UK's higher education funding schemes', paper presented at the International Conference on Increasing Accessibility to Higher Education: Some International Examples on Student Loans, University of Lisbon, 2 June.
Barr, N. (2008b), Personal note, June.
Barr, N. and I. Crawford (2005), *Financing Higher Education: Answers from the UK*, London: Routledge.
Bennett, J. (2003), *Teaching and Learning Science: A Guide to Recent Research and Its Applications*, London: Continuum.
Bento, J., J. Duarte, M.V. Heitor and W. Mitchell (2004), *Collaborative Design and Learning: Competence Building for Innovation*, Westport, CT and London: Praeger.
Clark, B.R. (1998), *Creating Entrepreneurial University: Organizational Pathways of Transformation*, Oxford: Pergamon.
Conceição, P. and M.V. Heitor (1999), 'On the role of the university in the knowledge-based economy', *Science and Public Policy*, **26** (1): 37–51.
Conceição, P. and M.V. Heitor (2005), *Innovation for All? Learning from the Portuguese Path to Technical Change and the Dynamics of Innovation*, Westport, CT and London: Praeger.
Conceição, P. and M.V. Heitor (2007), 'Do we need a revisited policy agenda for research integrity? . . . an institutional perspective?', World Conference on Research Integrity, Calouste Gulbenkian Foundation, Lisbon, Portugal, 16–18 September.
Conceição, P., M.V. Heitor and B.-Å. Lundvall (eds) (2003a), *Innovation, Competence Building, and Social Cohesion in Europe: Towards a Learning Society*, Cheltenham, UK and Northampton, MA, USA: Edward Elgar.
Conceição, P., M.V. Heitor, G. Sirilli and R. Wilson (2004), 'The swing of the pendulum from public to market support for science and technology: is the US leading the way?', *Technological Forecasting and Social Change*, **71** (5): 553–78.
Conceição, P., M.V. Heitor and F. Veloso (2003b), 'Infrastructures, incentives and institutions: fostering distributed knowledge bases for the learning society', *Technological Forecasting and Social Change*, **70** (7): 583–617.
Cooke, P. and R. Huggins (1996), 'University–industry relations in Wales', Working Paper, Center for Advanced Studies in the Social Sciences, University of Wales, Cardiff (UWCC).
David, P. (2007), 'The historical origin of "open science": an essay on patronage, reputation and common agency contracting in the scientific revolution', Stanford Institute for Economic Policy Research, Stanford, CA.
David, P. and S. Metcalfe (2007), 'Universities and public research organizations in the ERA', prepared for the EC (DG-Research) Expert Group on 'Knowledge and Growth', June.
Ernst, R. (2003), 'The responsibility of scientists, a European view', *Angewandte Chemie International Edition*, **42**: 4434–39.
European Commission (2003), 'The role of the universities in the Europe of

knowledge', COM 5 February 58 final, available at: http://eur-lex.europa.eu/ LexUriServ.do?uri=Com:2003:0058:FIN:EN:pdf.

European Commission (2007), *Science Education Now: A Renewed Pedagogy for the Future of Europe*, M. Rocard, P. Csermely, D. Jorde, D. Lenzen, H. Walberg-Henriksson, and V. Hemmo (eds), Directorate-General for Research, Science, Economy and Society, EUR Report 22845, European Commission.

Gago, J.M. (ed.) (2007), *The Future of Science and Technology in Europe*, Portuguese Ministry of Science, Technology and Higher Education.

Gago, J.M. and M.V. Heitor (2007), 'A commitment to science for the future of Portugal', in J.M. Gago (ed.), *The Future of Science and Technology in Europe*, Portuguese Ministry of Science, Technology and Higher Education.

Gallagher, Michael (2008), Personal note, March.

Hasan, A. (2007), 'Independent legal status and universities as foundations', paper prepared for the Portuguese Ministry of Science, Technology and Higher Education.

'Increasing human resources for science and technology in Europe', (2004), April, available at: http://europa.eu.int/comm/research/conferences/2004/sciprof/pdf/ hlg_report_en.pdf.

Limoges, C., H. Nowotny and M. Gibbons (1994), *The New Production of Knowledge*, London: Sage.

Lundvall, B.-Å. and B. Johnson (1994), 'The learning economy', *Journal of Industry Studies*, **1** (2): 23–42.

Mansell, R. and W.E. Steinmueller (2000), *Mobilizing the Information Society*, Oxford: Oxford University Press.

Miller, S., P. Caro, V. Koulaidis, V. Semir, W. Staveloz and R. Vargas (2002), Report from the Expert Group: 'Benchmarking the Promotion of RTD Culture and Public Understanding of Science', available at: http://www.jinnove.com/ upload/documentaire/PP-fe-106.pdf.

National Academy of Engineering (NAE) (2003), *The Impact of Academic Research on Industrial Performance*, Washington, DC: NAE Press.

National Research Council (2000), 'How people learn: brain, mind, experience and school', J.D. Bransford, A.L. Brown, and R.R. Cocking (eds), Committee on Developments in the Science of Learning, Commission on Behavioral and Social Sciences and Education, National Research Council, Washington, DC.

Neave, G. (1995), 'The stirring of the prince and the silence of the lambs: the changing assumptions beneath higher education policy, reform and society', in D.D. Dill and B. Sporn (eds), *Emerging Patterns of Social Demand and University Reform: Through a Glass Darkly*, Oxford: Pergamon.

Nelson, R.R. (2004), 'The market economy, and the scientific commons', *Research Policy*, 33: 455–71.

OECD (2002), *Frascati Manual: Proposed Standard Practice for Surveys on research and Experimental Development*, Paris: OECD.

OECD (2006), 'Evolution of student interest in science and technology studies: Policy Report', OECD, Global Science Forum, Paris, May.

OECD (2007a), *Main Science and Technology Indicators*, Paris: OECD.

OECD (2007b), *Review of National Systems of Tertiary Education – Portugal*, Paris: OECD.

OECD (2009a), *The OECD Innovation Strategy*, Paris: OECD.

OECD (2009b), *Regions at a Glance*, Paris: OECD.

Oliveira, P., P. Conceição and M.V. Heitor (1998), 'Expectations for the university in the age of the knowledge based societies', *Technological Forecasting & Social Change*, **58** (3): 203–14.

Papert, S. (1991), 'Situating constructionism', in I. Harel and S. Papert (eds), *Constructionism*, Norwood, NJ: Ablex, pp. 1–11.

Pavitt, K. (1987), 'The objectives of technology policy', *Science and Public Policy*, **14**: 182–8.

Pavitt, K. (1998), 'The social shaping of the national science base', *Research Policy*, **27** (8): 793–805.

Piaget, J. (1973), *To Understand Is to Invent: The Future of Education*, New York: Grossman.

Reeve, M. and M. Rotondi (1997), *From the Center: Design Process at SCI-Arc*, New York: Monacelli Press.

Rodrigues, M.J. (ed.) (2002), *The New Knowledge Economy in Europe: A Strategy for International Competitiveness and Social Cohesion*, Cheltenham, UK and Northampton, MA, USA: Edward Elgar.

Rosenberg, N. (2002), 'Knowledge and innovation for economic development: should universities be economic institutions?', in P. Conceição, D.V. Gibson, M.V. Heitor, G. Sirilli and F. Veloso (eds), *Knowledge for Inclusive Development*, Westport, CT: Quorum.

Rosenberg, N. and R.R. Nelson (1996), 'The roles of universities in the advance of industrial technology', in R.S. Rosenbloom and W.J. Spencer (eds), *Engines of Innovation*, Cambridge, MA: Harvard Business School Press.

Saxenian, A. (1986), *Regional Advantage: Culture and Competition in Silicon Valley and Route 128*, Cambridge, MA: Harvard University Press.

UCLA (1997), *The American College Teacher: National Norms for the 1995–96 HERI Faculty Survey*, Los Angeles, CA: Higher Education Research Institute of the University of California at Los Angeles.

University Technology Enterprise Network (UTEN), Portugal (2009).

Vest, C.M. (2007), *The American Research University: From World War II to World Wide Web: Governments, the Private Sector and the Emerging Meta-university*, Los Angeles, CA: University of California Press.

von Hippel, Eric (2005), *Democratizing Innovation*, Boston, MA: MIT Press.

Ziman, J. (1968), *Public Knowledge: The Social Dimension of Science*, Cambridge: Cambridge University Press.

Ziman, J. (1978), *Reliable Knowledge: An Exploration of the Grounds for Belief in Science*, Cambridge: Cambridge University Press.

Ziman, J. (2000), *Real Science: What It Is, and What It Means*, Cambridge: Cambridge University Press.

12. Technology transfer and commercialization in Russia

Nikolay Rogalev

1 INTRODUCTION

The start-up of innovative activity in Russia will be examined from the late 1980s to the present. The country had already recognized a necessity for change toward a market-oriented economy with new methods not so much focused on development as focused on technology transfer from scientific research centers and universities to industry. The first seminar for Technoparks and Business Incubators took place in Tomsk, Siberia, in 1989. Apart from Russian members, a number of reputable experts from Europe, the United States, and Canada participated in the seminar. This seminar in large measure laid the foundation for Russia's innovation development.

2 HISTORY AND TRENDS OF TECHNOLOGY TRANSFER IN RUSSIA

Set-up and Development of Science and Technology Parks

The innovation activity started in the university environment via innovative science and technology programs and via the organization of university science parks at leading higher education institutions. In 1990, the first science parks were founded in Tomsk as part of the Tomsk higher education institutions and the Tomsk Scientific Center of Siberian Division of the Academy of Sciences of the USSR and in Zelenograd as part of the Moscow Institute of Electronic Technology (MIET). More recently, university-related science parks were founded in Saratov, Moscow, St Petersburg, and Ufa. The Higher School Science and Technology Park Association (hereinafter called the Technopark Association) was also founded in 1990. From the time of its foundation, the Technopark Association has consolidated efforts of higher education institutions and university science parks.

During 1993–96, the Technopark Association managed to attract financing through the European Bank for Reconstruction and Development, the Know-How Fund under the UK government, TASIS and TASIS-BISTRO programs, and the Eurasian Fund for the fulfillment of international educational projects training manager teams from both leading and novice Russian science parks.

For the period under review, about 50 science parks were founded within the Russian higher education system. More than 20 university science parks obtained national and public accreditation provided by the Technopark Association. As a result of the accreditation process, the Association determined science park development levels and specified fields for improvement.

Undoubtedly, the overwhelming majority of the founded science parks were neither large-scale nor efficient, and they did not fulfill the role played by science and technology parks located in the United States, the United Kingdom, Germany, France, the People's Republic of China (PRC), and Finland. Nevertheless, during this period a number of Russian science parks found their niche as an innovation pool for the country, created an environment supporting innovation business activity, and maintained a fair level of functionality. The science parks established firm relations with partners, regulatory and government authorities, and promoters. They also provided funds in support of micro-entrepreneurship and employed specially trained personnel in the field of innovation management, technology transfer, and commercialization of scientific research results. Moreover, the science parks worked on solutions for the social and economic problems in the region.

For the period under review, the Ministry of Education and Science initiated 12 programs for the support and development of domestic science parks, innovation micro-entrepreneurship, and their support infrastructures. The most of the programs make the Technopark Association responsible for program elements associated with the development of the higher education institution innovation structure. Currently the higher education system incorporates a full-scale innovation infrastructure which comprises:

- 16 regional centers for training of experts in the field of innovation entrepreneurship;
- 12 regional informational and analytical centers;
- 10 regional innovation centers;
- 12 regional scientific and technical entrepreneurship development assistance centers;
- 44 science parks, including 21 accredited university-based science parks; and
- 30 innovation technology centers.

The higher education institutions have more than 2,000 structures, including small innovation and service enterprises, supporting innovation activity. These structures provide employment opportunities for more than 20,000 people, two-thirds of whom are university teaching staff and research workers.

The Technopark Association and university technology parks have a direct bearing on the innovation infrastructure development in their regions. The Technopark Association carried out a composition analysis of 22 science parks that were part of its association from 2002–06, and the results showed that 92 percent of science parks in Russia were university based, while only 4 percent were based on industry and academic scientific research institutes and 4 percent were enterprise based. Statistical information on 41 science parks categorized them as follows (Shukshunov, 2002):

1. science parks founded on the basis/as part of technical universities: 55 percent;
2. science parks founded on the basis/as part of conventional universities: 37 percent;
3. science parks founded on the basis of industry or academic scientific and research institutes: 4 percent;
4. Science parks founded on the basis of industrial enterprises: 4 percent.

The number of small business entities 'settled' in science parks varies. On average, one science park accommodates 12 small business entities mainly of an innovative nature.

Some key characteristics of the development of science parks include:

1. The vast majority of science parks have no permanently allocated lands. Only four of 22 examined science parks own their land. In this respect, Russian science parks do not meet requirements specified for science/technology parks abroad.
2. The vast majority of science parks occupy rather modest industrial premises, which vary from 4,000 to 56,000 square meters of floor space. In this respect, Russian science parks do not fully meet the requirements specified for science/technology parks abroad, except for the MIET science and technology park in Zelenograd. Unfortunately, except for the MIET science parks, there is no sign of action as far as the expansion of science park material and technical base is concerned.
3. The science parks provide few employment opportunities for people who want to conduct innovation research. Only 12 of 22 science parks have job creation numbers that exceed 200.

Table 12.1   Best technopark's major parameters

Parameter	Size
Occupied land	0.21–3.2 ha
Facilities	4.0–60.0 sq.m.
Jobs created	360–2700
Cumulative sales	18–180 $m
Number of tenants	6–55
	Average: 12

4. The volume of product and services sales offered by small businesses
    of the 22 most successful science parks is equal to an annual output of
    10.2 billion rubles (more than US$40 million). Even so, the predomi-
    nant contribution is made by only five science parks.

The major parameters of science parks running to date are given in
Table 12.1 (Shushunov, 2002).

On the strength of the university-based science park performance
indicators, the following science parks are incontestable leaders among
university-based science parks:

1. Zelenograd science and technology park of MIET (Moscow Institute
    of Electronic Technology);
2. science park of MSU (Moscow State University);
3. science park of MPEI (Moscow Power Engineering Institute);
4. technology park in Moskvorechye of MEPHI (Moscow Engineering
    Physics Institute);
5. technology park of SPSETU (St Petersburg State Electrotechnical
    University);
6. Tomsk Tekhnopark;
7. science and technology park of Volga-Tekhnika (Saratov State
    Technical University);
8. Technopark Ritm of the State Academy for Innovations;
9. Tekhnopark LTA of the St Petersburg State Forest Engineering
    Academy; and
10. Technology Park Uralsky of USTU (UPI) (Ural State Technical
    University).

Due to the financial and material and technical support from the federal
government of the Russian Federation and regional authorities, these
science and technology parks have every reason to receive a boost within

Table 12.2   Assistance fund budget, 2005–2011

Year	2005	2006	2007	2008	2009 plan	2010 plan	2011 plan
Fund budget (rbl m)	840.00	1,075.50	1,335.00	1,650.67	2,446.38	3,149.73	3,652.23
Fund budget ($m)	30.00	39.50	52.15	66.03			

the next two to three years, thus keeping pace with the well-known science parks abroad and becoming the largest science and technology parks in Russia.

Foundation for Assistance to Small Innovative Enterprises

The next step on the road of support for infrastructure development was the creation of the Foundation for Assistance to Small Innovative Enterprises in 1994 and the subsequent innovation activity development in Russia. The Foundation mission specified by the government Decree No.65 of February 3, 1994, remains invariant over a period of 15 years: small business development in the science and technology spheres and encouragement of competition by means of financial support for high-efficiency knowledge-intensive projects developed by small businesses.

The Foundation started its activity not at the 'seed' stage but with companies who were already present in the market, had passed the formation stage, experienced early sales, and made a name for themselves, but their development was 'unstable'. They needed assistance, hence the name of the Fund, that is, the Foundation for Assistance to Small Innovative Enterprises (Bortnik, 2008). In general, this approach worked very well: many of the Fund-supported small innovative enterprises (SIEs) became market players in different high-tech industrial sectors. Later on, with the growth of the Fund budget (Table 12.2) the number of annually financed projects increased (Polyakov, 2008).

Fund activity scaling is well demonstrated by the resources' provision level which the Fund had at its disposal to implement its plans. Its budget was generated based on a certain percentage of federal science budgetary means. As of the Fund's foundation date, this percentage was 0.5 percent. With the Fund's activity development, scientific and technological community acceptance, and consideration of the Fund's results this percentage grew to 1.5 percent by 2008.

After 10 years of activity, the Fund launched the START program aimed at supporting innovative small business enterprises and financing initial stages of company development. At the same time, venture funds accumulated disproportionately large amounts of money, but the entrepreneurial community was unprepared and failed to put forward appropriate projects. Furthermore, because of the science funding shortfall during the preceding years, there was a deficiency of young talented reseachers. The START program successfully targeted youths. These circumstances and the changed financial condition of the Fund resulted in its involvement in 'pre-seed' stages along with the existing support of currently operating companies.

Later, the Fund successfully launched and implemented such programs as PUSK (university–business partnership) and TEMP (technologies for small businesses) based on public–private partnership principles in the innovation sphere. The programs aim to develop mutually beneficial cooperation among higher educational institutions and the state science sector and small innovation businesses. The largest Fund program is START. Each year around 1,500–2,000 enterprises and applicant teams claim to receive funds under the START program.

With the purpose of positive environment financing (including social environment) and technological entrepreneurship development the Fund has developed and, together with the Ministry of Education and Science, the Federal Agency for Science, and the Federal Agency for Education, since 2006 it has been implementing a pre-seed program, UMNIK, which aims to involve young people in innovation activity. Every year, about 1,000 winners of the program receive grants for research and development (R&D) activities amounting to 200,000 rubles (US$8,000) per year for developing their innovation ideas. Specific features of the major Fund programs are given in Table 12.3.

In general, the efficiency of the Fund program is assessed using such indicators as the number of innovative small companies in high-tech business, the number of newly issued and applied (commercialized) patents, and the expansion rate of Fund-supported companies.

A 2008 sample survey of small innovation companies supported by the Fund suggests the following basic conclusions. First, SIE sales revenue indicated stable growth in the number of companies with sales revenues from 20 to 40 million rubles (US$0.8–1.4 million). The annual increase in the production of small innovation business financed by the Fund exceeds 20 percent per year. Second, the head count showed an increasing number of workers/employees whose primary work location is a small business. Thus, for a group of small companies with personnel capacity of 20 to 40 people, the number of workers/employees considering their company as the principal place of business has almost doubled. Furthermore, the

Table 12.5   Major performance indicators of ICTs

Parameter	Total	Average for ITC
Number of ITCs	30	
Tenants	962	32
Jobs Created	17,820	594

innovation technology centers were created. Originally four ITCs were developed and numbers peaked during 1999 with the creation of 13 centers. The first ITCs were created as part of already well-known university-based science parks. Later growth of ITCs was maintained mainly through the initiative and support of such projects within the region.

Currently, there are 25 innovation technology centers in 12 regions, which consolidate more than 970 small innovation enterprises. Major targets and goals of the ITCs are:

- development of a system for enhancement of innovation business efficiency;
- improvement of the existing innovation complex infrastructure;
- improvement of regulatory framework of and legal groundwork for small innovation enterprises' activity;
- integration of Russian ITCs into the European network of innovation centers; and
- development of new finance facilities for innovation projects and infrastructure.

The major performance indicators of ITCs including their constituent 900 innovation enterprises are shown in Table 12.5.

Following a Decree by the President of the Russian Federation of July 22, 2005, and the results of a competition conducted by the Ministry of Economic Development and Trade, a technology and innovation economy zone was established in Zelenograd. The ITC represented by the Zelenograd ITC participated in setting up this special economic zone, whose purpose was to ensure competitive industrial product sales growth. The zone development focuses on:

- developing breakthrough technologies with multiplicative effects and as a base for development and output of high-tech products;
- increasing product marketability level significantly;
- developing full-scale infrastructure as a support for technical and innovation activity;

- developing systems for continuous multilevel education and targeted personnel training; and
- enhancing coordination levels among education, science, and production entities.

There are currently four technical and innovation zones being developed: Zelenograd; Dubna town, in the Moscow region; in St Petersburg; and Tomsk in Siberia. The specified projects are at the initial stage of implementation.

3 MAJOR ISSUES OF TECHNOLOGY TRANSFER IN RUSSIA

Macroeconomics Variables

The overall microeconomic tendencies during 1985–2007 can be divided into several stages. The first stage, from 1985 to 1990, is marked by an increase in negative economic trends: production output rates slowed down, investment activity died, and many five-year planned performance indicators were not met. The second stage, from 1991 to 1998, is characterized by negative changes in the national economy, which affected all public activity spheres, specifically, politics, economy, and industry. The third stage is a phase of dynamic and successful development up until the financial crisis of 2008. Figure 12.1 shows the time history assessment of GDP from 1985 to 2007 (Goskomstat of Russia, 1996, 1998).

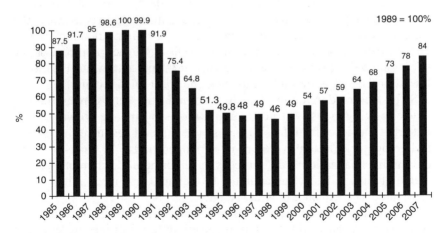

Figure 12.1   Relative change in GDP

Cutbacks in manufacturing output starting from 1990 were to some extent structural. The industry development dynamics were mostly affected by the purchasing power of consumers that was determined by their financial standing. Starting from the end of 1993, suspensions in production were mainly associated with a lack of consumers' financial means. On the one hand, the lack of financial means was responsible for a limited demand for manufactured goods, and on the other, it influenced the ability to finance the working capital (that is raw materials and component items) required for the organization of sound industrial processes. Raw material industries and fuel and energy sectors were affected by the current market conditions to a lesser degree. This can be explained by their export orientation and also the high level of material and energy intensity of domestic manufacturing. As a result, the percentage of raw material industries in general industrial production grew substantially. The share of products generated by raw material industries and the fuel and energy sectors within the general national economy structure increased, while the share of the manufacturing sector decreased.

The negative dynamics of innovation is quite obvious. The level of innovation activity of enterprises specified in Gohberg et al. (1996) as a specific weight of companies involved in the development and implementation of innovations (development and implementation of new or improved products, technological processes) was decreasing. According to various estimates, the specific weight is now about 3–9 percent, whereas in the late 1980s this index varied between 60 and 70 percent for the enterprises of the former USSR.

The presence of Russia in the international market of science-intensive products is insignificant. According to the 2008 Ministry of Education and Science report, 'Science and Technology: State and Perspectives', the share of Russian science-intensive products in the international market is about 1 percent. In the total Russian export volume, the specific weight of science-intensive products does not exceed 1.5–2 percent, which is the next lowest order compared with the average index for OECD countries.

So the observed trends in the majority of industry sectors are marked by a deteriorating industry structure and a move toward the growth of raw material and resource-intensive industries, mineral resources, and low-technology orientation in export–import operations. As far as technology commercialization is concerned, the trends here are characterized by incredibly low industry susceptibility to technological innovations which are a direct consequence of R&D activity.

As a result of economic reforms in Russia, the early 1990s were characterized by a sharp stratification of society in terms of income level and a general decline in the economy. After the recession in 1998, the GDP showed steady growth as a result of favorable commercial opportunities in the international raw material market. However, the GDP remained below its historical maximum up until 2006.

Doubling the GDP within 10 years is considered to be one of the main goals of Russian policy. This task was announced in President Vladimir Putin's address to the Federal Assembly on May 16, 2003. To accomplish this target, it is sufficient that real GDP should grow by 7.2 percent per year, which had been the case before 2008, when the average annual GDP growth was 7.3 percent. From that point over the next five years (from 2002 to the beginning of 2008), growth amounted to 42 percent. Yet, it is not clear what will happen to the economy when the global recession is over.

Fiscal and Tax Policy to Encourage Innovations

One of the negative issues impeding the realization of scientific and innovation activity is a gradual decrease in tax relief offered to scientific and innovation organizations with respect to such considerable taxes as value-added tax (VAT), profit tax, and property tax. Table 12.6 presents a list of currently existing tax incentives and those that had been in force before the tax legislation reform in 2001–04, with respect to activity connected with R&D, generation, and use of intellectual property.

It is clear from the analysis that the number of tax incentives is small when compared to the previous years. It is evident that innovation activity that is no longer stimulated by tax incentives is doomed to slow development.

For comparison purposes, regulatory management of innovation activity tax incentives in the United Kingdom allows for a reduction in the taxable base according to the amount spent on research and experimental developments during the year when the funds were spent (Mizhinsky, 2005). The Canadian internal revenue code provides for the possibility of 100 percent deduction from taxable sums spent on financing current expenditures on R&D and investments in equipment for R&D activity (Barabashev and Bromberg, 2004).

Intellectual Property Challenges

It is obvious that the normative legal base in Russia is currently under-developed, namely the normative legal base of innovation activity carried out by state scientific research institutes and universities, including activity on commercialization and technology transfer. Legislation is lagging, when compared to the rate of innovation activity carried out by institutions of

Table 12.6   Previous and current tax incentives

Tax type	Previous situation	Current situation
VAT	Tax exemption for sale of scientific and study book products, and also editorial, publishers, and polygraphic activity on its performance and realization for public and science organizations. (subpara. 17, para. 3, Art. 149 NK RF FZ of August 05, 2000) Tax exemption for patent-license transactions (except for agency operations) connected with industry property units, and also obtaining authors' rights (para. 1, Art. 5 VAT Law)	Tax exemption 12a for public training and scientific institutions with regard to R&D activity (budgetary and economic agreement-based organizations) (para. 3.16, art. 149, Tax code of the RF)
Profit tax	Public educational and scientific research institutions were allowed to reduce the taxable profit by sums spent on R&D and training process (paragraph G, and additional para. 1, Art. 6 of Enterprise and Organization Profit Tax Law - ceased to be in force by virtue of Federal Law of August 06, 2001) Exclude from taxable base cost of machines and equipment, developmental prototypes, experimental samples, and other articles transferred for tests and experiments, or submitted free of charge to a scientific organization in the course of contract (order) fulfillment for production of scientific and technical products in accordance with contract (order) provisions (Art. 2 Organization Profit Tax Law – ceased to be in force) For other organizations: Reduce the taxable profit by sums spent on R&D by no more than 10% of taxable income (para. 1, Art. 6, Enterprise and Organization Profit Tax Law – ceased to be in force by virtue of Federal Law of August 06, 2001)	No tax exemption
Property tax	Tax exemption for scientific and educational institutions with respect to property used for the purpose of scientific activity (para. 16, Art. 381 NK RF – ceased to be in force by virtue of Federal Law of November 11, 2003)	Tax exemption for property of national scientific centers (para. 15, Art. 381, Tax code of the RF)

Table 12.6   (continued)

Tax type	Previous situation	Current situation
	Tax exemption for enterprises which R&D contracts sales amount is no less than 70% (Art. 4, Enterprise Property Tax Law – ceased to be in force)	
Land tax	Tax exemption for scientific and educational institutions with respect to land plots under buildings and structures used for the purpose of scientific activity (para. 8, Art. 395, Tax code of the RF ceased to be in force by virtue of Federal Law of November 11, 2004)	No tax exemption

higher education. The legislation is primarily oriented toward higher education institution scientific and training activity and considers intellectual property rights, though the intellectual property commercialization and management process itself is ignored.

An analysis of the Russian Federation regulatory legal acts with respect to the legal status of institutions reveals a number of contradictions:

- *The procedure that determines ownership of intellectual property (IP) is under dispute*   Formerly the IP rights were vested in the executor, but according to the current regulatory acts a contractor can buy them (based on license contract, cession of rights) from the state client on a competitive basis. If commercialization is successful, the contractor is supposed to charge an amount out of the income to the state client. Thus, the property right is limited on the part of the R&D customer, and the procedure itself is neither developed nor proven.
- *IP realization procedure is disputable, that is the IP power of disposition is disputable*   Even if a public institution obtained such IP rights, it is still problematic to realize the right, that is, sell a license or found a company manufacturing the products with application of the IP. There is a contradiction between the Civil and Fiscal Codes.
- *Opportunity for institutions to establish subsidiary companies is also disputable*   Public higher education institutions, scientific research institutes, and development design offices producing innovations while being public organizations are not able to put into practice one of the most efficient methods of commercialization, that is, establish spin-off companies.

Thus, the main task of legislation is to determine clear and unambiguous procedures for securing rights in R&D results and rights to disseminate such results and IP by all participants of the elaboration process. On behalf of the institutions that have no independent property, the existing regulatory legal acts shall be amended or the legal status of these institutions shall be determined in such a manner that they have the right to acquire and dispose of these rights without imposed limitations.

The analysis of legal and economic conditions for IP commercialization opportunities in Russia conducted by the author and his colleagues and also an analysis of IP management approaches demonstrated by higher education institutions make it possible to distinguish two groups of problems which impede commercialization: problems beyond institute/university control and problems within institute/university control (that is, the problems that can be solved by the institution). We have specified the basic problems beyond institution control (Solomatova, 2007).

The problems that can be solved by an institute/university independently are:

1. *Insufficient understanding of IP's role in higher education institution activity and lack of knowledge about its application* Because they are involved in educational and scientific activities, such institutions often underestimate the role of IP in higher education institution activity and its impact on main types of activity. If a university policy is oriented toward commercialization of university IP, then training programs for university personnel should become an integral part of the university's incentive mechanisms.
2. *Imperfection of IP development mechanisms* The life cycle of a scientifically intensive product creation includes phases of marketing and patent research, R&D, patenting, design of the product's prototype, fitting-out, and industrial assimilation. Therefore, it is necessary to consider investigation results at any stage of the product life cycle as a potentially commercialized article in the future and take corresponding measures on protection of rights for these results (ensure ownership of proprietary information, monopoly over the rights, and so on).
3. *Imperfection of mechanisms controlling rights in IP objects* Imperfection of IP object development mechanisms creates a weakness in IP controlling mechanisms. An organization has the opportunity to control IP, so it is necessary for it to be authorized to have corresponding rights. In this connection, the organization will legally secure its own proprietary rights. This problem can be subdivided into several subproblems:
    a. imperfection of legislative mechanisms;
    b. imperfection of organizational and economic mechanisms;

c.   worsening of university material and technical bases; and
d.   personnel policy of universities, including motivation mechanisms.

Based on the experience of successful universities, the conclusion can be drawn that without encouragement of managing IP, it is impossible to obtain efficient IP control and commercialization of technologies. For this reason, it is very important to motivate employees to get involved in the commercialization process together with the university.

In recent years, the model of interaction with industry has changed. Under the conditions of the former Soviet planned economy, a break-through technology development from a university was recommended for implementation by an industrial ministry, and corresponding orders and circular letters were issued to charge specific enterprises with the imple-mentation of specific developments at a specific cost. Thus, the role of the university ceased at the developmental prototype stage. Now there are no such directives, and an industry comprising enterprises characterized by a variety of property, subordination, and size factors does not need a devel-opmental prototype, but a production sample, which can be operated by personnel and serviced under a guarantee.

It is the task of small business enterprises focused on solving specific technical and engineering problems to transform university research results into a manufacturing sample. For this reason, it is necessary to learn how to work with small innovation companies, since in the future these very companies will generate a significant number of orders for investigations of an industrial nature (Rogalev, 2004).

4   COLLABORATION BETWEEN SCIENCE (UNIVERSITIES AND RESEARCH CENTERS) AND SMALL INNOVATIVE COMPANIES

Analysis of the activities carried out by universities and higher education institutions, which are believed to have achieved the best results in the commercialization of their IP, permits one to identify the potential and prerequisites that are essential for efficient IP commercialization. They include:

*   focus on innovation-based development, which ensures growing state support, including financial backing, for universities and higher education institutions that carry out innovative activities;
*   encourage legislative developments that stimulate universities and higher education institutions to carry out innovative activities,

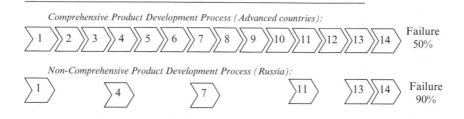

Note: 1: Concept; 2: Concept development; 3: Pre marketing research; 4: Technology analysis; 5: Market research; 6: Business analysis (SWOT); 7: Product development; 8: α-testing; 9: β-testing; 10: Test marketing; 11: Small manufacturing; 12: Final business plan; 13: Large manufacturing; 14: Market entry.

Figure 12.2   New product development steps

technology transfer, commercializing technologies, and setting up technological companies;

● make available a project database cataloging the performance of R&D activities that might require inventory;

● develop innovative infrastructure elements (technology parks, technology transfer centers, and other similar facilities) and make available certain legal and regulatory instruments that eliminate inconsistencies and compensate for legislative deficiencies; and

● highlight successful cases of IP commercialization, namely successful licensing or spin-off companies.

Figuratively speaking, the innovation process is a chain of subsequent events in which innovation develops from an inspirational idea all the way to a specific commercial marketable product, technology, or service that is further distributed through practical application. However, many companies fail to accomplish all the required steps in full measure. Figure 12.2 shows a typical product development process in companies, which carries out the full product development cycle (14 stages) as is normal in developed countries, contrasted against the usual product development process in Russian companies (six stages). In developed countries, this is a comprehensive and meticulous process that includes analytical support. In Russia, the majority of companies omit such stages as concept development, test marketing, and business analysis. Consequently, the new product can prove to be unsalable. As a result, the level of product development failure in Russia amounts to 90 percent compared to 50 percent in developed countries (Shukshunov et al., 2004).

More than 10 years ago, the author carried out a number of surveys and

Table 12.7   Major barriers to company growth ('very important' +
'important' factors)

Factor	Author's study, 1997	Studies of other researchers, 2004–08
1. Cost of capital and loan term	> 60%	> 30%
2. Personal skill	> 55%	> 12%
3. Search for financing sources, lack of own money	> 80%	> 50%
4. Manufacturing investment	> 50%	> 25%
5. High cost of innovative products development and marketing	> 50%	> 50%

used the results to write the book *Technology Innovations at a Technical University*. Among other things, the author reviews the results of his studies on the establishment and development of spin-off companies at one of the major Russian technical universities: the Moscow Power Engineering Institute (MPIE-TU). The studies identified the main obstacles that hinder the development of new companies. In his survey, the author also used data obtained by other researchers (Yevtushenkov, 2004; Akperov and Petrashov, 2008).

Table 12.7 provides a comparison of results obtained from the surveys carried out for the purposes of the author's studies, on the one hand, and the data received from other sources, on the other. The main criterion for the comparison was the aggregate of the 'very important' and 'important' factors. The comparison allows us to arrive at a simple conclusion that over the past decade the main issues, including the cost of capital, the credit payment period (loan term), the search for business development financing, the manufacturing investment, and the high cost of innovation have retained their relevance. However, they have somewhat lost their significance in the context of a considerable economic growth and availability of financial resources. As for innovations, such as the development of new products and services, the problem still exists.

5   TECHNOLOGY TRANSFER MODELING: THE CASE OF MPEI SCIENCE PARK

Infrastructure Development

Transformation of the planned economy inherited from the former USSR and the transition of Russia to a free market was impossible without the construction of a legal framework to support the development of business and private property rights, including legal instruments for IP protection. Lack of appropriate laws to regulate issues related to patents, copyrights, trade secrets, and foreign investments, on the one hand, and the lack of appropriate infrastructures to support small businesses, especially technology-based enterprises, on the other, forced universities to develop their own policies aimed at encouraging the implementation of technological innovations through setting up companies and creating a beneficial environment for their successful growth.

An impressive breakthrough of technology development regions in market-oriented economies, including the successful growth of Silicon Valley in California (US), Austin, Texas (US), and a Japanese program for the development of 19 technopoleis, as well as newly emerging opportunities of becoming a small business owner, gave rise to a spontaneous, booming development of business activities in different layers of the Soviet and post-Soviet society, including the scientific and technological communities. Many research scientists and engineers strove to develop and market technology-based products and services making use of the research and engineering projects they had carried out in state-run institutions. However, since the majority of technologies were fully owned by the state or by the university, as was the case with the projects developed by the MPEI Technical University faculty, the problem of technology transfer became one of the biggest stumbling blocks.

In its attempt to solve the problems of a spin-off company's formation and IP protection, the MPEI University developed a policy within existing legal limitations that was expected to satisfy the interests of the company founders, on the one hand, and of the university, on the other. According to this policy, all issues related to the formation of new MPEI spin-off companies were to be considered by a specially formed committee. The committee studied potential ideas, products and services, contributions of the parties, and other technical and economic aspects of the newly formed companies. The committee, together with the authors, determined technology fees, estimated the share of the company assets owned by the university, and determined the procedure for the use of the resources shared by the company, the university, administrative offices and departments. Direct cash investments, transfers of equipment, and provision of access to shared university facilities were regarded as the university's contribution to the company's initial property. Cash payments received from the company for the use of university resources are distributed among the MPEI University Scientific and Research Division, academic divisions, schools, and departments. In the context of the joint efforts made by businesses, the academic (scientific and research) community

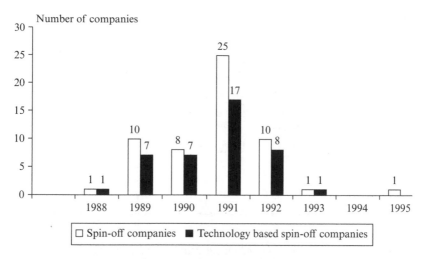

Figure 12.3   *MPEI Spin-off company formation (set up with participation of its Research Division and Business Association)*

and the government for the development of high technologies, the MPEI University regards its innovative activities as an integral part of its academic research and manufacturing complex. Figure 12.3 shows the trend in the formation of the spin-off companies, which were set up with participation of the university.

As we can see from Figure 12.3, the onset of the spin-off companies' formation falls during 1988 and peaks during 1991. The majority of the companies that formed over that period were technologically focused. Another characteristic feature of that period consists in the quick realization of the need for the creation of innovative business support elements. In 1991, the university founded its own commercial bank, and in 1992, it opened Izmaylovo Science Park.

The MPEI was the first higher education establishment to found its own bank, which was set up to improve the application of university and its subsidiaries' funds, increase the promptness of banking operations, provide administrative offices and departments with opportunities to enjoy credit facilities on an independent basis (and on attractive terms), and create conditions for the consolidation of funds belonging to the university and to its subsidiary organizations for the implementation of large-scale research and technology projects and the management of social issues. Thus, the infrastructure formed by the MPEI for the support of small businesses and technology enterprises provided basic conditions for the commercialization of innovative technologies and business incubation.

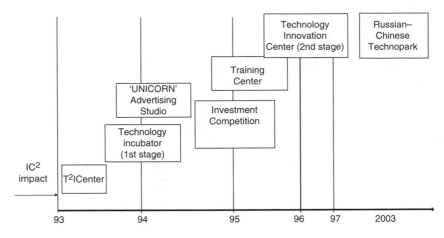

Figure 12.4   MPEI Izmaylovo Science Park development

Implementation of the technology enterprise development strategy resulted in the formation of the core system elements, which defined the technology commercialization infrastructure based on the MPEI Izmaylovo Science Park. Technology commercialization elements of the Science Park include the Technology Transfer and Innovation Center (T²I Center), the Unicorn Advertising Studio engaged in company promotion, the Investment Projects Competition, the Science Park Technology Incubator, the Science Park Training Center, the ITC, and the Russian–Chinese Druzhba Technopark. Figure 12.4 shows the stages of the infrastructure development.

In this chapter, we shall discuss only those core infrastructure elements that made the most significant contribution in technology transfer and commercialization in Russia:

- *T²I Center*: is largely focused on scientific research in the field of technology innovation, transfer, management, and strategy development. Its principal foreign partner is the Innovation, Creativity and Capital Institute (IC² Institute) of the University of Texas at Austin, US. Indeed, implementation of this project gave an impetus to all further activities.
- *Izmaylovo Science Park Technology Incubator*: combines the functions of the MPEI technology-based spin-off businesses' incubation infrastructure and those of a practical laboratory for technology commercialization mechanisms implementation.
- *Izmaylovo Science Park Training Center*: carries out short- and

medium-term training of entrepreneurship, university research scientists, members of the academic staff and students in the sphere of innovative business, and technology commercialization.

- *ITC*: focuses on the implementation of a large-scale freestanding project for the development of an infrastructure to provide support for medium and small knowledge-intensive businesses. The ITC was opened within the framework of the Joint Program for the Stimulation of Innovative Activities, of which the MPEI Technical University was an active participant. MPEI ITC center became one of the first four centers of this kind in Russia.
- *Russian–Chinese Druzhba Technopark*: was opened on the initiative of the Russian and Chinese governments to intensify the processes of scientific, technical, and innovative cooperation among the two countries' research and academic institutions and innovative companies.

The above facilities are basic elements of the technology commercialization infrastructure. The concept makes provisions for their further development, including the extension of the ITC incubator premises and the development of new syllabuses.

The formation of extended information networks with Russian and foreign partners has become an important aspect of the science park infrastructure development activities. Izmaylovo Science Park Training Center is first and foremost focused on the training of specialists involved in the development of technology-based businesses who require expert knowledge in this field. The project was developed on the basis of existing experience in teaching similar programs in the United States and the United Kingdom, customized to meet the requirements of the Russian economic environment. The core Technology Commercialization program is unique in terms of text materials, videos, and sample business plans.

The Technology Commercialization Training Course is targeted toward small innovative businesses employees, research scientists, and university students involved in research and technology projects that market promotion and conversion into commercial products or services. Upon completion of the course, the trainees have sufficient knowledge of and acquire certain practical skills in technology commercialization, the creation and management of technology-intensive companies, the fundamentals of marketing, company management, financial management, IP protection, and technology transfer. Direct results of the project implementation include professional development and acquisition of new knowledge that promotes the development of innovative business in Russia.

All preparatory work for the development of the core training program

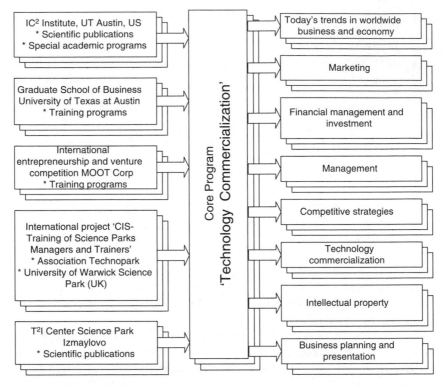

Figure 12.5   Sources and modules of the core technology commercialization program

was done on the basis of the analysis of MBA syllabuses offered by the Graduate School of Business of the University of Texas at Austin, US, specialized syllabuses developed by the IC^2 Institute, and practical experience acquired at special teacher-training courses organized within the framework of the international CIS–Training of Science Park Managers and Trainers project, carried out by the Technopark Association and Warwick University Science Park (UK) and sponsored by the European Bank for Reconstruction and Development and the TACIS Program (Rogalev, 1997). Importantly, the training program was developed in the light of the findings of the research carried out by the T^{2}I Center. Figure 12.5 shows the core Technology Commercialization program sources and study units.

Over the years, the MPEI Science Park has developed into a significant and efficient innovation infrastructure. All businesses within the park are innovative companies. Their activities are based on the transfer of innovative technologies from research organizations or from the MPEI Technical

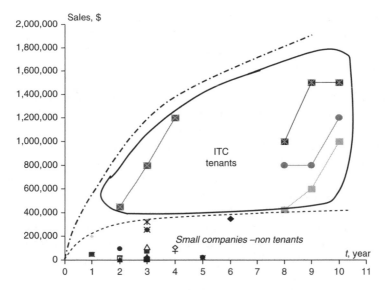

Figure 12.6 Companies' growth nurturing

University mainly through the creation of companies whose rapid growth is testament to the high efficiency of the created infrastructure for company development. The author and his colleagues carried out research on the stages of innovative companies' growth in various industrial sectors (Tabachny et al., 2002).

The research focused on the companies financed by the Foundation for Assistance to Small Innovative Enterprises. The results obtained during the course of the research were compared with the development results achieved by the companies that joined the MPEI Science Park Innovation Technology Center as shown in Figure 12.6. The figure shows that the companies supported by an efficient infrastructure exhibit considerable growth, being on average 2.5–3 times greater than the level shown by the businesses that lack such comprehensive support. These results are in full accordance with the reports on the ITC activities, from which it follows that the turnover of ITC companies is three times higher than the turnover of the companies within the Science and Scientific Services sector at large.

The MPEI Science Park activities can be illustrated through, a number of major technology transfer projects. One of the most important conditions for the successful accomplishment of the park's mission related to the commercialization of research and technology projects is close cooperation with the MPEI Technical University. The essential factors include direct support provided by the university during the initial development period of the park's structure and assistance in establishing contacts with committed ministries and agencies, as well as the use of university infrastructure and longstanding experience in the sphere of technology commercialization.

In view of the park's sufficiently extensive experience of interacting with knowledge-intensive companies, the park and the university can both gain from a natural division of responsibilities within the framework of their partnership with regard to the selection of the most commercially promising technological projects and delivery of further assistance in the process of their commercialization. In the context of this division, the park undertakes the development of closer cooperation with the businesses, while the university focuses on its own divisions and departments. The efficiency of interaction among innovative businesses and university departments and research divisions is continuously improved through implementation of a Program for the Development of Cooperation between Innovative Companies and MPEI Divisions. Cooperation occurs in a variety of ways:

- through employment, practical training, and research opportunities, including work on graduation projects and dissertation research, provided by the companies for MPEI students and members of the academic staff;
- through training in the sphere of innovation activities;
- through R&D contracts; and
- through special cooperation projects.

The program has been successfully implemented since its launch in 2004, and has achieved the following results. Annually:

- 180–220 members of the MPEI academic and research faculty are employed by the science park companies;
- 20–25 university graduates are recruited by the companies;
- 20–30 students and company employees receive innovation training;
- the companies and the Innovation Technology Center have established eight academic scholarships and fellowships for MPEI undergraduate and postgraduate students;
- one of the science park companies provides a $10,000 research grant for the MPEI academic staff; and
- three university laboratories are fitted with equipment manufactured by the companies.

The aggregate annual financial support is estimated at US$1.4–1.8 million, which amounts to 9–12 percent of the companies' annual turnover. This is very high, as in the top innovative companies in the world this indicator does not exceed 15 percent.

One of the most successful technology transfer projects is a series of package schemes for Energy Consumption Metering and Energy Saving (implemented within the framework of the Communal Services Reform). Implementation of this project has involved the following companies:

- Intechenergo M: energy audit;
- IVK Sayany: energy accounting meters manufacturing;
- Cycle Plus: electronic converters for an electrical drive of different types;
- ESCoTek: design and assembly of instruments for energy measuring and energy consumption management; and
- Intesco: service maintenance of integrated energy metering systems and dispatch control.

The project has produced the following outputs and results:

- nurturing of two new technology-based companies with a total of 153 new jobs;
- establishing partnership relations with nine engineering services and energy-saving equipment suppliers;
- creation of 17 energy-efficiency zones in Moscow covering over 900 housing blocks and 35,000 Moscow residents;
- 214 housing blocks managed by the Moscow Department of Housing and Communal Services are currently being fitted with heating management systems; and
- realization of a complex of regional energy-saving schemes.

The project was highly appreciated at the national level and won the Russian Federation Government Science and Technology Award. This prestigious annual award is a government decoration that is conferred on 30 research organizations in recognition of their important contributions to the development of science and technology.

The third major project is the development of the Russian–Chinese Druzhba Technopark opened following a decision of the Russian and Chinese governments in 2003.

Key targets of the project are:

- to promote cooperation in the field of science and technology and improve its efficiency;
- to expand scientific and technological exchange;

- to establish information support for the development of cooperation between the two countries; and
- to promote development of joint projects and creation of joint ventures to commercialize R&D outputs.

Main results to date:

- creation of the Russia–China Marketing Information System (web portal, inquiry line, videoconferencing);
- development of request and project databases (Research, Development, Finished Products, and Creation of Joint Ventures). Currently they cover 600 projects, 120 customer inquiries, 300 negotiations, and 48 agreements;
- organization of 17 international trade fairs;
- creation of an Innovations Academy, which performs the function of an educational cooperation platform; and
- launch of four major priority projects of paramount importance for Russia and China in the spheres of power generation, medicine, and innovative materials, each with a budget of US$1.2–2 million.

This shows that some system-based projects for technology transfer and commercialization have been successfully implemented in Russia's complicated economic environment.

6   MAJOR CHALLENGES OF RUSSIA FOR INNOVATION

The need for the development of an innovation economy was proclaimed in Russia at the highest government level several years ago. The goals and objectives of the government policy in the sphere of innovation were formulated during 2002–06 in several official concept and policy documents, including the Annual Message of the Russian Federation President to the Federation Council and the Key Concepts of the RF Innovation Policy, as well as in several innovation strategies, industrial development strategies, innovation programs, and projects. The Annual Message of May 10, 2006, emphasized the idea that 'in today's highly competitive global economy, the economic development of the country should largely be determined by its scientific and technological advantages'. Thus, the government has formulated the following medium-term strategy goals: development of a balanced scientific research sector and efficient innovation system that will serve to promote technological modernization of the economy and improve its competitiveness through the introduction of new technologies; and transformation of the national science potential into one of the main resources of sustainable economic growth.

There have been three very important benchmark studies initiated by the government and carried out with its participation over the 2005–06 period. In 2005, experts from the Ministry of Education and Science requested that their German colleagues from the Federal Ministry of Economics and Labor carry out an assessment of the state of innovation in Russia. The German experts gave a favorable opinion of the Strategy for the Development of Science and Innovation in the Russian Federation up to the year 2010 and pointed out the need for the improvement of legislation and control instruments and the development of the applied research sector.

In the *Economic Review of the Russian Federation: Sustainable Growth: Major Challenges* prepared by the OECD (Organisation for Economic Co-operation and Development) in 2006, Russian and foreign experts involved in the review of Russian innovation policy arrived at the conclusion that Russia has a great potential for the promotion of a more efficient innovation policy. OECD experts believed that the Russian state research sector has a huge growth potential. However, it needs restructuring in order to reduce the number of direct recipients of the federal funds allocated for R&D activities, provide financing of particular projects rather than of research institutes, and promote commercialization of research outputs.

The World Bank report on the state of the Russian economy, which was published in 2006 under the title *Russian Economic Report No. 13*, devotes a whole chapter to innovation entitled, 'Promotion of innovation economy development in Russia'. In this report, the World Bank experts recognize the commitment of the Russian government to promote diversification of the Russian economy, develop competitive sectors other than raw material industries, and nurture a knowledge-based or 'innovation' economy. However, their general assessment of the measures undertaken to promote innovation is rather controversial. The government demonstrates a very positive attitude toward the innovation economy, but the results of its activities prove that the national economy has shown no signs of departure from the model based on the trade in raw materials, oil, and gas. The authors of the report arrive at the conclusion that the prospects of the Russian 'national economic model' seem to be in accord with the continuous focus on the exploitation of natural resources, and express doubts that this course will contribute to the development of a competitive and innovative economy.

The authors (Ivanova et al., 2008) analyzed the national innovation policy pursued by the government over the last few years. The results of their research once again confirmed that the fuel and energy sectors, along with construction, trade, and communication services, make a dominant contribution to Russia's economic growth. They also identified the importance of intensifying innovative activities as a means for ensuring diversification of the economy.

Among the challenges that require solutions for the successful development of innovative activities in Russia, the researchers name three major issues:

1. *Increasing planned R&D expenditures to 2.5 percent of GDP by 2015 and increasing off-budget expenditures to 70 percent of national R&D expenditures*   At the beginning of the twenty-first century, despite sustainable growth of the Russian economy and improvement of its macroeconomic indicators, science and innovation expenditures have been increasing too slowly to record any real growth with regard to GDP.
2. *Increasing the number of innovation-active enterprises*   Since 1991, the number of innovation-active enterprises has been consistently decreasing and currently does not show any significant growth trend. One of the most critical issues for start-up companies is access to capital.
3. *Reformation and modernization of the research sector*   There has been no significant shift in the direction of innovative development or R&D outcomes in the above sector. Nor do its characteristics demonstrate significant improvement or capability for a dynamic innovative development.

On the other hand, the number of foreign companies that sign contracts with Russian research organizations for the development of innovative projects is growing. International financing accounts for 10 percent of all expenditures related to the development of innovative projects in the Russian Federation. The major foreign investors are the United Kingdom, the United States, and some Asian countries (China, Japan, and South Korea).

Shukshunov (2008), a well-known Russian expert in the field of innovative activities, identifies the shortcomings in the development of innovative activities in Russian institutions of higher education as follows:

1. For the most part, the existing new innovative structures, including university technoparks, remain small-scale facilities without serious support from federal, regional, or local public authorities.

Consequently, they cannot replace the experimental-design bureaus with pilot facilities set up at technical universities between 1970 and the1990s, which played an important role in the development of new knowledge-based technology, especially of defense-related technology and equipment.

2. Technical universities and their innovative structures produce very few significant technologies, products, materials, or systems that can make a technological breakthrough on the regional, industrial, or national level.

3. University innovative structures (technoparks, innovation technology centers, and so on) are insufficiently integrated into university academic and research complexes. For this reason, they do not participate in the final R&D cycle during which new developments turn into innovations.

4. Innovation activities carried out at universities are not focused on the development of major corporate projects in cooperation with other universities, technoparks, and ITCs. Meanwhile such projects could accumulate their potential in the search for a comprehensive solution to the issues of the region's technological and social development. All the talk about universities and technoparks being the pivots of the social, economic, and technological development of regions and industries has no basis.

5. Universities, with some minor exceptions, have not modernized their management system to bring it in line with the new innovative activity or incorporated new structures that support innovative activity and provide targeted integration with the structures outside the university for the purposes of innovation development.

6. Only 20–25 percent of Russian universities are committed to the development of innovative activities and innovation structures.

Sharing the concerns expressed by the authors, I would like to present my own opinion on the development of an innovation economy in Russia. After a very long break, in 2005, the country set up a Medium-Term Program for the Social and Economic Development of the Russian Federation (2005–08). For the first time in the country's history, the strategic goal of the program is the development of its human capital, the resource that determines the economic growth of the country to a much greater extent than financial capital or natural resources. Without claiming great coherence or fullness of detail with regard to the issues awaiting solution, I would like to single out a number of indispensable measures, which need be taken into consideration (Rogalev and Klimenko, 2005).

Measures of a general nature include the following:

- First, it is necessary to develop a program for technological forecasting of the country's evolution within the framework of the major global scientific and technological trends adjusted for Russia's specific features and national security issues in which the national system of education and science (including higher education) should have its own clearly defined place. It is necessary to bear in mind that education, as compared to science, receives priority financing and that the amount of funding allocated for education is 2.5–3 times higher than financial resources provided for science.
- Second, universities should recognize and accept today's national and global realities, give up their 'resigned attitude', and focus on the need for dramatic changes, which will help them to succeed in the globalized world and adapt to new trends. They should shape public opinion with regard to the importance of education, science, and innovative activities for the country's present and future by addressing the President of the Russian Federation, the Russian government, the Federation Council, the State Duma, and other channels of influence.
- Third, higher education authorities should concentrate educational, research, and innovation resources in a limited number of the largest and most advanced universities with due consideration for the territorial distribution of Russia's educational, scientific, technological, and industrial potential. In developed countries several selected universities, which have accumulated a 'critical mass' of lecturers and research scientists, get 60–65 percent financing of research activities. Why should Russia not follow this example?
- And finally, it is necessary to start the integration of education, science, and innovative activities through the development of a national innovation system.

Measures in the sphere of education should include without limitation:

- reform of the teaching system, which implies transition from the model based on studying facts to the model that 'teaches students to learn' accompanied by the introduction of a continuous education system;
- measures aimed at combining the best features of the existing Russian and the preceding 'Soviet' system of public education with the advanced approaches used in western educational systems (distance learning techniques, greater focus on controlled individual work, American MBA syllabus, and so on) to create a competitive system that will train specialists for the development of an innovation economy;

- recruitment of academic and research personnel, development of competitive salaries that will permit universities to compete with industry and business in terms of job attractiveness;
- transformation of the university management system for the purposes of managing universities as innovative market economy entities;
- training for university executives with the purpose of advanced management technique implementation;
- focus on the training of innovative technology designers and project developers instead of specialists qualified for operation and maintenance of the existing industrial equipment that for the most part is worn out and outdated; and
- introduction of business-customized distance learning (in companies and on location at internal and extra-mural courses) through E-learning programs based on a clear and acceptable educational technology.

Measures in the sphere of research and development should include without limitation:

- a focus on priority directions of the global and Russian scientific and technological development;
- 'escape' from diluted and void results in applied research to clear practical and commercial applications;
- use of federal financing in the sphere of applied research to focus on the solutions for major applied problems, organization of teamwork at universities and other higher education institutions, realization of the program-based targeted approach for the achievement of the goals set by the Medium-Term Program for Russia's Development;
- integration with sectoral and academic research centers for the purposes of research and training; and
- clear procedures for IP items protection for the purpose of their further commercial application within the innovation cycle framework.

Measures in the sphere of innovative activities should include without limitation:

- organization of an integral innovation diffusion channel at universities covering the whole innovation cycle from idea generation to finished product marketing;
- organization of training and refresher courses in the sphere of

innovation business for university executives, middle managers, graduate, and doctoral students;

- expansion of innovation business infrastructure and updating of the existing infrastructure by adding the missing elements required for the development of a comprehensive innovation structure;
- concentration of innovative technological companies within innovation infrastructures;
- development of technologies and implementation of innovative projects within priority directions of scientific and technological advancement;
- integration of education, science, and innovation business for the purposes of dealing with Russia's social and economic challenges;
- development of interaction among innovative businesses and university departments with regard to participation in the academic and research processes, adjustment of the training models for the purposes of preparing specialists required by the new economy and promotion of university research output into the market with the help of innovative companies; and
- transition from a fragmentary to an integral national innovation system within a higher education structure.

The results of this study highlight that the fundamental elements of a national innovation system in Russia have been developed and the modeling of technology transfer and commercialization have shown a high efficacy of efforts that have been undertaken. However, for a large-scale expansion of achieved results and further progress toward a knowledge economy, the government should develop clear policies and have implementation programs in place to build up an integral national innovation system for knowledge, technology creation, and its transformation into wealth through technology transfer and commercialization in the marketplace.

REFERENCES

Akperov, I.G. and A.V. Petrashov (2008), 'Transfer of innovation technologies: readiness, hindrances, possibilities', *Innovations*, **115** (5): C106–12.
Barabashev, A.G. and G.V. Bromberg (2004), *Intellectual Property and State: International Experience*, Moscow: INIC Rospatent.
Bortnik, I.M. (2008), 'Fund for the promotion: logic of development', *Innovations Magazine*, December: 1–2.
Gohberg, L.M., I.A. Kuznetsova and L.E. Mindeli (1996), *Innovations in Industry Sectors: Statistical Digest*, Moscow: CISN.

Goskomstat of Russia (1996), *Statistical Yearbook of Russia: Statistical Digest*, Moscow: Lotos.

Goskomstat of Russia (1998), *Russia in Figures: Concise Statistical Digest*, Moscow: Goskomstat publisher.

Ivanova, N.I., I.G. Dezhina, N.V. Shelyubskaya and L.K. Pipiya (2008), 'Analysis of innovation policy and assessment of its results: Russia', *Innovations*, **115** (5): 56–72.

Mizhinsky, M.Yu, (2005), 'Legal regulation of the tax exemption procedure for the purposes of promoting research and experimental activities in the UK', *Innovations*, **8**: 36–42.

Polyakov, S.G. (2008), '15th anniversary of the fund for the promotion of the development of small businesses in the sphere of science and technology', *Innovations Journal*, December: 3–9.

Rogalev, N.D. (1997), *Technology Innovations at a Technical University*, Moscow: MEI (MPEI).

Rogalev, N.D. (2004), 'On innovative activities in MPEI', from a report by M. Firsanovka, MEI (MPEI).

Rogalev, N.D. and A.V. Klimenko (2005), *Modern Day Universities: Teaching, Research, and Technological Innovation Models*, Moscow: MEI (MPEI).

Shukshunov, V.E. (2002), 'The state of innovative activities in Russian higher education and the tasks for their further development and improvement of their efficiency', Collected materials of the All-Russian research/practice conference: 'The state and prospects of innovation activities development in the Russian system of public education', Krasnodar, Russia, Moscow–September 8–11, pp. 21–32.

Shukshunov, V.E. (2008), 'Report on the state and prospects of university technopark development in Russia', paper presented at conference: 'State and prospects of university technoparks development in the context of providing integration of university research sector, education and production and for the promotion of small and medium business creation', Zvenigorod, October 1–3.

Shukshunov, V.E., A.V. Pavlenko and E.A. Nyrkov (2004), *Conceptual Basis for the Dvelopment of Hiher Edcation System Novocherkassk*, Novocherkassk: YuRGTU NPI: 11–17.

Solomatova, M.V. (2007), 'Development of legal, organizational and economic mechanisms for a technical university intellectual property management', Candidate of Economic Sciences diss., Moscow Power Engineering Instituite.

Tabachny, E.M., N.D. Rogalev and O.P. Akhmedzhanova (2002), 'Product diffusion analysis and modeling', *Vestnik*, **4**: 57–62.

Yevtushenkov, V.P. (ed.) (2004), *Policy for the Improvement of Russia's Economy Competitiveness National Report*, Moscow: RSPP.

13. The experience in the United States: a university perspective

Patricia G. Greene and Mark P. Rice

1 INTRODUCTION

The consistent overarching motivation for technology transfer activities is the betterment of society; in an ideal sense, the technology is intended to improve the life of individuals and/or organizations. From a university's perspective, which is the focus of this chapter, a programmatic or at least a systematic approach to technology transfer is intended to contribute to that societal betterment with concern for the benefit of the university as a close second (AUTM, 2008a).

In an era of decreasing public and private funds to support post-secondary education, technology transfer activities are likely to become yet more important as a potential source of support to underwrite other university activities that need to be subsidized. More specifically, many institutions around the world look to technology transfer as a method of creating, or at least enhancing, opportunities for moving technology from the developer of that technology into the market. Over the years, the primary stakeholders have included the federal government, universities, and industries. The motivations, practices, policies, and funding models have changed over time to reflect various endogenous and exogenous factors. The 2009 IC^2 Fellows workshop, 'Global Perspectives on Technology Transfer and Commercialization', on technology transfer practices around the world show the ever-increasing scale and scope of technology transfer activities, complete with a variety of evolving approaches. This chapter will provide an overview of the practice of technology transfer in the United States in order to provide a point of comparison and learning for the ongoing discussion.

For the reasons suggested above, the process of crossing the technology transfer intersection is of great interest to stakeholder individuals and organizations, including industry, academia, and government. As this interest continues to grow around the world, a number of questions remain based upon past practices, current accomplishments, and future objectives:

- How is technology identified?
- How is technology evaluated?
- Who participates in the technology development process?
- What technology is selected for the market?
- Who pays for the process (and how)?
- Who supports the process (and what does that include)?
- How is the process assessed?

The purpose of this chapter is to review and investigate current processes and practices as well as the emerging questions and issues surrounding technology transfer across the United States. We use two qualitative methodologies to support the chapter. First, a content analysis to identify current issues is used to develop a semi-structured interview format. Second, a series of expert interviews is used to explore and challenge those identified issues. We conclude with a consideration of emerging issues and models for the future that might be useful for global applications.

Technology transfer and commercialization can be defined in a variety of ways. The Association of University Technology Managers (AUTM), arguably the leading trade association in this field, describes technology transfer as 'the term given to the practice of licensing research institution-owned intellectual property to commercial and non-profit organizations' (AUTM, 2008a). The governmental approach is a bit simpler, according to the Robert C. Byrd, National Technology Transfer Center (2009): 'Technology Transfer involved moving a technology developed for one organization or environment into another'.

To further the purposes of this chapter, we shall adopt the commercialization definition used by the IC^2 Institute: '[T]he process of creating and transferring intellectual property generated at the university into the private, for-profit sector'. The two differences between the AUTM and the IC^2 Institute definitions are that IC^2 explicitly looks to transferring into the 'private, for-profit sector' while AUTM intentionally includes non-profit organizations. AUTM also is specific about the licensing activity while IC^2 more broadly includes the creation of the intellectual property as well as the transfer activities, which expands the type of activities included in technology transfer.

In the fiscal year 2007, US technology transfer programs sent 686 new products into the market and helped launch 555 new companies. This equates to almost two new products and one and a half new businesses every day of the calendar year (AUTM, 2008a). The AUTM further reports that US$48.8 billion were reported as research expenditures in 2007, plus 5,109 licenses and options signed, and 3,622 patents issued.

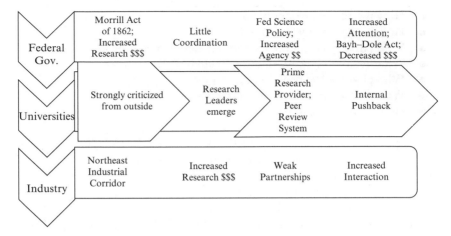

| Federal Gov. | Morrill Act of 1862; Increased Research $$$ | Little Coordination | Fed Science Policy; Increased Agency $$ | Increased Attention; Bayh–Dole Act; Decreased $$$ |

| Universities | Strongly criticized from outside | Research Leaders emerge | Prime Research Provider; Peer Review System | Internal Pushback |

| Industry | Northeast Industrial Corridor | Increased Research $$$ | Weak Partnerships | Increased Interaction |

Source: Adapted from Matkin (1990).

Figure 13.1   Timetable of the emergence of technology transfer

2   HISTORICAL OVERVIEW

Modern technology transfer practices have been a long time in the making. One of the more thoughtful overviews of the evolution of technology transfer is found in Gary Matkin's (1990) treatment of the relationship between technology transfer and universities. Matkin posits that the evolution of these practices emerged from the educational philosophy of the United States, particularly as it concerns higher or post-secondary education (see Figure 13.1). One line of thought in the mid-1880s was that universities in the United States did not place enough emphasis on the natural sciences and lacked a strong enough orientation on a practical and career-oriented education. The comparison was made with the model of the more career-focused advanced training in the European schools, in which the US schools found to be lacking (ibid. 1990). The Morrill Act of 1862 was an explicit policy decision toward a more utilitarian approach, providing federal grants to schools if the state maintains 'at least one college where the leading subject shall be, without excluding other scientific and classical studies . . . to teach such branches of learning as are related to agriculture and the mechanic arts' (ibid., 17). This explicitly practice-based, applied approach led to changes in the relationships between universities and industry, and universities and government research activities. One of the foremost early examples was the emergence of the Northeast Industrial Corridor in the late 1800s. This corridor, a network of industry and university partnerships, marked a significant change in the types of relationships created among these very different types of organizations.

The next major step in the early 1900s prompted by these policy and organizational relationship changes was the rise of the research universities. Early on, 15 universities recognized the federal government as a source of increased research dollars and began to organize faculty, students, and their research differently from before to avail themselves of this emerging source of funding. Notably, the first institutional line item for research is attributed to the University of California in 1915 (Matkin, 1990).

Despite the fact that government funding at this time came from a variety of agencies and offices and was not explicitly coordinated, the early research institutions learned the systems and continued to become stronger, pursuing grants across agency boundaries. The National Research Council was created during the era of the First World War and began to play a significant role in starting to better coordinate government research spending. At the same time, various industries also began committing more research dollars to advance the development of new products and services.

By the time of the Second World War, the government had advanced to establish a Federal Science Policy to further guide research spending even though most of the government spending continued to come through individual agencies. The role of the other players, industry and academic, also shifted. While industry partnerships existed, they were generally considered to be weak while the universities continued to strengthen their position as the prime providers of the research. It was also during this time that the peer review system took strong root as a significant aspect of the research process, a factor that continues to play a role in today's practices.

The Bayh–Dole Act, formally known as the University and Small Business Patent Procedures Act, was passed in 1980 and is generally identified as one of the most critical drivers in the advancement of US technology transfer. This act for the first time gave university researchers the option for ownership of government-sponsored inventions (albeit with stipulations regarding the exercise of options, patenting, and so on). The Bayh–Dole Act also gave explicit preference to small businesses, defined as those with less than 500 employees (Sandelin, 2006).

While the universities had been active in the technology transfer domain for many years, the Stanford Office of Technology was one of the first official offices to organize the university's technology transfer functions. Stanford's office was founded in 1969 and to date has issued 6,000 invention disclosures, 1,700 patents, 2,500 licenses, and US$1.1 billion in royalties (ibid.). The best-known firm to emerge from this process to date is Google.

New programs continued to emerge at a steady pace for the next two decades. However, the growth rate in US programs has slowed. AUTM reports only 12 new university programs initiated since 2001 (AUTM, 2008a). This might be because the type of school most likely to participate in technology transfer has already started its program. What is compelling is that while the launch of new programs is slowing in the United States, a growing global interest in designing, launching, and also refining technology transfer programs is evident, including the broad international participation in conferences such as the 2009 IC^2 Fellows workshop.

3   KEY PLAYERS IN THE UNITED STATES

For the purposes of this chapter we are going to start at the bottom of our list of questions and work backwards. This approach allows us to consider the important aspects of technology transfer while building on the premise that what is being measured is actually important. We shall go on to identify the list of those institutions most active in this area. From that list we review overall processes and approaches. To conclude this section we revisit a study by Innovation Associates (Palmintera et al., 2007) in order to include a consideration of practices based upon those not in the list of usual subjects.

How the Process Is Assessed: Rankings

Assessment measures in higher education often become rankings lists that are bemoaned or celebrated depending on an institution's spot in the rankings. For technology transfer, the primary rankings lists and lists of ranking criteria are produced by the AUTM and more industry-specific criteria by the Milken Institute and the Kauffman Foundation. AUTM uses the following metrics to compare and contrast programs (AUTM, 2008a):

- Licensing FTE;
- Research Expenditures;
- Licenses & Options Executed;
- Start-ups;
- Disclosures;
- US Patents Issued;
- New Patent Applications; and
- License Income.

These metrics can be viewed as assessments of both process and outcome as well as metrics of inputs and outputs. These particular metrics also

Table 13.1   Comparison by select ranking metrics

Licensing & options	Start-ups	License income
Univ. of Washington/ Res Fdn	Univ. of California System	NYU
Univ. of Georgia	MIT	Columbia
MIT	Univ. of Utah	Univ. of California System
Iowa State	Columbia	Northwestern
North Carolina State	Univ. of Washington/Res Fdn	Wake Forest
	Univ. of Colorado (tie)	Univ. of Minnesota
	Univ. of Kentucky Res Fdn (tie)	Univ. of Washington/Res Fdn
	Northwestern (tie)	MIT

suggest different sets of 'leaders in the field' depending on which metric is under consideration. If approaching from the metric of 2007 Licenses & Options Executed, the leaders are the University of California System (231; note this is an aggregate measure for the system as opposed to an individual educational institution), the University of Washington/ Washington Research Foundation (203; note combined reporting for the university and the research foundation), the University of Georgia (125), MIT (116), Iowa State (113), and North Carolina State University (106) (AUTM, 2007).

If considering from the metric of Start-ups, the top players change somewhat and now include the University of California System (38), MIT (24), the University of Utah (18), Columbia (12), the University of Washington/Washington Research Foundation (11), and a group tied at 10 (University of Colorado, University of Kentucky Research Foundation, and Northwestern).

The top players change yet again if assessing from the perspective of License Income in 2007 (AUTM):

$791,210,587	New York University
$135,632,417	Columbia
$97,593,575	University of California System
$85,298,599	Northwestern
$71,226,905	Wake Forest University
$63,315,910	University of Minnesota
$63,283,697	University of Washington/Washington Research Foundation
$61,600,000	MIT

Other types of measurement used are often closely tied to the mission and motivation of the university. For instance, the North Carolina system uses measures including SBIR grants, venture capital disbursed per $1,000 of gross state product, the number of venture capital deals as a share of high-tech business establishments, and also the number of academic patents per 1,000 S&E doctorate holders in academic institutions (Office of Technology Management, 2008). This set of metrics ties directly to their economic development goal for their state and speaks to a broad and strategic approach.

What Is the Technology Transfer Process?

One long-time participant in the field, the University of Illinois at Champaign-Urbana (UIC) is explicit and articulate about its process to the point of including its process diagram in the technology transfer reports. This model serves well as an overall description of the general process (Office of Technology Management, 2008, 7). The process follows these steps:

1. Intellectual property disclosures are the entry to the system built to encourage early disclosure in innovations. The motivation behind doing this early is to obtain patent protection as quickly as possible.
2. Screening the evaluation determines whether the disclosure is for an idea or an actual business opportunity. The UIC system includes target timelines for every step of the process. This particular internal review process is targeted to be completed within six weeks of the technology transfer office receiving the disclosure.
3. Assessment of the technology builds on the initial screening and is often done with internal and external advisors. This part of the process determines whether or not the transfer process will continue.
4. Marketing is next done to investigate the most appropriate licensing partners.
5. License negotiations are conducted by the Office of Technology Management.
6. Compliance function for monitoring by the Office of Technology Management is initiated.

Notably, UIC explicitly states that ultimately there should be a return to the inventor.

It is not only the schools on these top lists that are active in the technology transfer arena. A recent study supported by the National Science Foundation and conducted by Innovation Associates (Palmintera et al., 2007) intentionally explores other institutions that have created unique ways to also participate in technology transfer activities. The report selected a set of exemplars and investigated the unique ways in which they were able to compete, generally without large R&D budgets or extensive supporting infrastructure. The exemplars included: Alfred University, Brigham Young University, Florida Agricultural and Mechanical University, Iowa State University, Montana State University, Rensselaer Polytechnic Institute, Springfield Technical Community College, the University of Akron, the University of Central Florida, and the University of North Carolina at Charlotte.

The process of technology transfer as modeled by UIC is not necessarily how these other exemplars work. The Innovation Associates study identified a varied set of attributes and processes for these schools that better fits who they are, why they exist, and how they function. These attributes include such things as the explicit development of an entrepreneurial culture, the identification and focus on research niches, collaboration with various government agencies at different levels, as well as with industry partners, the creation of institutional incentives for technology transfer and entrepreneurial activities, including hiring and promotion policies, and the design of a linked network of resources for technology start-ups (ibid., 2007).

4 CONTENT ANALYSIS

Much discussion occurs on a regular basis to advance technology transfer activities around the world. AUTM's periodical, *Technology Transfer Tactics* (AUTM, 2008b), reports on current issues and debates for the industry. These topics reflect unresolved recurring issues and emerging issues for the field. In order to identify the top current concerns in the field, we used a qualitative methodology, content analysis, to explore the 2008 editions of these reports. The content analysis was conducted using NVivo software and reviewed the entire contents of the 12 publications. The top five issues identified from the content analysis are:

- New models: examples of new ways of doing things, including new ways of collaborating within and across university boundaries.
- Intellectual property: anything related to patent policies and practices.
- University bureaucracy: ways in which the university structures and practices impact technology transfer.
- Global issues: how schools are trying to increase the range of their partnerships and size of their markets.

- Valuation models: both for technologies and also for technology transfer practices.

Once these top issues were identified, the next phase in the research process was to conduct a series of expert interviews to validate the issues and investigate the future of technology transfer.

5   FINDINGS: THE EXPERTS SPEAK

To explore more fully the issues identified through the content analysis of the 2008 issues of AUTM's periodical, *Technology Transfer Tactics*, we identified a set of industry experts for in-depth interviews. While we assembled a sample of convenience, we were able to structure the sample to ensure diversity along the dimensions sponsorship (public versus private), geography (east coast, central United States, and west coast), and size. Our sample included two large public universities (University of Texas and University of Massachusetts), one public university of more modest size (Georgia Institute of Technology), one large private university (University of Southern California), and one small private university (Rensselaer Polytechnic Institute). For more information about the respondents who participated in the interviews see Appendix 13A.

For each of the five prominent issues in technology transfer in the United States, we asked our respondents four questions:

- Do you agree that this is a major issue?
- What are the major dimensions, characteristics, and elements of the issue?
- Can you briefly describe an example of this issue at your institution?
- Can you identify one or more best practices related to this issue?

In addition we asked the following questions to conclude each interview.

- Can you identify one or more best practices related to this issue?
- What trends in technology transfer do you see emerging, if any?

Issue 1: New Models of Technology Transfer

All respondents acknowledged that the new models of technology transfer are a major issue or topic of interest. With respect to dimensions, characteristics, and elements, several respondents cited the emerging importance of intra- and inter-institutional collaboration. Examples cited included the partnership between Massachusetts Technology Transfer Center (MTTC) and Massachusetts Association of Technology Transfer Offices (MATTO), and also Universities of Upstate New York Technology (UNYTECH). Collaboration was seen as important with respect to identifying and specifying cross-disciplinary problems to solve, strengthening internal and external communication, and sharing of resources in support of technology transfer as a means of dealing with resource limitations or shortfalls.

With respect to resources, universities are attempting to be more proactive in delivering a broader set of services to support technology commercialization, particularly in supporting start-ups through advising, mentoring, investing, and showcasing to external sources of resources and expertise through a variety of university sponsored forums and web portals. The internal support takes a variety of institutional forms, such as incubators, technology parks, and centers for innovation/entrepreneurship. University culture was also cited as an important dimension in the emergence of new models, particularly because technology transfer is not seen as being within the primary mission of a university though it has the potential to be a revenue generator. This is reflected in differing expectations/goals for the technology transfer function inside and outside university, as well as different perspectives with respect to relative time to take action.

Generally respondents seemed to indicate that standard industry practices have not yet evolved into 'best practices'. One aspect of new models is the emergence of new approaches to evaluating technologies and making decisions regarding patenting (networks, commercial advisory boards, and internal counsels of experts) but generally these all have significant room for improvement.

Issue 2: Intellectual Property (IP) Policies and Practices

There was widespread agreement among respondents that IP policies and practices encompass an imperfect system as they are often written in a way that is unclear, ambiguous, and sometimes internally inconsistent. Perspectives and practices vary across industries, for example, life sciences versus IT versus other high-tech industries. Lack of clarity increases inefficiencies of processes and can drive researchers to behaviors that are self-serving and that run counter to the protection of institutional IP rights. Consistent, swift, and appropriate enforcement is an important objective but performance might be less than ideal. Lack of sufficient resources, complemented by inadequate internal communications, might result in inefficient and inappropriately timed implementation of IP processes. It was clear from the comments of the respondents that while they recognized the inevitable limits to the commitment of financial resources to technology transfer, they saw this constraint as compromising their ability to fulfill their missions. In addition to restricting their capacity of protecting IP, these restrictions constrained efforts to market the IP and hence harvest the value that had been captured. Even more challenging as a result of resource constraints was the difficulty of recruiting and developing technology transfer talent.

Collaboration, which was recognized in the previous section as an important new model, brings with it the challenge of resolving joint ownership issues inherent in multi-institutional research. Divergence of interests between universities and corporate sponsors might lead companies to focus support on R&D that does not compromise their own potential IP interests. In addition, companies prefer to pre-value technology as part of the funding process, whereas universities do not want to undervalue technology before it is developed. Typically a comprehensive and consistent evaluation process is lacking, hampering the ability of technology transfer professionals to make smart decisions about all forms of IP and moving forward with commercialization.

Once again, respondents seemed unable or unwilling to cite best practices. Comments related to this question focused on communications (concise, crisp, and clear policies; frequent seminars with faculty) and evaluation. (Columbia University's evaluation system using graduate students was cited as a novel approach.)

Issue 3: University Bureaucracy

This topic elicited strong reactions and general agreement that university bureaucracy creates challenges for effective management of the university's technology transfer function. One respondent seemed to capture the frustration of the respondents when he characterized the impact of university bureaucracy in the following way:

> Huge. Especially in a public university. The patent system [US Patent and Trademark Office and the Patent Cooperation Treaty] is inherently filled with forms and processes. The Bayh–Dole Act requires disclosure of commercial efforts for federal funds. Taken together and put in the context of a large university, this easily becomes the primary focus of any office – just processing forms.

Specific comments characterizing the components of this meta-issue include the challenges of managing real legal concerns, the difficulty of addressing the need for expeditious and responsive action, and the context in which the technology transfer office must operate.

Universities are typically very complex and very political organizations. Organizational rigidities can make collaboration among departments a challenge and turf wars one of the cultural norms. Institutional decisions can be revisited and commitments undone as a result of changes in leadership. Decision-making processes might be overly complex. One respondent bemoaned the absence of a central IP signature authority, requiring too many reviews and approvals for simple things. The tension between the need for entrepreneurial flexibility and disciplined implementation of clear and consistent IP policies is captured in the statement below from one of our respondents:

> Faculty startups require strong flexibility from the campus with respect to the faculty's time [and] efforts, IP rights, and consulting agreements. Huge gains can be derived. Ideally a startup would use a portion of the faculty's lab and the faculty would have an equity stake. This aligns the incentives and allows for very capital efficient business. However, this also represents a conflict of interest due to the faculty/student and faculty/startup relationships. Getting this resolved can either take a long time (hampering the startup) or be ignored, causing longer term issues.

Issue 4: Global Issues

Reactions of our respondents to global issues were mixed: two of the six respondents saw global issues as a major issue; two saw global issues as an emerging issue; one took global issues as a given, that is, just one of the issues he had to consider routinely; and the final respondent declared that global issues was not a major issue. The comments of the respondents reflected concerns about variation in policies, practices, and norms around the world and the challenges of deciding where to file disclosures, particularly given limited financial resources. One respondent described it as a triage process – trying to maximize protection and opportunities to license while dealing with financial limitations. The concept of limited resources was extended to include the shortage of personnel with the competencies required to explore commercial needs in both the present and the future. Respondents reflected on the increased difficulty of making patenting decisions given uncertainty about whether a technology could or should be patented in other countries and whether potential licensees could be identified. Concern was also expressed about potential domestic political repercussions related to licensing IP to foreign competitors of US companies.

The respondents were mostly silent with respect to best practices, with one respondent stating: 'Unknown. Would love to hear some'. It appeared that the 'common' rather than 'best' practice, presumably reflecting limited financial resources, is reflected in the following comment: 'Shop to US companies first, then pursue foreign partners'. With respect to patenting in countries outside the US, another respondent stated, 'Europe, maybe. Won't go beyond that unless we have a licensee who is willing to pay for it'.

Issue 5: Valuation Models

Perspectives on the relative importance of valuation for both technologies and technology transfer practices were split: two respondents saw valuation models as a major issue; two did not; and the remaining two did not offer a perspective on its relative importance. However, the follow-on comments to the remaining three questions revealed that valuation models are problematic on a number of dimensions. As indicated above, licensees prefer predictability and hence want the valuation and the terms of the licensing arrangement established at the front end before funding for additional R&D is committed. One respondent characterized the problem as follows: 'Valuation models only work well with existing markets. Our stuff is very early, often with nascent or non-existent markets and only pending patents. It's too difficult to figure out how valuable a *typical* patent might be years before products have evolved and with ever changing markets'.

As indicated in the section above on IP practices and policies, norms vary across industries. Exclusive licenses are common in the life sciences. By comparison, in the IT world cross-licensing is common. Outside of life sciences, some companies just do not want to deal with universities.

One respondent indicated that performance metrics for evaluating the technology transfer office were lacking and much more work needed to be done in this area. On that note, several respondents reflected on problems with inexperienced and/or unskilled personnel working in this arena. Another respondent stated: 'University people have little concept of external market valuation condition and changes to those conditions. Valuation at most stages of transfer is considered perceptual and not "real". Universities are always looking at short term cash versus long term reward or their economic development responsibility'. Another respondent stated: 'Too many new tech transfer offices are started up with unrealistically high expectations. They end up asking for too much for too little, try[ing] to impose "punitive" milestone payments and hav[ing] staff with the wrong, [no] or little experience'. The issue of staff competence and the need for improved training also emerged in comments about potential missed issues.

Though in one case a respondent recommended a best practice to be developed in reaction to current weaknesses in valuation models, the respondents collectively offered no examples of existing best practices. One respondent did acknowledge the efforts by AUTM through its Better World Project, launched in 2005, to 'promote public understanding of how academic research and technology transfer benefits you, your community and millions of people around the world'.

6 DISCUSSION: EMERGING TRENDS IN TECHNOLOGY TRANSFER IN THE UNITED STATES

Given the significant challenges of licensing early-stage technologies to established firms who seek impact in the short term, universities are increasing their focus on start-ups as the means to develop technologies and serve as engines to direct sponsored research back to the laboratories. This approach is complemented by increased efforts to develop IP further within an institution to increase its value prior to commercialization. Early on, technology transfer offices were consumed with administration-focused tasks: disclosures, patent filings, publication reviews, and so forth. Technology transfer offices have increasingly realized that without a valid licensor, there is no point in patenting. This has led to ever more outward-facing offices with an increased scope of activities, including hiring marketing and business development professionals as well as entrepreneurs who are willing to work inside the university and help bridge the 'talent divide' between university research and commercial markets. This trend has extended to nascent programs designed to develop technology transfer professionals with a broader range of skill sets.

7 FUTURE RESEARCH

In reviewing the insights gained from our initial content analysis of *Technology Transfer Tactics* and the subsequent in-depth exploration with industry veterans, it is our view that the following research topics could provide useful insights, processes, structures, and methodologies supporting trends in technology transfer:

- How can the processes, systems, and structures through which IP is created, developed, and commercialized be enhanced?
- How can the cadre of people who are highly skilled at managing these processes, systems and structures be expanded?
- What metrics and assessment processes are most useful for determining inputs and outputs?
- How does technology transfer fit into an entrepreneurial ecosystem for greenfield start-up ventures and for corporate ventures?

Uncertainty Framework (O = Organizational;
R = Resource; T = Technological; M = Market

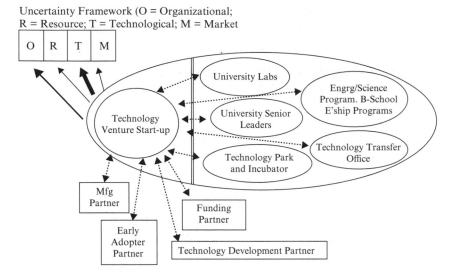

Source: Model developed by Mark P. Rice.

*Figure 13.2   Technological venture Start-up in the context of a university-
based entrepreneurship ecosystem*

To advance this research agenda, we propose a conceptual model of a
university-based entrepreneurship ecosystem with the focus on the transfer of university IP through a technology start-up (see Figure 13.2).

The model encompasses the common challenge that most technology-
driven start-up ventures have difficulty confronting, that is, the need to
move beyond technology development and to confront the entire innovation and entrepreneurship uncertainty framework, including technical,
market, organizational, and resource uncertainties (Rice et al., 2008).
Further, it suggests that the technological entrepreneur needs to be adept
at accessing resources and competencies not only within the university-
based entrepreneurship ecosystem but also via outreach to the extended
and complementary ecosystem beyond the university. Hence the technological entrepreneur needs to be skillful in developing and managing
internal and external relationships. Therefore issues related to the development of organizational processes, structures, and systems (including
performance metrics and assessment systems) apply broadly to the entire
ecosystem: to the technology transfer function, to the portfolio of commercialization activities, and to the individual ventures.

We began this chapter by presenting the consensus that the primary
value of technology transfer should be for the good of society. However,

the fact remains that most of the research, assessment processes, and criteria focus on an economic perspective. In 2007 the AUTM convened a meeting to more explicitly consider other ramifications of technology transfer activities, including those relating to social and policy issues. The group concluded with nine primary points of consideration (AUTM, 2007), which we believe complement the key issues derived from our content analysis exercise and in-depth interviews discussed earlier:

1. Universities should reserve the right to practise licensed inventions and to allow other non-profit and government organizations to do so.
2. Exclusive licenses should be structured in a manner that encourages technology development and use.
3. Universities should strive to minimize the licensing of 'future improvements'.
4. Universities should anticipate and help manage technology transfer-related conflicts of interest.
5. Universities should ensure broad access to research tools.
6. Universities should consider enforcement action carefully.
7. Universities should be mindful of export regulations.
8. Universities should be mindful of the implications of working with patent aggregators.
9. Universities should consider including provisions that address unmet needs, such as those of neglected patient populations or geographic areas, giving particular attention to improved therapeutics, diagnostics, and agricultural technologies for the developing world.

Though some of these key issues are clearly tactical, an underlying strategic theme is apparent. Technology transfer offices and their university sponsors should aspire to accomplish more than protecting IP and generating licensing revenue for the inventor and the university. Technology transfer offices should seek opportunities to enhance technology development and use in advancing the human condition globally.

BIBLIOGRAPHY

Association of University Technology Managers (AUTM) (2007), *In the Public Interest: Nine Points to Consider in Licensing University Technology*, White Paper developed by AUTM, available at: www.autm.net/Nine_Points_to_ Consider.htm.
Association of University Technology Managers (AUTM) (2008a), *U.S. Licensing Activity Survey: FY: 2007*, ed. Robert Tieckelmann, Richard Kordal and Dana Bostrom, available at: https://portal.rfsuny.org/portal/page/portal/The%20

Research%20Foundation%20of%20SUNY/home/What_we_do/strategic_plan
ning/autm_us_licensing_activity_survey_fy_2007.pdf.

Association of University Technology Managers (AUTM) (2008b), *Technology Transfer Tactics*, available at : http://www.autm.net/source/subscriptions/index.cfm?fuseaction=home.loginForm.

Gruber, William H. and Donald G. Marquis (eds) (1969), *Factors in the Transfer of Technology*, Cambridge, MA: MIT Press.

Matkin, Gary W. (1990), *Technology Transfer and the University*, New York: American Council on Education and Macmillan.

National Technology Transfer Center (2009), available at: www.nttc.edu/about/techtransfer.asp (accessed March 2009).

Office of Technology Management (2008), *Advancing Innovation in North Carolina: An Innovation Framework for Competing and Prospering in the Interconnected Global Economy*, Prepared at the Direction of the North Carolina Board of Science and Technology, 2008 Annual Fiscal Report, University of Illinois, available at: http://www.ncscitech.com/PDF/reports/Advancing_Innovation_in_NC_Full_Report.pdf.

Palmintera, D., J. Joy and E.X. Lin (2007), 'Technology Transfer and Commercialization Partnerships', Report of Innovation Associates supported by National Science Foundation grant number EEC-0413603.

Rice, Mark P., Gina Colarelli O'Connor and Ronald Pierantozzi (2008), 'Implementing a learning plan to counter project uncertainty', *Sloan Management Review*, Winter, 54–62.

Sandelin, J. (2006), 'Bayh/Dole and beyond – strategies and tactics', *Know IP*, **3** (8), Module 3, June, Stockholm Network.

Snyder, S., M.M.E. Johns, J.J. Mongan and J.R. Utaski (2003), 'Accelerating Technology Transfer and Commercialization in the Life and Health Sciences', Final Report of the Panel of Advisors on the Life Sciences, Ewing Marion Kauffman Foundation, Kansas City, MO.

APPENDIX 13A

Table 13A.1   Interview respondents

Institution	Individual respondent	Relevant experience
Georgia Institute of Technology	Steven Derezinski	Founder and Past Director, Georgia Tech VentureLab; Former CEO of SmallBizPlanet. com; and Managing Director, Platform Technology Ventures
Rensselaer Polytechnic Institute	Charles Rancourt	Director (Retired), RPI Office of Technology Commercialization
University of Massachusetts	Tom Chmura	Vice President of Economic Development
University of Massachusetts	William Rosenberg	Executive Director of Commercial Ventures and Intellectual Property
University of Southern California	Joe Koepnick	Senior Director of Innovation Advancement and Business Development
The University of Texas at Austin	Laura Kilcrease	Former Executive Director, The University of Texas IC^2 Institute's Center for Commercialization and Enterprise and Founder and Former Executive Director Austin Technology Incubator

Index